Non-Western Educational Traditions
Alternative Approaches
to Educational Thought and Practice

Sociocultural, Political, and Historical Studies in Education
Joel Spring, Editor

Non-Western Educational Traditions
Alternative Approaches
to Educational Thought and Practice

Second Edition

Timothy Reagan
The University of Connecticut

 LAWRENCE ERLBAUM ASSOCIATES, PUBLISHERS
2000   Mahwah, New Jersey   London

Lawrence Erlbaum Associates, Inc., Publishers
10 Industrial Avenue
Mahwah, NJ 07430

Cover design by Kathryn Houghtaling Lacey

Library of Congress Cataloging-in-Publication Data

Reagan, Timothy G.
Non-western educational traditions : alternative approaches
    to educational thought and practice /
    Timothy Reagan.—2nd ed.
        p. cm.
    Includes bibliographical references and index.
    ISBN 0-8058-3450-8 (pbk. : alk. paper)
    1. Comparative education. 2. Education—Philosophy.
    3. Educational anthropology. I. Title
LB43 .R43 2000
370'.9—dc21   99-054729
                                                                CIP

Books published by Lawrence Erlbaum Associates are
printed on acid-free paper, and their bindings are chosen for
strength and durability.

Printed in the United States of America
10 9 8 7 6 5 4 3 2 1

This book is dedicated to my father,
Gerald Reagan,
with thanks for everything

Contents

List of Figures

Preface

In all societies, throughout human history, people have educated their children. Indeed, one of the fundamental characteristics of human civilization is a concern for the preparation of the next generation. From one generation to the next, we seek to pass on what we know and have learned, hoping to ensure not merely the survival of our offspring, but of our culture as well.

The history of education, as it has been conceived and taught in the United States (and generally in the West), has focused almost entirely on the ways in which our own educational tradition emerged, developed, and changed over the course of the centuries. This is, of course, understandable, but it means that we have ignored the many ways that other societies have sought to meet many of the same challenges. In this book, an effort is made to try to provide a brief overview of a small number of other, non-Western approaches to educational thought and practice. An understanding of the ways that other peoples have tried to educate their children, as well as what counted for them as "education," may help us to think more clearly about some of our own assumptions and values, as well as to help us to become more open to alternative viewpoints about important educational matters.

Unlike most areas traditionally included in the training of educators, very few individuals have had any real exposure to non-Western educational traditions, and so the audience for this book is a very broad and diverse one. The book was written to be accessible to both preservice and inservice teachers, but may also be of interest to advanced students in graduate programs as well as faculty members. Although both the book as a whole and particular sections of the book may be of considerable interest to educators in other societies, the book is written from the perspective of American readers and presupposes that readers are, at the very least, familiar with the Western educational tradition.

ORGANIZATION OF THE BOOK

Non-Western Educational Traditions: Alternative Approaches to Educational Thought and Practice consists of nine chapters dealing with a wide variety of different, non-Western cultural and historical educational traditions. In chapter 1, a theoretical foundation and base for the study of non-Western educational traditions is offered. In the next chapter, a broad overview of traditional, indigenous African educational thought and practice is offered. Chapters 3 and 4 move our focus away from Africa and onto indigenous educational thought and practice in two distinctive settings in the Americas. In chapter 3, an examination of the educational thought and practice of the Mayas and Aztecs is used as a case study of indigenous education in Mesoamerica, while in chapter 4, the indigenous North American experience is discussed. Traditional educational thought and practice in imperial China is the focus of chapter 5, with a special emphasis on the role of the imperial examination system. Chapter 6 provides an overview of the educational tradition embedded in Hinduism and Buddhism. Chapter 7 presents an overview of educational thought and practice among the Rom. Although technically not non-Western in important ways, including its relationship to the so-called "Judeo-Christian" tradition, the Muslim educational heritage is similarly excluded in large part from Western histories of educational thought and practice, and so its inclusion in a book of this sort is certainly defensible. Therefore, chapter 8 presents a survey of traditional Islamic educational thought and practice. Finally, the last chapter in *Non-Western Educational Traditions: Alternative Approaches to Educational Thought and Practice* summarizes some of the major themes and issues discussed in the book and suggests future areas for scholarly exploration. At the end of each chapter, there are a number of questions for reflection and discussion, as well as recommendations for further readings.

NEW IN THE SECOND EDITION

This second edition of *Non-Western Educational Traditions: Alternative Approaches to Educational Thought and Practice* has allowed me the opportunity to revisit a number of areas, to expand and clarify points that I felt were not sufficiently clear in the first edition, to update chapters as needed, and to improve (I hope) the pedagogical usefulness of the text. In chapter 3 ("Training 'Face and Heart': The Mesoamerican Educational Experiment") a section on Mayan education has been added. One entirely new chapter has been written (chapter 7, "'Familiar Strangers': The Case of the Rom").

ACKNOWLEDGMENTS

Writing a book is an undertaking like few others, in that it is profoundly personal and individual, but at the same time it requires considerable patience and support from many others. I am deeply grateful to many colleagues for their help and assistance throughout the writing of this work. In particular, I would like to thank Naomi Tutu, Patricia Weibust, Tom Jones, Chuck Case, Eva Díaz, Frank Stone, Kay Norlander, Cheryl Spaulding, and Tom DeFranco, all at the University of Connecticut, as well as Larry Klein and Daniel Mulcahy at Central Connecticut State University, Rose Morris at the Human Sciences Research Council in Pretoria, and Claire Penn at the University of the Witwatersrand. I am also very thankful for the insights and challenges provided by many of my doctoral students, and especially those of Beatrice Ndu Okwu, Terry A. Osborn, Hsiung-Huei Lee, Eliana Rojas, Sharon Wilson, Gerda Walz-Michaels, Joe Veth, Adama Sow, and Kamala Willey. The librarians at the University of Connecticut, as well as those at Central Connecticut State University, the University of Hartford, The Ohio State University, the Human Sciences Research Council, and the University of the Witwatersrand, were incredibly supportive as well, tracking down difficult-to-find material and making every effort to be helpful. My friends Tammy Wood and Ann Randall provided many cups of coffee and worthwhile discussion on many of the topics covered in this book, and I am also more grateful to them than I can say. Naomi Silverman, at Lawrence Erlbaum Associates, has been a wonderful friend and supporter from the beginning of this project. The reviewers of the manuscript provided many useful and helpful ideas and questions, and I would like to thank Robert H. Kim, Western Washington University; Maenette Benham, Michigan State University; and Tove Skutnabb-Kangas, The University of Roskilde, Denmark. Finally, and as always, I want to thank Jo Ann, Joshua, Bryan, and Kimberly.

—*Timothy Reagan*

It is not for him to pride himself who loveth his own country, but rather for him who loveth the whole world. The earth is but one country, and mankind its citizens.
—Bahá'u'lláh

1

An Introduction to the Study
of Non-Western Educational Traditions:
A Philosophical Starting Point

Most books and courses that deal with the history and philosophy of education include few, if any, references to indigenous educational ideas and practices in Africa and the Americas, and relatively few references to those of Asia. While for some time now there have been calls for the inclusion of the perspectives of women and people of color in studies of the history and philosophy of education, such efforts, where they have taken place, have often entailed little more than the addition of vignettes indicating the contributions of women and people of color to the Western tradition. In other words, the idea that there might be valuable insights to be gained from a serious examination of non-Western educational traditions themselves—indeed, that these traditions might be fully comparable to the Western tradition in their unique richness and diversity—is one that has been rarely voiced. Furthermore, where non-Western educational ideas and practices have been discussed, they are often subjected to a treatment roughly comparable to the "Orientalism" discussed by Edward Said with regard to the Western (and specifically, Anglo-French-American) response to Islam and the Islamic world. Said argued that:

> Orientalism can be discussed and analyzed as the corporate institution for dealing with the Orient—dealing with it by making statements about it, authorizing views of it, describing it, by teaching it, settling it, ruling over it: in short, Orientalism as a Western style for dominating, restructuring, and having authority over the Orient. … European culture gained in strength and identity by setting itself off against the Orient as a sort of surrogate and even underground self.[1]

In other words, when scholars *do* try to examine non-Western educational thought and practice, all too often they tend to do so through a lens that not only colors what they see, but also reifies the object of study—making it, in essence, part of "the other" and hence alien. Reification results not only in the distortion of what one is trying to understand, but also in its subjugation to one's own preexisting values and norms. This problem is not, of course, unique to the study of educational thought and practice; it is a common criticism of Western scholarship about the non-Western world in general. For example, in his discussion of the study of indigenous African religions by Western scholars, the Ugandan poet Okot p'Bitek wrote of the "systematic and intensive use of dirty gossip" in place of solid and sensitive scholarship.[2] In a similar vein, the anthropologist Adam Kuper wrote of *The Invention of Primitive Society* by 19th- and 20th-century anthropologists and social theorists in the West.[3] In terms of traditional African educational practices, A. Babs Fafunwa commented that, "Because indigenous education failed to conform to the ways of the Westernised system, some less well-informed writers have considered it primitive, even savage and barbaric. But such contentions should be seen as the product of ignorance and due to a total misunderstanding of the inherent value of informal education."[4]

The same, of course, can be argued with respect to Western treatment of indigenous educational ideas and practices in Asia, the Americas, and elsewhere. In short, when we speak of the history of educational thought and practice, what we have actually meant in the past has been the history of *Western* educational thought and practice, and the effect of our meaning has been, in essence, to delegitimatize the many alternatives found elsewhere in the world. In other words, it is discourse itself—the way that one talks, thinks about, and conceptualizes educational thought and practice—that is at issue. As Stephen Ball noted in a discussion of the work of the French philosopher Michel Foucault, "Discourse is a central concept in Foucault's analytical framework. Discourses are about what can be said and thought, but also about who can speak, when, and with what authority. Discourses embody meaning and social relationships, they constitute both subjectivity and power relations."[5]

The underlying purpose of this book, then, is to begin the process by which the existing discourse in the history of educational thought and practice can be expanded in such a way as to provide a starting point for the development of a more open and diverse view of the development of various approaches to educational thought and practice. Needless to say, this work is intended to be only a beginning. If the study of the various educational traditions discussed here is to be taken seriously, these traditions (and many others as well) will require, and are certainly entitled to, the same sort of concern that has long been accorded the Western tradition. Furthermore, given their differences from the Western tradition, it is essential that we all learn to invite and to listen to the "multiple voices" and perspectives that can enlighten our understanding of these traditions, just as we must learn to recognize that different groups may, as a consequence of their sociocultural contexts and backgrounds, possess "ways of knowing" that, although different from our own, may be every bit as valuable and worthwhile as those to which we are accustomed.[6] As Carol

Gilligan suggested with respect to "woman's place in man's life cycle" in her book, *In a Different Voice: Psychological Theory and Women's Development:*

> At a time when efforts are being made to eradicate discrimination between the sexes in the search for social equality and justice, the differences between the sexes are being rediscovered in the social sciences. This discovery occurs when theories formerly considered to be sexually neutral in their scientific objectivity are found instead to reflect a consistent observational and evaluative bias. Then the presumed neutrality of science, like that of language itself, gives way to the recognition that the categories of knowledge are human constructions. The fascination with point of view that has informed the fiction of the twentieth century and the corresponding recognition of the relativity of judgment infuse our scientific understanding as well when we begin to notice how accustomed we have become to seeing life through men's eyes.[7]

A very similar kind of argument can be made with respect to the differences in perspective and worldview in various non-Western cultural and historic traditions. To be sure, this argument is, at the present time, speculative in nature with respect to many of the traditions to be discussed in this book, while in the case of women there is now a growing body of fairly compelling empirical evidence. My hope would be that others, from a wide array of different backgrounds, would challenge, modify and add to the base that is offered here, and that someday the study of the Aztec *calmécac* and *telpochcalli*, of the imperial Chinese examination system and its content, and the role of various African initiation schools, among others, might be as commonly taught in courses in the history of educational thought as the study of Plato, Rousseau, and Dewey is today. Having said this, I also want to stress that I am not arguing that Plato, Rousseau, and Dewey (among others) should be eliminated; they, and many others, are important figures in the development of our own historical tradition, and certainly merit serious study. My focus here is not on replacing the Western tradition, but rather on trying to expand our understanding of education, broadly conceived, through the examination and study of other approaches to educational thought and practice with which many of us tend to be less familiar. Ultimately, of course, as we better understand the educational traditions of other societies and cultures, we will also be forced to reexamine and to reflect on our own tradition in somewhat different ways—and this will be immensely beneficial to our understanding of our own traditions.

THE CHALLENGE OF ETHNOCENTRISM

As we begin the process of trying to broaden our perspectives on the history of educational thought and practice, it is important for us to understand that the activity in which we are engaged will inevitably involve challenging both our own ethnocentrism and the ethnocentrism of others. Basically, *ethnocentrism* refers to the tendency to view one's own cultural group as superior to others—a tendency common to most, if not all, human societies. However, in contemporary scholarly discourse, one seldom comes across such blatant ethnocentrism. Rather, what is far more common is simply the practice of using one's own society and sociocultural practices as the "norms" by which other societies are viewed, measured, and evaluated. Ethnocentrism of this kind takes two somewhat distinct forms: cultural ethnocentrism and epistemological ethnocentrism.[8]

Cultural ethnocentrism refers to manifestations of ethnocentrism in individual scholars and their work, as well as to the sociocultural context that has helped to form and support such individual and idiosyncratic biases. In other words, we see examples of cultural ethnocentrism when writers and scholars allow common biases, prejudices, and assumptions to color their work in various ways. Racism, sexism, linguicism, ageism, and so on, all contribute to cultural ethnocentrism, most often in ways that are unconscious. Thus, the topics that a scholar chooses to explore, the questions that are asked about the topic, the framework within which hypotheses are constructed, how conflicting evidence is weighed, and even what counts as evidence, can all be affected by personal biases.

This brings us to the second sort of ethnocentrism, *epistemological ethnocentrism*, which deals not so much with individual assumptions and biases, but rather, with those common to an entire field of study. With epistemological ethnocentrism, we are concerned with what the philosopher of science Thomas Kuhn called the dominant "paradigm" in our own field of study.[9] A paradigm, on Kuhn's account, is far more than merely a model or a theory. As Patton explained:

> A paradigm is a world view, a general perspective, a way of breaking down the complexity of the real world. As such, paradigms are deeply embedded in the socialization of adherents and practitioners: paradigms tell them what is important, legitimate, and reasonable. Paradigms are also normative, telling the practitioner what to do without the necessity of long existential or epistemological consideration. But it is this aspect of paradigms that constitutes both their strength and their weakness—their strength in that it makes action possible, their weakness in that the very reason for action is hidden in the unquestioned assumptions of the paradigm.[10]

Thus, the dominant paradigm in a field of study at any given point in time essentially establishes the parameters within which "legitimate" discourse may take place. Kuhn explained the significance and power of the dominant paradigm in a field of study as follows:

> Scientists work from models acquired through education and through subsequent exposure to the literature often without quite knowing or needing to know what characteristics have given these models the status of community paradigms. ... That scientists do not usually ask or debate what makes a particular

problem or solution legitimate tempts us to suppose that, at least intuitively, they know the answer. But it may only indicate that neither the question nor the answer is felt to be relevant to their research. Paradigms may be prior to, more binding, and more complete than any set of rules for research that could be unequivocally abstracted from them.[11]

In the case of the study of the history and philosophy of education, the dominant paradigm has focused almost entirely on a single educational tradition, to the exclusion of virtually all others, as was mentioned earlier in this chapter. The study of traditional, indigenous educational practices has been reduced to the study of "socialization" and "acculturation," and has been left to anthropologists and others. Because scholars have tended to equate "education" with "schooling," and because they have consistently focused on the role of literacy and a literary tradition, many important and interesting—indeed, fascinating—traditions have been seen as falling outside of the parameters of "legitimate" study in the history and philosophy of education. Furthermore, even in the study of the Western educational tradition itself, scholars have been somewhat remiss in examining aspects of the traditions that seem to fall outside the bounds of their expectations. For example, even recent works concerned with educational thought and practice in classical antiquity generally ignore the formidable work of Martin Bernal, who has, since the early 1980s, been arguing that the civilization of classical Greece has deep and important roots in Afroasiatic cultures.[12] Similarly, until fairly recently the contributions of women to the Western educational tradition were largely ignored, in part as a result of overlooking the contributions of specific individual women, but even more, by defining *education* in such a way as to eliminate from discussion what might be called the "reproductive" (as opposed to the "productive") aspects of education.[13] Thus, although throughout virtually all of the Western historical tradition women have played the central role in raising children and in educating them, this was largely ignored in formal studies of the development of the Western educational tradition.[14]

Although dangerous and pernicious, cultural ethnocentrism is actually somewhat easier to challenge than epistemological ethnocentrism, since individual scholars in a particular field at the same point in time may differ to a considerable degree with respect to issues related to cultural ethnocentrism. Thus, many scholars today are far more sensitive to issues of gender, race, and ethnicity than others, while nonetheless working within the same epistemologically ethnocentric paradigm.

An example in which both cultural and epistemological ethnocentrism can be clearly seen was written in the mid-1970s by H. M. Phillips, and is presented here:

In Africa, education was extremely limited and associated with the very small numbers who were in contact with Islam over the land routes and later with Eu-

ropeans in the ports or administrative centres already starting to be set up in
those parts of Africa which were colonized. But basically the continent as a whole
was still completely underdeveloped and tribal. African potential, though great,
was late in being mobilized.[15]

The epistemological ethnocentrism of this passage can be seen, for instance, in
its conflation of "education" with "formal schooling" to the obvious detriment
of traditional education in Africa, which has been informal in nature and
closely tied to the social life of the community.[16] By assuming, as Phillips did,
that "education" and "schooling" are synonymous constructs, one dramatically
distorts the reality of the African experience. The passage also displays elements of cultural ethnocentrism, especially in its presentation of colonialism
and imperialism (whether Islamic or Western) as essentially progressive in nature, while indigenous practices, ideals, and so on are seen as "underdeveloped" and "primitive"—spoken of only in terms of "potential," suggesting the
need for "development."

    In short, as one considers both cultural and epistemological ethnocentrism
in the study of the history of educational thought and practice, there is good
reason to believe that perhaps it is time to begin to challenge the dominant paradigm in the field, in roughly the same way that an increasing number of educational researchers have challenged the traditional, essentially positivistic,
paradigm in educational research, seeking to replace it with a naturalistic,
interpretivist qualitative paradigm.[17] In the case of the history and philosophy
of education, the paradigmatic challenge must rest in large part on the reality
of diversity, and the lack of any "universal" tradition—a theme about which
Paul Ricoeur, in his book *History and Truth*, wrote:

> When we discover that there are several cultures instead of just one and conse-
> quently at the time when we acknowledge the end of a sort of cultural monopoly,
> be it illusory or real, we are threatened with destruction by our own discovery.
> Suddenly it becomes possible that there are just *others*, that we ourselves are an
> "other" among others.[18]

The recognition that one's own tradition is simply one among many (and not
necessarily even *primus inter pares*,[19] at that) will be, for many people, a difficult one to accept, and yet that is precisely what is required if the study of the
history of educational thought and practice is to be more than a parochial arti-
fact. Furthermore, in order better to understand the many educational traditions that exist and have existed in the world, it will be necessary to expand
substantially the methodological tools at the disposal of scholars, using not
only the standard methods of historical and philosophical scholarship, but increasingly, those of such disciplines as anthropology, cultural studies, linguistics, sociology, comparative literature, archeology, and others. Our
scholarship, in short, must become far more interdisciplinary in both theory
and practice than has been true in the past.

THE ROLE OF CONSTRUCTIVIST EPISTEMOLOGY IN THE STUDY
OF NON-WESTERN EDUCATIONAL TRADITIONS

As our discussion of ethnocentrism in general, and of epistemological ethnocentrism in particular, makes clear, a critical component of the study of non-Western educational traditions must necessarily be that of epistemology, especially with respect to our view of the *nature of knowledge*. In this book, two important assumptions are made about knowledge: the first is that knowledge is, to some degree, relative, in that it is both reasonable and indeed appropriate for us to talk about "multiple perspectives" on reality.[20] Thus, in order to make sense of the events and debates of the American Civil Rights Movement, for instance, one would need to understand the perspectives of the various actors in that movement: civil rights workers (both black and white), hard-core segregationists, politicians, and everyday black and white people living in different parts of the United States. It is important to note that while we need to recognize all of these perspectives (and indeed many others as well), that does *not* mean that we presuppose that all perspectives should be treated as equally valid. To grant the *legitimacy* of an individual's or a group's perspective is by no means the same as granting its *accuracy*.[21] In short, what we do when we accept the idea of "multiple perspectives" is to admit that a single event or set of events can be understood in very different ways by different groups and individuals—and that it is important to take into account as many of these different perspectives as possible in any serious examination of the event or events.

The second assumption that is made here is that knowledge is *constructed* by each individual.[22] In other words, "knowledge" is not something that is "out there" that we need to grasp; rather, it is something that we ourselves build based on our own background, experiences, prior understandings, and the data before us. This means that each of us will construct our own knowledge in a unique manner, and that each of us will, therefore, have idiosyncratically derived understandings of reality (and, hence, we see the need for the recognition of "multiple perspectives"). It is important to stress here that constructivist epistemology is more than simply an alternative to other approaches to epistemology; rather, it entails a rejection of some of the core assumptions that have been shared by Western epistemology for some two and a half millennia.[23] As von Glasersfeld argued, "the crucial fact [in understanding constructivism is] that the constructivist theory of knowing breaks with the epistemological tradition in philosophy,"[24] which is why it has been labeled not merely postmodernist, but *postepistemological* by some writers.[25]

Up to this point, we have discussed constructivism as a single entity; in reality, it has become fairly commonplace in discussions of constructivism to distinguish between what are often taken to be two fundamentally distinct, competing *types* of constructivism.[26] The first type of constructivism, radical constructivism, is fundamentally an epistemological construct that has been most clearly and forcefully advocated in the work of Ernst von Glasersfeld.[27] Radical constructivism has its philosophical roots in Piaget's genetic episte-mology,[28] and is essentially a cognitive view of learning in which "students ac-tively construct their ways of knowing as they strive to be effective by restoring coherence to the worlds of their personal experience."[29] Radical constructivism is premised on the belief that an individual's knowledge can never be a "true" representation of reality (i.e., in an observer-independent sense), but is rather a construction of the world that the individual experi-ences. In other words, knowledge is not something that is passively received by the learner; it is, quite the contrary, the result of active mental work on the part of the learner. Thus, from a radical constructivist perspective, knowledge is not something that can merely be conveyed from teacher to student and any pedagogical approach that presumes otherwise must be rejected.

The alternative to radical constructivism is social constructivism, which has as its primary theoretical foundation, the work of Lev Vygotsky.[30] Social constructivism, while accepting the notion that the individual does indeed construct his or her own knowledge, argues that the process of knowledge con-struction inevitably takes place in a sociocultural context, and that therefore knowledge is in fact *socially* constructed. As Driver and her colleagues argued with respect to science education, "it is important ... to appreciate that scien-tific knowledge is both symbolic in nature and also socially negotiated. ... The objects of science are not phenomena of nature but constructs that are ad-vanced by the scientific community to interpret nature."[31]

The tension between radical and social constructivism, between the per-sonal and the social construction of knowledge, is to a significant extent more apparent than real, and in any event, is certainly amenable to resolution on a practical level, criticisms to the contrary notwithstanding.[32] As Paul Cobb as-serted, "the sociocultural and cognitive constructivist perspectives each con-stitute the background for the other,"[33] and von Glasersfeld recognized that "we must generate an explanation of how 'others' and the 'society' in which we find ourselves living can be conceptually constructed on the basis of our sub-jective experiences."[34] Ultimately, even D. C. Phillips, a leading critic of the philosophical foundations of radical constructivism,[35] agreed that:

> It is worth stressing that these philosophical issues do not have to be settled be-fore the business of education can proceed. I suspect that von Glasersfeld and I are very close in the kinds of educational attitudes and practices that we endorse. If you are about to undergo brain surgery, you do not have to wait until surgeons reach agreement about the thorny philosophical issues surrounding the body–mind problem. Similarly, a student can manipulate geological samples without having to settle upon a defensible philosophical account about the na-ture of the existence of these samples.[36]

Perhaps the most reasonable way to articulate the common, shared elements of radical and social constructivism is to talk about learning as "socially mitigated but personally constructed," a formulation that at the very least moves us away from a strong bifurcation of radical and social constructivism. Finally, it is important to keep in mind that not only is reality a social and individual construction in a certain sense, but further, that any academic discipline is itself the result of both personal and social construction.[37] As Gunnarsson argued:

> Scientific language and discourse emerge in a cooperative and competitive struggle among scientists to create the knowledge base of their field, to establish themselves in relation to other scientists and to other professional groups, and to gain influence and control over political and socioeconomic means. In every strand of human communication, language and discourse play a role in the formation of a social and societal reality and identity. This is also true both of the different professional and vocational cultures within working and public life and of the formation of different academic cultures.[38]

THE CONCEPT OF "TRADITION" AND ITS LIMITS

This book is about non-Western educational traditions, and throughout we talk about "tradition" in a number of very different ways. Patricia Weibust compellingly argued that the concept of "tradition" is a far more complex one than is generally recognized. She suggested that "tradition" can come in three very different, and in fact logically distinct, forms: the historical tradition (that is, what really took place historically), the defined tradition (what members of the culture believe to have taken place historically), and the contemporary tradition (the way in which the tradition is manifested in people's lives today), and furthermore, that "tradition" is best understood not in static terms, but rather as an on-going process.[39] This distinction is a powerful and useful one as a heuristic device and analytic tool. However, in practice the three kinds of tradition are often far from distinct, and it is very difficult indeed to distinguish among them in many of the instances which we examine. Our task becomes even more complex in this regard when one considers that some of the traditions which we study here are living ones, while others continue to exist in very truncated forms, if at all. Thus, while we are concerned primarily with the historical tradition in each of the cases we examine, the defined tradition may well function as a limitation to our understanding, and, in some cases, confusion may arise between the historical, defined, and contemporary traditions. Finally, as we talk about different traditions, it is important that we keep in mind that traditions are in fact processes that continually change, develop and evolve, and that at best, we are looking at a snapshot of a tradition at a particular point in time.

THE WESTERN/NON-WESTERN DICHOTOMY

The title and organization of this book would appear to create a dichotomy between Western and non-Western traditions and practices. It is important that we note that such a dichotomy, although heuristically useful, is in fact misleading. As Swartz noted, "The categories 'Western' and 'Non-Western' are our creations, and reflect neither the diversity of beliefs (often mutually contradictory) that people hold, nor the commonalities that exist across apparently very different groups of people."[40] The problem is really one of oversimplification: Although there may be certain similarities from one non-Western culture to another, there are also bound to be significant and relevant differences, just as there are significant and relevant differences among different Western traditions. Furthermore, individuals often tolerate (and even thrive upon) mutually contradictory beliefs—thus, people in Western traditions may well hold stereotypic non-Western beliefs, and vice versa. Finally, the distinction itself is potentially problematic ideologically, in that the terms "Western" and "non-Western" may (and often do) reflect biased and loaded assumptions. In other words, even the labels that we are using may lead us to errors akin to those identified by Said with respect to "Orientalism."

If the labels "Western" and "non-Western" are such a problem, then why use them? The answer to this very reasonable question is actually quite simple: The biases inherent in the terms are in fact a significant and telling component of the phenomenon that we are concerned with studying. The assumptions and stereotypes that need to be challenged are already present, and if our language reflects them, then it may be useful to recognize the biases that are inherent in the language that we use. Thus, what begins as a false dichotomy can emerge as an effective way of challenging and reforming racist and ethnocentric assumptions and biases, both conceptually and linguistically.

LEARNING FROM ORAL TRADITIONS

An important element in the process of expanding our perspectives on the history of educational thought and practice is learning more about the many ways in which different societies pass on their traditions, histories, and so on. Although many of the societies that we will examine in this book do have written traditions, similar to those found in the Western tradition, others have relied primarily or exclusively on oral traditions. Written traditions have many advantages, but so do oral ones—advantages that our own society, for the most part, lost long ago. In his landmark work, *Oral Tradition as History*, Jan Vansina argued that:

> The marvel of oral tradition, some will say its curse, is this: messages from the past exist, are real, and yet are not continuously accessible to the senses. Oral traditions make an appearance only when they are told. For fleeting moments they can be heard, but most of the time they dwell only in the minds of people. The utterance is transitory, but the memories are not. No one in oral societies doubts that memories can be faithful repositories which contain the sum total of past human experience and explain the how and why of present day conditions. *Tete*

are ne nne: "Ancient things are today" or "History repeats itself." … How it is possible for a mind to remember and out of nothing to spin complex ideas, messages, and instructions for living, which manifest continuity over time, is one of the greatest wonders one can study, comparable only to human intelligence and thought itself. Because the wonder is so great, it is also very complex. Oral tradition should be central to students of culture, of ideology, of society, of psychology, of art, and, finally, of history.[41]

And, one might well add, of students of education, since education plays a key role both in the perpetuation of any oral tradition (as it does in the perpetuation of any written tradition) and in helping to determine the content of that tradition.[42]

It is important to understand that oral and written traditions are *different*, and that each is useful and valuable in its own right. Neither is intrinsically superior to the other in all ways; each has its own strengths and each has its own limitations.[43] It is also important for us to bear in mind that much of the Western tradition has its origins in oral traditions—the epic poetry of Homer,[44] Anglo-Saxon heroic poetry,[45] the Irish epics,[46] even the synoptic Gospels,[47] all have their origins in oral, rather than written, traditions.[48]

Finally, the fact that we attempt to discuss oral traditions in a written text is itself something of a paradox. As Karl Kroeber commented about the study of American Indian tales, "one must ask if any *written* text can accurately produce an *oral* recitation."[49] The problem is that oral literature is, by its very nature, dependent on *performance*. As Ruth Finnegan explained in her discussion of oral literature in Africa:

Oral literature is by definition dependent on a performer who formulates it in words on a specific occasion—there is no other way in which it can be realized as a literary product … without its oral realization and direct rendition by singer or speaker, an unwritten literary piece cannot easily be said to have any continued or independent existence at all. In this respect the parallel is less to written literature than to music and dance; for these too are art forms which in the last analysis are actualized in and through their performance and, furthermore, in a sense depend on repeated performances for their continued existence.[50]

Thus, when we discuss oral traditions in a book like this one, we are at best dealing with a mere shadow of the true reality of the oral text (somewhat analogous to Plato's "allegory of the cave"). The risks of such an undertaking are made clear in the following story, an example of "dissident humor" in the former Soviet Union:

Standing on Lenin's tomb in Red Square, Stalin was acknowledging the acclamation of the masses. Suddenly he raised his hands to silence the crowd.

"Comrades," he cried. "A most historic event! A telegram of congratulations from Leon Trotsky!"

The crowd could hardly believe its ears. It waited in hushed anticipation.

"Joseph Stalin," read Stalin. "The Kremlin. Moscow. You were right and I was wrong. You are the true heir of Lenin. I must apologize. Trotsky."

A roar erupted from the crowd.

But in the front row a little Jewish tailor gestured frantically to Stalin.

"Psst!" he cried. "Comrade Stalin."

Stalin leaned over to hear what he had to say.

"Such a message! But you read it without the right *feeling*."

Stalin once again raised his hands to the still excited crowd. "Comrades!" he announced. "Here is a simple worker, a Communist, who says I did not read Trotsky's message with the right *feeling*. I ask that worker to come up on the podium himself to read Trotsky's telegram."

The tailor jumped up on the podium and took the telegram into his hands. He read:

"Joseph Stalin. The Kremlin. Moscow."

Then he cleared his throat and sang out:

"You were *right* and I was *wrong*? *You* are the true heir of Lenin? *I* must *apologize*?"[51]

Needless to say, the tailor's rendition of the telegram conveyed a radically different meaning to the text—a meaning disguised by the written text, and best made clear in an oral rendition. The use of italics in the text may help us to reproduce the oral event, but it requires a performance to really make sense. It is just such risks that we must be sensitive to when we examine any oral tradition or written rendering of an oral "text." In addition, it is essential that we keep in mind"that all texts are in some sense intertextual, all discourses interdiscursive, requiring a Foucaultian archaeology to uncover and explicate how it is that they are multiply formed."[52]

E.T., THE LOST CONTINENT OF ATLANTIS, AND CANNIBALISM: SOME REFLECTIONS ON CREDIBILITY AND "OTHERNESS"

One of the more interesting aspects of studying non-Western cultures is the variety of ways in which the impressive accomplishments of such cultures and societies have often been either rejected altogether, diminished in importance, or attributed to other civilizations and sources. For example, the ruins and ancient mine shafts of Great Zimbabwe in southern Africa were claimed to have been the creation of some mysterious civilization in the distant past, perhaps related to the Carthaginians or some other ancient people, perhaps even the product of some extraterrestrial culture—*anyone*, in short, other than the ancestors of the indigenous Africans living in the area today.[53] It was simply inconceivable to many people that these incredible remnants of a once-great civilization could have been produced by people who were, in the words of the South African historian George McCall Theal, "fickle barbarians, prone to robbery and unscrupulous in shedding blood."[54] Such views were common in the late 19th and early 20th centuries, not just about Africa but also about the indigenous peoples of Asia and the Americas,[55] and might perhaps be dismissed as mere historical oddities, except that many of the elements of these views (and much of the work of the historians who proposed and supported them) has continued to be circulated, studied, and taught in spite of the overwhelming rejection of such ideas by academic historians and archeologists.[56]

The same tendency also appears, often overlapping "New Age" rhetoric and practice, in efforts to explain Mesoamerican and other non-Western civilizations by proposing ties to Atlantis, ancient Egypt, Stonehenge, and to various extraterrestrial sources. Such efforts date back at least to the 19th century,[57] but have become increasingly popular in the years following the initial publication of Erich von Däniken's *Chariots of the Gods*.[58] A quick trip to my local bookstore offered a selection of recent examples of such works including not only a number of follow-up works by von Däniken,[59] but also Maurice Cotterell's *The Supergods: They Came on a Mission to Save Mankind*,[60] about the Maya; David Furlong's *The Keys to the Temple*,[61] which ties the pyramids in Egypt to Mayan temples and to Marlborough Downs; and José Argüelles' *The Mayan Factor: Path Beyond Technology*,[62] which purports to use Mayan sources to explain harmonic convergence (among other things). Although these works, and those like them, tend to include ties to Atlantis, ancient Egypt, the Mayas, and the Incas, and, of course, extraterrestrial contacts, they also share another common theme: They are all based on the idea that various aspects of human civilizations (almost always non-Western civilizations, interestingly enough) cannot be explained by "normal" human history, sociocultural development, and so on. Instead, they all posit some sort of *deus ex machina* who, it is asserted, must have been responsible for the emergence of the great non-Western civilizations. The problem with such explanations, apart from the fact that they are simply pseudoscience in the garb of scholarship[63]—no small problem in its own right, to be sure—is that they also serve to support and reinforce beliefs and ideologies that are demonstrably racist in both origin and nature. In short, to assume or presuppose that the indigenous peoples of Mesoamerica, for instance, needed help from escaping Atlanteans, planet-hopping extraterrestrials, or whomever, would inevitably seem to suggest that they were not themselves capable of creating the civilizations whose ruins and remnants remain so impressive even today. This, it seems to me, does these people, the civilizations that they created, their descendants, and indeed, all of us as human beings, a serious injustice. It is far better, I would suggest, and certainly more credible in any meaningful sense of the term, to suppose that human beings in many different times and places have been able to create great civilizations, as well as architectural, artistic, musical, and literary feats.[64]

If there sometimes seems to be a reluctance to believe that various indige-nous peoples, or their ancestors, could have been the creators of great civiliza-tions, there is no similar reticence in believing that such people might be capable of horrible atrocities of various sorts. To be sure, human beings in many times and places have behaved in awful ways and done things that certainly de-serve condemnation (child sacrifice and abandonment, both not uncommon in the ancient world,[65] come to mind here, as of course does the Holocaust in our own century). However, it may be the case that we have been far too quick, and perhaps too gullible, in believing some of the more extreme claims about other peoples and societies. One example here is that of cannibalism. We know beyond any reasonable doubt that cannibalism has taken place in certain ex-treme situations; the question is whether there have been cultures in which rit-ualized cannibalism has been relatively commonplace. As Martin Gardner argued:

> No one denies that during life-and-death emergencies, such as starving after a shipwreck or airplane crash, or during times of extreme famine, individuals may choose to eat human corpses rather than die. No one denies that there have been occasions among primitive peoples when, after a military victory, the body of a once-feared enemy leader was ritually devoured, either out of revenge or out of a belief that the enemy's powers would be acquired by the eaters. ... The big ques-tion is this: Has cannibalism ever been a *common* custom?[66]

Although some anthropologists continue to maintain that ritual cannibalism is indeed found among some groups,[67] other scholars have begun to reject such claims and to argue that they are in fact the result of "pure folklore, fabricated by the desire of one culture to feel superior to another."[68] Although this debate is still an active and unresolved one in anthropology, it nevertheless does pro-vide us with a strong reason for being careful about believing claims of extreme practices on the part of other cultures, peoples, and societies.

COMMONALITY AND DIVERSITY IN NON-WESTERN TRADITIONS

The role of oral traditions is a common theme in many of the different societ-ies that are examined in this book, and the commonality of this theme raises an important question. If different non-Western societies share many features, such as the role of an oral tradition, a communal approach to the education of children, a reliance on nonformal kinds of educational experiences, and so on, then to what extent are they really different traditions? Is it, in short, really necessary for us to study many different non-Western traditions, or would it not be sufficient for us to simply study one tradition in detail?

This is an important question, and one that does not have a simple answer. The different educational traditions that we explore in this book do indeed share many common features, but they also differ in significant ways. One way to think about this that may prove useful is to draw an analogy to a concept used in contemporary linguistics. Linguists distinguish among different kinds of linguistic "universals" (that is, properties and characteristics common to all languages). The most important distinction made in linguistics in this regard is that between what are called "absolute universals," that "are properties all languages share," and "relative universals," that "are general tendencies in language."[69] In other words, there can be no exceptions to absolute universals, while there may be exceptions to relative universals. Furthermore, the way in which such universals are manifested in particular languages may differ dramatically. The study of non-Western educational traditions is in fact fairly similar to the study of the diverse languages used by human beings around the world. While there are likely to be certain absolute universals (such as the goal of helping the child to become a "good person," albeit perhaps defined in different ways), and while there are also likely to be relative universals (such as a concern with treating other people with respect), the ways in which such universals are in fact manifested in any particular culture—as well as the means by which the society seeks to accomplish these goals—will be very distinctive.

The purpose of studying non-Western educational traditions is both to help us understand the common principles that underlie all educational undertakings and to understand the different means that human beings have devised to accomplish these principles. Such understanding is of course valuable in its own right, but it may also have profound effects on the way in which we view diversity and difference writ large, and as it impacts our own personal and professional lives. An understanding of Aztec education, for instance, is unlikely to have an immediate and direct use for the classroom teacher—there is no likelihood whatsoever that a teacher will have to deal with a child whose parents wish him to be prepared to enter a *calmécac*. Nevertheless, an awareness of how the Aztecs educated their children, both in terms of the goals that guided their educational system and the means that they used to achieve these goals, may well help each of us as educators to develop a more critical and sensitive understanding of the educational goals and methods used in our own society.

CONCLUSION

In short, the unifying theme of this book is that it is neither idealistic nor unrealistic to suggest that we can learn much from non-Western educational traditions. As Ali Mazrui argued in the first of his BBC Reith Lectures with respect to Africa and its relations with the West, "I cannot help feeling that it is about time Africa sent missionaries to Europe and America, as well as teachers, engineers, doctors and ordinary workers. ... It is indeed time that Africa counter-penetrated the western world."[70] Perhaps it is time not only for Africa, but for the non-Western world in general, to begin penetrating the study of the history of educational thought and practice. It is with this goal in mind that this book was written.

QUESTIONS FOR REFLECTION AND DISCUSSION

1. What are the implications of Edward Said's notion of "Orientalism" for what should be taught in the public schools in our society? For what classroom teachers should know?
2. In this chapter, it is asserted that "schooling" and "education" are by no means synonymous concepts. In our own society, how do these concepts differ? What are the implications of these differences for "public education" and "public schooling"?
3. When Paul Ricoeur writes that when "we acknowledge the end of a sort of cultural monopoly ... we are threatened with destruction by our own discovery," what does he mean? What are the implications of this claim for the curriculum in the public schools? For the curriculum in teacher education programs?
4. Although our own culture is predominantly a written rather than an oral culture, one could nevertheless make a strong case for one or more oral traditions coexisting and paralleling the written tradition. What would the elements of such oral traditions be in our own society? How are these traditions passed on from one generation to the next? Are there some oral traditions in our society that are not transgenerational? What are the implications of your answers for the classroom teacher?
5. The concept of "multiple perspectives" is a very powerful one that can help us make sense of many different social, political, and cultural conflicts. Identify three current controversies in the news, and explain how the concept of "multiple perspectives" can assist us in understanding what is taking place in each of these controversies.
6. What are the implications of constructivist epistemology, as discussed in this chapter, for our understanding of history? What are its implications for teaching and learning in the classroom context? In informal educational settings? How does constructivist epistemology differ from that proposed by Plato?
7. In order to test the author's claim that even the terms "Western" and "non-Western" may contain hidden biases, construct a list of adjectives that seem to you to intuitively fit in each of these two categories. What conclusions can you draw from this experience?
8. What does it mean when we say that, "To grant the *legitimacy* of an individual's or a group's perspective is by no means the same as granting its *accuracy*"? Can you provide examples of legitimate perspectives that may not be accurate? How is this possible?
9. In a recent book, critical of "pseudoscientific" claims about history and archeology, Francis Harrold and Raymond Eve write that many popular books, articles, movies, and so on, about historical issues (and especially

about human origins and past civilizations), "make claims about the past which are simply wrong—sometimes spectacularly so."[71] Can such a claim be reconciled to the notion of "multiple perspectives" and constructivist epistemology, and if so, how?

10. Do you think that Ali Mazrui was serious when he called for Africa to send missionaries to Europe and America? If you think he was serious, what kinds of messages do you think that such missionaries might carry? If you think that he was speaking metaphorically, what are the implications of the metaphor?

RECOMMENDED FURTHER READINGS

Edward Said's book *Orientalism* (New York: Vintage, 1978) provides a powerful and challenging perspective on how cultural expectations and biases can influence and distort the way that we make sense of the "other," as does his more recent *Culture and Imperialism* (New York: Vintage, 1993). Also quite useful in helping us to understand traditions different from our own is Jan Vansina's *Oral Tradition as History* (Madison: University of Wisconsin Press, 1985). A fascinating perspective on the concept of democracy as it has emerged in various non-Western societies is provided in Raul Manglapus' *Will of the People: Original Democracy in Non-Western Societies* (New York: Greenwood, 1987). Finally, although dealing with issues of mental health rather than education, *Culture and Mental Health: A Southern African View* (Cape Town: Oxford University Press, 1998), by Leslie Swartz, is an incredibly powerful example of the kind of critical response to Western biases in scholarship and practice that is being advocated here.

NOTES

1. Edward Said, *Orientalism* (New York: Vintage, 1978), 3. Also relevant and useful in this regard are Lisa Lowe, *Critical Terrains: French and British Orientalisms* (Ithaca, NY: Cornell University Press, 1991); Bryan Turner, *Orientalism, Postmodernism, and Globalism* (London: Routledge, 1994); John J. Clarke, *Oriental Enlightenment: The Encounter Between Asian and Western Thought* (London: Routledge, 1997); Robert Young, *White Mythology: Writing History and the West* (London: Routledge, 1990); Gyan Prakash, "Writing Post-Orientalist Histories of the Third World: Perspectives from Indian Historiography," *Comparative Studies in Society and History* 32 (1990): 383–408.

2. Okot p'Bitek, *African Religions in Western Scholarship* (Nairobi, Kenya: East African Literature Bureau, 1971), 22.

3. Adam Kuper, *The Invention of Primitive Society: Transformations of an Illusion* (London: Routledge, 1988). Also of interest in this regard is Henrika Kuklick, *The Savage Within: The Social History of British Anthropology, 1885–1945* (Cambridge, England: Cambridge University Press, 1991).

4. A. Babs Fafunwa, *A History of Education in Nigeria* (London: Allen & Unwin, 1974), 17. See also Alan Williamson, "Decolonizing Historiography of Colonial Education: Processes of Interaction in the Schooling of Torres Strait Islanders," *International Journal of Qualitative Studies in Education* 10, 4 (1997): 407–423.

5. Stephen Ball (ed.), *Foucault and Education: Disciplines and Knowledge* (London: Routledge, 1990), 2.

6. Mary Field Belenky, Blyth McVicker Clinchy, Nancy Rule Goldberger, and Jill Mattuck Tarule, *Women's Ways of Knowing: The Development of Self, Voice, and Mind* (New York: Basic Books, 1986).

7. Carol Gilligan, *In a Different Voice: Psychological Theory and Women's Development* (Cambridge, MA: Harvard University Press, 1982), 6.

8. See V. Mudimbe, *The Invention of Africa: Gnosis, Philosophy, and the Order of Knowledge* (London: Currey, 1988), 19.

9. See Thomas Kuhn, *The Structure of Scientific Revolutions*, 2nd enlarged ed. (Chicago: University of Chicago Press, 1970); Thomas Kuhn, *The Essential Tension: Selected Studies in Scientific Tradition and Change* (Chicago: University of Chicago Press, 1977).

10. Michael Patton, *Utilization-Focused Evaluations* (Beverly Hills, CA: Sage, 1978), 203.

11. Kuhn, *The Structure of Scientific Revolutions*, 46.

12. See Martin Bernal, *Black Athena: The Afroasiatic Roots of Classical Civilization, Volume 1: The Fabrication of Ancient Greece, 1785–1985* (New Brunswick, NJ: Rutgers University Press, 1987); Martin Bernal, *Black Athena: The Afroasiatic Roots of Classical Civilization, Volume 2: The Archeological and Documentary Evidence* (New Brunswick, NJ: Rutgers University Press, 1991). See chapter 2 for a detailed examination of the issues surrounding Afrocentrism and Afrocentric perspectives in contemporary American education.

13. Jane Roland Martin, "The Ideal of the Educated Person," in Daniel DeNicola (ed.), *Philosophy of Education: 1981* (Normal, IL: Philosophy of Education Society, 1982), 3–20.

14. See Jane Roland Martin, *Reclaiming a Conversation: The Ideal of the Educated Woman* (New Haven, CT: Yale University Press, 1985).

15. H. M. Phillips, quoted in Niara Sudarkasa, "Sex Roles, Education and Development in Africa," *Anthropology and Education* 13, 3 (1982): 281.

16. Traditional African educational thought and practice is discussed in detail in the next chapter.

17. See Yvonna Lincoln and Egon Guba, *Naturalistic Inquiry* (Newbury Park, CA: Sage, 1985); Michael Patton, *Qualitative Evaluation and Research Methods*, 2nd ed. (Newbury Park, CA: Sage, 1990). An interesting example of a scholarly effort to challenge epistemological ethnocentrism is Robbie Davis-Floyd and Carolyn Sargent (eds.), *Childbirth and Authoritative Knowledge: Cross-Cultural Perspectives* (Berkeley: University of California Press, 1997).

18. Paul Ricoeur, *History and Truth* (Evanston, IL: Northwestern University Press, 1965), 278.

19. "First among equals"—the way in which the role of the Pope with respect to the other Bishops of the Church is traditionally discussed.

20. See Lincoln and Guba, *Naturalistic Inquiry*, 70–91; David Erlandson, Edward Harris, Barbara Skipper, and Steve Allen, *Doing Naturalistic Inquiry: A Guide to Methods* (Newbury Park, CA: Sage, 1993), 5–28. See also Jonathan Jansen (ed.), *Knowledge and Power in South Africa: Critical Perspectives Across the Disciplines* (Johannesburg: Skotaville, 1991) for a detailed examination of the role of epistemology and perspective in critical scholarship.

21. See Harvey Siegel, *Rationality Redeemed? Further Dialogues on an Educational Ideal* (New York: Routledge, 1997), 130–133. This point also leads to the issue of the trustworthiness of observations in general, and of naturalistic research in particular. See Lincoln and Guba, *Naturalistic Inquiry*, 289–331. A fascinating and powerful example of the phenomena being discussed here is provided in Marshall Sahlins' book, *How "Natives" Think: About Captain Cook, For Example* (Chicago: University of Chicago Press, 1995).

22. See Catherine Fosnot (ed.), *Constructivism: Theory, Perspectives, and Practice* (New York: Teachers College Press, 1996); Yasmin Kefai and Mitchel Resnick (eds.), *Constructionism in Practice: Designing, Thinking, and Learning in a Digital World* (Mahwah, NJ: Lawrence Erlbaum Associates, 1996); Thomas Duffy and David Jonassen (eds.), *Constructivism and the Technology of Instruction* (Hillsdale, NJ: Lawrence Erlbaum Associates, 1992); Virginia Richardson (ed.), *Constructivist Teacher Education: Building a World of New Understandings* (London: Falmer Press, 1997); and Nel Noddings, *Philosophy of Education* (Boulder, CO: Westview, 1995), 115–119. Two recent works in the philosophy of mathematics are outstanding examples of the implications of constructivist epistemology for how we conceptualize various fields of study: see Stanislas Debaene, *The Number Sense: How the Mind Creates Mathematics* (New York: Oxford University Press, 1997); Reuben Hersh, *What is Mathematics, Really?* (New York: Oxford University Press, 1997). For a powerful and critical theoretical examination of social constructivism, see Finn Collin, *Social Reality* (London: Routledge, 1997).

23. See Kenneth Gergen, *Towards Transformation in Social Knowledge* (New York: Springer-Verlag, 1982). Also of relevance here is Kenneth Gergen, "Social Construction and the Educational Process," in Leslie Steffe and Jerry Gale (eds.), *Constructivism in Education* (Hillsdale, NJ: Lawrence Erlbaum Associates, 1995), 17–39.

24. Ernst von Glasersfeld, "A Constructivist Approach to Teaching," in Leslie Steffe and Jerry Gale (eds.), *Constructivism in Education* (Hillsdale, NJ: Lawrence Erlbaum Associates, 1995), 6.

25. See Nel Noddings, "Constructivism in Mathematics Education," in Robert Davis, Carolyn Maher, and Nel Noddings (eds.), *Constructivist Views on the Teaching and Learning of Mathematics* (Reston, VA: National Council of Teachers of Mathematics, 1990), 7–18.

26. See Paul Cobb, "Where is the Mind? Constructivist and Socioculturalist Perspectives on Mathematical Development," *Educational Researcher* 23 (1994): 13–20; Paul Cobb, "Where is the Mind? A Coordination of Sociocultural and Cognitive Constructionist Perspectives," in Catherine Fosnot (ed.), *Constructivism: Theory, Perspectives, and Practice* (New York: Teachers College Press, 1996), 34–52; L. Magadla, "Constructivism: A Practitioner's Perspective," *South African Journal of Higher Education* 10 (1996): 83–88.

27. Among Ernst von Glasersfeld's works, those which are most helpful in this regard include his "An Introduction to Radical Constructivism," in Paul Watzlawick (ed.), *The Invented Reality: How Do We Know What We Believe We Know?* (New York: Norton, 1984), 17–40; "Cognition, Construction of Knowledge, and Teaching," *Synthese* 80 (1989): 121–140; "Questions and Answers about Radical Constructivism," in Kenneth Tobin (ed.), *The Practice of Constructivism in Science Education* (Hillsdale, NJ: Lawrence Erlbaum, 1993), 23–38; "A Constructivist Approach to Teaching"; *Radical Constructivism: A Way of Knowing* (London: Falmer Press, 1995); "Footnotes to 'The Many Faces of Constructivism'," *Educational Researcher* 25 (1996): 19.

28. Jean Piaget, *L'epistémologie génétique*, 3rd ed. (Paris: Presses Universitaires de France, 1979); H. Sinclair, I. Berthoud, J. Gerard, and E. Venesiano, "Constructivisme et psycholinguistique génétique," *Archives de Psychologie* 53 (1985): 37–60.

29. Cobb, "Where is the Mind? A Coordination of Sociocultural and Cognitive Constructionist Perspectives," 34.

30. Lev Vygotsky, *Mind in Society: The Development of Higher Psychological Processes* (Cambridge, MA: Harvard University Press, 1978); Lev Vygotsky, *Thought and Language* (Cambridge, MA: MIT Press, 1986). See also Luis Moll (ed.), *Vygotsky and Education: Instructional Implications and Applications of Sociocultural Psychology* (Cambridge, England: Cambridge University Press, 1990).

31. Rosalind Driver, Hilary Asoko, John Leach, Eduardo Mortimer, and Philip Scott "Constructing Scientific Knowledge in the Classroom," *Educational Researcher* 23 (1994): 5.

32. See, for example, William Cobern, "Contextual Constructivism: The Impact of Culture on the Learning and Teaching of Science," in Kenneth Tobin (ed.), *The Practice of Constructivism in Science Education* (Hillsdale, NJ: Lawrence Erlbaum Associates, 1993), 51–69; Jere Confrey, "How Compatible are Radical Constructivism, Sociocultural Approaches, and Social Constructivism?" in Leslie Steffe and Jerry Gale (eds.), *Constructivism in Education* (Hillsdale, NJ: Lawrence Erlbaum Associates, 1995), 185–225; R. E. Young, "The Epistemic Discourse of Teachers: An Ethnographic Study," *Anthropology and Education Quarterly* 12, 2 (1981): 122–144.

33. Cobb, "Where is the Mind? A Coordination of Sociocultural and Cognitive Constructionist Perspectives," 48.

34. von Glasersfeld, "A Constructivist Approach to Teaching," 12.

35. See Denis C. Phillips, "The Good, the Bad, and the Ugly: The Many Faces of Constructivism," *Educational Researcher* 24 (1995): 5–12.

36. Denis C. Phillips, "Response to Ernst von Glasersfeld," *Educational Researcher* 25 (1996): 20.

37. See Britt–Louise Gunnarsson, Per Linell, and Bengt Nordberg (eds.), *The Construction of Professional Discourse* (London: Longman, 1997).

38. Britt–Louise Gunnarsson, "On the Sociohistorical Construction of Scientific Discourse," in Britt–Louise Gunnarsson, Per Linell, and Bengt Nordberg (eds.), *The Construction of Professional Discourse* (London: Longman, 1997), 99. For extensions of the implications of this argument, see Eva Krugly–Smolska, "An Examination of Some Difficulties in Integrating Western Science into Societies with an Indigenous Scientific Tradition," *Interchange* 25, 4 (1994): 325–334; Janice Raymond, "Medicine as Patriarchal Religion," *Journal of Medicine and Philosophy* 7 (1982): 197–216.

39. See Patricia Weibust, "Tradition as Process: Creating Contemporary Tradition in a Rural Norwegian School and Community," *International Journal of Qualitative Studies in Education* 2, 2 (1989): 107–122.

40. Leslie Swartz, *Culture and Mental Health: A Southern African View* (Cape Town: Oxford University Press, 1998), 92.

41. Jan Vansina, *Oral Tradition as History*, rev. ed. (Madison: University of Wisconsin Press, 1985), xi.

42. See Louis–Jean Calvert, *La tradition orale* (Paris: Presses Universitaires de France, 1984), 9–25. See also Russell Kaschula (ed.), *Foundations in Southern African Oral Literature* (Johannesburg: Witwatersrand University Press, 1993); Graham Furniss and Liz Gunner (eds.), *Power, Marginality and African Oral Literature* (Cambridge, England: Cambridge University Press, 1995); Gary Gossen, *Chamulas in the World of the Sun: Time and Sace in a Maya Oral Tradition* (Prospect Heights, IL: Waveland, 1974).

43. The relationship between written and oral texts and traditions is also of considerable interest in this regard. See Jack Goody, *The Interface Between the Written and the Oral* (Cambridge, England: Cambridge University Press, 1987); Anita Rampal, "A Possible 'Orality' for Science?" *Interchange* 23, 3 (1992): 227–244.

44. See Geoffrey Horrocks, *Greek: A History of the Language and Its Speakers* (London: Longman, 1997), 17–23; Maurice Balme and Gilbert Lawall, *Athenaze: An Introduction to Ancient Greek, Book I* (New York: Oxford University Press, 1990), 74–75.

45. See James Hulbert, *Bright's Anglo–Saxon Reader* (New York: Henry Holt, 1935), cvi–cxv. Also relevant here are Robert Diamond, *Old English: Grammar and Reader* (Detroit, MI: Wayne State University Press, 1970); Richard Hamer, *A Choice of Anglo–Saxon Verse* (London: Faber & Faber, 1970); Bruce Mitchell, *An Invitation to Old English and Anglo–Saxon England* (Oxford, England: Blackwell, 1995); Bruce Mitchell and Fred Robinson, *A Guide to Old English*, 5th ed. (Oxford, England: Blackwell, 1992).

46. Colin Graham, *Ideologies of Epic: Nation, Empire, and Victorian Epic Poetry* (Manchester, England: Manchester University Press, 1998).

47. See Vansina, *Oral Tradition as History*, 159–160.

48. See Colin Renfrew, *Archeology and Language: The Puzzle of Indo–European Origins* (Cambridge, England: Cambridge University Press, 1987), 21–23; in contrast, see Mzo Sirayi, "Oral African Drama in South Africa: The Xhosa Indigenous Drama Forms," *South African Theatre Journal* 10, 1 (1996): 49–61.

49. Karl Kroeber, "The Art of Traditional American Indian Narration," in Karl Kroeber (ed.), *Traditional Literatures of the American Indian: Texts and Interpretations* (Lincoln: University of Nebraska Press, 1981), 2.

50. Ruth Finnegan, *Oral Literature in Africa* (Nairobi, Kenya: Oxford University Press, 1970), 2. See also Ruth Finnegan, "Reflecting Back on *Oral Literature in Africa*: Some Reconsiderations after 21 Years," *South African Journal of African Languages* 12, 2 (1992): 39–47.

51. Joseph Telushkin, *Jewish Humor* (New York: Morrow, 1992), 121–122.

52. Christopher Candlin, "General Editor's Preface," in Britt–Louise Gunnarsson, Per Linell, and Bengt Nordberg (eds.), *The Construction of Professional Discourse* (London: Longman, 1997), ix.

53. This was the view promulgated, for instance, in Richard Hall's *Ancient Ruins of Rhodesia: Monomotapae Imperium*, 2nd ed. revised and enlarged (New York: Negro Universities Press, 1969); (original publication 1904). See Christopher Saunders, *The Making of the South African Past: Major Historians on Race and Class* (Cape Town: David Philip, 1988), 36–37; Stephen Howe, *Afrocentrism: Mythical Pasts and Imagined Homes* (London: Verso, 1998), 117–119.

54. Quoted in Ken Smith, *The Changing Past: Trends in South African Historical Writing* (Johannesburg: Southern, 1988), 37.

55. In the North American case, it was a commonplace belief in the 19th century that Native Americans were descended from the lost tribes of Israel. One variation of this view is represented, for instance, in the *Book of Mormon* (see Jan Shipps, *Mormonism: The Story of a New Religious Tradition* [Urbana: University of Illinois Press, 1985], 25–39). Others, most notably DeWitt Clinton, during the same period argued that the Indians had more likely come from Asia, perhaps with a possible link to the ancient Scythians, or had ties to the seafaring Carthaginians and Phoenicians. See Evan Cornog, "American Antiquity: How DeWitt Clinton Invented Our Past," *The American Scholar* 67 (1998): 53–61.

56. Theal's work, for instance, was widely cited and utilized by conservative historians well into the 1970s and 1980s, and its influence is clearly present in such works as C. F. J. Muller's *Five Hundred Years: A History of South Africa*, 5th ed. (Pretoria: Academica, 1986); and F. A. van Jaarsveld's *From Van Riebeeck to Vorster, 1652–1974* (Pretoria: Perskor, 1975). See also Saunders, *The Making of the South African Past*; Smith, *The Changing Past*. A significant exception and alternative to such works, albeit in a broader context, that is

worth mentioning here is Raul Manglapus' book, *Will of the People: Original Democracy in Non-Western Societies* (New York: Greenwood, 1987).

57. See, for example, Ignatius Donnelly's *Atlantis: The Antediluvian World* (New York: Dover, 1976), which was originally published in 1882.

58. Erich von Däniken, *Chariots of the Gods: Unsolved Mysteries of the Past* (New York: Berkley, 1968).

59. Erich von Däniken, *The Return of the Gods* (Shaftesbury, Dorset: Element, 1995); Erich von Däniken, *The Eyes of the Sphinx* (New York: Berkley, 1996); and Erich von Däniken, *Arrival of the Gods* (Shaftesbury, Dorset: Element, 1997).

60. Maurice M. Cotterell, *The Supergods: They Came on a Mission to Save Mankind* (London: Thorsons, 1997).

61. David Furlong, *The Keys to the Temple* (London: Piatkus, 1997).

62. José Argüelles, *The Mayan Factor: Path Beyond Technology* (Sante Fe, NM: Bear & Co., 1987).

63. See Francis Harrold and Raymond Eve (eds.), *Cult Archaeology and Creationism: Understanding Pseudoscientific Beliefs About the Past*, expanded ed. (Iowa City: University of Iowa Press, 1995).

64. This is not, of course, to deny the obvious and significant influences that different societies and civilizations have had on one another. The issue raised here is simply the need to distinguish between those cases where contact and the historical and archeological record make such influences possible or likely, and those instances where it is less likely or not at all likely. Demonstrating *possibilities*, especially in cases where the evidence is scarce to begin with, can obviously be done. Virtually anything is *possible;* the question is whether a claim is likely, probable, or credible.

65. See, for instance, John Boswell, *The Kindness of Strangers: The Abandonment of Children in Western Europe From Late Antiquity to the Renaissance* (New York: Pantheon, 1988), especially Part I.

66. Martin Gardner, "Is Cannibalism a Myth?" *Skeptical Inquirer* 22, 1 (1998): 14, my emphasis.

67. See Eli Sagan, *Cannibalism: Human Aggression and Cultural Form* (Santa Fe, NM: FirstDrum, 1993); Garry Hogg, *Cannibalism and Human Sacrifice* (London: Hale, 1990).

68. Gardner, "Is Cannibalism a Myth?" 14. For a clear and cogent articulation of this position, see William Arens, *The Man-Eating Myth: Anthropology and Anthropophagy* (New York: Oxford University Press, 1979).

69. David Crystal, *A Dictionary of Linguistics and Phonetics*, 3rd ed. (Oxford, England: Blackwell, 1991), 367.

70. Ali Mazrui, *The African Condition: The Reith Lectures* (London: Heinemann, 1980), 16.

71. Harrold and Eve (eds.), *Cult Archaeology and Creationism*, ix.

2

"A Wise Child is Talked to in Proverbs": Traditional African Educational Thought and Practice

The African continent is immense, not only in terms of its size but, more important, with respect to the cultural, linguistic, and ethnic diversity that characterizes the people who live in its various parts. As Richard Olaniyan observed, "with almost a thousand separate language groups, a variety of climatic regions and greatly different levels of social and economic development ... Africa is a continent of bewildering diversity and extraordinary dynamism."[1] This immensity and diversity might lead one to believe that it is not possible for us to discuss traditional "African" educational thought and practice in any meaningful way because there is bound to be considerable variation on such a topic from one group to another throughout the continent. This is an important issue, as Meyer Fortes made clear:

> Take, to begin with, the idea of African culture: by what criteria can we include, under this rubric, both the culture of the Kung Bushmen of the Kalahari—those gentle, peaceful, propertyless, hunting and collecting folk who have been so aptly described as "the harmless people" by Lorna Marshall—and the traditional patterns of life and thought of the sophisticated, materially wealthy, politically and socially complex, militarily organized kingdoms of West Africa—Ashanti and Benin, Yoruba and Hausa.[2]

To assume that such diversity makes impossible any discussion of "African" culture (an assumption that Fortes did not, in fact, make), however, would ignore, or at the very least distort, the many commonalities that unite the African experience. As Molefi and Kariamu Asante argued:

> Africa ... is one cultural river with numerous tributaries characterized by their specific responses to history and the environment. In this way we have always seen Europe after the Christian manifestations. England, Norway, Ireland,

France, Belgium, Germany, etc., were one culture although at the same time they were different. Asante, Yoruba, Mandinka are also one, though different in the historical sense. When we speak of unity in Africa, we are speaking of the commonalities among the people. Thus, a Yoruba who is different from an Ibo or Asante still shares more in common culture with them than with Thais or Norwegians. To the degree that the material conditions influence the choices people make, we Africans share similarities in behavior, perceptions, and technologies.[3]

In short, what we must seek in an examination of traditional African educational thought and practice[4] is what Cheikh Anta Diop, in his important book *The Cultural Unity of Negro Africa*, called the "profound cultural unity still alive beneath the deceptive appearance of cultural heterogeneity" present in Africa.[5] In this chapter, an attempt is made to identify and discuss some of the common characteristics and assumptions shared by much traditional education in Africa, while at the same time noting differences and variations that are related to sociocultural and geographic context.

THE GOALS OF TRADITIONAL AFRICAN EDUCATION

It is possible to identify a number of different goals that traditional African educational practices seek to achieve. For instance, Fafunwa, in his *A History of Education in Nigeria*, discussed what he termed the "seven cardinal goals of traditional African education," including:

1. to develop the child's latent physical skills;
2. to develop character;
3. to inculcate respect for elders and those in position of authority;
4. to develop intellectual skills;
5. to acquire specific vocational training and a healthy attitude towards honest labour;
6. to develop a sense of belonging and to participate actively in family and community affairs;
7. to understand, appreciate and promote the cultural heritage of the community at large.[6]

Taken together, these educational goals constitute a descriptive inventory of the characteristics of the "good person" for traditional African societies. Such an individual, on Fafunwa's account, will be one who "is honest, respectable, skilled, cooperative and conforms to the social order of the day."[7] Although much can be said in favor of such individuals, there is also a risk involved in encouraging conformity in societies that are no longer purely traditional in nature as is, of course, the case in most of contemporary Africa. It is such people, in fact, about whom the Nigerian novelist Chinua Achebe wrote rather critically in *A Man of the People*:

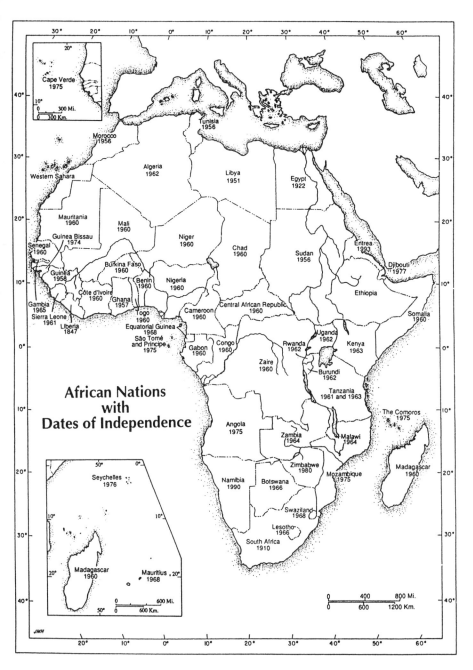

African Nations
with
Dates of Independence

FIG. 2.1. Contemporary Africa [From Phyllis M. Martin and Patrick O'Meara, *Africa*, 3rd ed. (Bloomington, IN; Indiana University Press, 1995), p. xv]. Reprinted with permission.

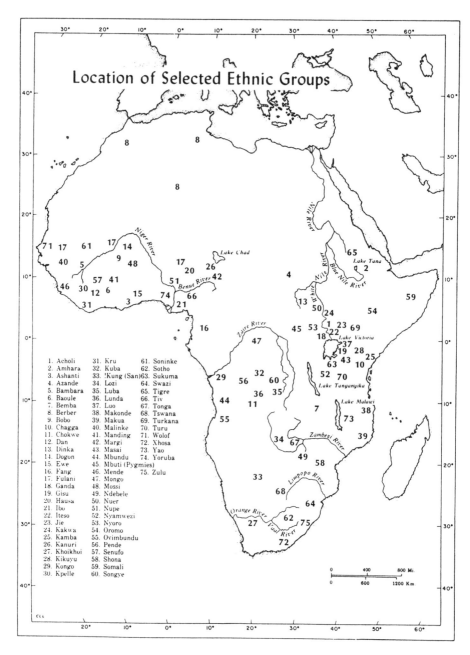

Location of Selected Ethnic Groups

1. Acholi	31. Kru	61. Soninke
2. Amhara	32. Kuba	62. Sotho
3. Ashanti	33. !Kung (San)	63. Sukuma
4. Azande	34. Lozi	64. Swazi
5. Bambara	35. Luba	65. Tigre
6. Baoule	36. Lunda	66. Tiv
7. Bemba	37. Luo	67. Tonga
8. Berber	38. Makonde	68. Tswana
9. Bobo	39. Makua	69. Turkana
10. Chagga	40. Malinke	70. Turu
11. Chokwe	41. Manding	71. Wolof
12. Dan	42. Margi	72. Xhosa
13. Dinka	43. Masai	73. Yao
14. Dogon	44. Mbundu	74. Yoruba
15. Ewe	45. Mbuti (Pygmies)	75. Zulu
16. Fang	46. Mende	
17. Fulani	47. Mongo	
18. Ganda	48. Mossi	
19. Gisu	49. Ndebele	
20. Hausa	50. Nuer	
21. Ibo	51. Nupe	
22. Iteso	52. Nyamwezi	
23. Jie	53. Nyoro	
24. Kakwa	54. Oromo	
25. Kamba	55. Ovimbundu	
26. Kanuri	56. Pende	
27. Khoikhoi	57. Senufo	
28. Kikuyu	58. Shona	
29. Kongo	59. Somali	
30. Kpelle	60. Songye	

FIG. 2.2 . Location of selected ethnic groups in Africa [From Phyllis M. Martin and Patrick O'Meara, *Africa*, 3rd ed. (Bloomington, IN: Indiana University Press, 1995), p. xvi]. Reprinted with permission.

Overnight everyone began to shake their heads at the excesses of the last regime, at its graft, oppression and corrupt government: newspapers, the radio, the hitherto silent intellectuals and civil servants—everybody said what a terrible lot; and it become public opinion the next morning. And these were the same people that only the other day had owned a thousand names of adulation, whom praise-singers followed with song and talking-drum wherever they went.[8]

Traditional African educational thought and practice is characterized not only by its concern with the "good person," however, but also by its interweaving of social, economic, political, cultural, and educational threads together into a common tapestry. In his book *Education in Africa*, Abdou Moumouni argued that traditional education in Africa is distinguished by these four features:

1. The great importance attached to it, and its collective and social nature;
2. Its intimate tie with social life, both in a material and a spiritual sense;
3. Its multivalent character, both in terms of its goals and the means employed; and
4. Its gradual and progressive achievements, in conformity with the successive stages of physical, emotional, and mental development of the child.[9]

Education, then, in the traditional African setting cannot (and indeed, should not) be separated from life itself. It is a natural process by which the child gradually acquires skill, knowledge, and attitudes appropriate to life in his or her community. Furthermore, in precolonial settings, such education was generally highly effective. As Moumouni argued:

The effectiveness of this education was possible because of its very close relationship with life. It was through social acts (production) and social relationships (family life, group activities) that the education of the child or adolescent took place, so that he was instructed and educated simultaneously. To the extent that a child learned everywhere and all the time, instead of learning in circumstances determined in advance as to place and time, outside of the productive and social world, he was truly in the "school of life," in the most concrete and real sense.[10]

An important facet of education conceived of in this way is that each and every adult in the community becomes, in essence, a teacher for any child with whom he or she has contact. Thus, writing about traditional education among the Igbo, Ambrose Okeke noted that:

Education in the wider sense of the term has all along been an essential factor in the way of life of the Igbo man. Parents, guardians, relatives and a wider circle of kinsmen in Igboland consider it a sacred trust of discharging their obligations as it concerned the socialization of the Igbo child. As a matter of fact, the entire village took part in this socialization process.[11]

Children learn adult roles, as well as the skills necessary for survival, in short, by imitating adults engaged in their daily activities, and by assisting parents and other adults as they engage in such activities.[12] Much is learned by the child through play and imitative games, as Duminy noted:

> The work and ways of the adult provided the material for the play of the child. Often, especially among girls, the imitative games (spontaneous imitation at first) gradually passed through a phase of diverted imitation to serious work. In various South African tribes (e.g., Sotho and Venda) it was customary for young children to build small houses and play at being grown up, imitating all the actions they had seen their elders do. Young girls were grinding soft stones between harder ones and young boys went through the whole ritual of their fathers "stock-farming" with their clay oxen.[13]

In fact, in the traditional African social context it is often virtually impossible to distinguish between "play," "learning," and other kinds of social activities:

> Among all peoples children learn by imitating their elders in play so that it is often difficult to distinguish between learning and play: the San boy is given a miniature bow and arrow as soon as he is able to handle them. The arrows are not poisoned and he plays at hunting, shooting field-mice, birds and hares; but when he kills a little duiker he is deemed ready to handle poisoned arrows.[14]

Furthermore, from early childhood, the African child in a traditional society is expected to participate in the economic life and activities of the community. As de Villiers and Hartshorne commented:

> Among peoples having non-specialized cultures children begin to participate at an early age in the economic activities of the adults according to their strength and skill. The Zulu girl tends her younger siblings, fetches water and firewood, cleans the home and, as she grows older, increasingly shares in the tasks she will one day perform as an adult. What she learns thus has a direct bearing on the knowledge and skills she will require in adulthood.[15]

With this general background to traditional African educational thought and practice in mind, we can now turn to more detailed discussions of several key components of such education. Specifically, we examine the role and place of the oral tradition in education, traditional education as moral education, the process of initiation, and the vocational aspects of traditional African education.

THE ORAL TRADITION IN AFRICAN EDUCATION

Traditional African societies are, by and large, oral ones, and this is true even where an established written literary tradition exists, as in the cases of such languages as Swahili, Zulu, Xhosa, and so on.[16] Writing about traditional education in East Africa, Mazrui and Wagaw noted that:

Yet another characteristic of most indigenous systems of education in East Africa is that they are based on the oral tradition rather than the written one. This is not to suggest that the written tradition has been entirely absent. On the contrary, both the Amharic literary culture and the Kiswahili literary culture are centuries old. But most "tribal" educational systems in Eastern Africa operated on the basis of the supremacy of the oral tradition, with only a minor role for the written word.[17]

An important aspect of traditional education in the African context has, therefore, been concerned with teaching children the oral tradition, as well as helping them to learn to use language creatively and effectively. In essence, such learning is a central feature of the intellectual training of the African child. With specific reference to traditional educational practice in Igboland, Okeke commented:

> The proverbs, the riddles, the ideation of *"chi"* and *"anyanwu la eseelu,"* the ability to distinguish between a killing herb and a healing one—all these constitute a veritable storehouse of intellectual exercise. Proverbs and riddles are used to hide a saying from the ordinary turn of mind. They help in selecting and analysing issues and problems of the moment. Traditional education exposed the Igbo to this training. So too do tongue-twisters used to train the child's capacity to retain the sequence of events.[18]

Proverbs feature prominently in virtually all traditional African cultures, and play important communicative and educational roles, as Boateng explained:

> Another means by which traditional education promoted intergenerational communication was through proverbial sayings. Proverbial sayings are widespread throughout Africa, and their themes bear strong similarity to one another. The educative and communicative power of proverbs in traditional Africa lies in their use as validators of traditional procedures and beliefs. Children are raised to believe strongly that proverbial sayings have been laid down and their validity tested by their forefathers.[19]

Furthermore, as Fajana argued,

> Proverbs which constituted an important intellectual mode of communication were used to develop the child's reasoning power and skill, and in expressing the deeper thoughts most essential in settling disputes and in decision-making processes. They had to be mastered if the child was to be fully developed and be able to cope with the various occasions when they had to be used.[20]

The basic idea underlying *proverbs* is that such sayings provide succinct, easily remembered summaries of important ideas and experiences that are part of the shared cultural knowledge of the community. Borland, writing about the oral culture of the Shona, noted that, *"Tsumo* [proverbs] embody the wisdom and experience of a people lacking written records in a concise, quotable and often amusing form. The free use of *tsumo* is the accepted way of winning an argument, and *tsumo* are therefore an integral part of Shona legal procedure which is conducted by argument."[21]

Proverbs can be used to discuss virtually any aspect of social life; in his discussion of Zulu proverbs, for instance, Nyembezi classified Zulu proverbs as falling into 10 categories, which are also applicable to proverbs found in most other African languages. The categories suggested by Nyembezi, together with examples of each type of proverb, are presented in Fig. 2.3.

Examples of proverbs from traditional African contexts abound, and many of them provide us with insight into both traditional education and social and cultural values and mores.[22] Consider, for instance, the Swahili proverb, *"Mgeni siki mbili, siku ya tatu mpe jembe"* [Your guest is a guest for two days; after that, give him a hoe], which conveys both practical advice and consider-

Category of Proverb	Content of Proverbs	Examples
Ubuntu	Treatment of people, good and bad behaviour, pride, ingratitude, etc.	A kindness is reciprocted. The stomach of a traveller is small.
Ukwethembeka Nokungethembeki	Faithfulness and unfaithfulness, deception, cunning, etc.	He cries with one eye. A crime is always denied.
Ubuhlobo Nobutha	Friendship and enmity.	The harshness of young people is repaid. The one offended never forgets; it is the offender who forgets.
Impumelelo, Inhlanhla, Namashwa	Good fortune, misfortune, troubles, uncertainty, despair, futile labour, failure and encouragement.	She has married her lover. To see once is to see twice.
Ubuqhawe Nobugwala	Bravery and cowardice.	An elephant is stabbed by all before it falls.
Emakhaya	Home life, marriage, heredity, relatives, child–parent relationships, etc.	A small pot is like the big one. A minister does not beget a minister.
Ukewedlula Kwemihla	Passage of time, aging, etc.	Old age does not announce itself. Death has no modesty.

FIG. 2.3. Categories and examples of Zulu proverbs [From C. Nyembezi, *Zulu Proverbs* (Johannesburg: University of the Witwatersrand Press, 1974), pp. 46–48]. Reprinted with permission.

able insight into interpersonal relations. A great deal can also be learned by examining proverbs that relate to the relationship between parents and children, as in these Igbo examples:

Akukwo nnewu talu, ka nweya nata. [The leaf that the big goat has eaten, will be eaten by his kids.]

Ezinkpolo nada ezinkpolo. [From good seed falls good seed.]

Ainy elur ike ili owa iru nabo. [We can't eat the world on two sides; i.e., you can't have both many children and a lot of money.][23]

For our purposes here, it is perhaps useful to consider proverbs common in southern Africa that relate directly to education:

If you take a knife from a child, give him a stick.

The teacher sometimes commits adultery himself.

The dry stick kindles the green ones.[24]

These proverbs provide us with considerable insight into the educational philosophy that underlies traditional African education, though it is important to keep in mind that proverbs are often notoriously difficult to translate. As Taban lo Liyong noted about Acoli proverbs, "the meaning of deep Acoli proverbs are made very light by their rendition into English word for word, rather than sense for sense, or proverb for proverb."[25] Furthermore, the use of proverbs in educating children, as well as in indirect social communication in general is, by its very nature, context specific. Thus, if one sees two reasonably well-matched Zulu boys fighting, one might say, "*Kubamben' ingwe nengonyama*" [the leopard and the lion are fighting]. Similarly, to describe two children who simply do not get along, one would use a proverb contrasting two animals that are natural enemies, such as:

Yinkuku nempaka. [It is a fowl and a wild cat.]

Yikati negundane. [It is a cat and a mouse.]

Yinja nekati. [It is a dog and a cat.][26]

Vast amounts of information can be thus conveyed quickly and creatively, and the use of proverbs in childrearing is widespread throughout Africa. As the Twi say, after all, "A wise child is talked to in proverbs."[27]

Finally, proverbs are sometimes used in various types of wordplay. For example, speakers of Teke in the Congo often engage in a specialized kind of linguistic behavior called *Bisisimi*, which can be roughly translated as "the language of the wise."[28] *Bisisimi* involve the competitive chanting of proverbs, as opposed to their common use in everyday speech, and is found primarily in specialized settings, such as mourning ceremonies, festive gatherings, and acts of divination.[29] Nkara described the process of *Bisisimi* as follows:

> In most contexts, participants sit in a circle, in the *mbong* (sort of communal shed in villages), in the shade of a big tree and sometimes around a fire at night. To begin with, participants converse in everyday Teke. After an hour or so, depending on the occasion, they start using *Bisisimi*. ... The addresser or initiator stands up and starts an *Isisimi*. The other participants chant either a part of it or the whole *Isisimi* as they clap hands following the rhythm of the chant. A small drum is sometimes beaten by one of them. As soon as any other participant realizes that he is the object of the *Isisimi* he responds immediately in kind. If he fails or happens to be in no position to respond, a friend or relative of his may come to his rescue.[30]

Furthermore, it is important to understand that, in some cases, *Bisisimi* may go far beyond being merely a game: "The use of *Bisisimi* ... may be regarded as a contest of wits or a verbal game, but this game may also turn into a kind of occult fight when the use of *mpaana* [psychic power] is involved. In such cases, it is believed that the loser may suffer physically."[31]

Another example of the way in which oral cultures are transmitted and language used creatively in traditional African education is the use of riddles, word games, puzzles, and tongue-twisters. All of these activities, which are common throughout most of Africa, are examples of what we might call "critical thinking activities," encouraging as they do innovative, creative, and difficult uses of various symbol systems. For instance, in Shona culture *zvirahwe*, or riddles, are widely used by and with children. Examples of Shona riddles, and their correct responses, include:

1. Question: *Nzira mbiri dzinoenda mugomo?* [Two paths lead up the mountain?]
   Answer: *Mhino.* [Nostrils.]
2. Question: *Imba imiri nebango rimwe?* [The house is supported by one pole?]
   Answer: *Howa.* [Mushroom.]
3. Question: *Shumba mbiri dzakaririra gomo?* [Two lions waited on the hill?]
   Answer: *Nzeve.* [Ears.][32]

Riddles can also be used to teach a great deal of information about the natural world, as these Ndebele riddles make clear:

1. Question: *Ngabantwana bami bakha indlu banganamanzi?* [My children burning a house without water?]
   Answer: *Mmuhlwa.* [Termites.]

2. Question: *Ngesitimela sami asikhambi esiporweni?* [By my train that does not go on the railway track?]
   Answer: *Lisongololo.* [Millipede.]
3. Question: *Ngomntwa'mi unamehlo amakhulu usaba ukuqalana nomkhayo?* [By my person with big eyes who is afraid of facing the light?]
   Answer: *Sirhulurhulu.* [Owl.][33]

Finally, riddles can reinforce social and cultural knowledge, as the following Yoruba riddle demonstrates:

Question: *A be ori, a be idi re, sibe-sibe o nsowo ola?* [We cut off the top and the bottom, yet it produces wealth?]
Answer: *Ilu.* [Drum.][34]

Word games can include a wide variety of different kinds of linguistic activities, but are generally concerned with the players' speed and continuity, although such games can also depend heavily on knowledge of the social and natural worlds, as was the case with riddles. For example, a common word game is for children to quiz one another about the names for different kinds of trees, plants, animals, and so on.[35] Another common type of word game is one in which children must engage in repetition (or alteration) of words, either real or invented, in some series or sequence. Such a game strengthens the memory and helps to develop mental acuity and speed.

Similar games often serve to teach and reinforce mathematical concepts. For instance, "The Yoruba have developed a system of counting and have used a variety of human experiences to promote practice and dexterity in enumeration. The Yoruba child is introduced early in life to counting by means of concrete objects, counting rhymes, folklore, plays, and games, at home and on the farm."[36] An example of one of the counting rhymes that Yoruba children are likely to learn, and which is fairly typical of such rhymes, is:

Rhyme	Translation
Eni bi eni	One is one
Eji bi eji	Two is two
Eta metagba	Three, spin calabash
Erin woroko	Four crooked
Arun igbodo	Five, pestle pounding
Efa ti ele	Six of ele
Aro nbaro	Cymbal, which cymbal?

Aro mbata	Cymbal, bata drum
B'oo da k'esan	If one is missing [out of ten fingers]
Gbangaba l'ewa	Ten exposed.[37]

Puzzles are also used in childrearing and education, and take several different forms. Two distinct examples of puzzles are "dilemma tales" and "arithmetic puzzles."[38] Although similar to proverbs in certain ways, both dilemma tales
and arithmetic puzzles are distinctive in nature. Bascom explained the difference among riddles, arithmetic puzzles, and dilemma tales: "Put concisely, riddles are to be answered; arithmetic puzzles are to be solved; dilemma tales are
to be resolved."[39] Kubik, writing about both dilemma tales and arithmetic puzzles among the Valuchazi in Eastern Angola and Northwestern Zambia, argued
that dilemma tales are:

> A genre of oral literature; as a prose narrative that ends in an open question, a di-
> lemma, for the audience to resolve. Thus, in contrast to ordinary folktales, a di-
> lemma tale is not brought to a conclusion by the narrator, but it ends on a
> question which is followed by a lively discussion by the audience.... in dilemma
> stories the aim is to stimulate discussion. A problem has to be resolved.[40]

Arithmetic puzzles, on the other hand, are stories in which a logical or mathematical challenge is presented to the listener. As with dilemma tales, both children and adults can participate in the discussion. It is important to note here,
as did Kubik, that in spite of its intellectual complexity (one arithmetical puzzle discussed by Kubik involved 11 steps) and potential metaphysical implications, "This is a leisure-time activity and arithmetic puzzles serve to stimulate
the intellect and test the mathematical capabilities of the participants."[41]

Thus far, we have considered the oral nature of traditional African societies
primarily in terms of its role in intellectual training, but also of great significance
is the content of the oral tradition. It is through fables, myths, and legends that
much of the history of the community, as well as its values and beliefs, is passed
on from one generation to the next. As Boateng commented, "Myths played an
active part in the African's everyday life and were a vital social force ... myths
and legends not only supplied accounts of the group's origin but related prece-
dents to present-day beliefs, actions, and codes of behavior."[42]

The African child learns fables, myths, and legends in a variety of settings
and from a host of different adults, including especially the village storyteller.
As N. Uka explained:

> By listening to the village story-teller [the child] acquires a knowledge of the
> past. Every tale is a parable; it is not just history but an educational story. The sto-
> ries are manifestations of the tribal memory, the origin and history of the group,
> the deeds of their great men and women, their victories and defeats in war, their

experiences which led to individual and group success and those which led to individual and group failure.[43]

Similarly, in describing the training of bori musicians among the Hausa, Besmer reported that:

> One common but informal institution for these lessons is the evening gossip sessions held inside or immediately in front of most Hausa compounds. A boy old enough to have "sense" (which the Hausa say should come to him by the time he is five or six years old) normally sits on the outside of the group presided over or attended by his father. Talking is the popular pastime and storytelling is an art, elderly bori musicians regularly claiming to be experts at both. The day's events are discussed and the society's problems solved during these sessions, and when spirits are the topic tale after tale is enjoyed by young and old alike. "Have I ever told you the secret of so-and-so's wealth?" or "Do you know the reason why such-and-such is a strange place?" an old man might ask. If his audience should reply "no" he would then ask them how many ears they had. Each listener would answer "two" and he would retort, "Well increase them to three and listen to this," the signal that a "true" story was about to be told.[44]

This oral tradition includes not only the history of the community, however, but also serves to "sustain morality, ritual, law, and sanctions against offenders."[45] It is manifested in everyday life in a variety of ways, none clearer than in the praise-songs or praise-poems (*izibongo*) that are sung to honor individuals, groups, and so on.[46] As Schapera noted:

> Praise-poems ... are composed not only about chiefs, headmen, famous warriors, and other prominent tribesmen, but about ordinary commoners also, including women; there are, in addition, praise-poems of tribes and subdivisions of tribes (such as wards and lineages), of domestic animals (notably cattle), of wild animals (including birds and insects), of trees and crops, of rivers, hills, and other scenic features, and of such inanimate objects as divining-bones. In modern times some have even been composed about schools, railway trains, and bicycles.[47]

In order to understand many praise-poems, however, let alone to be able to compose one, an individual must possess a broad historical and cultural knowledge of the community, as well as a good grasp of the language of the community.[48] The recitation of such *izibongo* remains a way of maintaining and transmitting the oral tradition, and it is a feature of traditional African education to which we will return later in the chapter.

TRADITIONAL EDUCATION AS MORAL EDUCATION

One of the central features of traditional education throughout Africa is its concern with the formation of the child's character. Fafunwa, discussing the education of the Yoruba, described this concern with character formation as "the corner-stone of African education."[49] Furthermore, Moumouni argued that:

Moulding character and providing moral qualities are primary objectives in traditional African education. Almost all the different aspects of education of the child and adolescent aim towards this goal, to a greater or lesser degree. In the family, parents concern themselves with the bearing, manners, honesty and integrity of the child. Outside the house, games, the society of his friends in the same age group, and the demands they make on each other, constitute a real source of character-building. Sociability, integrity, honesty, courage, solidarity, endurance, ethics and above all the concept of honour are, among others, the moral qualities constantly demanded, examined, judged and sanctioned, in ways which depend on the intellectual level and capacities of the child and adolescent.[50]

The responsibility for teaching the child the moral and spiritual values of the community, as well as for ensuring his compliance with those values, as indicated in the above passage, rests first of all with the child's mother and immediate family, but ultimately is the concern of the entire community.[51] As Okeke noted with regard to the Igbo, "Everyone in the home, in the village and in the community wanted the Igbo child to be sociable, truthful, brave, humble, have stamina and be of unreproachable conduct at all times. For this reason, everyone joined in correcting or praising any child whenever and wherever he failed or succeeded in showing acceptable norms of behaviour."[52]

Among the more important aspects of character training common in traditional African education is its emphasis on respect for elders.[53] As Fafunwa commented in terms of the Nigerian experience:

Age is an important element in the life of the African. Reverence for those who are older is particularly strong among the Yoruba. Seniority confers social and economic privileges, especially in the sharing of spoils, prizes, wealth, etc. The elder is assumed to be a man (or woman) of wisdom and is expected to demonstrate this in speech and action if he is to keep his position among those who look up to him for leadership. Age is such a vital factor among many ... ethnic groups that a man (or woman) will overstate his age rather than understate it. Moreover, a young man or woman is not expected to look an elder straight in the face for this is considered a sign of disrespect.[54]

It is important to note that the concept "elders" here refers not only to those chronologically older than the individual, but also to "those who are in authority, particularly the chief, the cult leaders, the diviners, relatives (especially uncles) and older neighbours,"[55] and furthermore, that respect in this regard entails, among other things, obedience. It also involves appropriate forms of address and ritual greetings, which play an important role in many African societies,[56] and even distinct forms of language in some cases.[57]

THE PROCESS OF INITIATION

Perhaps the best-known, and arguably the most misunderstood, aspect of traditional African education is that of initiation. The process by which the adolescent is formally transformed, socially and spiritually, into an adult varies considerably from one African society to another, and a few traditional societies (for instance, the Akans[58] and the Shona[59]) do not even have a formal initiation process at all. Nonetheless, initiation remains a common, although less often observed, practice today as a result of increasing urbanization and Westernization, throughout much of eastern, western, and southern Africa, and traditional African initiation practices do share significant common features and characteristics. As Benjamin Ray argued in his book *African Religions*:

> The most elaborate rites of passage usually concern the initiation of the young into adulthood. In this way a society not only socializes its young by outwardly moving them into new roles of social responsibility, but also transforms them inwardly by molding their moral and mental disposition towards the world. This is what African societies consider to be the primary purpose of initiation rituals.[60]

African initiation ceremonies and practices are different from comparable rites of passage in the West, however, in that they make public what Westerners see as intensely private: "Besides being a test of courage and the completion of education, initiation is also a collective ceremony. In European societies, reaching puberty is a private matter. Each girl and boy goes through adolescence to sexual maturity alone. In Africa the long initiation ceremonials dramatize this change and make it a social ritual."[61]

Although the process of initiation is divided into different stages by various African societies, for most groups the initiation process includes the following components:

- Separation of the initiates from the community, under the leadership of a specially selected adult,
- Both formal and informal instruction about adult duties, responsibilities, and obligations,
- Instruction in the folklore, legends, and history of the community,
- Observation of selected food, behavioral, and sexual taboos and restrictions,
- Instruction in aspects of sexuality and sexual relations in preparation for marriage,
- Physical markings, commonly permanent in nature, and
- Circumcision (often for both males and females).

In addition, male initiation very often involves tests of physical and mental endurance, including various kinds of torture, which "is regarded as a test of fortitude and a conditioning to pain and discomfort which the new life in which the individual finds himself will bring in its train."[62]

Finally, a lasting feature of the initiation process in many societies is the establishment of a peer group, or "age-set."[63] Such age-sets are among the more important nonkin groupings found in traditional African societies and are found in virtually all parts of sub-Saharan Africa. In essence, such age-sets are male association groups based on contemporaneity and reinforced by the bonding that takes place during the initiation process. As Olaniyan explained:

> A man belongs to that set of men who are his age mates, and their set moves through the several age-grades as the men go through life, beginning with their initiation into manhood as adolescents. Membership in an age set is not voluntary, and it carries with it both obligations and privileges. Typically, age sets pass through some four grades comprising (1) newly initiated men in a training period; (2) the warrior grade responsible for defence; (3) adult men responsible for governing; and (4) the society's elders.[64]

The initiation process, which in many ways is the pinnacle of traditional African educational practice, represents a huge investment on the part of the community. As Raum noted:

> The first thing that strikes an educationist is that initiation is a tremendous pedagogic effort. There is the ritual isolation of the company of initiands in a camp set apart "in the wilderness." There is the appointment of the requisite personnel: the master of the rite, or owner of the lodge, teachers of different rank, the operator, assistants and supervisors, the carriers of food to the camp. The master of the rite has to be a man of charisma to be able to transmit special qualities to the inmates of the camp; teachers and assistants must be ritually pure. The economic preparations for initiation are often on a grand scale.[65]

Although the initiation "school" and the ceremonials related to it are, then, clearly very important and costly to the community, they are also limited in their objectives. As van der Vliet observed, "The initiation schools ... do not mark the final stage of the development of the individual; they do, however, equip and entitle him to accept the roles which maturity will bring."[66] In short, the process by which adolescents are initiated into adulthood serves a variety of functions in traditional African societies, including religious, political, psychological, and educational ones. The initiation schools do not, however, seek to address what might be called the vocational aspects of adulthood. As Blacking argued with respect to the Venda, "Formal ... education in traditional Venda society was never intended to give people technological training for earning a living."[67] With this point in mind, we can now turn to a discussion of how the vocational needs of both the community and the individual are met in traditional African education.

VOCATIONAL ASPECTS OF TRADITIONAL EDUCATION

The preparation of children for their future economic roles in the society is an important element in traditional African educational thought and practice. To some extent, of course, many vocational skills and a great deal of knowledge related to and necessary for such skills are acquired simply by observation, imitation, and participation as the child interacts with his or her parents on an everyday basis. Such would, for instance, be the case for many agricultural and domestic types of activity. For other occupations in traditional societies, however, various kinds of apprenticeship are employed. Generally speaking, vocational preparation in traditional African education has been divided on the basis of type of occupation into three broad categories: agriculturally-related occupations, trades and crafts, and the professions.[68]

Agricultural activities have been the basis for the vast majority of traditional agricultural societies, although some groups (such as the Masai in Kenya and Tanzania) have relied on animal husbandry instead.[69] Agricultural knowledge and skills have been passed on from one generation to the next most often by involving children in all aspects of agricultural production from early on. Gradually, the child is given increasing responsibilities as he becomes proficient at the tasks related to agricultural production, often being given his own small farm to tend. Here, Ishumi describes the Yoruba custom:

> At the time the young farmer was learning these techniques, he would work with his guardian all day. But by about 12–15 years when he should have mastered these techniques he would be given some evenings free to work on his own farm. At first, it might be two evenings in the week, later this would be extended to all afternoons. This in itself was a lesson in responsibility and the foundation for independent existence. From now, the boy had his own chicken, product of his own effort which he could dispose of according to his wishes. By the time he was married, between 20–25, he could stand on his own as a farmer.[70]

The experience of boys and girls in this regard differed somewhat, reflecting the later occupational division that would divide them as adults. As Sudarkasa explained, however:

> Typically, in indigenous African societies, the occupational roles of women were different from but complementary to the roles of men.... Very often men and women worked in the same occupation (for example, in farming or trading), but the tasks undertaken tended to be sex specific (for example, preparing the land for farming versus tending the crops or trading in one line of goods as opposed to another). There does not seem to be a basis for holding that women's occupations were considered to be "inferior" to those of men, although such occupations were usually thought to be inappropriate for men, just as men's occupations were normally considered inappropriate for women. The point here is that the maintenance of separate occupational domains for the two sexes did not automatically imply a hierarchical relationship between those two domains.[71]

If agricultural and domestic occupations are learned largely from parents through imitation and informal participation, and thus, as Sudarkasa noted, "did not usually involve formal apprenticeships," more formal apprenticeship arrangements have been common for many crafts and professions in the traditional African society.[72] Among the more common crafts learned through some type of apprenticeship system are "weaving (for instance, baskets and cloth), hunting, carving, sculpturing, painting and decorating, carpentry, building, hair-plaiting, dress-making, boat-making, mat-making, dying, isusu-collecting (cooperative banking), food-selling, wine-tapping, and a host of other trades and crafts."[73] It is important to note, however, that such craft skills and knowledge are generally passed on within specific families, as Callaway, writing about Nigeria, explained:

> This vast apprenticeship training system began as a part of a wider educational process in which the indigenous societies of Nigeria passed on their cultural heritage from one generation to the next. The skills "owned" by a family were highly valued, and in some lines such as native medicine, secrets were zealously guarded.... Evidence of the passing on of skills within families is still strong.[74]

Ogundijo noted several important features of indigenous apprenticeship practices, not the least of which are that "children were not free to choose the trade of the their liking, for they were bound to follow the guidance of their parents. For effective training, parents always apprenticed their children to their relatives, friends or competent craftsmen."[75]

Not only were trades and crafts learned through the apprenticeship system, but so too were the professional occupations of traditional African societies. Included under the general category of "professional occupations" are such social roles as "doctors, priests, witch doctors, civil servants, village heads, chiefs and kings, tax collectors, heralds, judges, councillors, police and messengers, shrine-keepers, soldiers, etc."[76] Unlike most trade and craft occupations, at least some of these professions have traditionally been what Nadel called "free professions," which means that one could become a member of the occupation not only through birth, but also through merit. As Nadel commented about the Nupe kingdom in Nigeria, "It is not surprising that a rich and complex culture like Nupe should possess its clearly defined 'free professions'—its professional scholars, scientists and artists, or, in a terminology more akin to the native conception, its mallams, barber-doctors, and drummers and dancers."[77]

An intriguing example of such "free professionals" in the traditional African context, and one that has important implications for many contemporary African societies as well, is that of traditional healers. Traditional healers in Africa provide an important alternative to western medicine—both in terms of providing a kind of medical care where Western facilities are not available, and as socially and psychologically powerful alternatives and/or additions to Western medicine, especially, although by no means exclusively, in rural areas. Twumasi and Warren have divided traditional healers in Ghana and Zamiba into four main groups: traditional birth attendants, faith healers, herbalists, and spiritualists/diviners.[78] Although there are obviously variations in this model from one part of sub-Saharan Africa to another, these basic divisions work reasonably well to categorize different kinds of traditional healers. Traditional birth attendants actually have a far broader range of activities and responsibilities than the label would suggest: these individuals, almost universally women, serve not only as midwives, but also as specialists in obstetrics, sex education, and contraception. Their role is, in addition, both medical and spiritual; it is quite common for them to function as godmothers for the children whom they deliver, and they also often have a role to play in puberty ceremonies. Faith healers are generally tied to specific religious movements, such as the syncretic churches, millennial churches, and thaumaturgical churches, and can be either Christian or Muslim in origin and focus. Herbalists are traditional healers who make use of herbs in addressing medical problems; treatment procedures are generally fairly similar to those employed in Western medical practice. Finally, spiritualist healers, who are most often tied to particular shrines, are indigenous priests, priestesses, ritual, and cult leaders, who specialize in divination and spiritual possession.[79] In many parts of Africa today, traditional healers are in the process of organizing and gaining professional status,[80] and it is very important to keep in mind that the services that they provide are often valuable and effective—in some instances, far more so than would be Western medical alternatives. A powerful example of the way in which traditional and Western medical care can overlap and coexist is provided by Leslie Swartz, who reported that:

> At one time I was receiving three different treatments for a severe allergy: cortisone (from biomedicine), a treatment based on anthroposophical medicine (a form of healing with a spiritual component), and homeopathic remedies. I had faith in none of the three approaches to help me on its own, and I knew that practitioners from the three approaches would not approve of my using all three simultaneously but, probably quite irrationally, I thought that if I tried everything at once, it might work. (It did!) At that time, my discomfort was such that I was not thinking logically. I was also not acting in terms of any worked-out ideology of care. I was simply desperate. And this need for treatment, of some kind or another, together with what happens to be reasonably accessible to people, will help determine how people use resources.[81]

Traditional healers are selected and trained in a wide variety of ways. In a fascinating description of the process by which traditional healers acquire their professional competence among the Zezuru in Zimbabwe, for instance, Pamela Reynolds reported the following ten-stage "life cycle" for traditional healers:

Childhood
1.   Prior to his death, a healer may designate his heir. The heir need not have been born yet; he or she is identified as, perhaps, the healer's son's first child of either sex.

2.   Special ties are established between the child and the healer, often between grandparent and grandchild. Most children are taught to classify plants into three categories: poisonous plants, edible plants, and plants that must not be tampered with because they belong to the shades.

3.   This instruction is enlarged upon from the age of nine. The healer instructs the child in the identification and naming of herbs. The child assists the healer in the preparation and administration of medicines. The child is expected to help during treatment sessions, including those in which the healer is possessed.

Young Adulthood
4.   At about the age of 13, the child begins to collect herbs and prepare medicines alone. He may begin to gather herbs on his own initiative. While the healer is away, the child often treats patients, according to the healer's instructions.

5.   The process of "matriculation" begins. It is characterised by illness and dreams, in which universal symbols like water, flying, and pythons appear, often as a test of courage. Western and traditional experts are consulted. The patient may stay with a healer for long periods, even for a number of years.

6.   The spirit identifies itself, his demands are met and symptoms of illness fade away.

7.   Soon thereafter the healer begins to treat in his own right. He gradually accumulates power and respect and a reputation for success in certain areas of divination and healing.

Middle Age
8.   The healer is fully fledged. He begins to lead ritual occasions and bring out the spirits of others. In describing this stage of their life cycle, many healers admit training others but deny having been trained when they had their spirits brought out.

Old Age
9.   A time of seniority follows. There is substantial evidence that grandchildren are trained to assume the healing role after the healer's death.

Death
10.   Death is followed by the eventual possession of a kin member, often after a period of intense rivalry within the family.[82]

An interesting exception to the generally formal, apprenticeship-based training assumed for the professions is that of the *imbongi*, or praise-poet, among groups such as the Zulu and Xhosa in Southern Africa.[83] The *imbongi* is in many ways a unique figure in traditional society; his role is part historian, part counselor, part social and political critic. The *imbongi* fulfills a role similar to that played by the medieval bard, relying both on the established oral tradition and his own ability to improvise in creating the appropriate *izibongo* (praise-poem) for the occasion. The *imbongi* is granted remarkable freedom in what he can say in his *izibongo*. As Opland explained, "It is generally accepted that the *imbongi* enjoys license in his poetry to use ribald language otherwise unacceptable in public.... Not only can the *imbongi* use ribald language, he also enjoys the license to criticize with impunity persons in positions of power."[84]

Technically not a "professional" since he is not actually paid for his services, the *imbongi* is, to a very great extent, born rather than made. As Opland noted about the Xhosa *imbongi*:

There is no formal apprenticeship or training for an *imbongi*; he needs the tacit acceptance of the people to become an *imbongi*; rarely is he officially appointed *imbongi* by the chief, merely acknowledged or recognized if he chooses to present himself; and though he may associate himself intimately with the chief and the affairs of the great place, as *imbongi* he is never paid a salary by the chief. Aspirant *iimbongi* [plural] may listen to and learn from others, but they do not attach themselves to a practicing *imbongi* in order to learn their craft. The process is strictly informal: There are no guilds of poets; *iimbongi* do not form a separate class or caste; their status is not hereditary ... no amount of training can make an *imbongi* of a boy lacking a special talent.[85]

It must be remembered that the *imbongi*, however interesting as a social and cultural phenomenon, is atypical of the norm for vocational training in traditional African societies. Virtually all individuals in such societies learn occupational roles through either imitation of parents or apprenticeship training or, most commonly, a combination of the two.

AFROCENTRISM AND THE ROMANTICIZATION OF AFRICA

In recent years, especially in the United States, there has been a significant scholarly and academic movement advocating what has been called "Afrocentricity" or, more commonly in everyday discourse, the adoption and utilization of an "Afrocentric" worldview.[86] This movement has had a powerful impact on elements of public schooling in the United States, including contributing to the creation of curricular materials and even the establishment of entirely "Afrocentric" schools, and has, perhaps inevitably, resulted in considerable controversy and debate.[87] The fundamental focus of the emphasis on Afrocentrism is not so much on either historical or contemporary African reality, however, as much as it is on the articulation of a philosophical system containing its own historical framework for understanding the African past and present. Thus, for its supporters, Afrocentrism is not merely an interdisciplinary approach to the study of Africa, but is a unique discipline in its own right—a discipline whose rhetoric often seems almost evangelical in nature. In essence, the Afrocentric movement, which is identified most closely and powerfully with the work of Molefi Asante,[88] is an example of what can be called "romantic nationalism." Romantic nationalism refers to the efforts of any particular national or ethnic group to create a favorable historical record of their past and is a commonplace development throughout the world. It is hardly surprising that various groups seek to understand their pasts in the most positive light, and it is just as understandable that we all look for heros and wonderful accomplishments in our pasts. As Stephen Howe noted:

> Virtually every European state and ethnic group has drawn on and abused the discipline of archaeology in its search for historical roots, often involving straightforwardly racist ideas about the origins and destiny of itself and its neighbours....

In the cases I know best, those of Britain and Ireland, very long histories of ut-
terly fantastic racial myth and ideas about the national pasts and origins can be
traced, involving all the elements of mysticism, claims of racial primacy and superiority, and promiscuous borrowings from esoteric lore.[89]

There can be little doubt that the historical contributions of Africa in general, and of people of African descent in particular, have been overlooked, ignored, and even distorted. There should also be little question that much of
this phenomenon, especially during the past two or three centuries, is a consequence of racism of various sorts and manifestations.[90] Recent efforts to raise
such issues, and to help us come to a better, clearer, and more accurate picture
of the African past and present, as well as of the contributions of that past and
present to other civilizations (including our own), are very valuable and should
be commended. At the same time, however, it is clear that there are elements
of historical distortion and misrepresentation,[91] just as there are clear instances of pseudoscientific claims,[92] in parts of the growing Afrocentric literature. These concerns have been well-documented elsewhere[93] and need not be
explored here. What does need to be emphasized, however, is that even if cor-
rections and modifications of some of the claims of the Afrocentric movement
are needed, this should in no way blind us to the very real need for serious consideration of and reflection on the contributions of Africa to world civilization.
In order to accomplish this, it is important that we not over-romanticize
precolonial institutions and practices in Africa, as Mazrui noted in a critique of
the "Négritude" movement common especially in Francophone Africa: "The
mood of this branch of African romantic thought is one of nostalgia, yearning
for an innocence which is eternally lost. All that can be done now is to make the
best of a bad job, try to save some of the values of old Africa, and find a synthesis between these and the influences which have come with colonialism and
modernity."[94]

CONCLUDING THOUGHTS

In this chapter, an overview of several key components of traditional African
educational thought and practice has been presented. Although such practices
are less and less commonly found in modern Africa, it is not at all clear that this
is due to any intrinsic flaw in either the theory or practices that underlie such
traditional conceptions of education. Rather, this is arguably the result of a rejection of all things traditional in favor of Western models, a practice whose
risks are vividly evoked in p'Bitek's moving poem, "Song of Lawino":

Listen Ocol, my old friend,

The ways of your ancestors

Are good,

Their customs are solid

And not hollow

They are not thin, not easily

breakable

They cannot be blown away

By the winds

Because their roots reach deep

into the soil.

I do not understand

The ways of foreigners

But I do not despise their

customs.

Why should you despise yours?[95]

Although, as was noted earlier, it is important that we not take an overly romantic or naive view of the African past, it is also important that this past not
be rejected wholesale. As Okeke persuasively argued, "It is my belief that traditional education should serve as the springboard from which formal education takes off. Anything short of this shall continue to plague us and continue to
make formal education non-functional and divorced from the social, political
and economic realities of Igboland."[96]

In short, much can be learned from the African educational tradition that
could benefit contemporary educational thought and practice throughout the
continent. Indeed, there are useful and valuable lessons for non-Africans as
well. The communal responsibility for the education of the young, the effective use of the oral tradition in passing on various sorts of knowledge, the centrality of concerns with moral or character training in the education of the
young, the importance of a sense of belonging for the child, and the view of education as an integral component of social life (rather than as something separate from the daily lives of most adults) are all areas in which our own society
might gain insight about the problems and challenges that we face today.

QUESTIONS FOR REFLECTION AND DISCUSSION

1. How does the focus in traditional African education with respect to
   moral education or character training differ from various contemporary
   Western approaches to and concerns about moral education? In what
   ways is the traditional African approach similar to calls for a return to
   "traditional values" in our own society?

2. Contemporary Western societies are, for the most part, literate, rather than oral, societies, and yet, one could argue that the advent of much recent technology will change the way in which we view literacy. In what ways do we still possess an "oral culture," and how is that culture passed on to children? To what extent is modern technology utilized in this process? Do you believe that literacy will actually be necessary in the future, or will technological innovation make possible the development of a nonliterate but nonetheless "modern" society?
3. Does the concern in traditional African education with preparing children to accept and function in the *status quo* conflict with the goals of education for a democratic society? With the goal of producing "critical thinkers"?
4. What, in your view, are the greatest strengths of traditional African education? What are its greatest weaknesses?
5. What are the contemporary American equivalents of traditional African initiation schools? In what ways do we prepare individuals for, and mark "rites of passage" in our own society?
6. How does the preparation and training of a traditional healer, as outlined in the chapter for the Zezuru in Zimbabwe, compare to that of the physician in the West? What are the similarities and differences between the two? How can these be explained?
7. One could argue that the social and political role played by the Xhosa *imbongi* is similar to that played historically by the court jester in the West. Is there a similar role or occupation in contemporary Western societies? If so, how does this role compare to the status of the *imbongi*?
8. "Romantic nationalism" is briefly mentioned in this chapter in the context of the discussion of Afrocentrism. How does this concept relate to issues raised in chapter 1? What are the implications of this idea for the study of non-Western societies and civilizations in general?
9. How many proverbs can you recall from your own childhood? Write as many of them down as you can, and then, using Fig. 2.3 (Categories and examples of Zulu proverbs) as a model, try to construct an organizational framework for proverbs in our own tradition. How might such a framework be used in a classroom setting?
10. What lessons can you draw for your own classroom practice from what you have learned about traditional African education?

RECOMMENDED FURTHER READINGS

There are a number of good general introductions to Africa and African studies broadly conceived. Especially useful are Basil Davidson's *Africa in History*, revised and exp. ed. (New York: Macmillan, 1991); Davidson's edited *African Civilization Revisited: From Antiquity to Modern Times* (Trenton, NJ: Africa World Press, 1991); Philip Curtin, Steven Feierman, Leonard Thompson, and

Jan Vansina's *African History: From Earliest Times to Independence*, 2nd ed. (London: Longman, 1995); and Sanford Ungar's *Africa: The People and Politics of an Emerging Continent*, rev. ed. (New York: Simon & Schuster, 1986). Also useful for students seeking a better understanding of life in Africa are novels, and among the best for this purpose are the works of the Nigerian author Chinua Achebe, such as *Things Fall Apart* (London: Heinemann, 1958), *No Longer at Ease* (London: Heinemann, 1960), *Arrow of God* (London: Heinemann, 1974), and *A Man of the People* (London: Heinemann, 1966), all of which are now easily obtainable in North America.

NOTES

1. Richard Olaniyan, "African History and Culture: An Overview," in Richard Olaniyan (ed.), *African History and Culture* (Lagos, Nigeria: Longman, 1982), 1.
2. Meyer Fortes, "Foreward," in Eric Ayisi (ed.), *An Introduction to the Study of African Culture*, 2nd ed. (London: Currey, 1979), vii. See also Jean Jolly, *Historie de continent Africain*, 2 vols. (Paris: Éditions l'Harmattan, 1989).
3. Molefi Asante and Kariamu Asante (eds.), *African Culture: Rhythms of Unity* (Trenton, NJ: Africa World Press, 1990), ix–x.
4. See the discussion of Patricia Weibust's work on the concept of "tradition" in chapter 1.
5. Cheikh Anta Diop, *The Cultural Unity of Negro Africa* (Paris: Presence Africaine, 1962), 7; the same point is made in Diop's later revision of this work, *The Cultural Unity of Black Africa* (London: Karnak House, 1989). See also Cheikh Anta Diop, *Civilization or Barbarism: An Authentic Anthropology* (Chicago: Hill, 1991); Kwame Appiah, *In My Father's House: Africa in the Philosophy of Culture* (New York: Oxford University Press, 1992); Heinz Kimmerle, *Philosophie in Afrika—Afrikanische Philosophie* (Frankfort/Main, Germany: Campus Verlag, 1991).
6. A. Babs Fafunwa, *A History of Education in Nigeria* (London: Allen & Unwin, 1974), 20. See also S. Nwosu, "Pedagogic Problems in Africa Today," in Joseph Okpaku, Alfred Opubor, and Benjamin Oloruntimehin (eds.), *The Arts and Civilization of Black and African Peoples: Volume 6, Black Civilization and Pedagogy* (Lagos, Nigeria: Center for Black and African Arts and Civilization, 1986), 103–105; A. Okeke, "Traditional Education in Igboland," in F. Chidozie Ogbalu and E. Nolue Emenanjo (eds.), *Igbo Language and Culture*, vol. 2 (Ibadan, Nigeria: University Press, 1982), 15–26; Abiola Irele (ed.), *African Education and Identity* (Ibadan, Nigeria: Spectrum Books, 1992).
7. Fafunwa, *A History of Education in Nigeria*, 20.
8. Chinua Achebe, *A Man of the People* (Ibadan, Nigeria: Heinemann, 1966), 148.
9. Abdou Moumouni, *Education in Africa* (New York: Praeger, 1968), 15.

10. Moumouni, *Education in Africa*, 29.

11. Okeke, "Traditional Education in Igboland," 15.

12. Eric Ayisi, *An Introduction to the Study of African Culture* (London: Currey, 1979), 48–49.

13. P. Duminy, *African Pupils and Teaching Them* (Pretoria: van Schaik, 1973), 30–31.

14. Stephné de Villiers and S. Helena Hartshorne, "Education," in A. C. Myburgh (ed.), *Anthropology for Southern Africa* (Pretoria: van Schaik, 1981), 147–148.

15. de Villiers and Hartshorne, "Education," 147.

16. See, for example, M. Katengo and G. Mwale, "Can Traditional Education Be Integrated with the Modern Educational System?" in Steven Moyo, Tobias Sumaili, and James Moody (eds.), *Oral Traditions in Southern Africa*, vol. 6 (Lusaka, Zambia: Division for Cultural Research, Institute for African Studies, University of Zambia, 1986), 456–481.

17. Ali Mazrui and Teshome Wagaw, "Towards Decolonizing Modernity: Education and Culture Conflict in Eastern Africa," in *The Educational Process and Historiography in Africa* (Paris: UNESCO, 1985), 40.

18. Okeke, "Traditional Education in Igboland," 19; Mary Bill, "Rhythmical Patterning of Tsonga Children's Traditional Oral Poetry," *South African Journal of African Languages* 11, 4 (1991): 133–143.

19. Felix Boateng, "African Traditional Education: A Tool for Intergenerational Communication," in Molefi Asante and Kariamu Asante (eds.), *African Culture: Rhythms of Unity* (Trenton, NJ: Africa World Press, 1990), 117.

20. A. Fajana, "Traditional Methods of Education in Africa: The Yoruba Example," in Joseph Okpaku, Alfred Opubor, and Benjamin Oloruntimehin (eds.), *The Arts and Civilization of Black and African Peoples: Volume 6, Black Civilization and Pedagogy* (Lagos, Nigeria: Center for Black and African Arts and Civilization, 1986), 45.

21. C. H. Borland, "The Oral and Written Culture of the Shona," *LIMI: Bulletin of the Department of Bantu Languages, University of South Africa* 8 (1969): 8.

22. C. Nyembezi, *Zulu Proverbs* (Johannesburg: University of the Witwatersrand Press, 1974), 46–48; see also Northcote W. Thomas, *Proverbs, Narratives, Vocabularies and Grammar: Anthropological Report on the Ibo-Speaking Peoples of Nigeria, Part III* (New York: Negro Universities Press, 1969).

23. Thomas, *Proverbs, Narratives, Vocabularies and Grammar*, 9.

24. Cited in O. F. Raum, "An Evaluation of Indigenous Education," in P. A. Duminy (ed.), *Trends and Challenges in the Education of the South African Bantu* (Pretoria: van Schaik, 1967), 103.

25. Taban lo Liyong, *The Last Word* (Nairobi: East Africa Publishing House, 1969), 141.

26. Nyembezi, *Zulu Proverbs*, 91.

27. Boateng, "African Traditional Education," 117.

28. See J. Nkara, "*Bisisimi* or the Language of the Wise," *South African Journal of African Languages* 12, 4 (1992): 144.

29. Nkara, "*Bisisimi* or the Language of the Wise," 144.

30. Nkara, "*Bisisimi* or the Language of the Wise," 145.

31. Nkara, "*Bisisimi* or the Language of the Wise," 144.

32. Borland, "The Oral and Written Culture of the Shona," 9.

33. D. Mahlangu, "*Imiraro*: Ndebele Riddles," *South African Journal of African Languages* 8 (Supplement 1) (1988): 154–155.

34. Fajana, "Traditional Methods of Education in Africa," 54.

35. See Borland, "The Oral and Written Culture of the Shona"; Okeke, "Traditional Education in Igboland."

36. Fafunwa, *A History of Education in Nigeria*, 28.

37. Fajana, "Traditional Methods of Education in Africa," 55.

38. See William Bascom, *African Dilemma Tales* (The Hague: Mouton, 1975); Gerhard Kubik, "*Visimu vya mukatikati*: Dilemma Tales and 'Arithmetical Puzzles' Collected among the Valuchazi," *South African Journal of African Languages* 10, 2 (1990): 59–68; Gerhard Kubik, "A Luchazi Riddle Session: Analysis of Recorded Texts in a South-Central African Bantu Language," *South African Journal of African Languages* 12, 2 (1992): 51–82.

39. Bascom, *African Dilemma Tales*, 12.

40. Kubik, "*Visimu vya mukatikati*," 60–61.

41. Kubik, "*Visimu vya mukatikati*," 67.

42. Boateng, "African Traditional Education," 113.

43. N. Uka, "Continuity and Change: A Challenge to African Educators," in Joseph Okpaku, Alfred Opubor, and Benjamin Oloruntimehin (eds.), *The Arts and Civilization of Black and African Peoples: Volume 6, Black Civilization and Pedagogy* (Lagos, Nigeria: Center for Black and African Arts and Civilization, 1986), 131.

44. Fremont Besmer, *Horses, Musicians, and Gods: The Hausa Cult of Possession-Trance* (Zaria, Nigeria: Ahmadu Bello University Press, 1983), 44.

45. Boateng, "African Traditional Education," 115.

46. For a distinction between *izibongo* and *izithakazelo*, or clan praises among the Zulu, see D. Mzolo, "Social Function of Clan Praises," in A. Nkabinde (ed.), *African Linguistics and Literature* (Johannesburg: Lexicon, 1988), 132–138.

47. I. Schapera, *Praise-Poems of Tswana Chiefs* (Oxford, England: Oxford University Press, 1965), 1; see also Daniel Kunene, *Heroic Poetry of the Basotho* (Oxford, England: Oxford University Press, 1971).

48. See Schapera, *Praise-Poems of Tswana Chiefs*, 25.

49. Fafunwa, *A History of Education in Nigeria*, 21.

50. Moumouni, *Education in Africa*, 22.

51. See Nathaniel Fadipe, *The Sociology of the Yoruba* (Ibadan, Nigeria: Ibadan University Press, 1970).

52. Okeke, "Traditional Education in Igboland," 18.

53. See Fafunwa, *A History of Education in Nigeria*, 24–26; Nwosu, "Pedagogic Problems in Africa Today"; Virginia van der Vliet, "Growing Up in a Traditional Society," in W. Hammond-Tooke (ed.), *The Bantu-Speaking Peoples of Southern Africa* (London: Routledge & Kegan Paul, 1974), 224.

54. Fafunwa, *A History of Education in Nigeria*, 19.

55. Fafunwa, *A History of Education in Nigeria*, 25.

56. See Fafunwa, *A History of Education in Nigeria*; Borland, "The Oral and Written Culture of the Shona"; S. Guma, *The Form, Content and Technique of Traditional Literature in Southern Sotho*, 2nd ed. (Pretoria: van Schaik, 1977).

57. See Rosalie Finlayson, "*Hlonipha*: The Women's Language of Avoidance among the Xhosa," *South African Journal of African Languages* (Supplement 1)(1982): 35–59; Rosalie Finlayson, "Linguistic Terms of Respect among the Xhosa," in Peter Raper (ed.), *Names 1983: Proceedings of the Second South African Names Congress* (Pretoria: Human Sciences Research Council, 1986), 128–138.

58. See Ayisi, *An Introduction to the Study of African Culture*, 47.

59. See Borland, "The Oral and Written Culture of the Shona."

60. Benjamin Ray, *African Religions: Symbol, Ritual, and Community* (Englewood Cliffs, NJ: Prentice-Hall, 1976), 91. Also of interest here are John Mbiti, *African Religions and Philosophy*, 2nd ed. (Oxford, England: Heinemann, 1989), 118–129; Geoffrey Parrinder, *Religion in Africa* (Harmondsworth: Penguin, 1969); E. Adegbola (ed.), *Traditional Religion in West Africa* (Nairobi, Kenya: Uzima, 1983).

61. Jacques Macquet, quoted in P. Boe, "Circumcision: The Rites of Manhood in the Bille Tribe," in E. Adegbola (ed.), *Traditional Religion in West Africa* (Nairobi, Kenya: Uzima Press, 1983), 88.

62. Ayisi, *An Introduction to the Study of African Culture*, 47.

63. See Ayisi, *An Introduction to the Study of African Culture*, 46; also relevant here is Olaniyan, *African History and Culture*, 30–31.

64. See Ayisi, *An Introduction to the Study of African Culture*, 46; Olaniyan, *African History and Culture*, 30–31.

65. Raum, "An Evaluation of Indigenous Education," 99–100.

66. van der Vliet, "Growing Up in a Traditional Society," 241.

67. Blacking, quoted in van der Vliet, "Growing Up in a Traditional Society," 235.

68. See Fafunwa, *A History of Education in Nigeria*, 30–31. See also Olaitan Obanewa, *Education of the Children and Youth in Ile-Ife: A Comparison of Formal and Non-Formal Systems of Education* (M.Ed. thesis, University of Ife, Nigeria, 1973), and Okeke, "Traditional Education in Igboland," 20–22.

69. See A. Ishumi, "Black Civilization and Pedagogy: A Search for Modern Methods," in Joseph Okpaku, Alfred Opubor, and Benjamin Oloruntimehin (eds.), *The Arts and Civilization of Black and African Peoples: Volume 6, Black Civilization and Pedagogy* (Lagos, Nigeria: Center for Black and African Arts and Civilization, 1986), 67.

70. Ishumi, "Black Civilization and Pedagogy," 51.

71. Niara Sudarkasa, "Sex Roles, Education and Development in Africa," *Anthropology and Education* 13, 3 (1982): 280.

72. See Sudarkasa, "Sex Roles, Education and Development in Africa," 280–281.

73. Okeke, "Traditional Education in Igboland," 21.

74. Quoted in Fafunwa, *A History of Education in Nigeria*, 30.

75. M. Ogundijo, *Indigenous Education in the Ejigbo District of Oshun Division in the Pre-Colonial Days and the Coming of the Missionaries* (B.A. thesis, Faculty of Education, University of Ife, Nigeria, 1970), 11–12.

76. Fafunwa, *A History of Education in Nigeria*, 30; see also Okeke, "Traditional Education in Igboland," 21.

77. Quoted in Fafunwa, *A History of Education in Nigeria*, 37.

78. Patrick Twumasi and Dennis Warren, "The Professionalisation of Indigenous Medicine: A Comparative Study of Ghana and Zambia," in Murray Last and C. L. Chavunduka (eds.), *The Professionalization of African Medicine* (Manchester, England: Manchester University Press, 1986), 118.

79. Twumasi and Warren, "The Professionalisation of Indigenous Medicine," 118.

80. See Murray Last and C. L. Chavunduka (eds.), *The Professionalization of African Medicine* (Manchester, England: Manchester University Press, 1986). There is a growing recognition of the value of many indigenous medical practices and beliefs in many parts of the world. See, for instance, Arthur Kleinman, *Patients and Healers in the Context of Culture: An Exploration of the Borderland Between Anthropology, Medicine, and Psychiatry* (Berkeley: University of California Press, 1980); Charles Leslie and Allen Young (eds.), *Paths to Asian Medical Knowledge* (Berkeley: University of California Press, 1992); Paul Brodwin, *Medicine and Morality in Haiti: The Contest for Healing Power* (Cambridge, England: Cambridge University Press, 1996).

81. Leslie Swartz, *Culture and Mental Health: A Southern African View* (Cape Town: Oxford University Press, 1998), 92. Also relevant here is Robin Horton, "African Traditional Thought and Western Science," in Bryan Wilson (ed.), *Rationality* (New York: Harper & Row, 1970), 131–171.

82. Pamela Reynolds, "The Training of Traditional Healers in Mashonaland," in Murray Last and C. L. Chavunduka (eds.), *The Professionalization of African Medicine* (Manchester, England: Manchester University Press, 1986), 170–172.

83. See Jeff Opland, *Xhosa Oral Poetry: Aspects of a Black South African Tradition* (Cambridge, England: Cambridge University Press, 1983); Jeff Opland, "Xhosa *izibongo*: Improvised Line," *South African Journal of African Languages* 10, 4 (1990): 239–251; Russell Kaschula, "The Role of the Xhosa Oral Poet in Contemporary South African Society," *South African Journal of African Languages* 11, 2 (1991): 47–54; Trevor Cope (ed.), *Izibongo: Zulu Praise Poems* (Oxford, England: Oxford University Press, 1968); David Rycroft and A. Bhekabantu Ngcobo, *Say it in Zulu* (Pietermaritzburg: Lan-

guage and Reading Laboratories, University of Natal, 1981), Part II, Appendix I; Noleen Turner, "Comparison of the *Izibongo* of the Zulu Royal Women, Mnkabayi and Nandi," *South African Journal of African Languages* 8, 1 (1988): 28–33; W. J. Pretorius, "A Comparative Look at the Development of Heroic Poetry in Northern Sotho," *South African Journal of African Languages* 10, 3 (1990): 125–131.

84. Opland, *Xhosa Oral Poetry*, 66–67.

85. Opland, *Xhosa Oral Poetry*, 64–65.

86. See Molefi Asante, *Afrocentricity*, rev. ed. (Trenton, NJ: Africa World Press, 1988); Molefi Asante, *Kemet, Afrocentricity and Knowledge* (Trenton, NJ: Africa World Press, 1990). Perhaps the most extensive articulation of Afrocentrism (although one with serious limitations as well) is Marimba Ani, *Yurugu: An African-Centered Critique of European Cultural Thought and Behavior* (Trenton, NJ: Africa World Press, 1994). For a fascinating historical study of the evolution of Afrocentrism, see Wilson J. Moses, *Afrotopia: The Roots of African American Popular History* (Cambridge, England: Cambridge University Press, 1998).

The Afrocentric literature should be distinguished from more general *African* scholarship, especially with respect to philosophic scholarship. See, for example, P. H. Coetzee and A. P. Roux (eds.), *The African Philosophy Reader* (London: Routledge, 1998); and Emmanuel Chukwudi Eze (ed.), *African Philosophy: An Anthology* (Oxford, England: Blackwell, 1998).

87. Although much of the debate has taken place in the popular media, there has also been a critical scholarly response to Afrocentrism. This critical scholarly response includes Mary R. Lefkowitz and Guy MacLean Rogers (eds.), *Black Athena Revisited* (Chapel Hill: University of North Carolina Press, 1996); Mary Lefkowitz, *Not Out of Africa: How Afrocentrism Became An Excuse To Teach Myth As History* (New York: Basic Books, 1996); Stephen Howe, *Afrocentrism: Mythical Pasts and Imagined Homes* (London: Verso, 1998).

88. Molefi Asante is Professor and Chairperson of the Department of African American Studies at Temple University, and one of the most prolific Afrocentric scholars. In addition to Asante's own work, see Howe, *Afrocentrism: Mythical Pasts and Imagined Homes*, chapter 17. A more sympathetic treatment of Asante's work, especially in terms of its pedagogical implications, can be found in Joel Spring, *The Intersection of Cultures: Minority Education in the United States* (New York: McGraw-Hill, 1995), 135–141.

89. Howe, *Afrocentrism: Mythical Pasts and Imagined Homes*, 7.

90. This has been one of the more significant contributions of Martin Bernal's work, for instance. See Martin Bernal, *Black Athena: The Afroasiatic Roots of Classical Civilization, Volume 1: The Fabrication of Ancient Greece, 1785–1985* (New Brunswick, NJ: Rutgers University Press, 1987); Martin Bernal, "Animadversions on the Origins of Western Science," *Isis*, 83 (1992): 596–607.

91. See Howe, *Afrocentrism: Mythical Pasts and Imagined Homes*; Lefkowitz, *Not Out of Africa.*

92. See, for example, Bernard Ortiz de Montellano, "Multiculturalism, Cult Archaeology, and Pseudoscience," in Francis Harrold and Raymond Eve (eds.), *Cult Archaeology and Creationism* (Iowa City: University of Iowa Press, 1995), 134 –151; Howe, *Afrocentrism: Mythical Pasts and Imagined Homes*, 259–264; Robert Palter, "*Black Athena*, Afrocentrism, and the History of Science," in Mary R. Lefkowitz and Guy MacLean Rogers, *Black Athena Revisited* (Chapel Hill: University of North Carolina Press, 1996), 209–266. Martin Bernal has offered powerful rejoinders to many of his critics that are also worth noting here. See, for instance, Martin Bernal, "Response," *Journal of Women's History* 4, 3 (1993): 119–135; Martin Bernal, "Response to Edith Hall," *Arethusa* 24, 2 (1991): 203–214.

93. See Howe, *Afrocentrism: Mythical Pasts and Imagined Homes.*

94. Ali Mazrui, *The African Condition: The Reith Lectures* (London: Heinemann, 1980), 11.

95. Okot p'Bitek, *Song of Lawino and Song of Ocol* (Ibadan, Nigeria: Heinemann, 1967), 41.

96. Okeke, "Traditional Education in Igboland," 25.

3

Training "Face and Heart": The Mesoamerican Educational Experience

Mesoamerica has been the home of a number of distinct, but related, civilizations since human beings first began settling in the area millennia ago. Although there is evidence of human habitation in Mesoamerica at least as far back as 25,000 years ago, it is possible that people were living in the area as early as 40,000 years ago.[1] By 1500 B.C.E., we know that the indigenous peoples of Mesoamerica had undergone the transition from hunter and gathering societies to settled agricultural village societies,[2] and it is with this development that Mesoamerican history (rather than prehistory) can be said to have begun. The history of Mesoamerica can, in turn, be divided into four very broad stages: the Formative Period (1500 B.C.E. to 150 C.E.), the Classic Period (from around 150 C.E. to around 900 C.E.), the Early Post-Classic Period (from around 900 C.E. to 1250 C.E.), and the Late Post-Classic Period (from 1250 C.E. to 1519 C.E.).[3] It was during the Formative Period that the elaboration of a set of core cultural beliefs and practices emerged. This set of core cultural beliefs and practices was first manifested in the Olmec civilization, which Jacques Soustelle called the "mother civilization" of Mesoamerica,[4] but was modified, reformulated, changed, and developed over the history of Mesoamerican civilizations.[5] As Adams argued, "the Olmec ... did invent and diffuse much of the cultural equipment used and reformulated in later cultures."[6] Indeed, it was the Olmecs who provided the cultural matrix within which Mesoamerican civilization developed and evolved:

> The touching continuity of indigenous Mexican civilization in spite of the often bloody upheavals of its history, and the indelible imprint still preserved in the depths of its nature despite the changes of the modern era, are ample justification for the attempt being made by archaeologists to return to the earliest sources of this autochthonous civilization. With the Olmecs we catch a glimpse of the decisive mutation that made Mexico and Mesoamerica a cultural high-pressure area.... Pre-Conquest Mexico would not have been what it was—and even the Mexico of the twentieth century would not be what it is—if

these men of long ago had not begun to erect their stelae and to sculpt their bas-reliefs in the depths of torrid jungles, more than three thousand years ago.[7]

Among the civiliztions that developed in Mesoamerica were not only the Olmecs, but the Toltecs, the Mayas, and the Aztecs, among others.[8] Soustelle provided a vivid analogy for understanding the relationships among these groups: "The Aztecs have often been compared to the Romans, the Mayas to the Greeks. It has been said that the Toltecs played in Amerindian antiquity a role comparable to that of the Etruscans in Italy. The Olmecs, for their part, remind us of the Sumerians: like them long unknown, like them precursors, like them buried beneath ruins many thousands of years old and hidden from our eyes by the traces of peoples who succeeded them."[9] Although a powerful description, this analogy is only in part valid, since the cultural relationship among the peoples of Mesoamerica was far, far closer than that among the comparison civilizations that Soustelle identifies. Furthermore, the relationship among these different civilizations was one that was recognized by the members of the societies themselves, as can be seen in the following passage taken from the *Códice Matritense de la Real Academia*, which describes the development of Nahuatl philosophy from the Toltec period to that of the Aztecs:

Those who

carried with them

the black and red ink,

the manuscripts and the pictures,

wisdom [*tlamatiliztli*].

They brought everything with them:

the song books and the music of the flutes.[10]

In any event, Mesoamerica presents us with a fascinating collection of related cultures that emerged, grew, developed, and, to some extent, disappeared over a period of some three millennia. While it would be impossible for us to examine seriously and in detail the educational thought and practice of each of these civilizations, we can focus our attention on two of the civilizations of Mesoamerica. First, we will examine what little is known of Classic Mayan educational thought and practice, and then we will turn to the more abundant literature concerned with educational thought and practice in Aztec society.

EDUCATIONAL THOUGHT AND PRACTICE IN CLASSIC MAYAN SOCIETY

In recent years, our knowledge about and understanding of classical Mayan society and civilization have undergone dramatic changes. As Michael Coe wrote in the late 1980s:

The past two decades have seen great advances in our knowledge of Maya civilization in both the Preclassic and Classic epochs, often in ways that earlier generations of scholars would not have approved. From a picture of the Maya that emphasized peaceful theocracies led by priest astronomers, ruling over relatively empty "ceremonial centers," we now have highly warlike city-states led by grim dynasts obsessed with human sacrifice and the ritual letting of their own blood. Although traditional "dirt" archeology has contributed to our current view of the ancient Maya, the contributions of epigraphy and art history have been, in my opinion, truly revolutionary.[11]

This revolutionary rethinking of both the general nature and the details of ancient Mayan society has continued up to the present time.[12] If we know a great deal more today about the history and politics of the Maya, however, our knowledge about their views about childrearing and education, as well as of their specific educational practices and institutions, remains largely conjectural in nature.[13] What we do know, or at least what we now believe, is based largely on assumptions about the general nature of ancient Mayan society. For instance, Norman Hammond has written that:

We now have abundant evidence that Classic Maya society was divided into a number of layers, with rulers at the top and common people, some of them peasants, at the base of the social pyramid. It has become clear that this complex and many-layered society must have had a great many specialists and that any one layer in the pyramid could have embraced a range of occupations, many pursued as full-time economic specialties.[14]

To Hammond's observations we can add the presence of a highly complex written literature, produced by scribes, as well as obvious evidence of architectural, engineering, mathematical, and astronomical knowledge, not to mention what were clearly highly ritualized religious practices—all of which would strongly suggest the operation of some sort of formal educational system for at least some individuals in ancient Mayan society.[15] This formal educational system need not have been schooling as we understand it, however, as Robert Sharer explained:

There is no evidence that the ancient Maya had formal schools. But it is certain that children selected on the basis of social status or aptitude were trained for specialized roles in society by an apprentice system. Scribes, priests, artists, masons, and other occupational groups recruited novices and trained them.[16]

In addition to such conjectural sources, we also know something about the way in which the Maya lived at the time of the Conquest, largely due to the work of the second Bishop of Yucatán, Diego de Landa. De Landa recorded, in considerable detail, the society and way of life of the indigenous peoples of the Yucatán, based both on his own observations and information he received from

native informants, in his work *Relación de las cosas de Yucatán*.[17] Such information provides us with invaluable insights into the kinds of childrearing practices
that were carried over from the time of the Classic Mayan civilization (many of
which continue even to the present). We also possess a limited number of Mayan codices,[18] as well as the *Popol Vuh*,[19] a work of great literary and historical
value that has been called "the Sacred Book of the ancient Quiché Maya."[20]
While these sources by no means provide us with a clear picture of ancient Mayan educational thought and practice, they do provide some limited insight into
the role played by education in Maya society, and the purposes that the ancient
Maya believed should be served by childrearing and education.[21]

For the ancient Maya, education was, at its heart, religious in nature. As Ana
Luisa Izquierdo argued in *La educación maya en los tiempos prehispánicos*,

> The destiny of Mayan man and his role on earth find their ultimate plenitude
> through religious fulfillment. Attainments such as wisdom, social integration or
> personal success are only recognized when they are geared toward the fulfillment
> of the intrinsic and spiritual mission. So, if all the vital actions of Mayan man had
> a religious orientation, likewise education had its long-term and short-term ob-
> jectives, as well as its ultimate goal, in sacred fulfillment. Because of this, the
> ways of shaping children and adolescents were deeply entrenched in the religious
> meaning of life, and were characterized by it.[22]

Mayan childrearing and education were clearly grounded in a fairly conservative social and educational agenda. The point of proper education, from a Mayan perspective, was conformity to one's society and an acceptance of one's
place within that society.[23] Custom and religion governed virtually all parts of
an individual's life-cycle, and both formal and informal education were no exception to this rule.[24] This was achieved by learning from the priests and elders
in society, generally orally.[25] Thus, "for the Mayas, the process through which it
was assured that an individual made a concept, an idea, or a value his own, was
the memorization of the words contained in it."[26] While such an approach to
learning might have many advantages, it was clearly not oriented to encouraging what we would today call "critical thinking."

An interesting aspect of Mayan educational thought is that of its epistemology and implicit learning theory. In the *Popol Vuh*, the creation of the first human beings is described in considerable detail. Four human beings were
created by the gods Tepeu and Gucumatz in order to nourish, sustain, and worship the gods. When first created, these men had all of the characteristics of
the gods themselves:

> They had the appearance of men, they were men; they talked, conversed, saw
> and heard, grasped things; they were good and handsome men, and their figure
> was the figure of a man. They were endowed with intelligence; they saw and in-
> stantly they could see far, they succeeded in seeing, they succeeded in knowing
> all that there is in the world. When they looked, instantly they saw all around
> them, and they contemplated in turn the arch of heaven and the round face of

the earth. The things hidden they saw all, without first having to move; at once they saw the world, and so, too, from where they were, they saw it. Great was their wisdom; their sight reached to the forests, the rocks, the lakes, the seas, the mountains, and the valleys. In truth, they were admirable men ... [27]

The gods, however, were not entirely pleased with their creation; they were concerned that men could know all and see all, as they themselves could, and so decided to impose some limits on their creations. Thus, according to the *Popol Vuh*, "the Heart of Heaven blew mist into their eyes, which clouded their sight as when a mirror is breathed upon. Their eyes were covered and they could see only what was close, only that was clear to them. In this way the wisdom and all the knowledge of the four men, the origin and beginning, were destroyed."[28] This account is fascinating on a number of grounds, not the least of which are the intriguing parallels to the Biblical account of the destruction of the Tower of Babel and to the theory of knowledge expounded by Plato.

THE AZTEC CASE

When Hernán Cortés and his men first arrived in Mexico in 1519, they were astounded by the civilization that greeted them. Unlike earlier contacts between Europeans and indigenous peoples in the Western hemisphere, in their introduction to the Aztec civilization,[29] Cortés and his followers faced a highly sophisticated, urban culture in full flower—a civilization, in fact, that in many ways compared favorably to that of any 16th-century European society. As Cortés himself wrote to the Spanish king, "these people live like those in Spain, and in as much harmony and order as there, and considering that they are barbarous and so far from the knowledge of God and cut off from all civilized nations, it is truly remarkable to see what they have achieved in all things."[30] This was remarkably high praise from the man who was, more than any other single individual, responsible for the destruction of the Aztec world—or, as the Aztecs themselves would have termed it, the "time of the fifth sun."[31]

Education, both formal and informal, was an important and well-developed part of Aztec society.[32] As Miguel León-Portilla commented, "The written sources on the educational practices of the Nahuas are so abundant that a book could be written on that subject alone. Such a book might reconstruct—as did Jaeger's *Paideia* for the ancient Greeks—through the educational system all the richness and profundity of the Nahuatl concept of man."[33] And yet, despite its noteworthy successes, no mention whatever of the educational thought and practice of the Aztecs appears in the standard works in the history of education in the English-speaking world. While a thorough analysis of education in the "time of the fifth sun" is far beyond the scope of this chapter, what is possible is to present a general overview of Aztec education as it existed at the time of the arrival of the Spanish in the early 16th century.

THE AZTEC WORLD

The Aztecs were relative latecomers to the valley of Mexico, building their society on the cultural, religious, and intellectual foundations, as well as on the
architectural ruins, of earlier civilizations, especially that of the Toltecs. Furthermore, their rise to prominence was, in the words of Muriel Weaver, "a dramatic rags-to-riches tale."[34] The Aztecs first arrived in the area of the Valley of
Mexico in the early 13th century, by which time the more desirable areas
around the lakeshore were already settled by other Nahuatl- and
Otomí-speaking peoples, as well as by the descendants of earlier refugees from
Teotihuacań and Tula, among others.[35] Indeed, the awareness of their late arrival, as well as of their status as outsiders, remained with the Aztecs until the
arrival of the Spanish. Cortés himself recorded that Monteuczoma, in their
first conversation together, commented that, "From the records which we
have long possessed and which are handed down from our ancestors, it is
known that no one, neither I nor the others who inhabit the land of Anahuac,
are native to it. We are strangers and we came from far outer parts."[36]

The new arrivals were not greeted with open arms by those already settled
in the area, and in the early years after their arrival in the Valley of Mexico, the
Aztecs were driven from one area to another around the western part of the
lake. As Jon Manchip White wrote:

> [T]hey were looked upon as little more than squatters.... Nor was it simply the
> case that they were backward and brutish: they were downright squalid. Their
> little uncouth tribal war-god, Huitzilopochtli, was already notorious for the
> number of fresh, bleeding hearts he required, and his worshippers did not seem
> to be particular about where they got them. They gained a reputation for every
> kind of murder and brutality.[37]

Finally, the Aztecs arrived at Culhuacan, one of the established cities in the
Valley. The Culhua permitted the Aztecs to settle at Tizapan, about 6 miles west
of Culhuacan, in an inhospitable area where they fully expected that the Aztecs
would, "perish ... eaten by the serpents, since many dwell in that place."[38] Instead, the Aztecs prospered, ultimately acquiring not only access to the cultural
heritage of the Toltecs, but also to claims of Toltec lineage as a result of intermar-
riage with the inhabitants of Culhuacan. The Aztecs also became mercenaries
for the Culhua, and were so successful in this role that they eventually came to
represent a serious threat to the Culhua. The tensions between the Culhua and
the Aztecs were forced to a head when the Aztecs requested:

> the hand of one of Culhuacan's rulers, a beautiful girl whom they promptly killed
> and flayed. Her father arrived to attend her wedding, only to be confronted by a
> priest dancing in her flayed skin. Fighting broke out at once, and the [Aztecs] re-
> treated into the swamps of the lagoon, finally reaching the safety of a

reed-covered island near the center of what is now Mexico City. There they rested. Huitzilopochtli [the Aztec war god] appeared before one of the priests, ordering him to search for a cactus where a great eagle perched. This, said the god, was a place he had named Tenochtitlán, the "Place of the Fruit of the Prickly Pear Cactus."[39]

Thus was Tenochtitlán, the capital city of the Aztec Empire, established, probably around 1345.[40] The Aztecs now experienced a period of growth and consolidation, culminating in the defeat of the city of Azcapotzalco in 1428, which "established the Aztecs as the dominant power in the Basin of Mexico."[41]

By the time of the arrival of Cortés and his men, the Aztec Empire was in many ways at its height,[42] consisting of some 15 million people and 489 tributary towns, which were in turn divided into 38 provinces for administrative purposes.[43] It was in actuality not so much an "empire" as it was a loose collection of culturally related but distinct principalities sharing (for the most) a common language[44] and united primarily by the paying of tribute to Tenochtitlán.[45] Under the Aztecs, local rulers continued to govern their communities, albeit under the auspices of the Aztecs. Characteristic of the Aztec approach to imperium was its emphasis on control of urban centers:

Because of the nature of Mesoamerican warfare and the limitations on political consolidation, conquest did not mean complete territorial control. Rather, conquest was of political centers. Control of territory per se was not a major consideration. Once a political center was dominated, so too were its dependencies, and tribute, flowing from dependency to cabecera to provincial capital, could be drained from an entire region simply by dominating the center.[46]

The empire was held together, in short, not by the establishment of military garrisons throughout its territories, nor by overt control from Tenochtitlán, but rather, by tribute to be paid to Tenochtitlán and well-developed commercial ties.[47] The paying of tribute as well as the commercial ties were both, in turn, strengthened by what might be termed *ideological hegemony*, as Hassig noted:

The Aztecs' reliance on hegemonic rather than territorial control produced an empire of distinctive character and vast expanse but loose control. Mesoamerican technological constraints limited the size, strength and duration of forays outside the empire, and such engagements took on strategic characteristics that varied with the political nature of the target. Furthermore, the Aztec Empire was essentially an alliance, and was expectedly fraught with rebellion. Nevertheless, the system functioned admirably within its cultural context, and through it the Aztecs expanded their domain to a size unprecedented in Mesoamerica.[48]

By 1519, Tenochtitlán was a large, thriving urban metropolis of some 200,000 people, with at least as many living in the satellite cities that surrounded it, making it far larger than any European city of the time.[49] The city was connected to the mainland by three elevated causeways, and was provided fresh water by a series of carefully engineered aqueducts.[50] Food came to the capital not only as tribute from the provinces, but also, and more important, from the *chinampas*, the island-gardens that made possible the intensive agricultural cultivation that supported the urban civilizations of the Valley of Mexico.[51]

The spiritual heart of the Aztec Empire was the Templo Mayor, the largest structure in the central plaza of Tenochtitlán,[52] which represented not only the ritualistic center of the empire, but even more, in its architecture itself was the embodiment of the Aztec view of the universe, as Eduardo Matos Moctezuma noted: "The Templo Mayor thus becomes the fundamental center where all sacred power is concentrated and where all the levels intersect. I propose that it not only occupies a privileged location but that in its architecture, form, and particular characteristics it also represents the entire Mexica conception of the cosmos."[53]

Aztec society was hierarchical in nature, characterized by rank and kinship.[54] The population was broadly divided into those of noble birth and those of common birth, although some degree of social mobility did exist—primarily as a result of success in commerce, military success, or entrance into the priesthood.[55] Gender also played a key role in individual identity in Aztec society,[56] as did ethnicity for those of non-Aztec ancestry. Central to social status in Aztec society, however, was military rank. As Hassig explained, "Military ranking was intimately tied to the overall social structure of Aztec society, and social ranking was intimately tied to political offices, the latter defining rights and requiring the holder to have a specified status."[57]

It is interesting to observe that although, as Nicholson noted, "the sharply aristocratic bias of the society as a whole, naturally correlated with a high degree of social stratification,"[58] this social stratification was manifested in practice by far greater expectations of those at higher social levels. For example, as Muriel Weaver argued:

> An interesting concept of Aztec law was that the severity of punishment was measured in accordance with the offender's station in life. A high priest would be put to death for a crime that might be tolerated if committed by a bondsman. That is, a man of high office assumed greater moral responsibilities and his conduct was expected to be beyond reproach.[59]

Also important in terms of the organization of Aztec society was the role played by the *calpulli*, the ancient territorial kinship groups to which every member of the society belonged. The *calpulli* "served as the interface between the citizens and the government,"[60] as well as maintaining religious and educational institutions and communally holding a certain amount of land.[61] As Fagan commented:

The *calpulli* was probably the most important social institution in Aztec society. It provided a mechanism by which people cooperated with one another and gave a large measure of security to everyone. The state used it not only to govern a teeming and diverse urban and rural population, but to recruit large numbers of people at short notice for public works or armies of conquest.[62]

Underlying virtually all aspects of Aztec society were the two closely inter-related pillars of Aztec society, militarism and religion.[63] For the Aztecs, warfare was a means not only of gaining personal glory, social status, and, ultimately, tribute and expanding territorial control, but even more, a kind of sacrificial activity. In fact, warfare involved two kinds of sacrifice, as one of the terms used by the Aztecs to refer to war makes clear: *teoatl tlachinolli*, which translates literally as "divine liquid and ashes."[64] The term itself incorporates a vast wealth of meaning:

> The first element signifies "blood," and the second is a shorthand statement for the practice of cremating dead warriors on the battlefield, a Toltec custom that released the fortunate soul like a sunburst to ascend into the heavens. War meant the spilling of human blood, which was by definition a liquor destined for the support of the gods; war, in other words, was an act of sacrifice carried out voluntarily by those who killed as well as by those who were killed.[65]

Indeed, the need for such sacrifice was so great that when real warfare was not possible or advisable, the Aztecs engaged in what was called a *xochiyaoyotl*, or "war of flowers."[66] The *xochiyaoyotl* was a ritual military contest, "in which the two sides set out to capture the maximum number of sacrificial victims from the other while inflicting a minimum of damage in other respects."[67]

Sacrifice was essential in the Aztec religious system, since it was the shedding of human blood that ensured "the continued existence of the cosmos."[68] The sun itself, as well as the other deities of the Aztec pantheon, were nourished by human blood.[69] As Davies suggested, "In general terms, the religion of the Aztecs was an elaborate defence mechanism, born not out of hope but of anxiety. Every aspect, and in particular human offering, implies a struggle to ward off disaster, whether immediate catastrophes such as crop failure or the ultimate doom of the Fifth, and last, Sun."[70] Such an understanding is also consistent with the Aztec view of history, as the noted scholar Miguel León-Portilla maintained:

> It was believed that the present sun, moon, stars and earth integrate the fifth universe within a series of ages, known to the Nahua people as "Suns." Four other Suns had emerged and come to an end through the machinations of the gods: the ages of Earth, Air, Water, and Fire. The present is that of *Olintonatiuh*, "The Sun of Movement," which began to exist and to move thanks to a primeval sacrifice of the gods, who, with their own blood, brought it into being and thus also gave life to a new generation of humans. This fifth age not only may perish but actually carries within itself the very principle of death and destruction.[71]

Another view of the role of sacrifice in Aztec religious thought is that offered by López Austin, who, on the account of Bernard Ortiz de Montellano:

> claimed that the relationship between god and man was mercantilistic: man gave blood, hearts, and fire to the gods, and was given in return crops, water, and freedom from disease and plagues. This claim is supported etymologically. The word for sacrifice to the gods is *nextlahualiztli* ("the act of payment"), and the offering of fire to the gods, *tlenamaca*, means "to sell fire."[72]

Such sacrifice occurred, of course, not only on the battlefield, but in the temples and in everyday life as well. The role of human sacrifice, and the related practice of ritual cannibalism, in Aztec society has been well documented,[73] and it is clear that such sacrifice involved both males and females, adults and children,[74] and as many as 20,000 human sacrifices a year may have taken place by the time of the arrival of Cortés.[75] Also important in Aztec life, however, was the practice of autosacrifice, which involved personal bloodletting. As Cecelia Klein argued, "In Aztec society, from all reports, virtually everyone, regardless of age, sex, or social class, was expected to bleed himself."[76] The practice of such autosacrifice, which the Aztecs believed to have originated with the god Quetzalcoatl, was in fact closely related to human sacrifice, and it appears to have served as a symbolic substitute for human sacrifice in some instances.[77]

Aztec religious thought entailed far more than just sacrifice, of course. Religion played a central role in social life in general, touching every aspect of the society.[78] In addition to the rituals performed in the temples, their religion provided the Aztecs with a well developed creation mythology, a powerful moral code, the basis for their political and economic social order, a complex view of life after death, a priesthood responsible for the maintenance of both the oral and written traditions of their society, the calendrical system used not only to maintain records but to make predictions, a highly developed astrological system, and the foundations for a metaphysical and ultimately philosophical worldview.[79] Thus, it is hardly surprising that religious concerns are in many ways at the heart of the Aztec notion of the educated person, the concept to which we now turn.

THE AZTEC CONCEPTION OF THE "EDUCATED PERSON"

The development of the individual's personality, which the Aztecs called "face and heart,"[80] played an important role in their conception of *education* and the *educated person*, although the primary focus of education was "the assimilation of individuals into the life and highest ideals of the community."[81] As one ancient text described what we would today call the "educated person":

In omacic oquichtli,

Yollotetl, yollotlaquavac,

ixlamati,

ixehyollo,

Mozcalia.

The mature man

is a heart solid as a rock,

is a wise face.

Possessor of a face, possessor of a heart,

he is able and understanding.[82]

The core values that were expected to guide the behavior of all individuals in Aztec society, regardless of social station, and which provide a clear indication of the Aztec view of what the "educated person" might look like include:

1. maintenance of control and discipline;
2. fluency of speech and good manners;
3. a composed and reserved attitude;
4. a sense of responsibility for the common people;
5. respect for one's elders;
6. interest in and knowledge of the gods; and
7. courage, submission to one's fate, a desire to die a heroic death rather than to die without having made a serious effort to expand and strengthen the Aztecs' supremacy.[83]

These core values are clearly intended to promote the general good of society, and have a social rather than individual focus, as one would expect. This focus can be seen vividly in the following model homily delivered by an Aztec father to his son:

Revere and greet your elders; console the poor and the afflicted with good works and words.... Follow not the madmen who honour neither father nor mother; for they are like animals, for they neither take nor hear advice.... Do not mock the old, the sick, the maimed, or one who has sinned. Do not insult or abhor them, but abase yourself before God and fear lest the same befall you.... Do not set a bad example, or speak indiscreetly, or interrupt the speech of another. If someone does not speak well or coherently, see that you do not the same; if it is not your business to speak, be silent. If you are asked something, reply soberly and without affectation or flattery or prejudice to others, and your speech will be well regarded.... Wherever you go, walk with a peaceful air, and do not make wry faces or improper gestures.[84]

Such homilies were common in Aztec society, and a number, especially targeting the children of the elite, have been preserved. Among the kinds of advice and instruction provided in these homilies are such warnings as:

"Do not throw thy feet much, nor raise thy feet high, nor go jumping, lest it be said of thee, lest thou be named fool, shameless."

"Thou art not to speak hurriedly, nor to pant, nor to squeak, lest it be said that thou art a groaner, a growler, a squeaker."

"Ignore [gossip]. Pretend not to understand the words. If thou canst not ignore it, respond not. And speak not; only listen, let what is said remain as said."

"Be not called twice, like the wind art thou to go."

"Thou art not to array thyself fantastically ... neither art thou to put on rags, tatters, an old loosely-woven cape."[85]

Similar messages were conveyed less directly, but perhaps more effectively, to children in Aztec society through the use of proverbs, conundrums, and metaphors.[86] For example, typical proverbs that children might hear include the following, reported in the *Florentine Codex:*

1. *Nonouian.* Here, there and everywhere. (This is said about a person who enters where he should not enter, sticks his hand where he should not stick his hand, and quickly takes part in whatever others are doing.)[87]
2. *Ayac xictili in tlalticpac.* No one on earth is an umbilical cord (i.e., to be thrown away). (We should not sneer at anyone; meaning, we should not disdain anyone even though he appears to warrant disdain, as he might be a wise man, or learned, or able.)[88]
3. *Tlacoqualli in monequi.* Moderation is proper. (We should not dress in rags, nor should we overdress. In the matter of clothing, we should dress with moderation.)[89]

The conundrums that characterized much of the verbal play of Aztec children, as Sullivan notes, "are like conundrums everywhere—charming, simple, and concerned with everyday things."[90] Some interesting examples of common conundrums, again drawn from the *Florentine Codex,* include:

1. *Zazan tleino, icuitlaxcol quiuilana, tepetozcatl quitoca. Aca quittaz tozazaniltzin, tla ca nenca uitzmallotl.* (What is it that drags its intestines as it ambles along the foothills of the mountain? Someone is sure to guess our riddle; it is a sewing needle.)[91]

2. *Zazan tleino, tezcatzintli acxoyacaletica. Tixtelolo.* (What is a little mirror in the middle of fir trees? Our eyes.)[92]
3. *Zazan tleino, tepetlamimilolli yitic ameia. Toyac.* (What is a mountain-
side that has a spring of water in it? Our nose.)[93]
4. *Zazan tleino, quauhtla calaqui nenepilotiuh. Tepuztli.* (What is it that
goes into a tree and its tongue is hanging out? An ax.)[94]

The purpose of Aztec education, in short, was largely to promote socially
appropriate, and basically conformist, behavior, and in this objective, it is clear
that Aztec education was remarkably successful.[95] As the Jesuit José de Acosta
noted in the latter part of the 16th century, "Nothing caused me so much ad-
miration and seems to me more worthy of praise and remembering than the
care and discipline with which the Mexicans raised their children. In effect, it
would be quite difficult to find a nation which in its times of paganism gave
more attention to this element of highest importance to the state."[96]

We turn now to an examination of how the Aztecs accomplished the making
of such "educated persons," first looking at the child's earliest years at home,
and then at the formal educational institutions of Aztec society.

THE EDUCATIONAL FUNCTIONS OF THE FAMILY IN AZTEC SOCIETY

As Fagan commented, "From the moment of birth, an Aztec child became
aware that the world was a place of hard work and suffering."[97] Early childhood education for the Aztecs was guided by the twin concerns of teaching
self-control and accommodation to adversity on the one hand and
self-knowledge and introspection on the other.[98] By the age of 4, both boys and
girls were performing chores around the home; boys began by carrying water
and accompanying their fathers to work and the market, girls by helping their
mothers in various household activities.[99] The nature of the activities in which
children were engaged became increasingly sophisticated as they grew older
and were given more responsibility; for girls, such training was intended to prepare them for their futures as wives and mothers, while for boys, the focus was
increasingly on learning their father's craft.[100] Children also learned the importance of learning to control their appetites during this early period—a lesson
reinforced by the relatively small food ration they were allowed.[101] Boys
learned to tolerate not only hunger, but also extremes of heat and cold, as preparation for their later lives as warriors.[102] Indeed, one of the goals of such experiences was to develop in each individual "a heart of stone" (*yolotetl*), a
necessary outcome for a society such as that of the Aztecs.[103]

Much of the concern of parents for their children during this early period in
their children's upbringing concerned what might be called "character education," with punishments for inappropriate behavior ranging from mere scold-

ing to beatings, being pricked with maguey spines, and, perhaps as a last result, being forced to inhale the fumes of burning chilis—punishments vividly portrayed in the Aztec manuscript, the *Codex Mendoza*.[104]

FORMAL SCHOOLING IN AZTEC SOCIETY

The first taste of formal schooling outside of the home that Aztec children had took place between the ages of 12 and 15, when both boys and girls attended the *cuicacalli* ("the House of Song").[105] Each *calpulli* maintained its own *cuicacalli*, in which the elderly members of the community taught the songs, dances, and music with which everyone in Aztec society needed to be familiar.[106] The *cuicacalli* took place toward the end of the day, about an hour before sunset, and children learned:

> the correct songs and orations for every major religious ceremony on the Aztec calendar. These incantations spoke of the Aztec cosmos, the creation, and the great migrations of the ancestors. They dealt with the roles of mortals on earth, and of the relationships between gods and humans. At the *cuicacalli* everyone learned about their cultural heritage and about the mystical and highly symbolic world that surrounded them.[107]

Attendance at the *cuicacalli* was, for all intents and purposes, compulsory, and absences were punished by law. In addition, it is clear that attendance at the *cuicacalli* was not left to chance or to the responsibility of the individual. Rather, as Fray Diego Durán explained,

> certain elders were appointed to pick up and lead the children to their classes. They were elected exclusively for this task in all the wards and were known as *teaanque*, which means "men who conduct boys." Old women appointed by the wards went to fetch the girls; these were called *cihuatepixque*, which means "keepers of the maidens" ... [108]

These same elders were then responsible for returning the children to their homes or schools, and for ensuring that nothing inappropriate took place during the journey.

For the sons of the common people, additional schooling normally took place in the *telpochcalli* (the "House of Youth"), in which the curriculum included the study of history, religion, ritual, proper behavior, and music, singing, and dancing.[109] The *telpochcalli*, however, was primarily concerned with preparing their charges for war, and the students in the *telpochcalli* engaged in extensive military training and even participation in real battles on occasion.[110] As Hassig explained:

> Beyond greater numbers, the Aztecs also had a fully professional corps of soldiers, the result of a formal educational system. Initially, the Aztecs offered for-

mal military training only to the elite, but within two decades of their emergence as an independent power, King Monteuczomah Ilhuicamina instituted training for all males.... The commoners' schools [the *telpochcalli*], located in each of the city's wards, were responsible for educating all the youths therein between the ages of fifteen and twenty years ... each commoners' school had a staff of accomplished veteran soldiers who trained the youths in military skills. Youths ... accompanied the army on its campaigns to teach them about battle, usually as burden bearers.[111]

Boys slept at the *telpochcalli* at night, and were required to perform a variety of different kinds of physical work necessary to the maintenance of the *telpochcalli*, but they ate their meals at home with their families, and spent part of their day with the fathers, continuing to learn the vocational skills they would someday need to support themselves.[112]

The sons of the nobility, on the other hand, generally attended the *calmécac*, which were attached to the temples and were under the direct control of the religious authorities.[113] The *calmécac* provided an academically superior education, focusing not only on the military skills needed by all Aztec males, but also on religious instruction, history, painting, music, law, astrology, mathematics, government, and architecture.[114] Also important in a *calmécac* education was learning to speak well; the Aztecs valued the ability to use what they called *qualli tlatolli* ("good language"), by which they meant noble (as opposed to common) speech, and even distinguished between *macehuallatolli* ("the language of the common people") and *tecpillatolli* ("lordly language").[115]

Since the Aztec writing system was "not a transliteration of spoken words but an elaborate code that was reserved to those who had learned its intricacies and the orations behind it,"[116] students at the *calmécac* spent much of their time memorizing vast quantities of historical and religious material.[117] This limitation of the Aztec literary tradition turned out to have significant benefits for us today as we try to understand more fully the Aztecs, as John Cornyn noted:

> The great body of the national literature was memorized in the Aztec schools over a period of scholastic life that was almost as long as our own. To this fact we owe the preservation of the very considerable body of Aztec metric compositions which have come down to us, for, had the Aztecs been able to write their literature, it would all have disappeared in the ruthless destruction of Indian libraries wrought by the Spanish conquerors and their native allies in the first few years after the conquest.[118]

Unlike in the *telpochcalli*, students in the *calmécac* lived at the school, in what has been suggested to have been an environment "more like that of a monastery than an ordinary school."[119] It was from the *calmécac* that the priests of Aztec society were drawn, as well as the senior government officials, military leaders, judges, and so on, and thus, the *calmécac* served an important role in "the spread of elite dogma and the consolidation of belief" in Aztec society.[120] Interestingly, while the patron god of the *telpochcalli* was Tezcatlipoca, the war god, the patron god of the *calmécac* was Quetzalcoatl, the Creator god who was also "the god of learning and culture, of ancient lore, the god of civilization itself."[121]

Although attendance at the *telpochcalli* and the *calmécac* was largely determined by social class background, there was nevertheless a certain degree of choice involved in the selection of the school one's son would attend.[122] It is well established that children of non-noble backgrounds attended the *calmécac*, primarily to become priests, just as it is documented that some children of the nobility attended the *telpochcalli*.[123] In any event, all young men in Aztec society, regardless of their social background, attended one or the other of these institutions.[124]

While all boys went on for further schooling, the *cuicacalli* was the end of formal schooling for many, and perhaps most, girls. There were, however, equivalent institutions to both the *telpochcalli* and the *calmécac* available for girls,[125] which were in fact located in the same complex as their male counterparts,[126] as we read about in the "Bancroft Dialogues":

> Likewise within the houses, where the ladies were in their quarters, the girls were taught all the different things women do: sweeping, sprinkling, preparing food, making beverages, grinding (maize), preparing tortillas, making tamales, all the different things customarily done among women; also (the art of) the spindle and the weaver's reed and various kinds of embroidery; also dyeing, how rabbit down or rabbit fur was dyed different colors. And in the same way (as with the boys) those who did something wrong or did not take care were severely punished. And they were all well cared for: no men, no matter who, entered there; taking care of them was the exclusive domain of the elderly noblewomen ... And the commoners were raised in the same way; the youths were raised in the school at the youths' house, and the girls at the women's temple, where the female penitents were enclosed and fasted.[127]

CONCLUSION

In short, formal schooling in Aztec society was well developed and effective. Perhaps most impressive was the fact that at a time when, in virtually every European society, schooling of any sort was limited to a small elite, in the Aztec world, mandatory universal schooling, for both boys and girls, and regardless of social class, was an established fact.[128] Furthermore, for the Aztecs "education" entailed a variety of different attributes; in fact, the Aztecs had two very distinct words for "education": *neixtlamachiliztli* ("the act of giving wisdom to the face") and *tlacahuapahualiztli* ("the art of strengthening or bringing up men").[129] Given this model of *education* and the *educated person*, it could certainly be argued that the Aztecs were far more successful in achieving their educational aims than are many contemporary societies.

QUESTIONS FOR REFLECTION AND DISCUSSION

1. know virtually nothing about the Olmecs and Toltecs with respect to their educational thought and practice. However, since they are part of the same broad cultural tradition as the Maya and the Aztecs, what kinds of generalizations do you think could be made about education and childrearing among these peoples?
2. Consider the account offered in the *Popol Vuh* of the creation of human beings. If one accepted this account, what would the social and educational implications be? How would this account affect one's conception of what constitutes an "educated person"?
3. In this chapter, it is suggested that ancient Maya was profoundly religious in nature. What are the parallels to other systems of education that are deeply religious? How did the Mayan experience differ from other religious approaches to education? How can you account for these differences?
4. Social class clearly played an important role in both informal and formal education in Aztec society. To what extent, and in what ways, was the educational system open to social class mobility, and how might this have strengthened Aztec society?
5. The Aztec conception of the *educated man* is discussed in detail in this chapter. What, given your knowledge of Aztec society, would have been the Aztec conception of the *educated woman*? How does this conception fit with the passage from the "Bancroft Dialogues" presented in the chapter?
6. In many ways, Aztec educational goals and practices are similar to those of a number of other societies historically. For example, what are the similarities to and differences from Spartan education? What about the educational ideals and institutions of Nazi Germany? How might the similarities that you have identified be explained?
7. Aztec schooling sought to promote the social status quo and to reproduce Aztec society. To what extent, and in what ways, is this true for contemporary schooling as well? Is this, in your view, a reasonable goal for schooling?
8. Music played a very important role in Aztec education. What purposes did music serve in Aztec schooling and society? How do these purposes compare to those offered for the study of music in our own society?
9. Since the Aztec writing system was "not a transliteration of spoken words but an elaborate code that was reserved to those who had learned its intricacies and the orations behind it," it was necessary for students to learn to use the written text as a support for the recall of memorized information. Can you think of any learning techniques that you have used that are similar to this? What kinds of learning is best promoted by such techniques?

10. This chapter concludes by noting that Aztec education may have been more effective than many contemporary systems of education. If this is true, is it in fact desirable? With what issues other than effectiveness might one be concerned in evaluating educational thought and practice?

RECOMMENDED FURTHER READINGS

An excellent overview of Aztec society for the beginner is Richard Townsend's *The Aztecs* (London: Thames and Hudson, 1992), while a somewhat more sophisticated account is provided in Inga Clendinnen's *Aztecs: An Interpretation* (Cambridge, England: Cambridge University Press, 1991). Among the best works describing the intellectual and cultural world of the Aztecs are Miguel León-Portilla's *Aztec Thought and Culture* (Norman: University of Oklahoma Press, 1963) and his *The Aztec Image of Self and Society: An Introduction to Nahua Culture* (Salt Lake City: University of Utah Press, 1992). Finally, both Davíd Carrasco, with Scott Sessions, *Daily Life of the Aztecs: People of the Sun and Earth* (Westport, CT: Greenwood, 1998) and Robert Sharer, *Daily Life in Maya Civilization* (Westport, CT: Greenwood, 1996) provide very good summaries of many educationally relevant aspects of Aztec life.

NOTES

1. Richard E. Adams, *Prehistoric Mesoamerica*, rev. ed. (Norman: University of Oklahoma Press, 1991), 22.
2. Adams, *Prehistoric Mesoamerica*, 23.
3. Adams, *Prehistoric Mesoamerica*, 24. See also Nigel Davies, *The Ancient Kingdoms of Mexico* (Harmondsworth: Penguin, 1982), 11–20.
4. Jacques Soustelle, *The Olmecs: The Oldest Civilization in Mexico* (Norman: University of Oklahoma Press, 1979), 1; Davies, *The Ancient Kingdoms of Mexico*, 61–62.
5. This cultural continuity can be seen, for instance, in the development of Mesoamerican religious thought. See Davíd Carrasco, *Religions of Mesoamerica: Cosmovision and Ceremonial Centers* (San Francisco: HarperSanFrancisco, 1990).
6. Adams, *Prehistoric Mesoamerica*, 85.
7. Soustelle, *The Olmecs*, 194.
8. See, for instance, Ronald Spores, *The Mixtecs in Ancient and Colonial Times* (Norman: University of Oklahoma Press, 1984).
9. Soustelle, *The Olmecs*, 1.
10. *Códice Matritense de la Real Academia*, VIII, fol. 192, r; quoted in Miguel León-Portilla, *Aztec Thought and Culture: A Study of the Ancient Nahuatl Mind* (Norman: University of Oklahoma Press, 1963), 23.
11. Michael D. Coe, *The Maya*, 4th ed. (London: Thames and Hudson, 1987), 7.

12. For recent scholarship on Mayan civilization, see Linda Schele and Peter Mathews, *The Code of Kings: The Language of Seven Sacred Maya Temples and Tombs* (New York: Simon & Shuster, 1998); Anthony Aveni (ed.), *The Sky in Mayan Literature* (New York: Oxford University Press, 1992); Michael Coe, *Breaking the Maya Code* (London: Thames and Hudson, 1992); David Freidel, Linda Schele, and Joy Parker, *Maya Cosmos: Three Thousand Years of the Shaman's Path* (New York: William Morrow, 1993); Charles Gallenkamp, *Maya: The Riddle and Rediscovery of a Lost Civilization*, 3rd ed. (New York: Penguin, 1985); Linda Schele and David Freidel, *A Forest of Kings: The Untold Story of the Ancient Maya* (New York: William Morrow, 1990); Robert Sharer, *The Ancient Maya*, 5th ed. (Stanford, CA: Stanford University Press, 1994); Robert Sharer, *La civilización maya* (México: Fondo de Cultura Económica, 1998). The classic presentation of the older "peaceful priest-astronomers" view of the Maya is given by Eric Thompson, *The Rise and Fall of Maya Civilization* (Norman: University of Oklahoma Press, 1954); see also Sylvanus Morley, *The Ancient Maya*, 3rd ed. (Stanford, CA: Stanford University Press, 1956); Paul Gendrop, *Les mayas* (Paris: Presses Universitaires de France, 1978).

13. That such claims are largely conjectural, however, has not prevented a number of scholars from speculating about educational matters in ancient Mayan civilization. See, for instance, Ana Luisa Izquierdo, *La educación maya en los tiempos prehispánicos* (México: Universidad Nacional Autónoma de México, 1983); Carlos Orellana, *Historia de la educación en Guatemala*, 5th ed. (Guatemala: Editoria Universitaria, Universidad de San Carlos de Guatemala, 1997), 19–39.

14. Norman Hammond, *Ancient Maya Civilization* (New Brunswick, NJ: Rutgers University Press, 1988), 180.

15. See, for example, Robert Sharer, *Daily Life in Maya Civilization* (Westport, CT: Greenwood Press, 1996); Robert Sharer, *The Ancient Maya*, 5th ed. (Stanford, CA: Stanford University Press, 1994); Robert Sharer, *La civilización maya;* Mary Ellen Miller, *The Art of Mesoamerica From Olmec to Aztec* (London: Thames and Hudson, 1986).

16. Sharer, *Daily Life in Maya Civilization*, 118.

17. Diego de Landa, *Relación de las cosas de Yucatán* (México: Editorial Porrua, 1959).

18. See Gualberto Alonzo, *An Overview of the Mayan World*, 11th ed. (Mérida, Yucatán, México: Author, 1993), 50–52; Nelly Solana, *Códices de México: Historia e interpretación de los grandes libros pintados prehispánicos* (México: Panorama Editorial, 1990).

19. An excellent Spanish version is Ermilo Abreu Gomez, *Popol Vuh* (Mérida, Yucatán, México: Producción Editorial Dante, 1996); for English, see Della Goetz and Sylvanus Morley, trans., *Popol Vuy: The Sacred Book of the Ancient Quiché Maya* (Norman: University of Oklahoma Press, 1950).

20. Goetz and Morley, *Popul Vuh*, ix.

21. See Orellana, *Historia de la educación en Guatemala*, 27–29.

22. Izquierdo, *La educación maya en los tiempos prehispánicos*, 13.

23. Izquierdo, *La educación maya en los tiempos prehispánicos*, 17.

24. See Sharer, *Daily Life in Maya Civilization*, 117–129; Sharer, *The Ancient Maya*, 481–488; Sharer, *La civilización maya*, 458–468.

25. See the discussion of the role of oral traditions in education in chapter 1.

26. Izquierdo, *La educación maya en los tiempos prehispánicos*, 18.

27. Goetz and Morley, *Popol Vuh*, 168.

28. Goetz and Morley, *Popol Vuh*, 169.

29. There is something of a terminological problem involved in discussing the Aztecs. First, as Fagan quite correctly noted, "At the time of the Spanish Conquest, the Aztecs called themselves either Tenocha Mexica or Tlatelolca Mexica, depending on which part of the capital they lived in. 'Mexica' could also be used alone, depending on the context" [Brian Fagan, *The Aztecs* (New York: Freeman, 1984), x]. Furthermore, the Aztecs were but one group among the closely related Nahuatl groups in Mesoamerica, and so one might also quite properly use the term "Nahuatl" to refer to them—as, indeed, Miguel León-Portilla does. However, "Aztec" is the most commonly and easily understood term used today for the people about whom I am writing, and so I have chosen to take the easiest way out for the benefit of the reader, as have many other writers on the Aztecs.

30. Quoted in Ross Hassig, *Trade, Tribute, and Transportation: The Sixteenth Century Political Economy of the Valley of Mexico* (Norman: University of Oklahoma Press, 1985), 4.

31. From the Aztec perspective, of course, the "time of the fifth sun" did not actually end with the Spanish Conquest—technically speaking, only the end of the world as we know it, on a predetermined date, would constitute the end of the "time of the fifth sun." However, in a very real social and political sense, the world of the Aztecs did indeed end in the early sixteenth century, as Brundage and others seem to implicitly recognize in utilizing the phrase "the fifth sun" to refer solely to the world of the Aztecs. See Burr Brundage, *The Fifth Sun: Aztec Gods, Aztec World* (Austin: University of Texas Press, 1979).

32. See Ruben Campos, *La producción literaria de los Aztecas* (México: Talleres Gráficos del Museo Nacional de Arqueología, Historia y Ethnografía, 1936), 65–72; F. Infante, *La educación de los Aztecas* (México: Panorama Editorial, 1983); Mina Markus, "Estudio comparativo entre la educación nahuatl y la griega," *Estudios de Cultura Náhuatl* 4 (1963): 281–292; P. Aizpuro, *Historia de la educación en la época colonial: El mundo indígena* (México: El Colegio de México, 1990); Jacqueline Sáenz, "Reto y educación en el México prehispánico," in J. Kathryn Josserand and Karen Dakin (eds.), *Smoke and Mist: Mesoamerican Studies in Memory of Thelma D. Sullivan, Part II* (Oxford, England: B.A.R., 1988), 681–695.

33. León-Portilla, *Aztec Thought and Culture*, 135. See also Miguel León-Portilla, *La filosofía Nahuatl: Estudio en sus fuentes* (México: Universidad Nacional Autónoma de México, 1966); Miguel León-Portilla, *Trece poetas del mundo azteca* (México: Universidad Nacional Autónoma de México, Instituto de Investigaciones Históricas, 1967).

34. Muriel Weaver, *The Aztecs, Maya, and Their Predecessors: Archeology of Mesoamerica*, 2nd ed. (New York: Academic, 1981), 420; see also Betty Bell (ed.), *Indian Mexico: Past and Present* (Los Angeles: University of California at Los Angeles, Latin American Center, 1967); Burr Brundage, *Two Heavens, Two Earths: An Essay Contrasting the Aztecs and the Incas* (Albuquerque: University of New Mexico Press, 1975); Davíd Carrasco, *Quetzalcoatl and the Irony of Empire: Myths and Prophecies in the Aztec Tradition* (Chicago: University of Chicago Press, 1982).

35. See Davies, *The Ancient Kingdoms of Mexico*, 167–171; John Thompson, *Mexico Before Cortez: An Account of the Daily Life, Religion, and Ritual of the Aztecs and Kindred Peoples* (New York: Scribner's, 1933), 23–27; Weaver, *The Aztecs, Maya, and Their Predecessors*, 420; Jacques Soustelle, *Les aztèques*, 6th ed. (Paris: Presses Universitaires de France, 1991).

36. Quoted in Burr Brundage, *A Rain of Darts: The Mexica Aztecs* (Austin: University of Texas Press, 1972), 22.

37. Jon Manchip White, *Cortés and the Downfall of the Aztec Empire: A Study in a Conflict of Cultures* (New York: St. Martin's Press, 1971), 93.

38. Quoted in Fagan, *The Aztecs*, 57–58.

39. Fagan, *The Aztecs*, 58.

40. See Davies, *The Ancient Kingdoms of Mexico*, 171; Weaver, *The Aztecs, Maya, and Their Predecessors*, 421.

41. Weaver, *The Aztecs, Maya, and Their Predecessors*, 422.

42. Although in many ways the Aztec Empire was indeed at its height in 1519, in other ways it was profoundly troubled. As Benjamin Keen noted:

Was Aztec society going through a moral crisis, a *crise de conscience*, on the eve of the Conquest? Certainly the native chronicles reveal a state of jangled nerves, of profound insecurity on the part of the Aztec leadership. Economic and social factors undoubtedly contributed to this state of affairs: chronic discontent of conquered peoples under the mounting burden of tribute demands, perhaps population pressure on exhausted soils, dissension between warrior nobles and increasingly powerful merchants, a decline of tribal solidarity as a result of growing inequalities of wealth and status. Yet ideological factors also played their part…. Aztec civilization has reached an impasse that perhaps could have been overcome only by a decisive advance in technology, of the kind that attended the invention of ironworking in the Old World. [see Benjamin Keen, *The Aztec Image in Western Thought* (New Brunswick, NJ: Rutgers University Press, 1971), 47–48].

43. Warwick Bray, *The Everyday Life of the Aztecs* (New York: Dorset, 1968), 25.

44. Throughout Mesoamerica, Nahuatl, the language of the Aztecs and related peoples, functioned as a *lingua franca*. See James Andrews, *An Introduction to Classical Nahuatl* (Austin: University of Texas Press, 1975); Jorge Suárez, *The Mesoamerican Indian Languages* (Cambridge, England: Cambridge University Press, 1983); Gunter Lanczkowski, *Aztekische Sprach und Überlieferung* (Berlin: Springer-Verlag, 1970).

45. See Frances Berdan, "La organización del tributo en el imperio azteca," *Estudios de Cultura Náhuatl* 12 (1976): 185–195; Hassig, *Trade, Tribute and Transportation*, 276–280.

46. Hassig, *Trade, Tribute and Transportation*, 104.

47. See Weaver, *The Aztecs, Maya, and Their Predecessors*, 451–455; see also Hassig, *Trade, Tribute and Transportation*.

48. Ross Hassig, *Aztec Warfare: Imperial Expansion and Political Control* (Norman: University of Oklahoma Press, 1988), 26; see also Ross Hassig, *Trade, Tribute and Transportation*, 92–103.

49. Fagan, *The Aztecs*, 109; Bray, *The Everyday Life of the Aztecs*, 98.

50. See Bray, *The Everyday Life of the Aztecs*, 98.

51. Fagan, *The Aztecs*, 84–89.

52. Fagan, *The Aztecs*, 99–103; Elizabeth Boone (ed.), *The Aztec Templo Mayor: A Symposium at Dumbarton Oaks, 8th and 9th October 1983* (Washington, DC: Dumbarton Oaks Research Library and Collection, 1987).

53. Eduardo Matos Moctezuma, "Symbolism of the Templo Mayor," in Elizabeth Boone (ed.), *The Aztec Templo Mayor: A Symposium at Dumbarton Oaks, 8th and 9th October 1983* (Washington, DC: Dumbarton Oaks Research Library and Collection, 1987), 191.

54. Diane Chase and Arlen Chase (eds.), *Mesoamerican Elites: An Archeological Assessment* (Norman: University of Oklahoma Press, 1992); Nigel Davies, *The Aztec Empire: The Toltec Resurgence* (Norman: University of Oklahoma Press, 1987), 106–116; Fagan, *The Aztecs*, 137–138; Friedrich Katz, *Situación social y económica de los Aztecas durante los siglos XV y XVI* (México: Universidad Nacional Autónoma de México, Instituto de Investigaciones Históricas, 1966), 123–149; H. Nicholson, "The Efflorescence of Mesoamerican Civilization: A Resume," in Betty Bell (ed.), *Indian Mexico: Past and Present* (Los Angeles: University of California at Los Angeles, Latin American Center, 1967), 46–71.

55. Hassig, *Aztec Warfare*, 28.

56. See Anna-Britta Hellbrom, *La participación cultural de las mujeres: Indias y mestizas en el México precortesiano y postrevolucionario* (Stockholm: The Ethnographic Museum, Monograph Series, Publication 10, 1967); Susan Kellogg, "Cognatic Kinship and Religion: Women in Aztec Society," in J. Kathryn Josserand and Karen Dakin (eds.), *Smoke and Mist: Mesoamerican Studies in Memory of Thelma D. Sullivan, Part II* (Oxford, England: B.A.R., 1988), 665–681.

57. Hassig, *Aztec Warfare*, 28.

58. Nicholson, "The Efflorescence of Mesoamerican Civilization," 64.

59. Weaver, *The Aztecs, Maya, and Their Predecessors*, 446.

60. Fagan, *The Aztecs*, 146; see also Claude Davies, *Los mexicas: Primeros pasos hacia el imperio* (México: Universidad Nacional Autónoma de México, Instituto de Investigaciones Históricas, 1973), 81–83; Jane Day, *Aztec: The World of Moctezuma* (Niwot, CO: Denver Museum of Natural History and Roberts Rinehart Publishers, 1992), 8–9.

61. See Katz, *Situación social y económica de los Aztecas durante los siglos XV y XVI*, 117–121; Day, *Aztec*, 8.

62. Fagan, *The Aztecs*, 148.

63. See Cecilia Klein, "The Ideology of Autosacrifice at the Templo Mayor," in Elizabeth Boone (ed.), *The Aztec Templo Mayor: A Symposium at Dumbarton Oaks, 8th and 9th October 1983* (Washington, DC: Dumbarton Oaks Research Library and Collection, 1987), 293–370; Brundage, *A Rain of Darts*, 96–102; White, *Cortés and the Downfall of the Aztec Empire*, 113–115.

64. Brundage, *A Rain of Darts*, 97.

65. Brundage, *A Rain of Darts*, 97.

66. Brundage, *A Rain of Darts*, 99–101.

67. Davies, *The Aztec Empire*, 93; see also R. Hassig, *War and Society in Ancient Mesoamerica* (Berkeley: University of California Press, 1992), 147–148.

68. Fagan, *The Aztecs*, 228.

69. Bray, *The Everyday Life of the Aztecs*, 171–175.

70. Davies, *The Ancient Kingdoms of Mexico*, 229–230.

71. Miguel León-Portilla, *Fifteen Poets of the Aztec World* (Norman: University of Oklahoma Press, 1992), 46.

72. Bernard Ortiz de Montellano, *Aztec Medicine, Health, and Nutrition* (New Brunswick, NJ: Rutgers University Press, 1990), 41.

73. See Brundage, *A Rain of Darts*, 101–107; Davies, *The Ancient Kingdoms of Mexico*, 228–231; Fagan, *The Aztecs*, 228–237; M. Othón de Mendizábal, "La cultura azteca y los sacrificios humanos," in Miguel León-Portilla (ed.), *De Teotihuacán a los Aztecas: Antología de fuentes e interpretaciones históricas* (México: Universidad Nacional Autónoma de México, Instituto de Investigaciones Históricas, 1971), 208–214; White, *Cortés and the Downfall of the Aztec Empire*, 119–121.

74. See Juan Berrelleza, "Offering 48 of the Templo Mayor: A Case of Child Sacrifice," in Elizabeth Boone (ed.), *The Aztec Templo Mayor: A Symposium at Dumbarton Oaks, 8th and 9th October 1983* (Washington, DC: Dumbarton Oaks Research Library and Collection, 1987), 131–143; Brundage, *The Fifth Sun*, 212–214; Davies, *The Aztec Empire*; Fagan, *The Aztecs*, 232; Miguel León-Portilla (ed.), *Ritos, sacerdotes y atavíos de los dioses: Textos de los informantes de Sahagun, 1* (México: Universidad Nacional Autónoma de México, Instituto de Historia, 1958).

75. Brundage, *The Fifth Sun*, 215; Fagan, *The Aztecs*, 230; see also Davies, *The Aztec Empire*, 218–221, for a description of the inflationary nature of human sacrifice in Aztec society.

76. Klein, "The Ideology of Autosacrifice at the Templo Mayor," 350.

77. Klein, "The Ideology of Autosacrifice at the Templo Mayor," 297.

78. See Bray, *The Everyday Life of the Aztecs*, 152–185; Weaver, *The Aztecs, Maya, and Their Predecessors*, 446–451; George C. Vaillant, *La civilización azteca: Origen, grandeza y decadencia* (México: Fondo de Cultura Económica, 1995), 142–156.

79. See Munro Edmonson, *The Book of the Year: Middle American Calendrical Systems* (Salt Lake City: University of Utah Press, 1988); Wayne Elzey, "Some Remarks on the Space and Time of the 'Center' in Aztec Religion," *Estudios de Cultura Náhuatl* 12 (1976): 315–334; Keen, *The Aztec Image in Western Thought*, 30–48; León-Portilla, *Ritos, sacerdotes y atavíos de los dioses*; León-Portilla, *Aztec Thought and Culture*, 1966; Alberto Lhuillier, "El pensamiento náhuatl respecto de la muerte," *Estudios de Cultura Náhuatl* 4 (1963): 251–261.

80. See Miguel León-Portilla, *Toltecáyotl: Aspectos de la cultura náhuatl* (México: Fondo de Cultura Económica, 1995), 192–193.

81. León-Portilla, *Aztec Thought and Culture*, 135.

82. Quoted in Markus, "Estudio comparativo entre la educación nahuatl y la griega," 292; see also Miguel León-Portilla, *The Aztec Image of Self and Society: An Introduction to Nahua Culture* (Salt Lake City: University of Utah Press, 1992), 189–196.

83. Rudolf van Zantwijk, *The Aztec Arrangement: The Social History of Pre-Spanish Mexico* (Norman: University of Oklahoma Press, 1985), 170–171.

84. Quoted in Davies, *The Ancient Kingdoms of Mexico*, 240.

85. Davíd Carrasco, with Scott Sessions, *Daily Life of the Aztecs: People of the Sun and Earth* (Westport, CT: Greenwood Press, 1998), 103.

86. See Thelma Sullivan, "Nahuatl Proverbs, Conundrums and Metaphors Collected by Sahagun," *Estudios de Cultura Náhuatl* 4 (1963): 93–178.

87. Sullivan, "Nahuatl Proverbs, Conundrums and Metaphors Collected by Sahagun," 97.

88. Sullivan, "Nahuatl Proverbs, Conundrums and Metaphors Collected by Sahagun," 99.

89. Sullivan, "Nahuatl Proverbs, Conundrums and Metaphors Collected by Sahagun," 121.

90. Sullivan, "Nahuatl Proverbs, Conundrums and Metaphors Collected by Sahagun," 95.

91. Sullivan, "Nahuatl Proverbs, Conundrums and Metaphors Collected by Sahagun," 131.

92. Sullivan, "Nahuatl Proverbs, Conundrums and Metaphors Collected by Sahagun," 133.

93. Sullivan, "Nahuatl Proverbs, Conundrums and Metaphors Collected by Sahagun," 133.

94. Sullivan, "Nahuatl Proverbs, Conundrums and Metaphors Collected by Sahagun," 135.

95. See Infante, *La educación de los Aztecas*; León-Portilla, *Toltecáyotl: Aspectos de la cultura náhuatl*, 190–204.

96. Quoted in León-Portilla, *Aztec Thought and Culture*, 135.

97. Fagan, *The Aztecs*, 149–150.

98. See León-Portilla, *Aztec Thought and Culture*, 136.

99. Bray, *The Everyday Life of the Aztecs*, 58–59.

100. Fagan, *The Aztecs*, 151.

101. León-Portilla, *Aztec Thought and Culture*, 136.

102. See Campos, *La producción literaria de los Aztecas*, 65–66.

103. Diego Durán, *Book of the Gods and Rites and the Ancient Calendar* (Norman: University of Oklahoma Press, 1971), 294.

104. See Frances F. Berdan and Patricia R. Anawalt, *The Essential Codex Mendoza* (Berkeley: University of California Press, 1997).

105. Day, *Aztec*, 23; Fagan, *The Aztecs*, 151–153; Joyce Marcus, *Mesoamerican Writing Systems: Propaganda, Myth, and History in Four Ancient Civilizations* (Princeton, NJ: Princeton University Press, 1992), 50; Elizabeth Boone and Walter Mignolo (eds.), *Writing Without Words: Alternative Literacies in Mesoamerica and the Andes* (Durham, NC: Duke University Press, 1994); Bernardino Sahagun, *El Mexico antiguo: Selección y reordenación de la historia general de las cosas de Nueva España* (Caracas: Biblioteca Ayachucho, 1981), 165–166; Remi Siméon, *Dictionnaire de la langue Nahuatl ou Mexicaine* (Graz, Germany: Akademische Druck U. Verlagsanstalt, 1963), 120; Richard Townsend, *The Aztecs* (London: Thames and Hudson, 1992), 158.

106. Townsend, *The Aztecs*, 158.

107. Fagan, *The Aztecs*, 153.

108. Durán, *Book of the Gods and Rites and the Ancient Calendar*, 290.

109. Bray, *The Everyday Life of the Aztecs*, 63; Day, *Aztec*, 23; Infante, *La educación de los Aztecas*, 57–63; Marcus, *Mesoamerican Writing Systems*, 51; Townsend, *The Aztecs*, 158–159.

110. See Hassig, *Aztec Warfare*, 30–37.

111. Hassig, *War and Society in Ancient Mesoamerica*, 142.

112. Bray, *The Everyday Life of the Aztecs*, 62–63; Fagan, *The Aztecs*, 154; Sahagun, *El Mexico antiguo*, 163–166; van Zantwijk, *The Aztec Arrangement*, 144.

113. Bray, *The Everyday Life of the Aztecs*, 63; E. Calnek, "The Calmécac and Telpochcalli in Pre-Conquest Tenochtitlán," in J. Jorge Klor de Alva, H. Nicholson, and Eloise Caber (eds.), *The Work of Bernardino de Sahagun: Pioneer Ethnographer of Sixteenth-Century Aztec Mexico* (Albany: Institute for Mesoamerican Studies, State University of New York, 1988), 169–177.

114. See Bray, *The Everyday Life of the Aztecs*, 64; Infante, *La educación de los Aztecas*, 63–71; Marcus, *Mesoamerican Writing Systems*, 50–51; Townsend, *The Aztecs*. The study and practice of medicine were also well developed in Aztec society; see Bernard Ortiz de Montellano, *Aztec Medicine, Health, and Nutrition* (New Brunswick, NJ: Rutgers University Press, 1990).

115. León-Portilla, *Aztec Thought and Culture*, 140.

116. Fagan, *The Aztecs*, 198; see also Miguel León-Portilla, *Quince poetas del mundo náhuatl* (México: Editorial Diana, 1994), 11–24.

117. See Marcus, *Mesoamerican Writing Systems*, 50–51; Nelly Gutiérrez Solana, *Códices de México: Historia e interpretación de los grandes libros pintados prehispánicos* (México: Panorama Editorial, 1985).

118. John Cornyn, *The Song of Quetzalcoatl* (Yellow Springs, OH: Antioch Press, 1930), 9–10.

119. Bray, *The Everyday Life of the Aztecs*, 64.

120. Geoffrey Conrad and Arthur Demarest, *Religion and Empire: The Dynamics of Aztec and Inca Expansionism* (Cambridge, England: Cambridge University Press, 1984), 43.

121. Fagan, *The Aztecs*, 244.

122. Calnek, "The *Calmécac* and *Telpochcalli* in Pre-Conquest Tenochtitlán."

123. See Calnek, "The *Calmécac* and *Telpochcalli* in Pre-Conquest Tenochtitlán"; Hassig, *Aztec Warfare*, 34; León-Portilla, *Aztec Thought and Culture*, 137–138.

124. León-Portilla, *Aztec Thought and Culture*, 138.

125. See Bray, *The Everyday Life of the Aztecs*, 64; Day, *Aztec*, 33; Infante, *La educación de los Aztecas*, 71–74; Marcus, *Mesoamerican Writing Systems*, 51–52.

126. Durán, *Book of the Gods and Rites and the Ancient Calendar*, 83–85.

127. Frances Karttunen and James Lockhard (eds.), *The Art of Nahuatl Speech: The Bancroft Dialogues* (Los Angeles: UCLA Latin American Center Publications, 1987), 153–155.

128. See José Luis de Rojas, *México Tenochtitlan: Economía y sociedad en el siglo XVI* (México: El Colegio de Michoacán, Fondo de Cultura Econónica, 1988), 22, 24.

129. León-Portilla, *Aztec Thought and Culture*, 134–135.

4
"Finding the True Meaning of Life": Indigenous Education in North America

There is an extensive literature concerned with the education of Native American children,[1] and it includes a significant body of excellent historical works.[2] With very few exceptions, however, this historical literature deals with the education of Indian children after the arrival of European settlers. In other words, the focus of scholarship has been not so much on Native American education as it has been on the formal, Western schooling processes to which Indian children have been exposed (or, some would say, subjected). The history of the treatment of the indigenous peoples of North America is an important, and largely shameful, part of our history, and the historical studies of Indian education constitute a significant and potent piece of the broader history of American education. Our concern in this chapter, however, is not with the history of the interaction of Indians and others in North America, but rather, with the educational ideas and practices that existed before that interaction began, many of which continue to play roles in Native American cultural and childrearing practices even today.

In discussing Native American educational ideas and practices, we are faced with a problem very similar to that discussed in chapter 2 with respect to traditional African education. North America is geographically large, and the indigenous peoples of North America were and are very diverse culturally and linguistically (see Fig. 4.1). Some 250 distinct languages were spoken in North America when Europeans first arrived and, although many of these languages are now extinct, a significant number still survive.[3] American Indians, both in the past and the present, live in a wide variety of very different physical settings, and as a consequence have developed very different cultural patterns, norms, social structures, and behaviors. Indeed, even the separation of the peoples of Mesoamerica from those of North America is problematic not only geographically, but also culturally. There are clear similarities of thought and practice among all of the indigenous peoples of the Americas, although there are also significant differences. As Joseph Oxendine commented, "The great diversity

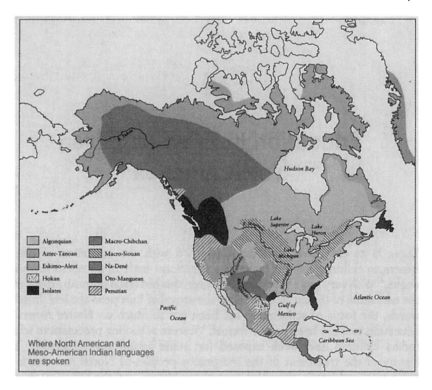

FIG. 4.1.   The diversity of Native America: where North American and
Mesoamerican languages are spoken [From David Crystal, *The Cambridge Encyclope-*
dia of Language (Cambridge, England, Cambridge University Press, 1987), p. 321.
Reprinted with permission.

among traditional Indian cultures makes it impossible to discuss Indian customs
… as a cohesive entity. Differences in languages, means of livelihood, social
structures, and traditions inhibit attempts to generalize absolutely about … cultural phenomena."[4] In fact, Carol Locust argued that it is the diversity of both
beliefs and practices among different Indian peoples that contributes to a general lack of understanding of Indians in our society. As she explained:

> One of the reasons many non-Indian people do not understand much about In-
> dian belief systems is that they vary from tribe to tribe and from clan to clan. For
> example, Apaches believe that supernatural spirits seek out an individual to be-
> come a medicine person. The Tohono O'odham, on the other hand, believe that
> one must be born into a lineage of medicine persons or must be a twin in order to
> become a medicine person.[5]

Nevertheless, just as in the case of sub-Saharan Africa it is possible to discuss a common, core unity in the midst of diversity, so too is this possible in the

case of Native Americans. There are, in fact, a common core of beliefs, and of remarkably similar practices, that are common to most (although by no means all) American Indians. This is true not only with respect to their belief systems, as Locust argued, but also with respect to traditional ideas about education and childrearing. This having been said, it is important to keep in mind that variation and diversity will nonetheless characterize the reality of American Indian thought and practice, and that the general claims offered here are just that—generalizations rather than absolutes. Furthermore, it is important to remember that even within a particular tribe, there may well be differences of opinion and practice related to clan distinctions, as well as differences related to the degree and amount of contact with other groups.[6]

Added to this complexity has been the tendency of historians to view American Indian history as synonymous with the history of contact with Europeans. As Calvin Martin noted:

> "There are two Indians of history," recently mused an eminent anthropologist: "one is the Indian of ethnology; the other, the Indian of recent history. The first is the Indian of cultural elements: the snowshoe, puberty ceremonies, kinship organization, and the potlatch. The second is the Indian of the mines, the *encomiendas*, the missions, and the fur trade."[7]

In order to understand traditional educational thought and practice, it is with the former, more anthropologically based, view of the Native American that we are concerned here. We turn now to a brief discussion of the underlying, core belief system of Native Americans.

THE CORE BELIEF SYSTEM OF AMERICAN INDIANS

Carol Locust identified 10 core beliefs that she believes are common to most Indian tribes in the United States, and which are probably valid for North American Indians in general. At the outset, of course, we need to recognize that any such list of "core beliefs" associated with a culture will be highly problematic. At best, a list of this sort can only provide us with a framework, and a limited framework at that, for making sense of the incredibly complex nexus of social, cultural, economic, political, and ideological factors that influence both individual and group identity and behavior. While any articulation of cultural beliefs and practices runs the risk of distortion and misrepresentation, such efforts can, if taken with a grain of salt, be nonetheless useful. The 10 core beliefs identified by Locust, which are basically an attempt to summarize the key elements of what many Indians would call the "Old Teachings," fall into this "problematic but useful" category, I think, and include:

1. American Indians believe in a Supreme Creator. In this belief system, there are lesser beings also.

2. Humans are threefold beings made up of a spirit, mind, and body.
3. Plants and animals, like humans, are part of the spirit world. The spirit world exists side by side with, and intermingles with, the physical world.
4. The spirit existed before it came into a physical body, and will exist after the body dies.
5. Illness affects the mind and spirit as well as the body.
6. Wellness is harmony in spirit, mind, and body.
7. Unwellness is disharmony in spirit, mind, and body.
8. Natural unwellness is caused by the violation of a sacred or tribal taboo.
9. Unnatural unwellness is caused by witchcraft.
10. Each of us is responsible for his or her own wellness.[8]

The overall focus of this set of core beliefs is on health, which may initially seem to be related to educational beliefs at best only tangentially. And yet this is, in fact, far from the case, because for Native Americans one's health is not only a physical condition, but a spiritual one as well. Furthermore, the separation of the spiritual from other aspects of culture not only does not exist in traditional Indian thought, it does not make sense *conceptually*. In other words, if we want to understand traditional Native American ideas about education and childrearing, we must begin with traditional Native Americans' ideas of good health and illness.[9]

Central to Native American educational thought and practice is the view of the human being as a threefold being, consisting of a spirit, a mind, and a physical body. Each of these parts has a role to play, but the roles are distinctive and are by no means of the same relative importance. As Locust explained:

> Of the three elements—spirit, mind, and body—the spirit is the most important, for it is the essence of the being. The instrument by which the spirit may express itself is the body. It can learn spiritual lessons and may progress toward the ultimate goal of being united with the Supreme Creator. The mind is the link between the spirit and the body and functions as an interpreter between the two.[10]

Education, understood in this context, should then involve all three of the elements of which each of us is composed and, furthermore, should aid in helping the individual to achieve the goal of *harmony*. Harmony has a somewhat distinctive meaning here, referring to: "the peaceful, tranquil state of knowing all is well with one's spirit, mind, and body. To be in harmony is to be at 'oneness' with life, eternity, the Supreme Creator, and oneself.... But harmony is not found within the environment, nor does it come from others; it comes from within and from the Supreme Creator."[11]

Although harmony is indeed associated with wellness, it is wellness of a spiritual sort.[12] Thus, learning to cope with various physical ailments may well be part of achieving harmony.[13] Just as harmony is the proper goal for education, the alternative—disharmony—is precisely what education ought to be concerned with preventing. Disharmony is the root cause for physical and psychological unwellness:

> One cannot be in a state of disharmony caused by suppressed anger, frustration, heartache, or fear without sooner or later developing unwellness in the physical body from that disharmony. Disharmony may be a vague feeling of things "not being right" in one's life, and a time of meditation may be needed in which to discover what is not right.[14]

Perhaps the most clearly articulated expression of this conception of harmony and disharmony can be found in the "pattern of the sacred circle." The sacred circle, which is also known as the "medicine wheel," the "sacred hoop," and the "peace symbol," is common to many North American Indian tribes, and is fundamentally concerned with representing and advocating balance and harmony in all aspects of life.[15] As Robert Regnier noted, the sacred circle "is a mirror which serves as a system of meaning reflecting the essential interconnectedness, harmony, and balance among all beings."[16] Although the exact nature of the manifestation of the sacred circle, as well as elements of its interpretation, do vary from group to group, there are nonetheless strong commonalities across tribes. Specifically,

1. As a closed formation, the circle symbolizes the totality, interconnectedness and unity of all things.
2. Divided in four equal quadrants by a line drawn from top to bottom and another one across the middle, the circle symbolizes harmony in the differences among entities, equality among the differences, and the unity of difference in one reality.
3. The solid circumference on which all points are equidistant from the centre differentiates this particular geometric representation from others that display symmetrical characteristics. Indeed, the equidistance of all points on the circumference of the medicine wheel reflects a notion of balance that is unhesitatingly equal and uncompromisingly symmetrical.[17]

The sacred wheel, then, is a visual and metaphorical reminder of the need to maintain balance and harmony in one's life and in the world. This need has been explained exceptionally clearly in the case of the Cree Indians by Fiddler and Sanderson:

> The concept of the sacred circle or way of life is supported by an underlying belief that the Creator created the world in balance and harmony and gave a purpose and power to all living things. All powers are eventually traced back to the Creator. It becomes the responsibility of mankind for keeping the world in order and following the sacred laws and way of life that was given to them by the Cre-

ator. Mankind was responsible to maintain this balance and harmony, defined in the Cree language as "Wanuskewin," by correctly carrying out the obligations that went with it. These obligations are passed on, and are reinforced through stories "acimowina" that told of events of long ago in which individuals restored harmony and balance to this world.[18]

The responsibility of each individual for his or her own wellness extends back beyond birth, since it is believed that each spirit chooses the body which it will inhabit. Thus, as Locust explained:

> In the case of a handicapped body, the spirit chooses the body knowing its limita-
> tions but choosing to use it for some purpose determined by that spirit and the
> Supreme Creator. Furthermore, tribal members envision the spirit inside a hand-
> icapped body as being whole and perfect and capable of understanding every-
> thing that goes on in the environment, even when it appears that the physical
> body cannot comprehend anything.[19]

Typical of this approach to education, and to individual differences, is the following quote from the Crow leader Plenty Crops:

> My people were wise.... They never neglected the young. Our teachers were
> willing and thorough. They were our grandfathers, our fathers, or uncles. All
> were quick to praise excellence without speaking a word that might break the
> spirit of a boy who might be less capable than others. The boy who failed at any
> lesson got only more lessons, more care, until he was as far as he could go.[20]

Such a view also has important implications for differences among learners, because such differences are not viewed normatively. Rather, they are simply taken to be part of nature and are dealt with accordingly. No sanction applies to the child who is less bright, nor does any particular reward accrue to those who are exceptionally bright. With this point in mind, we turn now to a discussion of the traditional educational beliefs and practices of the American Indians.

TRADITIONAL EDUCATIONAL BELIEFS AND PRACTICES

Traditional education among Native Americans was, for the most part, infor-mal in nature, taking place as an undemarcated part of social life in general.[21] Children learned the skills and knowledge necessary for successful survival as adults through observation and imitation as well as from direct instruction from parents and other adults.[22] Included among the skills and knowledge that children learned were gender-specific skills, attitudes, values, beliefs, and con-tent knowledge that encompassed vocational skills (hunting, fishing, trapping, agricultural skills, and so on, as appropriate to the tribe), social skills and be-haviors, and religious knowledge (including rituals, ceremonies, and so on).[23] All of this took place in a broadly spiritual context, which emphasized the need to live in balance with nature. As Jean Barman, Yvonne Hébert, and Don

McCaskill noted, "An emphasis was placed on maintaining reciprocal relationships between the individual and the natural environment in order to ensure the provision of the subsistence required to live."[24]

The ultimate purpose of traditional Indian education, however, was spiritual in nature, as our earlier discussion of the place of harmony and wellness would lead one to expect. Indeed, among the Nisga'a, for instance, there is a saying, *"Ts'im gan wilaak'il's wil luu sisgihl gandidils,"* which translates as "within the pursuit of knowledge, therein one will find the true meaning of life."[25] In other words, education comes to be seen as a "total way of life." As Jack Forbes commented in his discussion of traditional Native American philosophy:

> What is the purpose of education? ... [I]t is not primarily the acquisition of specific skills or factual knowledge. Rather it is learning how to be a human being. That is, how to live a life of the utmost spiritual quality. A person who has developed his character to its highest degree, and who is on that path, will also be able to master specific skills. But if they don't have that spiritual core, they will use those skills to hurt other people.... So knowledge without the spiritual core is a very dangerous thing.[26]

A central feature of traditional Indian education is its communal nature. Traditional educational practices were not separate from daily life, and teaching was an activity engaged in by all adults, and even by older children, in the community. As one Canadian elder noted, "In the old days not only your own elders would discipline you, but also an outsider would come in and lecture the young. This could happen anytime, just happen naturally."[27]

The responsibility for the education of the young, although a community one in the broadest sense, rested primarily on parents, relatives (in particular on maternal uncles in many tribes),[28] and on tribal elders. The role played by tribal elders is especially important in this regard, because it is the elders who function as both the repositories and transmitters of the cultural traditions of the community.[29] Elders are elders by virtue not only of age, but also as recognition by other members of the community; their role in the community has been a significant one:

> The elders, comprising the accumulation of tribal wisdom and experience, have always been a vital group in opinion-making, if not in actual decision-making. Many, if not all, of the political leaders depend on "their elders" for advice in decision-making. Some ... perform the role of adding the cultural perceptions to the decision-making process.[30]

Although the "entire question of the status, configuration, and function of elders in educational contexts is extremely nebulous and imprecise,"[31] it is nevertheless clear that their role historically was an incredibly important one with respect to the proper upbringing of children. As one contemporary elder recalled:

As children we learned from the very beginning, by teaching and discipline, and later on through lecturing, and also by example. You saw how your elders lived, how respectful they were of one another, and how they loved each other.... The training went on as a child grew older, became more severe, harder, tougher.... It became a habit to live in a sane, sensible way, and intelligent way.[32]

One facet of the educational role of the elder in traditional Native American education was in the passing on of ritual and ceremonial knowledge. Rituals and ceremonies of various sorts played and continue to play a very important role in most Native American cultures. As Gary Witherspoon noted with respect to the Navajo:

The Navajo term *nahaghá* ("ritual") labels a large and significant category of Navajo behavior which non-Navajos least understand, and thus constitutes a major dimension of the estrangement that divides Navajos and non-Navajos. Navajos possess and perform over sixty major rites and numerous minor ones. They perform rituals for blessing, for curing, and for purification. They bless (make immune to illness and tragedy) their land, their livestock, their crops, their homes, their property, their relatives, and themselves.[33]

Oratory often played an important role in ritual and ceremony, and was integrated, in speeches, myths, legends, folktales, chants, and so on, in virtually all aspects of traditional Indian social life.[34] As Oscar Kawagley noted, "Myths are the Alaska Native's tool for teaching. The human values that make me uniquely Yup'ik in cadence with the circadian and life rhythms of the universe are all slowly unfolded as my grandmother, and other elders, teach me through myths and legends."[35] In a similar vein, Joel Sherzer pointed out with respect to the Iroquois:

there was an ancient oratorical tradition which entered into all facets of traditional religious and political life, including death, curing, and agricultural ceremonies. Most Iroquois ceremonies involved many speakers, representing families, clans, or whole nations, making formal speeches. ... This oratory was a central feature of ritual and kept the Iroquois world spiritually alive and well.[36]

Indeed, the ability to use language creatively and effectively was among the key characteristics sought by many tribes in their leaders, and often such ability was at least as important as one's skills as a warrior or hunter.[37] A related point here is that traditionally Native American societies were oral ones, and so, as was the case with Africa, so too in North America was there an emphasis on the oral transmission and maintenance of knowledge. As Rik Yellow Bird explained, "Our system of learning was based on oral tradition although syllabics were used later. The nomadic lifestyle determined and strengthened the use of orally transmitted information.... "[38]

Although by no means a universal phenomenon, various initiation processes and ceremonies were quite common in traditional Indian societies, and such initiation ceremonies are often maintained today, although not uncommonly in modified ways. As Donald Miller wrote with respect to the Hopi:

> At about the age eight or nine, when children become involved in mischief, they are initiated into one of the ritual societies. This occasion arrives annually, usually during February, at the time of the Powamu ceremony.... Initiation marks the beginning of attaining adult social status. A child is sponsored by a set of ceremonial parents who guide him through the ritual and perform various functions at appropriate times as described below. This new relationship sets up future "ceremonial kinship ties" with subsequent rights, duties, and reciprocal obligations attached to them, thus adding an additional significant dimension to social cohesion.... During the initiation a child has his head washed in yucca suds by his ceremonial mother, after which he is given a new name. It is at this time that formal instruction is given about the gods.... During the day, those to be initiated are taken by their ceremonial fathers into one of the village kivas where instruction begins. Each child is brought forth before the whipper Kachinas [gods] who ritually purify by literally whipping the child's backside.... The ceremonial father may take some or all of the lashes for him, but if the child has been particularly naughty, the father will not interfere. The whipper Kachinas are believed to have ritual power to cleanse and to heal. Later, after an evening of ritual dancing, all non-initiates and women are dismissed from the kiva, after which the Kachinas remove their large masks to reveal themselves as fathers and "uncles" of the village. Initiation marks a turning point in Hopi life. It is not unlike a graduation ceremony—a rite of passage which ritually removes childhood and admits one to the greater responsibilities of an adult world.[39]

An important aspect of traditional Indian educational practice is that of children's play and games played by both children and adults.[40] Joseph Oxendine argued that the traditional play of Indian children can be organized into three broad, if overlapping, categories: games that functioned as preparation for adult activity, games in which toys were the focus of attention, and more formal games that were played by older children and adults.[41] We explore each of these types of play briefly here.

American Indian children, like children in all societies, often engaged in play that was imitative of adult activities. Such play was largely gender-specific in nature, with boys engaging in role playing related to such traditionally male roles as hunter, warrior, and athlete, while girls "played games that closely paralleled child-rearing, household chores, farming, or pastimes of their mothers."[42] As Ohiyesa commented with respect to play activities found among the Sioux, such play was:

> molded by the life and customs of our people; indeed, we practiced only what we expected to do when grown. Our games were feats with the bow and arrow, and foot and pony races, wrestling, swimming, and imitation of the customs and habits of our fathers. We had sham fights with mud balls and willow wands; we played lacrosse, made war upon bees, and coasted upon the ribs of animals and buffalo robes.[43]

Although imitation and role playing certainly comes naturally to children, this is not to say that it occurred independent of either adult supervision or input. Indeed, as George Pettitt observed more than 50 years ago:

> That these activities were recreational is beyond question, but that they were carried on as spontaneous uncontrolled imitations, either of adults or of slightly older juveniles, is hardly supported by the facts … it is clear that desired imitative activities are effectively fostered and undesired imitative activities neglected or discouraged.[44]

The second broad category of traditional play identified by Oxendine is play that involved the use of toys. Toys were both made by adults for children and by the children themselves. A wide variety of toys was made by adults for infants, including mobiles to be suspended over beds, colorful and noisy toys, feathers, and, at least in some tribes, rattles.[45] Typical toys for older children included bows and arrows, tops, noisemakers, and dolls. Very often such toys played roles in imitative activities, of course, and adults would engage in direct instruction (as in the case of archery) to help children learn how to use their toys properly.[46]

Finally, there were games played by both children and adults, generally of a "self-testing" nature. Among the more common games of this sort were tobogganing, playing string games (including "Cat's Cradle"), stilt walking, "battledoor" (also called "shuttlecock"), skin or blanket tossing, ring and pin, ball juggling, and hot ball.[47] These kinds of games involved challenging oneself, often both physically and intellectually, and so played an important educational as well as social role in traditional society.

TOWARD A PHILOSOPHY OF NATIVE AMERICAN EDUCATION

One might think that it would have made more sense in this chapter for us to begin with a discussion of the philosophy of Native American education, but in fact this would have been anachronistic. Although the indigenous peoples of North America obviously engaged in extensive educational and child-rearing practice (as indeed do all human societies), at no point did they seek deliberately to articulate what might be termed an "educational philosophy." Rather, their educational practices were guided by commonly shared assumptions about the nature of knowledge, the nature and purpose of human beings, and child development and learning theory—all of which overlapped and paralleled the core beliefs discussed earlier in this chapter.[48]

This does not mean, however, that it is not possible to discuss a Native American conception of philosophy of education in a useful and meaningful way. In recent years, for instance, Gregory Cajete, who is himself a member of the Pueblo tribe and a gifted educational scholar, has attempted to do just this by linking a model of indigenous Native American educational philosophy to contemporary educational practice in our society.[49] Cajete's work in this regard has been truly groundbreaking and challenges us to critically reexamine many of our fundamental assumptions about both the means and the ends of education, teaching, and learning. Cajete argued, in essence, that:

> a primary orientation of Indigenous education is that each person is their own teacher and that learning is connected to each individual's life process. Meaning is looked for in everything, especially in the workings of the natural world. All things comprising Nature are teachers of mankind; what is required is a cultivated and practiced openness to the lessons that the world has to teach. Ritual, mythology, and the art of storytelling—combined with the cultivation of relationship to one's inner self, family, community, and natural environment—are utilized to help individuals realize their potential for learning and living a complete life. Individuals are enabled to reach completeness by learning how to trust their natural instincts, to listen, to look, to create, to reflect and see things deeply, to understand and apply their intuitive intelligence, and to recognize and honor the teacher of spirit within themselves and the natural world. This is the educational legacy of Indigenous people.[50]

Embedded in such a description of Native American educational philosophy is an implicit and powerful critique of much contemporary educational practice in our society. Cajete has made this critique, which is in fact a call for an ecological conception of educational thought and practice,[51] explicit elsewhere in his work:

> The education that we experience today has been stripped of its former dimensions and soulful meaning and deep ecological understanding in favor of the methodological application of skill development and cognitive training. The honoring of soul, creativity, spontaneity, and play have given way to an almost complete monopoly of practical skill-based knowledge designed to weed out the dreamers and to ensure the perpetuation of the modern technologically oriented world. The goal of most of modern education is to define all aspects of human teaching and learning to such a precise degree and with such technical proficiency that education can be totally controlled from entrance to exit by the vested interests of the modern industrial-technocratic-political complex. This conceptual orientation has become so much the orientation of modern education that the only real opportunity for deep holistic learning is when one exits the system intentionally or by accident or through failure.[52]

The alternative, on Cajete's account, is an approach to education that must be guided by a number of key assumptions about appropriate and ecological educational practice:

- The environmental, social, and cultural crises that we face today cannot and will not be solved by the same education process that helped to create them.
- Ecological sustainability implies the recovery of civic and cultural wisdom.

- Sustainability has to be a focus for the content and process of postmodern education, as well as a defining element of knowledge.
- We must teach for cultural and ecological literacy and transactional competence in working with various dimensions of the crises.
- Students must be acquainted with the deeper levels of the environmental crisis.
- We must rekindle the innate reflection of our inborn feeling of connectedness to the natural world.
- We must begin to teach for a contemporary expression of the indigenous and ecologically possible human.[53]

In a nutshell, what Cajete is suggesting is that, "Learning is always a creative act. We are continuously engaged in the art of making meaning and creating our world through the unique processes of human learning. Learning for humans is instinctual, continuous, and the most complex of our natural traits. Learning is also a key to our ability to survive in the environments that we create and that create us."[54]

CONCLUSION

The spiritual nature of traditional Indian educational thought and practice permeates virtually all aspects of its educational practice. This can be seen most clearly, perhaps, in the way that the child is viewed and treated, and the respect that is to be accorded to each individual.[55] Beyond this, however, is the sense of kinship with not only other members of one's own community, but with the larger human community, and, indeed, with everything around us. As Jack Forbes wrote:

> So everything is like a big family. We are children of the Great Spirit, children of Mother Earth, children of the sky, and so on. We have that relationship, that kinship that is part of our identity. That is knowing who we are ... we live in a world of many circles and these circles constitute our identity and they go out to encompass every thing that there is in this Universe. That is our kinship. Those are our relatives. The Universe is a family and we have to deal with other things in that Universe with that in mind.[56]

Although the context in which traditional Native American educational thought and practice emerged and prospered for centuries has undergone dramatic change in the last few centuries, there is, nevertheless, much to be learned and even emulated not only in educational activities and programs for Indians themselves, but for all of us, as the previously quoted Forbes passage makes clear. Indeed, some scholars have argued that the very contemporary goal of sustainable development requires that we *re-learn* much of the indigenous educational tradition.[57] For educators, the implications of Native American educational thought and practice are in fact immense—not only in terms

of curricula, evaluation, teaching methodologies, and even teacher assessment,[58] but also, even more, for the epistemological assumptions that guide
our practice. For instance, Gloria Snively compellingly suggested that:

> If schools are to do justice to Native students they must not represent a culture
> that ignores and denigrates the indigenous culture. Oral traditions must be re-
> spected and viewed by the teacher as a distinctive intellectual tradition, not sim-
> ply as myths and legends. If the traditional beliefs, values, and ideas that have
> been taught to the children by their parents and grandparents are not important
> in the school curriculum, the message is obvious. Hence a textbook approach
> with emphasis on the scientifically accepted concepts only will not work. Text-
> books make fine resources for the teacher, but no textbook can comprise a viable
> science program for culturally different students. The spiritual stories and heri-
> tage of the Native community should become part of the school science experi-
> ence.... The current research suggests that the two traditions—Native oral
> tradition and western scientific thought—in combination provide a broader per-
> spective on the natural environment than either by itself.[59]

In other words, as Oscar Kawagley has argued, it is a serious mistake to suggest
that indigenous knowledge and "scientific" knowledge are incompatible in the
pedagogical setting. As he suggested,

> I propose that it is possible to teach Native youth mathematics and, more partic-
> ularly, the natural and physical sciences by capitalizing on the Native knowledge
> and skills that already exist in their culture. The natural sciences are nothing
> more than observation and mystical understanding of the interplay between Na-
> ture and man. The Native has perspicacious knowledge of Nature. The teacher
> must realize that these Native students entering school are not empty computer
> disks or sponges to be filled with facts and knowledge by the teacher.... Their
> culture provides a basis to progress in acquiring new knowledge, new skills, and
> introducing new ideas on how to increase the quality of life.... [60]

Such, then, is the challenge before us as we, as educators, learn to "look to the
mountain"!

QUESTIONS FOR REFLECTION AND DISCUSSION

1. Based on your reading, how do you believe that Native Americans would
   traditionally have defined an *educated person* in their societies? How
   does this view of an *educated person* differ from our contemporary
   view?
2. The American Indian view of the role of *elders* in both social life in general and in education in particular is arguably very different from that
   found in contemporary American society. What are the advantages of
   the Native American view of the role of the elder? What are its disadvantages?

3. Using the discussion of play activities as a component of traditional Native American education that was presented in this chapter as a guide, try to develop a similar classification system for play in contemporary American society. What differences do you find? How might these differences be explained?

4. The Indian concept of kinship, as expounded in the conclusion of this chapter, is potentially a very powerful one. What are its educational implications, both in terms of the aims of education and the content of education?

5. Reflect on the Native American concept of *disharmony*. What are the implications of this concept for society in general, and for the education of children in particular? Is the concept a pedagogically useful one in your view?

6. How might the concept of the sacred wheel be used to describe and change a classroom environment? What specific aspects of the classroom environment might be affected? What does this tell you about the nature and purposes of formal education in our society?

7. Explain the concept of an "ecology of education" in your own words, giving examples from classroom settings as well as from the perspective of the larger community. What are the implications of such an "ecology of education" for the classroom teacher? For the school principal? For the Board of Education member?

8. Oscar Kawagley is quoted in the chapter as arguing that, "The natural sciences are nothing more than observation and mystical understanding of the interplay between Nature and man." Do you agree? Why or why not?

9. In the chapter, Gloria Snively suggests that a combination of Native oral tradition and Western scientific thought can be effectively utilized in the teaching of science. What other school subjects and disciplines might also benefit from combinations of this sort? Are there subjects that could not involve such combinations?

10. Based on your readings, how do you think that the Western conception of "nature" differs from that of indigenous peoples in North America? What are the implications of these differences?

RECOMMENDED FURTHER READINGS

There are a number of excellent works that present a Native American view on both American history and contemporary American society. Especially valuable are Ronald Wright, *Stolen Continents: The "New World" Through Indian Eyes* (Boston: Houghton Mifflin, 1992); Alvin Josephy, Jr.'s *500 Nations: An Illustrated History of North American Indians* (New York: Knopf, 1994), as well as the recent revision of his 1968 *The Indian Heritage of America* (Boston: Houghton Mifflin, 1991); Alvin Josephy, Jr. (ed.), *America in 1492: The World of the Indian Peoples Before the Arrival of Columbus* (New York: Vintage, 1991);

and Dee Brown, *Bury My Heart At Wounded Knee: An Indian History of the American West* (New York: Bantam, 1971). For a detailed and explicit discussion of Native American educational thought and practice and its significance for contemporary education, see Gregory Cajete, *Look to the Mountain: An Ecology of Indigenous Education* (Durango, CO: Kivakí Press, 1994).

NOTES

1. There is a terminological problem with respect to the proper term for the indigenous peoples of North America. In this chapter, I have chosen to use both *Indian* and *Native American* interchangeably, as is a fairly common practice by such people themselves in the United States. In the Canadian setting, the term "First Nations" is now well-established as the appropriate term for the indigenous peoples of North America (and, indeed, of all indigenous peoples); see, for example, Robert Regnier, "Bridging Western and First Nations Thought: Balanced Education in Whitehead's Philosophy of Organism and the Sacred Circle," *Interchange* 26, 4 (1995): 383–415; Celia Haig-Brown and Jo-Ann Archibald, "Transforming First Nations Research with Respect and Power," *International Journal of Qualitative Studies in Education* 9, 3 (1996): 245–267. It should also be noted that the term *North America* is being used here in a common, but nonetheless inaccurate, way to refer to what is today the United States and Canada. Thus, the civilizations of Mesoamerica (which were geographically in North America) are excluded from our focus here.

2. See, for example, Margaret Szasz, *Education and the American Indian: The Road to Self-Determination, 1928–1973* (Albuquerque: University of New Mexico Press, 1974); Guy Senese, *Self-Determination and the Social Education of Native Americans* (New York: Praeger, 1991); K. Tsianina Lomawaima, *They Called It Prairie Light: The Story of Chilocco Indian School* (Lincoln: University of Nebraska Press, 1994); Ruth McDonald Boyer and Narcissus Gayton, *Apache Mothers and Daughters: Four Generations of a Family* (Norman: University of Oklahoma Press, 1992); Michael Coleman, *American Indian Children at School, 1850–1930* (Jackson: University Press of Mississippi, 1993).

3. See Joel Sherzer, "A Richness of Voices," in Alvin Josephy, Jr. (ed.), *America in 1492: The World of the Indian Peoples Before the Arrival of Columbus* (New York: Vintage, 1991), 251–275.

4. Joseph Oxendine, *American Indian Sports Heritage* (Champaign, IL: Human Kinetics Books, 1988), xiii.

5. Carol Locust, "Wounding the Spirit: Discrimination and Traditional American Indian Belief Systems," *Harvard Educational Review* 58, 3 (1988): 317.

6. Locust, "Wounding the Spirit," 317.

7. Calvin Martin, "Ethnohistory: A Better Way to Write Indian History," in Albert Hurtado and Peter Iverson (eds.), *Major Problems in American Indian History: Documents and Essays* (Lexington, MA: Heath, 1994), 23.

8. Locust, "Wounding the Spirit," 317–318.

9. There are also, of course, important implications here for health care and other service professions serving Native American communities; see, for instance, Madeleine McIvor, "Research into Traditional First Nations Healing Practices: A Beginning," *Canadian Journal of Native Education* 17, 2 (1990): 89–95.

10. Locust, "Wounding the Spirit," 318.

11. Locust, "Wounding the Spirit," 321–322.

12. Native American approaches to education are, in fact, profoundly spiritual in nature. See Gloria Snively, "Traditional Native Indian Beliefs, Cultural Values, and Science Instruction," *Canadian Journal of Native Education* 17, 1 (1990): 44–59. Also of interest here are Mary Atwood, *Spirit Healing: North American Magic and Medicine* (New York: Sterling, 1991); and Steve Wall, *Shadowcatchers: A Journey in Search of the Teachings of Native American Healers* (New York: HarperCollins, 1994).

13. See John Coulehan, "Navajo Indian Medicine: Implications for Healing," *Journal of Family Practice* 10 (1980): 55–61.

14. Locust, "Wounding the Spirit," 322.

15. Regnier, "Bridging Western and First Nations Thought," 387.

16. Regnier, "Bridging Western and First Nations Thought," 387.

17. Regnier, "Bridging Western and First Nations Thought," 387–388.

18. Quoted in Regnier, "Bridging Western and First Nations Thought," 388.

19. Locust, "Wounding the Spirit," 325.

20. Quoted in Jack Forbes, "Traditional Native American Philosophy and Multicultural Education," in *Multicultural Education and the American Indian* (Los Angeles: American Indian Studies Center, University of California, 1979), 10.

21. Jean Barman, Yvonne Hébert, and Don McCaskill, "The Challenge of Indian Education: An Overview," in Jean Barman, Yvonne Hébert, and Don McCaskill (eds.), *Indian Education in Canada, Volume 2: The Challenge* (Vancouver: University of British Columbia Press, 1987), 3.

22. See Donald Miller, "Hopi Education: Before Schools and Teachers," *Tennessee Education* 18, 2 (1988), 28–32.

23. Barman, Hébert, and McCaskill, "The Challenge of Indian Education: An Overview," 3.

24. Jean Barman, Yvonne Hébert, and Don McCaskill, "The Challenge of Indian Education," 3.

25. Alvin McKay and Bert McKay, "Education as a Total Way of Life: The Nisga'a Experience," in Jean Barman, Yvonne Hébert, and Don McCaskill (eds.), *Indian Education in Canada, Volume 2: The Challenge* (Vancouver: University of British Columbia Press, 1987), 64.

26. Forbes, "Traditional Native American Philosophy and Multicultural Education," 11.

27. Quoted in Beatrice Medicine, "My Elders Tell Me," in Jean Barman, Yvonne Hébert, and Don McCaskill (eds.), *Indian Education in Canada, Volume 2: The Challenge* (Vancouver: University of British Columbia Press, 1987), 146.

28. For an extensive discussion of the role of relatives in traditional American Indian education, see George Pettitt, *Primitive Education in North America* (Berkeley: University of California Press, 1946), 15–24. Published as part of the University of California "Publications in American Archaeology and Ethnology" series, this monograph is invaluable despite its dated and highly ethnocentric bias (and title!).

29. Medicine, "My Elders Tell Me," 142–152; see also Rik Yellow Bird, "Position Paper on Native Education," *Humanity & Society* 14, 3 (1990), 298–299; Teresa Scott Kincheloe, "The Wisdom of the Elders: Cross-Cultural Perspectives," *Journal of Thought* 19, 3 (1984), 121–127.

30. Quoted in Medicine, "My Elders Tell Me," 147.

31. Medicine, "My Elders Tell Me," 143; see also Miller, "Hopi Education: Before Schools and Teachers," 28–32.

32. Quoted in Medicine, "My Elders Tell Me," 145–146.

33. Gary Witherspoon, *Language and Art in the Navajo Universe* (Ann Arbor: The University of Michigan Press, 1977), 13.

34. Sherzer, "A Richness of Voices," 271. See also Karl Kroeber, "The Art of Traditional American Indian Narration," in Karl Kroeber (ed.), *Traditional Literatures of the American Indian: Texts and Interpretations* (Lincoln: University of Nebraska Press, 1981), 1–24.

35. Oscar Kawagley, "Yup'ik Ways of Knowing," *Canadian Journal of Native Education* 17, 2 (1990): 10.

36. Sherzer, "A Richness of Voices," 265.

37. Sherzer, "A Richness of Voices," 265.

38. Yellow Bird, "Position Paper on Native Education," 297.

39. Miller, "Hopi Education," 30–31.

40. See Steward Culin, *Games of the North American Indians* (New York: Dover, 1975).

41. Oxendine, *American Indian Sports Heritage*, 121.

42. Oxendine, *American Indian Sports Heritage*, 122.

43. Quoted in Oxendine, *American Indian Sports Heritage*, 123.

44. Pettitt, *Primitive Education in North America*, 41, 58.

45. Oxendine, *American Indian Sports Heritage*, 124. In some Native American cultures, rattles are viewed as sacred objects, and are used only in specific religious ceremonies. Thus, in these groups they would obviously be seen as inappropriate as children's toys.

46. See Pettitt, *Primitive Education in North America*, 41–44.

47. For detailed discussions of these games, see Oxendine, *American Indian Sports Heritage*, 131–137. An even more extensive examination of such games is provided in Culin, *Games of North American Indians*.

48. In fairness, I should note here that in my experience the same is in fact true of many educators today in our own society as well; very often discussions of "philosophy of education" among practitioners tend to be *post hoc* rather than actually guiding practice. This is not, of course, to say that this is the ideal. Philosophy of education, properly conceived and executed, can and should be

an immensely valuable and important tool for the classroom teacher. See, for instance, Timothy Reagan, "Educating the 'Reflective Practitioner': The Contribution of Philosophy of Education," *Journal of Research and Development in Education* 26, 4 (1993): 189–196.

49. See Gregory Cajete, "The Making of an Indigenous Teacher: Insights into the Ecology of Teaching" in Jeffrey Kane (ed.), *Education, Information and Transformation: Essays on Learning and Thinking* (Upper Saddle River, NJ: Merrill, 1999), 161–183; Gregory Cajete, *Look to the Mountain: An Ecology of Indigenous Education* (Durango, CO: Kivakí, 1994).

50. Cajete, *Look to the Mountain*, 227.

51. See David Orr, *Ecological Literacy: Education and the Transition to a Postmodern World* Albany: State University of New York Press, 1992).

52. Cajete, "The Making of an Indigenous Teacher," 175.

53. Cajete, "The Making of an Indigenous Teacher," 181.

54. Cajete, *Look to the Mountain*, 25.

55. See Forbes, "Traditional Native American Philosophy and Multicultural Education."

56. Forbes, "Traditional Native American Philosophy and Multicultural Education," 5–6.

57. See Orr, *Ecological Literacy*; Daniel Morales-Gómez, "Knowledge, Change and the Preservation of Progress," *IDRC Reports* 21, 1 (1993): 4–5; Neale MacMillan, "Indigenous Peoples Test the Waters," *IDRC Reports* 21, 1 (1993): 6–8; Deborah Carter, "Recognizing Traditional Environmental Knowledge," *IDRC Reports* 21, 1 (1993): 10–13; Paul Icamina, "Threads of Common Knowledge," *IDRC Reports* 21, 1 (1993): 14–16.

58. See Cajete, *Look to the Mountain*, 29–31 and 222–227; see also Sharon Nelson-Barber, "Considerations for the Inclusion of Multiple Cultural Competencies in Teacher Assessment: A Yup'ik Eskimo Case," *Canadian Journal of Native Education* 17, 2 (1990): 33–42.

59. Snively, "Traditional Native Indian Beliefs, Cultural Values, and Science Instruction," 56.

60. Kawagley, "Yup'ik Ways of Knowing," 13–14.

5

Developing the Chün-tzu: Confucius and the Chinese Educational Heritage

Elements of Chinese civilization can be traced back at least as far as 6,000 years, and perhaps considerably further.[1] By the time of the Shang dynasty (roughly 1700 B.C.E. to 1100 B.C.E.; see Fig. 5.1), schools and other social institutions of a complex culture had developed, as had the foundations for the examination system that would serve throughout the history of imperial China to select government officials.[2] Although Chinese civilization evolved, developed, and changed throughout its history, it nevertheless retained a core set of features that characterize it as a single cultural tradition. Although much of the Chinese cultural heritage has been rejected in contemporary China, much remains as well. In other words, much of the culture of China that still thrives has a direct link to the civilization that emerged nearly as long ago as those of ancient Egypt and Mesopotamia.[3] The difference, of course, is that while the civilizations of Egypt and Mesopotamia may be fascinating for us to study, the ties that bind modern people to them are, at best, very distant indeed, while the ties that bind modern Chinese people to their past remain powerful. Furthermore, as Michael Loewe wrote in his book *The Pride That Was China*, the impact of traditional Chinese civilization went far beyond the borders of China itself:

> China's achievements have been unique. Just as the glory that was Greece and the grandeur that was Rome have left their indelible mark on Europe, so have the features of China's traditional way of life nurtured the cultural growth of East Asia; for it was largely the ideas, beliefs and ideals of China that shaped the humanities of the east, with their counterparts to the spirit and grace of Greece and the dignity and organization of Rome.[4]

If traditional Chinese culture had such a significant impact on the historical development of Asia, it was able to do so in large part because of the values and institutions that underlie its educational system. This system had to address

Chinese Dynasties

Hsia Dynasty	21st to 16th centuries B.C.E.
Shang Dynasty	16th to 11th centuries B.C.E.
Western Chou Dynasty	11th century to 771 B.C.E.
Spring and Autumn Period	770 to 476 B.C.E.
Warring States Period	475 to 221 B.C.E.

First Unification

Ch'in Dynasty	221 to 207 B.C.E.
Western Han Dynasty	206 B.C.E. To 24 C.E.
Eastern Han Dynasty	25 C.E. To 220 C.E.
First Partition	
Three Kingdoms Period	220 C.E. To 265 C.E.
Shu Dynasty	
Wei Dynasty	
Wu Dynasty	

Second Unification

Western Chin Dynasty	265 C.E. To 316 C.E.
Eastern Chin Dynasty	317 C.E. To 420 C.E.
Sung Dynasty	420 C.E. To 479 C.E.

Second Partition

Northern and Southern Dynasties	479 C.E. To 581 C.E.
Ch'i Dynasty	
Liang Dynasty	
Ch'en Dynasty	
Northern Wei Dynasty	
Western Wei Dynasty	
Eastern Wei Dynasty	
Northern Ch'i Dynasty	
Northern Chou Dynasty	

Third Unification

Sui Dynasty	581 C.E. To 618 C.E.
T'ang Dynasty	618 C.E. To 907 C.E.

Third Partition

Five Dynasties Period   907 C.E. To 960 C.E.

   Later Liang Dynasty

   Later T'ang Dynasty

   Later Chin Dynasty

   Later Han Dynasty

   Later Chou Dynasty

Fourth Unification

Northern Sung Dynasty   960 C.E. To 1127 C.E.

Southern Sung Dynasty   1127 C.E. To 1279 C.E.

Liao Dynasty   916 C.E. To 1125 C.E.

Chin Dynasty   1115 C.E. To 1234 C.E.

Yuan Dynasty   1271 C.E. To 1368 C.E.

Ming Dynasty   1368 C.E. To 1644 C.E.

Ch'ing Dynasty   1644 C.E. To 1911 C.E.

                                      1912 C.E.
Establishment of the Republic

FIG. 5.1.   Chinese dynasties.

problems related to the size of the country (China has been, and remains, one of the largest countries in the world), its geographical diversity, the ethnic and linguistic diversity of its population (see Fig. 5.2),[5] and the tensions in an overwhelmingly agrarian society with large urban centers competing for resources. The traditional Chinese educational system was able to meet these challenges remarkably effectively for millennia. The endurance of Chinese civilization, as well as its intellectual, cultural, and artistic contributions to world civilization, in short, make it well worth an examination of the educational thought and practice that played a key role in its maintenance, transmission, and development.

The study of the history of Chinese educational thought and practice is in many ways somewhat easier to understand than that of many other non-Western societies. Not only are many facets of traditional Chinese education still maintained in Chinese communities around the world, but even more, there is a wealth of material related to the history of the Chinese educational tradition available. As Will Durant noted in *The Story of Civilization*, "China has been called 'the paradise of historians.' For centuries and millenniums, it has had official historiographers who recorded everything that happened, and much besides. We cannot trust them further back than 776 B.C.;

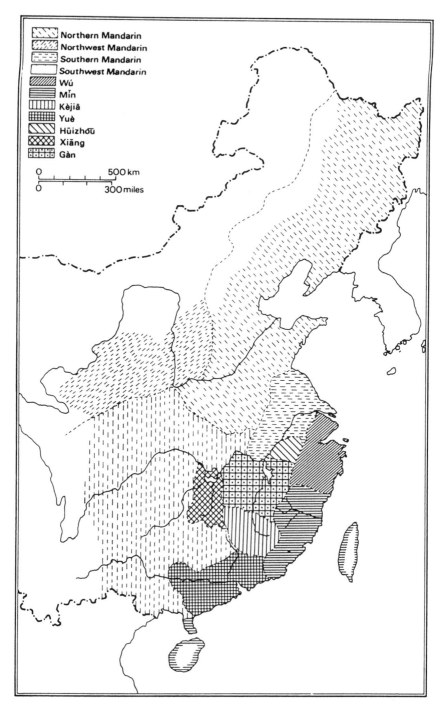

Legend:

Northern Mandarin
Northwest Mandarin
Southern Mandarin
Southwest Mandarin
Wú
Mǐn
Kèjiā
Yuè
Huīzhōu
Xiāng
Gàn

0   500 km
0   300 miles

FIG. 5.2.   Ethnic and linguistic diversity in China [From Jerry Norman, *Chinese* (Cambridge, England: Cambridge University Press, 1988), p. 184]. Reprinted with permission.

104

but if we lend them a ready ear they will explain in detail the history of China from 3000 B.C ... ."[6]

This abundance of sources means that the challenge in discussing traditional Chinese educational thought and practice is not one of trying to reconstruct the past from limited information, but rather, trying to sort through an incredibly complex and monumental historical record to identify the key issues that we need to address. In this chapter, we begin with a discussion of traditional Chinese educational thought, focusing on the special role of Confucian thought in that tradition. We then turn to the ways in which Confucian thought was manifested in practice in educational institutions and, even more, in the imperial examination system.

THE ROLE OF CONFUCIAN THOUGHT IN TRADITIONAL CHINESE EDUCATION

It would be impossible to discuss traditional Chinese educational thought without repeated reference to Confucian thought; indeed, to a considerable extent one could argue that traditional Chinese educational thought in large part *is* Confucian educational thought.[7] Tu Wei-Ming argued that, "Confucianism is still an integral part of the 'psycho-cultural construct' of the contemporary Chinese intellectual as well as the Chinese peasant; it remains a defining characteristic of the Chinese mentality,"[8] and, in a similar vein, Cheng Tien-Hsi commented, "the whole Chinese social system, or rather what may be called Chinese civilization and culture ... is saturated with the teachings of Confucius and those of Mencius, the sage next to him and the most brilliant exponent of his doctrines."[9] As Cheng Tien-Hsi implied, however, it is important that we distinguish between the body of teaching that can be reliably ascribed to Confucius himself, and the far broader body of theories and doctrines that developed after his death and which are today identified as *Confucian*.[10]

Confucius (whose real name was K'ung Ch'iu) was, according to tradition, born in the town of Ch'ü-fu, in the state of Lu, in the year 551 B.C.E., and died in the year 479 B.C.E.[11] Of relatively humble background, Confucius seems to have been largely self-educated, as well as both ambitious and relatively successful in his own time.[12] Living in a time of considerable social, political, and economic unrest and uncertainty, Confucius advocated a conception of the *good man* (*chün-tzu*)[13] that emphasized the twin qualities of benevolence (*ren*) and propriety (*li*). There is, in Confucian texts, an emphasis on the writings of Chinese antiquity, and his philosophy is often identified as a conservative one seeking a return to a more moral and just past.[14] This is especially interesting since, as Jacques Gernet observed about Confucius' work, "a body of teaching which aimed primarily at being faithful to tradition in fact threw up ideas that were new."[15]

The core of Confucian thought is found in a short text produced by Confucius' disciples after his death, called the *Lun-yü* or, more commonly in English, the *Analects*.[16] One interesting aspect of the *Analects* is the extent to which it continues to be generally accepted as authentic: although some parts of the *Analects* are almost certainly not genuinely original, there is a widespread agreement among scholars about the overall authenticity of the work.[17] It would be difficult to underestimate the significance of the *Analects* in the history of Chinese thought. As Patricia Ebrey wrote:

> Confucius' ideas are known to us primarily through the sayings recorded by his disciples in the *Analects*. This book does not provide carefully organized or argued philosophical discourses, and the sayings seem to have been haphazardly arranged. Yet this short text became a sacred book, memorized by beginning students and known to all educated people. As such it influenced the values and habits of thought of Chinese for centuries. Many of its passages became proverbial sayings, unknowingly cited by illiterate peasants.[18]

The closest analogy that one could draw to the role of the *Analects* in the Western tradition would probably be the role of the Bible. For us, regardless of our personal religious beliefs, the Bible provides a virtually limitless source of proverbs, folk wisdom, and references to people and events that color our language and fill our speech, as well as offering a framework within which much of our everyday experience is, both knowingly and unknowingly, organized. It would be inconceivable to be a member of Western civilization and not recognize reference to the burning bush, to Noah and the ark, to Lot's wife, or to the miracle of the loaves and fishes. The *Analects*, in short, have played a comparable role in traditional Chinese culture.

The notion of *li*, mentioned above, is a very important one in understanding Confucian thought.[19] Originally, the term referred merely to proper conduct in general, and in religious and ritualistic settings in particular, but for Confucius, it came to encompass far more than simply ceremonial correctness. Although ritual and its proper performance was an important aspect of Confucian thought,[20] *li* entailed both a knowledge of traditional practice and behavior, and a sensitivity that would allow their modification as required by contemporary circumstances.[21] In short:

> *Li* was in fact a kind of balance wheel of conduct, tending to prevent either deficiency or excess, guiding toward the middle path of socially beneficial conduct. Confucius stated it thus: "Courtesy, if not regulated by *li*, becomes labored effort; caution, if not regulated by *li*, becomes mere timidity; courage, if not regulated by *li*, becomes mere unruliness; frankness, if not regulated by *li*, becomes mere effrontery."[22]

It is important to keep in mind, however, that *li* is not just a Chinese version of the ancient Greek dictum, "Moderation in all things." Moderation, to be sure, is an important part of *li*, but the concept goes well beyond this. The goal of *li* is both a social and individual one, grounded in the proper expression of social and cultural tradition. Education is the means by which the individual learns what *li* will require in a particular situation; *li* is not so much character as the means by which character is manifested.

If *li* is the way in which character is manifested, the cultivation of character itself—defined in terms of virtues—is a significant component of education.[23] For Confucius, the *chün-tzu* will seek to develop what are called the "Five Constant Virtues": right attitude, right procedure, right knowledge, right moral courage, and right persistence.[24] Taken together, the practice of these virtues would lead to a new society based on justice and wisdom.[25] The nature of the *chün-tzu*, as described in the *Analects*, included the following characteristics:

> The Master said, (the good man) does not grieve that other people do not recognize his merits. His only anxiety is lest he should fail to recognize theirs. (Book I: 16)

> The Master said, In the presence of a good man, think all the time how you may learn to equal him. In the presence of a bad man, turn your gaze within! (Book IV: 17)

> The Master said, A gentleman is ashamed to let his words outrun his deeds. (Book XIV: 29)

Furthermore, Confucian moral thought is grounded in the concept of the five basic human relationships: ruler and subject, father and son, husband and wife, older brother and younger brother, and between friends.[26] Each of these relationships is hierarchical, with each individual tied and obligated to the other in keeping with his or her station. Thus, children are bound to their parents by filial piety, wives to husbands, subjects to rulers, and so on. However, it is important to understand that each of these relationships, as envisaged by Confucius, was to be one of mutual responsibility. As Ron-Guey Chu explained, "Filiality originates from one's sense of obligation or gratitude. It is a natural response to the parents' love and care for one—a consequence of their initial parental solicitude. Indeed, this kind of reciprocity underlies all human relationships."[27]

This reciprocity, although very much affecting both parties in the relationship, was nonetheless in no way intended to be one of equality. Wang Gungwu, for instance, commented that:

> In talking about reciprocity and reciprocal rights, I am talking about unequal reciprocity in a hierarchical structure. In short, duties and implicit rights were between unequals not between equals, and therefore the shares of both duties and rights were also necessarily unequal and this was implicit in the very concept of reciprocity.[28]

The analogy drawn by Confucius of the family to the state was built on precisely this same notion of the reciprocity of the ruled and the ruler. In essence:

> Confucianism thus built a new moral interpretation of the world upon the oldest and soundest foundation, the family system. It could be fitted to the political system, thus ensuring that monarchy, as an apotheosis of paternalism, would be the only conceivable form of government. The government must, however, be restrained and guided by ethical teaching and exercised in conformity with high moral principles.[29]

In summary, Confucian theory, especially as it was articulated and expanded by latter Chinese philosophers (most notably Mencius[30] and Chu Hsi[31]), provided what was taken by its proponents to be a powerful and compelling justification for a highly stratified social order that proved to be remarkably conservative and resistant to change. Confucius himself often distinguishes between the *chün-tzu* (here best translated as *gentleman*) and the common people, always to the detriment of the latter, and there can be little doubt that Confucian thought did indeed have a profoundly conservative effect on Chinese society—precisely, of course, as Confucius would have wished.

And yet, there is another side to Confucian theory and practice as it relates to the role of education in the social order. Education was the key to Confucius' view of how the ideal social order could be achieved, and he was far from naive about the intellectual and moral qualities of many of those born into positions of power and influence. In essence, Confucius believed that: "a good education would change men for the better, and that this should be available to those capable of benefitting from it. His remark that 'by nature men are nearly alike; but through experience they grow wide apart' supported the efficacy of schooling, and he was famed for his meritocratic outlook…. "[32]

Among Confucius' own pupils were individuals from virtually all social and class backgrounds, and he emphasized that wealth and honor were just "fleeting clouds."[33] Education should identify those of talent, and help them to become men fit to rule over others.[34] In other words, education for Confucius served a very pragmatic purpose—the creation of individuals who would be able to ensure better government. Indeed, Confucian philosophy in general has often been described by Western scholars as "this-worldly," in contrast to the "other-worldly" focus of much Western philosophical thought.[35] However, at the same time the purpose of education:

> was by no means narrowly practical. Although the end of education was to bring about good government, this did not mean that the end product of education should be an efficient administrator and nothing more. Far from it, he should, in fact, be as nearly as possible the ideal man, from every point of view. He definitely should not be a mere specialist in some particular technique…. Confucius' object was not successful careers but good government, and this he believed to be

possible only when government was administered by men who, in addition to being educated in the ordinary sense, were also endowed with integrity and poise.[36]

This brings us to one of the more criticized aspects of Confucian educational thought, which is its negative view of manual labor in general, and of agricultural pursuits in particular. Confucius himself once rebuked a student who had asked him about growing crops as a "little-minded man."[37] Thus, although education for Confucius had a practical focus, there were limits on how this practicality was to be manifested.

Although it is true that, to a considerable extent, the Confucian system in practice "reinforced the rigidly hierarchical social class structure" of imperial China,[38] it nevertheless did permit limited social class mobility based on talent, and was not incompatible with certain characteristics of a democratic social order. As H. G. Creel argued, Confucius appears to have believed, among other things, that:

- The proper aim of government is the welfare and happiness of the whole people.
- This aim can be achieved only when the state is administered by those most capable of government.
- Capacity to govern has no necessary connection with birth, wealth, or position; it depends solely on character and knowledge.
- Character and education are produced by proper education.
- In order that the best talents may become available, education should be widely diffused.
- It follows that the government should be administered by those persons, chosen from the whole population, who prove themselves to have profited most by the proper kind of education.[39]

Such a perspective is not only reminiscent of the view of the role of education in Plato's *Republic*, but is also very close to the view of education found in Thomas Jefferson's "Bill for the More General Diffusion of Knowledge,"[40] which proposed a system of tax-supported public education for the state of Virginia long before such schooling was in fact achieved.

Finally, it should be noted that although Confucianism has indeed played a central role in the development and evolution of Chinese culture, it has not been alone in providing a conceptual and philosophical context for Chinese educational thought and practice. Challenges to Confucianism, especially those of the "Legalists" in the years preceding the rise of the Han dynasty,[41] as well as the impact of Taoism, most clearly identified with Lao-tzu's *Tao Te Ching*,[42] also impacted Chinese educational thought in important ways. Nor, as suggested earlier, was Confucian thought static; rather, it evolved and changed over time, and the articulation of Confucian thought that we know today undoubtedly has at least as much to do with the later formulations of Mencius and Chu Hsi as with Confucius himself.[43] With this in mind, we turn now to a discussion of traditional Chinese educational practice.

TRADITIONAL CHINESE EDUCATIONAL PRACTICE

Traditional Chinese educational practice, as well as traditional views about the proper upbringing of children, focused on social adaptation and a deep-seated sense of politeness. As Jacques Gernet explained:

> Children were brought up to be affable, gentle and obedient. They were taught to prize self-restraint above everything else, and had to learn to be content with their lot and to live on good terms with relations, friends and strangers. The rules of politeness, widespread even among the lower classes, had no other aims but these.... Thus the rules of the art of living taught to children awakened in them a feeling of respect for elders and betters. They were taught not to answer back when their parents spoke to them, not to sit down if a superior—father, mother, a friend of the parents or someone senior to themselves—remained standing.... [44]

Although this may sound strict and repressive to some readers, in fact it would appear that early childhood in imperial China "was one of the happiest times of life"[45]—a time during which children had a great deal of personal freedom, and were far more likely to be spoiled than beaten or punished.[46] This relatively carefree existence ended as the child reached the age of seven, when formal schooling and expectations of other responsibilities began in earnest.

Schooling in imperial China reflected social class background to a very great extent. Although private schools existed for the children of merchants and artisans, as did private tutors, the focus of most schooling in China was on the preparation of the sons of the elite for the imperial civil service examinations.[47] It was this latter type of school that was actively supported by the government, largely out of self-interest, because it was from the ranks of successful examinees that government officials would come. Thus, it is not surprising to find that during the early years of the Ming dynasty, as China was recovering from a century of Mongol rule and civil strife, the government invested heavily in schooling: "To provide for the nation's needs, radical steps were taken to improve the means of training; no less than 1,200 local schools were established in the prefectures and counties, at the expense of the central government and with officially appointed teachers."[48]

Raymond Dawson argued in *The Chinese Experience* that, "Throughout imperial Chinese history emperors were regarded as the grand patrons of education, frequently paying formal visits to the national university, issuing edicts for the establishment of schools, and paying honour to Confucius as the 'first teacher.'"[49] Nonetheless, it is important not to overemphasize the role of the government in supporting education; elementary schooling remained primarily the province and responsibility of parents,[50] which inevitably meant that such institutions were generally neighborhood-based and somewhat informal in terms of their status. As the Reverend Justus Doolittle described the system in 1865, "There is no village tax nor any aid from government received for the support of schools. Each parent must pay the teacher for the instruction of his children."[51]

Furthermore, although the emperors were indeed presented in many Chinese historical records as patrons of educational institutions, the reality is somewhat more complex. Yuan Zheng explained:

> There is a wealth of historical data about Chinese education, but some of them are misleading. Almost all official historiographers in imperial China were Confucianists. To enhance the emperor's reputation and encourage rulers to devote attention to education, they would try hard to find activities of the emperor that could be described as support for education. They exaggerated the significance of these activities in the official history, hiding the fact that the emperor was indifferent to education.[52]

Rather, Yuan Zheng argues, the real test of commitment to education is to be found in financial support, and using this criteria, the support for education in imperial China would seem to have been more rhetorical than real much of the time.[53] In short, schooling in imperial China was available to those most able to pay for it, and the quality of basic education was to a significant degree reflected in one's social class background, and to one's geographic location as well, since "the closer government schools were to high-level authorities, the better their economic condition was."[54]

Preparation for the civil service examinations actually began well before the birth of a boy. Detailed advice was given to pregnant women to help them ensure the birth of a gifted son; the advice included sitting erect, avoiding strange food, and having poetry and classical literature read to her.[55]

The more formal education of the child began a bit later, around the age of 3, when the boy began learning to read his first characters.[56] Because of the complexity of written Chinese, the acquisition of literacy played an important and time-consuming role in the educational process. From the time he was able to hold a brush, the boy would copy characters from various books intended for use with children, among which were the *Three Character Classic* and the *Thousand Character Essay*. The former "is the world's longest surviving and best selling textbook and is still in print in China."[57] These books served two distinct kinds of educational purposes: First, they provided the child with the basic lexicon he would need to become literate, and second, they provided extensive moral education in keeping with the Confucian ethic.

Schooling as such began for the boy around the age of 7 or 8, after he had mastered the basic elements of literacy. Working with a tutor or teacher in a small group, he began an educational process that relied extensively on the memorization of the Four Books (which included both the *Analects* and the

Mencius, as well as two shorter works, the *Great Learning* and the *Just Mean*) and the Five Classics (which included the *Book of Changes, Book of Records, Book of Odes, Book of Rites,* and the *Spring and Autumn Record*).[58]

By the time he was 12, a boy would have memorized texts consisting of more than 400,000 characters[59]—and these texts were the same ones learned by every student preparing for the civil service examinations, assuring a broad and deep common intellectual base for each generation of Chinese officials. Once he had mastered the basic texts, the student would progress to the commentaries written about the texts, and finally, to learning the proper form for writing essays for the civil service examinations. This latter point is an important one; essay themes were set in the examinations, and examinees were required to produce what was called the "eight-legged essay"—a highly formal and rule-governed kind of writing that has been criticized for stressing technique over creativity. As Dawson commented, "This type of essay ... required technical expertise rather than intellectual distinction for its composition, so it has been a byword in modern times for the sterility and formalism of the classical tradition."[60]

Institutions of higher education provided additional schooling for small numbers of students in imperial China. Among the institutions of higher education were the National University, the Military Academy, the Imperial Academy, and a School of Medicine.[61] These state establishments were financially supported by revenues from lands that they owned (with which they had been endowed), and were impressive complexes:

> These great colleges were surrounded by vast grounds, and consisted of numerous buildings and single pavilions used for libraries, classrooms or temples for religious ceremonies. In the National University, which recruited the largest number of students ... there were twenty classrooms, a staff of fifteen, and nearly 2,000 students who lived in. The number of students, coming from all over China, had been fixed at 300 in the middle of the twelfth century; it was later increased to 1,000 and had reached 1,716 by 1270.[62]

Students were recruited for these institutions through competitive examinations, and their principle *raison d'être* was to prepare students for the imperial examinations.

While some boys and young men were engaged in this intensive educational undertaking, their sisters were educationally (and in a variety of other ways) less fortunate in traditional Chinese society. As John Cleverley wrote, "The world for many women was one of segregation and seclusion, often crippled by bound feet, and subject to child marriages arranged by parents."[63] Although there are a number of well-educated and politically powerful women in the long history of China, such women were clearly the exception rather than the rule.[64] For the most part, the role of the woman in traditional China was limited to the duties and obligations of being a wife and a mother, and her education was oriented toward these goals.

We turn now to an exploration of the nature and purposes of the imperial civil service examination, the focal point of traditional Chinese education and the feature of that education for which it is best known today.

THE IMPERIAL EXAMINATION SYSTEM

Written examinations to aid in the selection of government officials were used as early as the Han period (206 B.C.E. through 220 C.E.),[65] although it was only during the T'ang dynasty (618 C.E. to 907 C.E.) that they came to play a key role in the selection of such officials.[66] The purpose of the examination system was to ensure the quality of the civil service by making it more meritocratic, as well as to provide civil servants (as well as all educated people) with a common body of knowledge and experience on which they could draw.[67] Initially, the system coexisted with one of aristocratic privilege, in which recruitment to the civil service was based largely on heredity and recommendation. Under the usurper Empress Wu, however, this changed as the examination system was utilized as a political tool to challenge the power of the aristocracy, and by the eighth century the system operated as a highly effective, meritocratic means of providing a reasonably fair and objective means by which officials could be chosen.[68] As John Cleverley argued:

> The imperial civil service examination made it possible for a man from humble origin to move into a position of political power, and it also enabled districts to gain national prominence through their native sons. Because it served the cause of social mobility, it had an integrating and stabilising effect on Chinese life generally. Further, the infusion of new blood, which the examining process permitted, reduced the political power of the hereditary aristocracy and clans, and strengthened the throne.[69]

Although the examination system was not static over the long course of its existence, of course, it is nevertheless possible to present a general overview of how it operated, especially under the Ming and Ch'ing periods of Chinese history. Basically, the examination system consisted of tests at three distinct levels: the district examinations, the provincial examinations, and the metropolitan examinations.[70] The examinations were of increasing difficulty, and each required the candidate to have passed the preceding level (see Fig. 5.3). The first examination level, which was conducted in local cities by provincial education officials, granted successful examinees the title *hsiu-ts'ai* ("Flowering Talent"). Passing this first examination allowed one to wear special, distinctive clothing, as well as granting one's family a tax exemption, but more important, allowed one to progress to the next level of the examination system.[71]

Stage I: Preliminary Examinations

District-level (*hsien-k'ao*)
Prefectural-level (*fu-k'ao*)
Examination for *sheng-yüan* degree

Stage II: Provincial Examinations

Examination for *chü-jen* degree

Stage III: Metropolitan Examinations

Major examination (known as *Hui-Shih*) for chin- shih degree
Palace examination (*tien-shih*)

FIG. 5.3.   An overview of the Chinese Imperial Examination System.

The second level of the examination system consisted of a test given every 3 years in the various provincial capitals of the empire. The examination took place in a special complex, consisting of individual cells in which the candidates spent 9 days writing their answers to the set questions.[72] The cells, which contained only three boards to function as a shelf, desk, and chair, were too small to allow the individual to comfortably sleep at night (see Fig. 5.4). Successful candidates, who were generally a tiny fraction of those taking the examination, gained the title *chü-jen* ("Recommended Man"), and were now eligible for lower-level government appointments.

Next, metropolitan examinations were held in order to identify those scholars who would be suitable for higher posts in the government. Only 1 of 20 or 30 candidates at this level could hope to become a *chin-shih* ("Presented Scholar").[73] Finally, also at the metropolitan level, came the pinnacle of the examination system, the palace examination, which was, in theory if not in practice, presided over by the Emperor himself. At this final level, candidates did not fail, but rather, were ranked in order of merit.[74] Success at this level, while not ensuring career advancement, was nonetheless a necessary condition for it, as Dawson explained:

> Success in this rigorous competition did not, however, bring automatic appointment. It merely made one a member of a social and intellectual elite from among whom appointments were made. The top palace graduates would ... expect high

office after a period in the imperial secretariat; but there were not enough jobs to go round for those who were qualified.... [75]

The examinations were open to most men in Chinese society; excluded were members of certain occupations and, hardly surprising given the patriarchal nature of traditional Chinese society, women. Furthermore, there was no restriction on the number of times an individual might try to pass an examination, and so some men spent their entire lives attempting to pass the difficult examinations. Although the rewards for success in the examination system were great, so too were the challenges and expenses, and in practice few individuals from poor backgrounds could hope to succeed.[76]

If originally a creative and thoughtful solution to the complex and difficult challenge of providing the empire with the best possible civil servants and officials, over the course of the centuries the imperial examination system gradually declined as it "failed to preserve the freshness and ingenuity of earlier days."[77] To some extent, such an outcome was understandable. As Jacques Gernet explained, "As the sole means of access to political honours and responsibilities, the examinations served to inculcate in those who sat for them

Lines of Cells

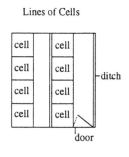

Inside of the Cells

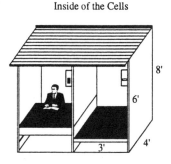

FIG. 5.4.   The Chinese Imperial Examination System: examination cells.

the virtues of devotion and submission indispensable to the autocratic empire. At the same time they also drained the energies of generations of the literati."[78]

Furthermore, the system was increasingly plagued by problems with cheating,[79] as well as by the narrowness of view encouraged by both the content of the examination (which excluded virtually all knowledge not related to the Classics) and its form (especially the "eight-legged essay" discussed earlier).[80] In any event, by the end of the 19th century, the examination system had come into widespread disrepute, and its abolition in 1905 came as a surprise to few.

SCIENCE AND TECHNOLOGY IN THE CHINESE TRADITION

Given our discussion thus far, one might be led to believe that the intellectual heritage of China had been focused exclusively on literary pursuits. Although not an uncommon assumption, this view is in fact demonstrably erroneous. In fact, the scientific and technological heritage of Chinese civilization is immense, and is, in its own way, every bit as impressive and significant as China's contributions in other areas.[81] Although modern science as we generally understand it essentially emerged in the Western Europe context during the Renaissance and the "scientific revolution," scientific studies, discoveries, and applications date back to the dawn of human history, and do so in virtually all human civilizations. [82] When compared with the scientific discoveries of the ancient Greeks, for instance, those of China often took place earlier and were more elaborately articulated and practically applied. In studying the history of science in the West, we are often guilty of dealing with scientific "discoveries" in much the same way that we have dealt with the "discovery" of the Americas by Christopher Columbus—which is to say, ignoring the fact that the "discovery" was such only to Europeans. For example,

> the triangle called by the name of Blaise Pascal was already old in China in 1300 [C.E.].... The system of linked and pivoted rings which we know as the Cardan suspension, after Jerome Cardan, really ought to be called Ting Huan's suspension because it had been used in China a whole thousand years before the time of Cardan.... Contrary to the usual ideas, mechanical clockwork began, not in early Renaissance Europe, but in T'ang China.... [83]

This tendency remained true throughout the medieval period and into the modern period; it is only in the last few centuries, in fact, that Western science has come to significantly outpace (and, indeed, to dominate and even replace) that of traditional Chinese science. The truly fascinating aspect of China's contributions in the scientific arena, then, in the words of one of the great historians of Chinese science, is that of how "the Chinese civilisation had been much more effective than the European in finding out about Nature and using natural knowledge for the benefit of mankind for fourteen centuries or so before the scientific revolution."[84]

Without a doubt, the most thorough and comprehensive study of traditional scientific thought and practice in China, in any language, is the landmark multivolumed work of the British scholar Joseph Needham and his collaborators, *Science and Civilisation in China.*[85] Although it would be neither possible nor desirable to fully document the wide range of traditional Chinese scientific, mathematical and technical discoveries and contributions here, Fig. 5.5 provides at least something of an idea of the variety and significance of such discoveries and contributions.[86]

Agriculture

Row cultivation
Intensive hoeing
Iron plow
Efficient horse harnesses
Rotary winnowing fan
Multi-tube seed drill

Astronomy and Cartography

Recognition of sunspots as solar phenomena
Quantitative cartography
Discovery of solar wind
Mercator map-projection
Equatorial astronomical instruments

Engineering

Cast iron
Double-action piston bellows
Crank handle
"Cardan Suspension"
Manufacture of Steel
Deep-drilling for natural gas
Belt-drive
Water power
Chain pump
Suspension bridge
Essentials of steam engine
"Siemens" steel process
Segmental arch bridge
Chain-drive
Underwater salvage operations

continued on next page

Domestic and Industrial Technology

Lacquer (the first plastic)
Strong beer
Use of petroleum and natural gas as fuel
Paper
Wheelbarrow
Sliding calipers
Fishing reel
Stirrup
Porcelain
Biological pest control
Umbrella
Matches
Chess
Brandy
Whiskey
Mechanical Clock
Printing
Playing cards
Paper money
Spinning wheel

Medicine

Circulation of the blood
Circadian rhythms in the human body
Endrocrinology
Deficiency diseases
Diabetes
Use of thyroid hormone
Immunology

Mathematics

Decimal system
Zero
Negative numbers
Extraction of higher roots and solutions of higher numerical equations
Decimal fractions
Use of algebra in geometry
Refined value of pi
"Pascal's" triangle

Magnetism

First compasses
Magnetic declination of the Earth's magnetic field
Magnetic remanence and induction

Military Inventions

Chemical warfare
Poison gas
Smoke bombs
Tear gas
Crossbow
Gunpowder
Flame-thrower
Grenades
Land mines
Sea mines
Rocket
Mortar
Guns
Repeating Guns

Physical Sciences

Geobotanical prospecting
First Law of Motion
Hexagonal structure of snowflakes
Seismograph
Geology
Phosphorescent paint

Transportation

Kite
Manned flight (using kites)
Relief maps
Contour transport canal
Parachute
Hot-air balloon
Rudder
Masts and sailing
Watertight compartments in ships

continued on next page

Helicopter rotor
Propeller
Paddle-wheel boat
Canal pound-lock

FIG. 5.5.   Selected Chinese scientific and mathematical discoveries and inventions.

CONCLUSION

Traditional Chinese educational thought and practice both reflected and helped to reproduce traditional Chinese society, as do all educational systems to some extent, and this was both its strength and weakness. Because traditional Chinese society was highly patriarchal and involved the oppression of girls and women in a number of ways, educational thought tended to pay little attention to the education of girls, and this meant that in practice girls were likely to receive little education beyond those things deemed necessary for wives and mothers to know. The social class organization of Chinese society was both hierarchical and fairly rigid, and again, both educational thought and practice reflected the social class structure of the society. If imperial Chinese society as a whole invested huge resources in education—and it did so throughout its history—these resources were far from equitably distributed. For some, educational endeavors would dominant their lives, whereas for the vast majority of the population, illiteracy was the norm.

At the same time, the system did in fact work well for most of its history to produce what was, in essence, as aristocracy of intellect. The system, although by no means truly meritocratic, did have features of meritocracy, and there were noteworthy instances of social class mobility based on intellectual skill and talent. China was well ahead of its time in terms of the development of a professional civil service based on talent rather than on birth. Finally, if traditional educational thought and practice in China was, as Gerald Gutek noted somewhat critically, "used for highly conservative maintenance purposes [and] not intended to promote social change,"[87] this was precisely what it was designed to do. The idea that the schools can, and should, contribute to social change flies in the face of Confucian teaching about the nature and purposes of the "good society." The point of traditional Chinese educational thought and practice was to ensure stability, and it did so effectively for most of its history.

QUESTIONS FOR REFLECTION AND DISCUSSION

1. An important theme in American education, since the time of the Common School Movement, has been on the role of the school in promoting

social change. Traditional Chinese education, as we have seen, placed its emphasis instead on social stability. To what extent is contemporary schooling in our society concerned with social maintenance, and to what extent is it concerned with promoting social change? How are each of these concerns manifested in practice?

2. The imperial civil service examination system ensured that all educated people in China would share a common educational background, based on knowing the same body of literature and having the same types of skills. What are the advantages of such a common educational background? What are the disadvantages?

3. How are national standards of the sorts that have been, and continue to be, developed in the United States similar to the Chinese notion of a common core of knowledge for all educated people? How do national standards in the U.S. context differ from the traditional Chinese model?

4. "Imperial China addressed the challenges posed by the presence of ethnic and linguistic diversity in a way that seems to share characteristics with both assimilationism and cultural pluralism." Respond to this claim, paying special attention to the role of social class and education.

5. The "eight-legged" essay consisted of a set format for responding to an examination question, and has been widely criticized for promoting an emphasis on form over content. To what extent do you believe that teaching students a particular form or format for the presentation of their ideas is a legitimate goal for education? Does the requirement of a particular form necessarily conflict with the educational goal of creativity?

6. Do you believe that a formal, institutionalized examination system such as that found in imperial China can be successfully utilized to promote meritocracy in a society? What are the constraints on such a system? In your view, is the goal of a meritocratic social order worth pursuing?

7. The concept of *li* is a very important aspect of traditional Confucian thought. In your own words, explain the basic concept of *li*, and then discuss how this concept would be manifested in practice in different kinds of societies.

8. In this chapter, it is noted that Confucius once rebuked a student as a "little-minded man" for asking about the growing of crops. Why do you think that Confucius responded in this manner? How does his response reflect important elements of traditional Chinese society?

9. In order to be admitted to a college or a university, an American student generally has to take either the SAT or ACT examination. In what ways is this requirement similar to the imperial examination system, and in what ways is it different?

10. What do you believe is the single most important lesson traditional Chinese educational thought and practice has for contemporary American education? Why?

RECOMMENDED FURTHER READINGS

There are several good general introductory works on Chinese history, including W. Scott Morton, *China: Its History and Culture* (New York: McGraw-Hill, 1995); John K. Fairbank, *China: A New History* (Cambridge, MA: Harvard University Press, 1992); Jacques Gernet, *A History of Chinese Civilization* (Cambridge, England: Cambridge University Press, 1982); and Immanuel C. Y. Hsü, *The Rise of Modern China* (New York: Oxford University Press, 1990). The best general introduction to Chinese education, both traditional and modern, is John Cleverley, *The Schooling of China: Tradition and Modernity in Chinese Education* (Sydney: Allen & Unwin, 1985). Among primary sources, D. C. Lau's excellent translations of *The Analects* (Harmondsworth: Penguin, 1979) and *Mencius* (Harmondsworth: Penguin, 1970) are very much worth reading.

NOTES

1. Jacques Gernet, *A History of Chinese Civilization* (Cambridge, England: Cambridge University Press, 1982), 37–38; Marcel Granet, *La civilisation chinoise: La vie publique et la vie privée* (Paris: Éditions Albin Michel, 1968); John Cleverley, *The Schooling of China: Tradition and Modernity in Chinese Education* (Sydney: Allen & Unwin, 1985), 1; Wolfgang Bauer, *China and the Search for Happiness: Recurring Themes in Four Thousand Years of Chinese History* (New York: Seabury, 1976); Henri Cordier, *Histoire général de la Chine*, 4 vols. (Paris: Geuthner, 1921).
2. Cleverley, *The Schooling of China*.
3. Gerald Gutek, *American Education in a Global Society* (New York: Longman, 1993), 178. See also Derk Bodde, *China's First Unifier: A Study of the Ch'in Dynasty as Seen in the Life of Li Ssu* (Hong Kong: Hong Kong University Press, 1967); Derk Bodde, *Essays on Chinese Civilization* (Princeton, NJ: Princeton University Press, 1981); Wolfram Eberhard, *A History of China* (Berkeley: University of California Press, 1977); Werner Eichhorn, *Chinese Civilization: An Introduction* (New York: Praeger, 1969); Mark Elvin, *The Pattern of the Chinese Past* (Stanford, CA: Stanford University Press, 1973); Ray Huang, *China: A Macro History* (London: Sharpe, 1988); Charles Hucker, *China's Imperial Past: An Introduction to Chinese History and Culture* (Stanford, CA: Stanford University Press, 1975); Michael Loewe, *Imperial China: The Historical Background to the Modern Age* (New York: Praeger, 1965); Henri Maspero and Jean Escarra, *Les institutions de la Chine: Essai historique* (Paris: Presses Universitaires de France, 1952); John Meskill with J. Mason Gentzler (eds.), *An Introduction to Chinese Civilization* (New York: Columbia University Press, 1973).

4. Michael Loewe, *The Pride That Was China* (New York: St. Martin's Press, 1990), xix.

5. See Gernet, *A History of Chinese Civilization*, 3–13; Jerry Norman, *Chinese* (Cambridge, England: Cambridge University Press, 1988).

6. Will Durant, *The Story of Civilization: Our Oriental Heritage* (New York: Simon and Schuster, 1963), 642. See, for example, Burton Watson, trans., *Records of the Great Historian of China* (2 vols.) (New York: Columbia University Press, 1961); Endymion Wilkinson, *The History of Imperial China: A Research Guide* (Cambridge, MA: Harvard University Press, 1973).

7. See David McMullen, *State and Scholars in T'ang China* (Cambridge, England: Cambridge University Press, 1988); Tadao Sakai, "Confucianism and Popular Educational Works," in William de Bary (ed.), *Self and Society in Ming Thought* (New York: Columbia University Press, 1970), 331–366; Don Wyatt, "A Language of Continuity in Confucian Thought," in Paul Cohen and Merle Goldman (eds.), *Ideas Across Cultures* (Cambridge, MA: Harvard University Press, 1990), 33–34; James Ball, *Things Chinese, or, Notes Connected With China*, 5th ed. (revised by E. C. Werner) (Shanghai: Kelly and Walsh, 1925); Chen Li-Fu, *Why Confucius Has Been Reverenced as the Model Teacher of All Ages* (New York: Center of Asian Studies, St. John's University, and the Institute of Chinese Culture, 1976); Cheng Hanbang, "Confucian Ethics and Moral Education of Contemporary Students," in Silke Krieger and Rolf Trauzettel (eds.), *Confucianism and the Modernization of China* (Mainz, Germany: Hase & Koehler, 1991), 193–202; William de Bary, *Neo-Confucian Orthodoxy and the Learning of the Mind-and-Heart* (New York: Columbia University Press, 1981); William de Bary, *The Liberal Tradition in China* (Hong Kong: Chinese University Press, 1983); Fu Shufang, "A Brief Account of the Positive Factors in Confucius' Thinking," in Silke Krieger and Rolf Trauzettel (eds.), *Confucianism and the Modernization of China* (Mainz, Germany: Hase & Koehler, 1991), 175–192; Kuang Yaming, "Modern Values of the Positive Elements in Confucius' Ideas Concerning the Study of Man," in Silke Krieger and Rolf Trauzettel (eds.), *Confucianism and the Modernization of China* (Mainz, Germany: Hase & Koehler, 1991), 7–17; I. Llasera, "Confucian Education Through European Eyes," in Ruth Hayhoe and Marianne Bastid (eds.), *China's Education and the Industrialized World* (London: Sharpe, 1987), 21–32; Vitalii Rubin, *Individual and State in Ancient China: Essays on Four Chinese Philosophers* (New York: Columbia University Press, 1976); B. Staiger, "The Image of Confucius in China," in Silke Krieger and Rolf Trauzettel (eds.), *Confucianism and the Modernization of China* (Mainz, Germany: Hase & Koehler, 1991), 116–125; H. Stumpfeldt, "Confucius and Confucianism: On Their History and Status and On Their Present Theoretical and Practical Potential," in Silke Krieger and Rolf Trauzettel (eds.), *Confucianism and the Modernization of China* (Mainz, Germany: Hase & Koehler, 1991), 18–28; L. Walton, "The Institutional Context of Neo-Confucianism: Scholars, Schools, and Shu-yüan in Sung- Yüan China," in William de Bary and John

Chaffee (eds.), *Neo-Confucian Education: The Formative Stage* (Berkeley: University of California Press, 1989), 457–492.

8. Tu Wei-Ming, "The Confucian Tradition in Chinese History," in Paul Ropp (ed.), *Heritage of China* (Berkeley: University of California Press, 1990), 136. See also Michael Bond and Kwang-Kuo Hwang, "The Social Psychology of the Chinese People," in Michael Bond (ed.), *The Psychology of the Chinese People* (Hong Kong: Oxford University Press, 1986), 213–266; Benjamin Schwartz, *The World of Thought in Ancient China* (Cambridge, MA: Harvard University Press, 1985); A. Sprenger, "Confucius and Modernization in China: An Educational Perspective," in Silke Krieger and Rolf Trauzettel (eds.), *Confucianism and the Modernization of China* (Mainz, Germany: Hase & Koehler, 1991), 454–472.

9. Cheng Tien-Hsi, *China Moulded By Confucius* (London: Stevens & Sons, 1947), 23.

10. Gernet, *A History of Chinese Civilization*, 88. See also Patricia Ebrey, *Confucianism and Family Rituals in Imperial China* (Princeton, NJ: Princeton University Press, 1991).

11. Herrlee G. Creel, *Confucius and the Chinese Way* (New York: Harper & Row, 1949), 25–26; Tu Wei-Ming, "The Confucian Tradition in Chinese History," 113–114.

12. Creel, *Confucius and the Chinese Way*, 25–26; Tu Wei-Ming, "The Confucian Tradition in Chinese History," 113–114.

13. The term *chün-tzu* literally means "son of a ruler," but is used in the more general sense of "gentleman." Even this translation is somewhat problematic, however, because it refers not so much to an assumed superiority of birth as to a superiority of character and behavior. See Arthur Waley, *The Analects of Confucius* (New York: Vintage, 1938), 34–38; Fung Yu-Lan, *A Short History of Chinese Philosophy* (New York: Free Press, 1948), 38–48.

It should be noted that the use of male pronouns here is deliberate and meaningful; the role of women in Confucian thought is restricted, in large part, to their roles as wives and mothers. Traditional Chinese society was very much patriarchal, and this was reflected in the place of women in the social order. See Patricia Ebrey, "Women, Marriage, and the Family in Chinese History," in Paul Ropp (ed.), *Heritage of China: Contemporary Perspectives on Chinese Civilization* (Berkeley: University of California Press, 1990), 197–223; Patricia Ebrey, "Education through Ritual: Efforts to Formulate Family Rituals During the Sung Period," in William de Bary and John Chaffee (eds.), *Neo-Confucian Education: The Formative Stage* (Berkeley: University of California Press, 1989), 277–306; Patricia Ebrey, *Confucianism and Family Rituals in Imperial China*.

14. See Creel, *Confucius and the Chinese Way*, 142–144; Ebrey, *Confucianism and Family Rituals in Imperial China*.

15. Gernet, *A History of Chinese Civilization*, 88.

16. D. C. Lau, trans., *The Analects* (Harmondsworth: Penguin, 1979).

17. Creel, *Confucius and the Chinese Way*, 291–294.

18. Patricia Ebrey (ed.), *Chinese Civilization* (New York: The Free Press, 1993), 17.

19. See Cheng Tien-Hsi, *China Moulded By Confucius*, 30–36.

20. See Ebrey, *Confucianism and Family Rituals in Imperial China*, 3–13.

21. Creel, *Confucius and the Chinese Way*, 85.

22. Creel, *Confucius and the Chinese Way*, 86.

23. Creel, *Confucius and the Chinese Way*, 129.

24. Howard Ozmon and Samuel Craver, *Philosophical Foundations of Education*, 5th ed. (Englewood Cliffs, NJ: Prentice-Hall, 1995), 93.

25. Ozmon and Craver, *Philosophical Foundations of Education*, 93.

26. Charles Commeaux, *La vie quotidienne en Chine sous les Mandchous* (Paris: Librairie Hachette, 1970), 162–194.

27. Ron-Guey Chu, "Chu Hsi and Public Instruction," in William de Bary and John Chaffee (eds.), *Neo-Confucian Education: The Formative Stage* (Berkeley: University of California Press, 1989), 272.

28. Wang Gungwu, *The Chineseness of China* (Hong Kong: Oxford University Press, 1991), 171.

29. Louis Heren, C. P. Fitzgerald, Michael Freeberne, Brian Hook, and David Bonavia, *China's Three Thousand Years* (New York: Collier Books, 1973), 23–24.

30. See D. C. Lau, trans., *Mencius* (Harmondsworth: Penguin, 1970); also useful is Tu Wei- Ming, "The Confucian Tradition in Chinese History."

31. See Peter Bol, "Chu Hsi's Redefinition of Literati Learning," in William de Bary and John Chaffee (eds.), *Neo-Confucian Education: The Formative Stage* (Berkeley: University of California Press, 1989), 151–185; William de Bary, "Chu Hsi's Aims as an Educator," in William de Bary and John Chaffee (eds.), *Neo-Confucian Education: The Formative Stage* (Berkeley: University of California Press, 1989), 186–218; M. Theresa Kelleher, "Back to Basics: Chu Hsi's *Elementary Learning (Hsiao-hsüeh)*," in William de Bary and John Chaffee (eds.), *Neo-Confucian Education: The Formative Stage* (Berkeley: University of California Press, 1989), 219–251; Ron-Guey Chu, "Chu Hsi and Public Instruction."

32. Cleverley, *The Schooling of China*, 4.

33. Cleverley, *The Schooling of China*, 4.

34. Creel, *Confucius and the Chinese Way*, 77.

35. See Wyatt, "A Language of Continuity in Confucian Thought," 33–34.

36. Creel, *Confucius and the Chinese Way*, 76.

37. Cleverley, *The Schooling of China*, 7.

38. Gutek, *American Education in a Global Society*, 179.

39. Creel, *Confucius and the Chinese Way*, 165–166.

40. See Steven Tozer, Paul Violas, and Guy Senese, *School and Society: Historical and Contemporary Perspectives*, 3rd ed. (New York: McGraw-Hill, 1998), 27–39; Gordon Lee, *Crusade Against Ignorance: Thomas Jefferson on Education* (New York: Teachers College Press, 1967).

41. Raymond Dawson, *The Chinese Experience* (London: Weidenfeld and Nicolson, 1978), 108–115; Gernet, *A History of Chinese Civilization*, 90–93.

42. See T. H. Barrett, "Religious Traditions in Chinese Civilization: Buddhism and Taoism," in Paul Ropp (ed.), *Heritage of China: Contemporary Perspectives on Chinese Civilization* (Berkeley: University of California Press, 1990), 138–163; Phyllis Chew, "The Great Tao," *The Journal of Bahá'í Studies*, 4, 2 (1991): 11–39; Liu Ts'un-Yan, "Taoist Self-Cultivation in Ming Thought," in William de Bary (ed.), *Self and Society in Ming Thought* (New York: Columbia University Press, 1970), 291–330; Chad Hansen, *A Daoist Theory of Chinese Thought: A Philosophical Interpretation* (New York: Oxford University Press, 1992); Gernet, *A History of Chinese Civilization*, 93–95.

43. See de Bary and Chaffee, *Neo-Confucian Education*.

44. Jacques Gernet, *Daily Life in China on the Eve of the Mongol Invasion, 1250–1276* (Stanford, CA: Stanford University Press, 1962), 151–152.

45. Gernet, *Daily Life in China*, 153.

46. Gernet, *Daily Life in China*, 153.

47. See Édouard Biot, *Essai sur l'histoire de l'instruction publique en chine et de la corporation des lettrés* (Paris: Benjamin Duprat, 1847); H. Galt, *A History of Chinese Educational Institutions*, vol. 1 (London: Arthur Probsthain, 1951); McMullen, *State and Scholars in T'ang China*; Cleverley, *The Schooling of China*, 15; William Ayers, *Chang Chih-tung and Educational Reform in China* (Cambridge, MA: Harvard University Press, 1971); James Liu (ed.), *Political Institutions in Traditional China: Major Issues* (New York: Wiley, 1974); Pei-yi Wu, "Education of Children in the Sung," in William de Bary and John Chaffee (eds.), *Neo-Confucian Education: The Formative Stage* (Berkeley: University of California Press, 1989), 307–324; Evelyn Rawski, *Education and Popular Literacy in Ch'ing China* (Ann Arbor: University of Michigan Press, 1979).

48. Loewe, *The Pride That Was China*, 145.

49. Dawson, *The Chinese Experience*, 20.

50. See Richard Smith, *China's Cultural Heritage: The Ch'ing Dynasty, 1644–1912* (Boulder, CO: Westview Press, 1983), 250.

51. Justus Doolittle, *Social Life of the Chinese*, vol. 1 (1865; Taipei: Ch'eng-Wen, 1966), 376–377; see also Isaac Headland, *Home Life in China* (London: Methuen & Co., 1914).

52. Yuan Zheng, "Local Government Schools in Sung China: A Reassessment," *History of Education Quarterly*, 34, 2 (1994): 213.

53. Yuan Zheng, "Local Government Schools in Sung China," 193–213.

54. Yuan Zheng, "Local Government Schools in Sung China," 212.

55. Cleverley, *The Schooling of China*, 16.

56. A few words about the nature of written Chinese are in order here. The Chinese writing system is not phonetic in the way that Western, alphabetically-based systems are. Rather, each Chinese character represents a single morpheme, and contains two elements, one of which carries semantic information and the other phonological information, which is used for sound value alone. Thus, the character for the word *liáng* ("wolf") contains the graph for "dog" on the left and a graph for the word *liáng* (literally meaning "good") on

the right. Thus, the combination gives the reader an idea of the semantic content, coupled with the appropriate sound. Although far more complicated to learn than an alphabetically-based system, the Chinese system has the advantage that it can be used to represent different spoken languages, which is, in essence, what has taken place historically, since China is in fact very diverse linguistically. An orthographic system such as that used by Chinese basically functions as a sort of written *lingua franca*, serving as an additional unifying force where spoken language would tend to work against unity. See Norman, *Chinese*, 58–63; S. Robert Ramsey, *The Languages of China* (Princeton, NJ: Princeton University Press, 1987), 134–137.

57. Cleverley, *The Schooling of China*, 17.

58. See Kiang Kang-Hu, *On Chinese Studies* (Shanghai: Commercial Press, 1934); S. Wells Williams, *The Middle Kingdom*, vol. 1 (New York: Scribners', 1907), 627–673.

59. Smith, *China's Cultural Heritage*, 47.

60. Dawson, *The Chinese Experience*, 34.

61. Gernet, *Daily Life in China*, 154–155.

62. Gernet, *Daily Life in China*, 154.

63. Cleverley, *The Schooling of China*, 27.

64. See Bettine Birge, "Chu Hsi and Women's Education," in William de Bary and John Chaffee (eds.), *Neo-Confucian Education: The Formative Stage* (Berkeley: University of California Press, 1989), 325–367; Ebrey, "Women, Marriage, and the Family in Chinese History."

65. Dawson, *The Chinese Experience*, 33.

66. Ebrey, *Chinese Civilization*, 128; see also Peter Bol, *"This Culture of Ours": Intellectual Transitions in T'ang and Sung China* (Stanford, CA: Stanford University Press, 1992), 36–48.

67. See Thomas H. C. Lee, *Government Education and Examinations in Sung China* (Hong Kong: Chinese University Press, 1985); Ping-Ti Ho, *The Ladder of Success in Imperial China* (New York: Columbia University Press, 1962); John Chaffee, *Education and Examinations in Sung Society* (Ph.D. dissertation, University of Chicago, 1979); Irene Bloom, *Knowledge Painfully Acquired: The K'un-chih chi by Lo Ch'in-shun* (New York: Columbia University Press, 1987); Joseph Needham, *Science in Traditional China: A Comparative Perspective* (Cambridge, MA: Harvard University Press, 1981), 23–24.

68. Dawson, *The Chinese Experience*, 33–34; see also Hsiung-Huei Lee, *Education in Taiwan During the Ch'ing Dynasty, 1683–1895* (Ph.D. dissertation, University of Connecticut, 1995), 193–272.

69. Cleverley, *The Schooling of China*, 19.

70. See Immanuel C. Y. Hsü, *The Rise of Modern China* (New York: Oxford University Press, 1990), 75. For a detailed discussion of the examination system, see Smith, *China's Cultural Heritage*, 47–51; also interesting is Doolittle, *Social Life of the Chinese*, chapters 15, 16, and 17.

71. Dawson, *The Chinese Experience*, 34.

72. Hsiung-Huei Lee, *Education in Taiwan During the Ch'ing Dynasty*, 217–222.

73. Dawson, *The Chinese Experience*, 36.

74. Dawson, *The Chinese Experience*, 36.

75. Dawson, *The Chinese Experience*, 36.

76. Hsiung-Huei Lee, *Education in Taiwan During the Ch'ing Dynasty*, chapter 5. See also Leon Stover, *The Cultural Ecology of Chinese Civilization: Peasants and Elites in the Last of the Agrarian Societies* (New York: Pica, 1974).

77. Dawson, *The Chinese Experience*, 34.

78. Gernet, *A History of Chinese Civilization*, 505. This is not to suggest, however, that the system was entirely unchanging or static; see, for example, Joanna Handlin, *Action in Late Ming Thought: The Reorientation of Lü K'un and Other Scholar-Officials* (Berkeley: University of California Press, 1983).

79. Cleverley, *The Schooling of China*, 20; Hsiung-Huei Lee, *Education in Taiwan During the Ch'ing Dynasty*, 212–216.

80. Cleverley, *The Schooling of China*, 20–21.

81. See Ho Peng Yoke, *Li, Qi and Shu: An Introduction to Science and Civilization in China* (Hong Kong: Hong Kong University Press, 1985). I am deeply indebted to the late Philip Steedman for bringing the work of Joseph Needham to my attention.

82. This is not, however, to suggest that science, even when passed from one cultural setting to another, in earlier times was in any meaningful way conceptually or epistemologically "universal." As Needham points out,

> The sciences of the mediaeval world were in fact tied closely to their ethnic environment, and it was difficult if not impossible for people of those different environments to find any common basis of discourse. For example, if Chang Heng had tried to talk to Vitruvius about the Tin and the Yang or the Five Elements, he would not have got very far, even if they could have understood each other at all. But that did not mean that it was impossible for inventions of great sociological importance to pass from one civilisation to another, and that they did, right through the Middle Ages. [see Needham, *Science in Traditional China*, 9].

This leaves open the question, of course, of the extent to which modern science, can be said to be "universal"; see, for instance, the work of the radical philosopher of science Paul Feyerabend, including his *Against Method*, 3rd ed. (London: Verso, 1993), *Farewell to Reason* (London: Verso, 1987), and *Three Dialogues on Knowledge* (Oxford, England: Basil Blackwell, 1989); as well as Alan Sokal and Jean Bricmont's powerful critique of postmodern philosophy of science, *Fashionable Nonsense: Posmodern Intellectuals' Abuse of Science* (New York: Picador, 1998).

83. Needham, *Science in Traditional China*, 10–12.

84. Needham, *Science in Traditional China*, 3.

85. *Science and Civilisation in China* is, by any definition, a monumental work, and can be overwhelming for the nonspecialist. An extremely useful abridged version of the work has now been produced; see Colin Ronan, *The Shorter Science and Civilisation in China, An Abridgement of Joseph*

Needham's Original Text, 4 volumes (Cambridge, England: Cambridge University Press, 1978–1994).

86. See Robert Temple, *The Genius of China: 3,000 Years of Science, Discovery, and Invention* (New York: Simon and Schuster, 1986).

87. Gutek, *American Education in a Global Society*, 179; see also, however, Marianne Bastid, "Servitude or Liberation? The Introduction of Foreign Educational Practices and Systems to China," in Ruth Hayhoe and Marianne Bastid (eds.), *China's Education and the Industrialized World* (London: Sharpe, 1987), 3–20.

6
"An Intelligent Man Attends on a Wise Person": Traditional Hindu and Buddhist Educational Thought and Practice

The Indian subcontinent is the home of three important, and related, cultural and religious traditions: Hinduism, Buddhism, and Jainism, each of which has educational traditions no doubt meriting a book of its own.[1] In this book, we examine the traditional educational thought and practices associated with two of these three religions. Specifically, in this chapter we explore selected aspects of the Hindu and Buddhist educational traditions.

THE ORIGINS OF HINDUISM

It is difficult both to identify the origins of Hinduism and to provide a succinct, clear summation of what the essence of Hinduism actually is. To some extent, these problems are related, since Hinduism is incredibly ancient and has been open to diversity and the assimilation of new ideas and practices throughout its long history.[2] According to Hindu tradition, the *Vedas* (or "body of knowledge") that constitute the sacred literature of Hinduism date back as far as 6000 B.C.E. in their oral form, while most historians would argue that the written literature, although not nearly as old as the tradition would suggest, nonetheless dates to around 1500 to 1000 B.C.E.[3] In fact, we know relatively little about the early history of Hinduism, and what today is called *Hinduism*[4] is actually the product of the blending of four distinct religious traditions. These four traditions, in chronological order of their impact of the development of Hinduism, are:

1. The religious and spiritual traditions of the original, indigenous people of the subcontinent, whose stone-age culture dates back some half million years,

2. The religious and spiritual traditions of the Indus civilization which encompassed much of Northern and Northwestern India,

3. The religious and spiritual traditions of the Dravidian culture, and
4. The Vedic religion, which was brought to the subcontinent by Aryan invaders roughly between 200 B.C.E. and 900 B.C.E.[5]

Later contacts with Jews, Christians, and Muslims, as well as with Buddhists whose religious tradition is related to and in part derived from that of Hinduism, have also impacted Hinduism in various ways, as have both Jainism and Sikhism. This openness to other religious traditions has not, however, meant that the fundamental essence of Hinduism has differed significantly through its long history. As Klaus Klostermaier noted in *A Survey of Hinduism*, "Despite its openness to many influences and the considerable changes that it has undergone throughout the ages, there is a distinct character, an unbroken tradition, and a unifying principle that allows Hinduism to be faithful to itself while inviting others to share whatever treasures they may possess."[6]

Hindus themselves call their religion *sanatana dharma*, which is generally translated as "eternal religion," although it might just as well be translated as "eternal truth." However, the term implies far more than the English translation.[7] *Sanatana* means "eternal" or "ageless" in the sense that the religion is believed by its practitioners to have always existed, and to be *the* religion.[8] *Dharma*, often translated simply as "religion," actually encompasses such concepts as "duty," "righteousness," and "natural law," thus suggesting a much broader understanding than that generally accorded the term "religion" in the West.[9] In fact, as Troy Organ argued in *The Hindu Quest for the Perfection of Man*, underlying the notion of *dharma* is a far more encompassing conception of the duties of the individual, involving "the total disciplinary methods of training the will, rather than to the moral rightness or wrongness of single acts as measured by a fixed law."[10]

Not only is the translation of *sanatana dharma* problematic, but the actual nature of the religion itself is somewhat difficult to define. Indeed, as Stephen Cross commented, "One of the ways in which Hinduism differs strikingly from those religions which we in the West are most used to is that it has no fixed minimum doctrine. There is no Hindu creed and no central authority.... Hinduism is not a tightly defined religion but rather the way of thought of an entire ancient and populous civilization."[11] As David Kinsley explained, "One cannot find the equivalent of a Hindu pope or an authoritative Hindu council.... Historically, Hinduism has never insisted on the necessity of a supreme figure in religious matters and has never agreed on certain articles of belief as essential for all Hindus. Throughout its long history, Hinduism has been highly decentralized."[12]

Further complicating this situation have been the close ties between Hinduism as a religious tradition and Indian nationalism in recent times.[13] Although certainly not all Indians are Hindu, and while there are of course non-Indian Hindus, for the most part there is a commonly assumed connection between

Hinduism and Indian cultural identity. To assume such a connection is hardly unreasonable because, as Arvind Sharma explained, "95 percent of the Hindus in the world live in India, over 80 percent of whose population is Hindu."[14] The contemporary reality of the situation is that Hinduism actually exists (or, perhaps more accurately, coexists) both as an ethnic religion and as a universal religion.[15] This has led to a degree of conceptual tension within Hinduism, as Sharma noted: "The ethnic and universal aspects of Hinduism thus together constitute the paradoxical axes of Hindu pluralism, keeping the map of Hinduism, as it were, forever on the drawing board of history."[16]

Identification of oneself as Hindu, then, inevitably depends less on doctrinal agreement than on self-definition and acceptance by the Hindu community, to a far greater extent than would be the case with most other religious traditions, especially those with which we in the West tend to be most familiar. This having been said, however, one common way of distinguishing Hindus from non-Hindus is that the former accept the authority of the *Vedas* in spiritual matters.[17] The centrality of the *Vedas* to Hinduism provides a valuable entry point for us as we try to understand Hinduism and the traditional educational thought and practice associated with Hinduism.

THE VEDIC TRADITION

The body of sacred writings in Hinduism is extensive, and includes a number of different kinds of literature. As Klostermaier pointed out, "No other living tradition can claim scriptures as numerous or as ancient as Hinduism; none can boast an unbroken tradition preserved as faithfully as the Hindu tradition. The sources of Hinduism are not only historical materials to be studied by the scholar of antiquity, they have been recited and studied by the faithful throughout the ages."[18] The two most significant of the elements in the sacred literature of Hinduism's "living tradition" are *shruti* and *smrti*,[19] each of which is now briefly discussed. We also consider the unique role of Sanskrit in the Hindu literary tradition.

Shruti

Shruti means "that which is heard," and is commonly associated primarily with the *Vedas*. The *Vedas* are believed to constitute divine revelation. As Fisher explained, "According to orthodox Hindus, the *Vedas* are not the work of any humans. They are believed to be the breath of the eternal, as 'heard' by the ancient sages, or *rishis*. The scriptures are thought to transcend human time and are thus as relevant today as they were thousands of years ago."[20]

Although the *Vedas* have been written down, they are first and foremost oral texts,[21] and there is a strong view in the Hindu tradition that they are best transmitted orally.[22] There are actually four distinct bodies of work that together make up the *Vedas*; specifically, there are the *Rig Veda*, the *Yajur Veda*, the *Sama Veda*, and the *Atharva Veda*.[23] Each of these *Vedas* is, in turn, divided into four parts, including devotional hymns (*Samhita* or *Mantra*), priestly texts (*Brahmanas*), forest treatises (*Aranyakas*), and philosophic texts (the *Upanishads*), which were actually produced later and are more correctly called *Vendantic* texts.[24]

The *Vedas* play a role in Hinduism that is in some ways similar to that of texts believed to be divinely inspired in other religions, but which is also different in important ways. As Sharma noted,

> The *Vedas*, by virtue of their historical priority and canonical primacy, play a very significant role in Hinduism but in unsuspecting ways.... The *Vedas*, for the tradition as a whole then, functioned as a symbol of the tradition and as the ultimate rather than the proximate basis of its beliefs and practices, for anything not inconsistent with the *Vedas* was considered admissible as Hindu. This negative criterion for orthodox inclusion once again attests to Hinduism's reluctance to limit itself.[25]

Smrti

Smrti is the body of religious literature in Hinduism that seeks to explain how the timeless spiritual truths of the *Vedas* are to be understood and applied in one's daily life.[26] In practice, the term *smrti*, which means "that which has been remembered," can be used either to refer to works that are basically codes of conduct, or "extended to embrace virtually all forms of sacred writings of human origin."[27] *Smrti*, at least in the former sense, consists of a variety of different books that seek to provide guidance for virtually all aspects of human life, the most widely accepted of which is the *Manusmrti* (the "Laws of Manu"). They tend to be highly prescriptive, complex, and analytic in nature but, as Sharma explained, there is an underlying reason for this: "Their passion for classification baffles modern readers. A 'method' may, however, underlie the 'madness.' Marriage is classified as being of eight kinds. A deep compassion perhaps underlies this classification, which is so exhaustive that it is virtually impossible for anyone to be born out of wedlock!"[28]

Although recognized by Hindus as being of human origin, *smrti* is arguably of considerably greater immediate importance than are the *Vedas* themselves for most Hindus, because it regulates daily life in a way that *shruti* does not.[29] Finally, it is worth noting that although Hindus accept *shruti* as divine scripture, Hinduism as it is generally recognized has, since the Classical Hindu Period (roughly 300 C.E. to 1200 C.E.) been characterized to a far greater extent by compliance with *smrti* than *shruti*.[30]

The Role of Sanskrit in the Vedic Tradition

Sanskrit, a language brought to India by the Aryan invaders of the subcontinent between 1500 B.C.E. and 1200 B.C.E., has played and continues to play an important role in Hinduism. The *Vedas* are written in Sanskrit, as are many other important religious writings. Although there is also an extensive religious literature in the various vernacular languages of India, Sanskrit remains very much the "sacred tongue *par excellence*" of Hinduism.[31] Furthermore, having ceased to function as a spoken language in daily life more than 2,000 years ago, Sanskrit was maintained for much of its history not merely as a sacred language, but as a sacred language of which knowledge was reserved for a small elite in Indian society who maintained both their religious and social status in part through their knowledge of it.[32]

Sanskrit, incidentally, is also important in another, far different, context. European scholars gained access to both the language and the texts written in Sanskrit only in the 18th century—an undertaking that had been quite difficult, since the Brahmins were hesitant to let foreigners (*mlecchas*) learn the sacred language. In 1786, a British scholar, Sir William Jones, delivered a paper on Sanskrit, in which he argued that the language bore striking similarities to Latin and Greek.[33] Jones noted that:

> The Sanskrit language, whatever may be its antiquity, is of a wonderful structure; more perfect than the Greek, more copious than the Latin, and more exquisitely refined than either, yet bearing to both of them a stronger affinity, both in the roots of the verbs and in the forms of grammar, than could possibly have been produced by accident; so strong indeed that no philologer could examine them all three, without believing them to have sprung from some common source, which, perhaps no longer exists.... [34]

The similarities identified by Jones were later explored in considerable detail and led to the discovery that Sanskrit, and many other languages as well, were indeed related. In fact, it proved to be the beginning of the discovery of the Indo-European language family, to which not only Sanskrit, but also English and the other Germanic languages, the Celtic languages, the Romance languages, the Slavic languages, the Hellenic languages, the Baltic languages, and the Indo-Iranian languages, all belong.

HINDU BELIEFS AND PRACTICES

As we have already seen, it is very difficult indeed to identify the core beliefs of Hinduism. However, keeping in mind that there is, and probably could be, no "creed" to which all Hindus subscribe, it is nevertheless possible to summarize some of the key beliefs that are most prevalent and common among Hindus. A good start in this effort has been made by the Himalayan Academy, an American Hindu organization, which identified the following "Nine Beliefs of Hinduism":

1. That there is "one, all-pervasive Supreme Being";

2. That there are "endless cycles of creation, preservation and dissolution" (that is, a cyclical view of time and history);
3. That "all souls are evolving" toward or seeking "*Moksha*" or "liberation";
4. That there is a "law of cause and effect" known as Karma;
5. That there is "reincarnation";
6. That there are "divine beings and forces" that require "temple worship" and "personal worship," or Puja, in the home;
7. That there is a need for "an awakened Master of Sat Guru" (that is, a reliable, personal teacher) for one's personal and ethical life;
8. That "all life is sacred" and that one should pursue "*ahimsa* or non-violence"; and
9. That "no particular religion teaches the only way to salvation about all others, but that all genuine religious paths are ... deserving (of) tolerance and understanding."[35]

Although this list is useful, it has also been carefully, and understandably, constructed to avoid, for the most part, issues that Americans might find problematic. It is not, however, universally accepted by Hindus—the need for a "guru," for instance, is by no means generally accepted as a core belief of Hinduism. One additional feature of Classical Hinduism that must be explicitly addressed here in order to help make sense of traditional Hindu educational thought and practice is that of the caste system that is so closely associated with Hinduism.

The Hindu caste system had its origins in the culture brought to India by the Aryan invaders, who, like other Indo-European peoples, divided their society into three classes of people: a priesthood, a class of warriors and rulers, and a class concerned with meeting the economic needs of the society (farmers, merchants, craftsmen, etc.). In addition, the Aryans developed a fourth class, who functioned as servants for the members of the other three classes. These four classes of people, called *varnas*, were called *Brahmins*, *Kshatriyas*, *Vaishyas*, and *Shudras*, respectively.[36] To this division of society, the Aryans added a fifth group, consisting of the indigenous people of India whom they had conquered, to whom were delegated various socially necessary but "impure" activities. This group were the "untouchables," because it came to be believed that even contact with them could pollute others. The social divisions among these five classes of people, which were established in the *Vedas*, were in practice replaced with an hereditary system based on *jati* (birth) in traditional Hindu society.[37] Thus, the divisions, which had always been hierarchical, came to be religiously sanctioned and, for the most part, permanent and binding in nature. Thus, what had begun as social classes gradually became castes. Over time, the caste system further developed, so that today there are actually more than 3,000 different castes, reflecting different trades, professions, backgrounds, and so on.[38] Although an understanding of traditional Hinduism certainly requires a familiarity with the caste system, especially in terms of traditional Hindu educational thought and practice, it is important to note that the caste system is not in fact part of the religion itself. As Cross noted, "The whole system has thus become attached in the popular mind, and in that of many foreign observers, to Hinduism, but in reality it has little to do with it. The caste system is a social phenomenon masquerading as religion."[39]

It is also possible for us to talk about Hinduism in terms of the legitimate goals for human life. Specifically, an important component of Hinduism has been what is termed the *doctrine of the four goals of life* or *purusharthas*.[40] These four goals include:

1. *Dharma* (the leading of a moral life);
2. *Artha* (the earning of wealth);
3. *Kama* (the enjoyment of the pleasures of the senses); and
4. *Moksha* (the seeking of liberation).[41]

Ideally, these four goals are to be reflected chronologically in one's life as distinct "stages of life," with *dharma* as the goal for one's first 25 years, followed by each of the other goals in its turn, although in practice most Hindus only progress through the first two.[42] The ultimate goal for the individual that underlies all of these four goals is, of course, the "quest for perfection,"[43] but the focus of this goal in Hinduism is on the process rather than on the product. As Organ argued in *The Hindu Quest for the Perfection of Man*, "Hinduism is a pursuit, an endeavor, a striving. According to the *Mahabharata* it is the 'pursuit of Brahman or self-knowledge' that is immortality. This continuous endeavor toward fulfillment is a promise, and, like all ideals, a forever falling short of the goal."[44]

We now turn to an examination of how individuals were educated for this pursuit in traditional Hindu society.

TRADITIONAL HINDU EDUCATIONAL THOUGHT

At the base of traditional Hindu educational thought is a deep concern with epistemology, or the theory of knowledge. Human beings are believed to be held captive by our ignorance, and thus, ways of knowing (*pramana*) become very important in Hinduism.[45] Hindu theologians and philosophers have identified six different methods of knowing: sense perception (*pratyaksha*), inference (*anumana*), authority (*shabda*), analogy (*upamana*), hypothetical supposition (*arthapatti*), and negation (*anupalabdhi*).[46] Although the ultimate purpose of epistemology in Hinduism is spiritual in nature, it is important to keep in mind that none of these six methods of knowing is intended to provide direct knowledge of the Absolute; rather, each is useful in assisting us to "discern the realities which are assumed to be manifestations of the Reality, and hence are instrumental in the quest for Absolute Reality."[47] Each of these methods of knowing is briefly discussed below:

1. *Pratyaksha*, or sense perception, is arguably the most important source of knowledge. It refers to those things that we learn by means of our senses (which, in Hinduism, are taken to include the five external senses—touch, taste, sight, sound, and smell—as well as an internal sense, mind [*manas*]).[48]

2. *Anumana*, or inference, refers to what might be called logical argument, and includes both inductive and deductive reasoning. Typical of *anumana* is the five-part syllogism characteristic of Hindu philosophy, which precedes the development of syllogistic reasoning in the West. The five-part syllogism includes the following steps:
   a. The thesis that is to be established.
   b. The reason for maintaining the thesis.
   c. The example of the reason.
   d. The application of the reason and example.
   e. The conclusion (that is, the thesis established).[49]

3. *Shabda*, or authority, is concerned primarily with scriptural authority, whether *shruti* or *smrti*. The study and analysis of the scripture plays an important role in Hinduism, and the concern with *shabda* led early on to extensive Hindu scholarship on the nature and structure of language. Religious knowledge is derived primarily from *shabda*.[50]

4. Analogical reasoning, or *upamana*, has a higher status in Hindu philosophical thought than it does in the West. Analogies are, in essence, comparisons of two things that share certain common characteristics, and suggest that because they share those characteristics, they are likely to share other characteristics as well. Basically, analogy in the West is used as a possible source for hypotheses, whereas in Hindu thought it is considered a possible source of knowledge.[51]

5. *Arthapatti*, or hypothetical supposition, is also sometimes called the "method of implication." It involves identifying a missing premise in a dilemma or argument. Thus, if a person is fasting during the day, but nonetheless is gaining weight, one would be led to suspect that he is eating at night.[52]

6. The last of the six methods of knowing is called *abhava*, or negation, and is, in a way, a sort of extension of *pratyaksha*, or sense perception. The idea here is that "non-existence ... can be known by non-cognition."[53] In other words, the fact that I do not sense *x* around me can be taken to be evidence for the non-existence of *x* in my immediate vicinity.

Beyond its epistemological concerns, traditional Hindu educational thought emphasizes the need to think of the individual apart from his or her social context. As Radha Mookerji explained in his monumental work *Ancient Indian Education*:

Hindu thought takes up the position that the individual as conceived in the context of social life, and the laws of the State, is essentially a psychological and biological fact. But the individual, in order that his ultimate datum of personality may be understood, must be viewed from other perspectives, those of his elemental nature, his potentiality for growth and transformation, his self-sufficiency, his capacity for effecting harmony between conflicting trends of impulses. Such a view of the self will necessarily take it out of its usual habitat. It means that the normal functions in terms of which the biological self ties itself to its material home must be checked so as to lay bare the core and kernel of one's being, the true self, the naked personality, stripped of the envelope with which it is shrouded by the accretions of passing impulses and emotions.[54]

In other words, the focus and purpose of education is on the spiritual growth and development of the individual, rather than on any particular instrumental goal or objective. However, the purpose of emphasizing the individual is in fact to move the learner beyond individuation, and toward emancipation. This involves moving away from the physical, material world around us, as well as beyond the limits of our own individual minds:

When the mind is withdrawn from the world of matter, and does not engage in individuation, Omniscience, the Knowledge of the Whole, dawns on it. Individuation shuts out omniscience. Individuation is concretion of the Mind. The Mind takes the form of the object in knowing it. It limits itself to the object, like the water rained down from the clouds limiting itself in a tank. Thus Individuation is Bondage. It limits vision, knowledge, omniscience.[55]

The goal of the traditional Hindu educational endeavor, then, will not be on the acquisition of bits of knowledge or on "objective knowledge," but rather on the knowledge of the totality of the universe. In short, rather than looking for the components of Knowledge, the point of education is to help us to find the source of Knowledge. We turn now to a discussion of how this search for Knowledge took place in traditional Hindu educational practice.

TRADITIONAL HINDU EDUCATIONAL PRACTICE

Given the very long history of Hinduism, it is hardly surprising that traditional Hindu educational thought has been manifested in practice in a variety of ways. Mookerji, for example, distinguished among the educational practices of the Rigvedic era, later Vedic educational practices, educational practices described in the Sutra literature, education in the time of Panini, and so on.[56] Although traditional Hindu education has, indeed, taken a variety of forms, there has also been an underlying unity that holds these different sets of practices together, and it is that underlying unity that is our focus here.

Hindu educational practice has focused on three distinct steps, discussed in detail in the *Upanishads*. Specifically, education is concerned with *shravana*, *manana*, and *nididhyasana*.[57] *Shravana* refers to the process of listening to one's teacher, and learning the oral tradition on which the Hindu religious tradition is largely based. It is *shravana* that provides the content base necessary for a person to become educated. *Shravana* is followed by *manana*, which involves reflection on that which is contained in the *shravana*. *Manana* is best understood as the process by which one begins to think about and reflect on the meaning of what one has learned, and is essentially an intellectual rather than a spiritual process. *Manana* is followed by *nididhyasana*, or "meditation," in which the goal is the realization of truth and the "consciousness of the One." Each in its own way, all of the different traditional Hindu educational practices follow this same general process of increasing spirituality.

Formal education in traditional Indian society was almost exclusively the domain of males, and of Brahmin males at that.[58] To be sure, exceptions did exist, and one can make a case from the extensive Hindu literature that learning was intended, at least in principle, to be a far more general endeavor. Sures Banerji, for instance, argued that, "In matters of education, the narrow barriers of the caste-system appeared to have crumbled down."[59] In terms of typical practice, however, this does not, in fact, seem to have been the case for much of Hindu history, when non-Brahmins and girls were generally excluded from the educational sphere.[60]

Brahmin education began when the boy was about 5 years old, with a ritual called *vidyarambha* (which means "knowledge beginning"). This involved learning the Sanskrit alphabet in a ceremonial way, and generally lasted about an hour.[61] The boy would then commence studying at home, reading and writing, practicing on simple texts, as well as learning basic arithmetic. At around the age of 8, the boy would undergo what is called the "sacred thread ceremony" (*upanayana*), which involved his new teacher whispering his *gayatri mantra* to him and beginning the more formal part of his education.[62]

Formal education then commenced, with the boy living in the home of his teacher. A teacher, or *guru*, would accept only a small number of students, thus ensuring that education remained the highly individualized undertaking that Hinduism required. The student, in this system,

> lived with the [teacher] as a member of his family, ministered to his needs, obeyed his *guru*'s commands implicitly and treated him with divine reverence. He wore his hair long, dressed simply, practised penances, and studied under the direction of the *guru*. He had to collect fuel and tend the sacred fires, look after the cattle, help in agriculture and attend to the running of the household. If the need arose he had to go begging on behalf of his master.[63]

At the age of 10, the boy would begin his study of the *Vedas* themselves, memorizing many texts and learning to perform the *samdhya* ("daily devotions") appropriately.[64] His education was also characterized by a commitment to sexual chastity, an important aspect of the vow of *brahmacharya* that the student had to take.[65] Adolescence, marked by a special ceremony called

keshanta ("the first shaving of the beard"), marked the end of formal education for many Brahmins.[66] For those who continued, study expanded and in-
tensified, and could last for as long as an additional 15 years.

Much traditional Hindu education took place as described above, in
ashramas run by individual teachers. As Mookerji noted, "the vital principle of
ancient Indian education was that of individual and intimate relationship between pupils and their teachers, as members of the same family, living in a
common home, the home of the teacher functioning as the school.... "[67] However, there were also notable educational institutions of a more formal, institution type in traditional Hindu society, often tied to temples and monasteries.[68]
Still, even in these more institutional settings, the focus of traditional Hindu
education was always on the individual and his personal spiritual growth.

SUMMARY

The Hindu educational tradition is both one of the oldest and one of the richest
in the world. It has functioned for millennia, in different forms, providing an education that emphasized the individual and his spiritual needs, even as it taught
that only by renouncing the self could one achieve unity with the whole of the
universe. Although sharing common roots with the West in the very distant past
(as reflected in the ties of the Sanskrit language to other Indo-European languages), Hinduism presents us with a very different view of both the *educated
person* and of the purposes of education than those with which most of us in the
West are most familiar and comfortable.[69] Furthermore, as we see in the next
part of this chapter, Hinduism also provides the foundation upon which Buddhism and, indeed, several other religious traditions, are based. In short, it is undoubtedly a good idea for us to reflect on the lessons that we can learn from the
wisdom of Hinduism and its educational tradition.

THE BUDDHIST TRADITION

Buddhism emerged in India during the period between the 7th and 5th centuries B.C.E., which was a time of intense intellectual ferment in the subcontinent.[70] Developing in the context of classical Hinduism, Buddhism shared
many common ideas and themes with Hinduism, even as it seems to have di-
verged from the Hindu tradition in significant ways.[71] Nonetheless, the distinction between Hinduism and Buddhism is often a difficult one to articulate
in practice. As Ananda Coomaraswamy wrote in his comparative study of the
two religions:

> The more superficially one studies Buddhism, the more it seems to differ from
> the Brahmanism in which it originated; the more profound our study, the more
> difficult it becomes to distinguish Buddhism from Brahmanism, or to say in what
> respects, if any, Buddhism is really unorthodox. The outstanding distinction lies

in the fact that Buddhist doctrine is propounded by an apparently historical founder.... Beyond this there are only broad distinctions of emphasis.[72]

As this passage suggests, the obvious starting point in trying to understand Buddhism is with its founder, the Buddha ("the Awakened One"). As Noble Ross Reat wrote in his book *Buddhism: A History:*

> Given his enormous historical significance, remarkably few Westerners are even vaguely acquainted with the Buddha or the religion he founded.... In terms of influence upon human history, the Buddha can be compared with only two historical individuals: Jesus and Muhammad, the founders of Christianity and Islam. As with Jesus and Muhammad, little is known of the early life of the Buddha, but in his later years as a teacher he stands out as one of the first figures ever to be recorded in history as a real, recognizable human personality rather than as a two-dimensional character in a mythologized narrative. In this sense, he is comparable to the Greek philosopher Socrates (fifth century B.C.E.) and to some of the figures in the *Hebrew Bible* or *Old Testament.*[73]

The man who became the Buddha was born in the village of Lumbini, in what is today Southern Nepal, and the most common dates for his life are 563 to 483 B.C.E. (though Chinese sources give the significantly later dates of roughly 445 to 365 B.C.E.).[74] His name was Siddhattha Gotama (also commonly written Gautama) and, as a prince, he was born into a life of privilege and comfort. He was a sensitive youth, concerned about human suffering around him, and so gave up his privileged life to become a wandering "seeker of truth." He studied meditation, and ultimately, at the age of 35, achieved what is known in Buddhism as the "Great Enlightenment" one night while sitting under the Bodhi tree (the "tree of enlightenment").[75] The "awakening" achieved by the Buddha, which can be achieved by others as well, is both difficult to attain and to describe. As Reat noted, "Buddhist doctrine emphasizes that the specific content of the Buddha's experience on the night of enlightenment—or the equivalent experience of an *arahat* [one who has achieved the awakening]—can never be conveyed by mere words."[76] In general terms, however, the Buddha is said to have experienced what are called the "three knowledges": "remembrance of his past rebirths in detail, ability to discern the past and future rebirths of other beings, and knowledge that he himself was free of all faults and illusions and would therefore never be reborn again. The 'third knowledge' is synonymous with the realization of nirvana."[77]

Although originating in India, Buddhism spread through Asia and has come to be identified more with other countries than with India itself. Buddhism remains the dominant religious tradition in Tibet, Sri Lanka, and Thailand, and has had a powerful impact both culturally and religiously in a number of other societies, including those of China, Korea, and Japan.[78] There are, as a consequence, many varieties and forms of Buddhism that coexist, both with each other and with other religious traditions.[79] As Malcolm Eckel noted:

If you have never thought of religion without thinking of God, or if you think that a religion has to have clear boundaries that separate insiders from outsiders, you will be intrigued and challenged by your encounter with Buddhism. For over two thousand years in Asia, and more recently in Europe and North America, the Buddhist tradition has brought joy, consolation, and meaning to human life without affirming the existence of a personal God, and it has found ways to exist side by side with other religious traditions without many of the great conflicts that have plagued religious life in the West.[80]

We turn now to an exploration of this intriguing and challenging religious tradition, focusing on the two major streams of Buddhism—Theravada and Mahayana Buddhism—and then moving on to a discussion of traditional Buddhist educational thought and practice.

AN OVERVIEW OF BUDDHISM

The core of Buddhism is expressed in what is called the *Triple Refuge* (*trisharana*), which is the basic "profession of faith" for the Buddhist. Every Buddhist recites the Triple Refuge (which is also sometimes called the *Three Jewels* or the *Three Treasures*) daily, and one becomes a Buddhist by reciting it three times. The Triple Refuge is as follows: "I go to refuge to the Buddha; I go for refuge to the Doctrine (*Dharma*); I go for refuge to the community (*Sangha*)."[81] Included in the Triple Refuge, then, are the place of the Buddha himself, the place of his teachings, and the role of the Buddhist community. We have already briefly discussed the Buddha, and so we now turn to the teachings of Buddhism.

Buddhism is, at its core, arguably less concerned with metaphysical and theological matters than with psychological ones.[82] The teachings of the Buddha are all basically concerned with human suffering and achieving freedom from that suffering.[83] Summarized in the Four Noble Truths, which are common to all of the different types of Buddhism, the teachings of the Buddha include the ideas that:

1. Human life inevitably involves suffering (*dukkha*),
2. Suffering arises from our desires (*samudaya*),
3. There is a state of being in which there is no suffering (*nirodha*), and
4. There is a way to achieve this state of being (*marga*).[84]

The way to achieve this state of being free from suffering is a systematic approach taught by the Buddha called the *Eightfold Path of Liberation*. As Mary Pat Fisher explained, "The Eightfold Path offers ways to burn up all past demerits, avoid accumulating new demerits, and build up merit for a favorable rebirth. Perfection of the path means final escape from the cycle of death and rebirth, into the peace of Nirvana."[85] The eight factors that comprise the Eightfold Path can be divided into three broad categories (known as *khandha*, or *pillars*), dealing respectively with wisdom (*panna*), ethics (*sila*), and meditation (*samadhi*).[86] The particular factors included in each of these three broad categories are discussed briefly next.

Wisdom

The factors included in this category include right understanding (*samma-ditthi*) and right intention (*samma-sankappa*). Right understanding refers to making sense of the world and questioning one's assumptions, within the framework provided by the Four Noble Truths. Right intention in essence involves the application of right understanding in one's life, and constitutes the core of Buddhist morality. Specifically, right intention includes renunciation (*nekkhama*), benevolence (*avyapada*), and nonviolence (*avihimsa*).[87]

Ethics

This category is concerned with conduct and the rules that underlie appropriate conduct. Taken as a whole, they seek to ensure that one's conduct is harmful neither to oneself nor to others. Specifically, the factors included here are right speech (*samma-vacha*), right action (*samma-kammanta*), and right livelihood (*samma-ajiva*). Right speech focuses on the need to avoid gossip, lying, slander, and other kinds of idle or hurtful language. Right action involves what are known as the Five Precepts (*sikkha-pada*) in Buddhism, which include the avoidance of violence toward any living thing, stealing, harmful speech, sexual misconduct, and abuse of drugs and alcohol.[88] Right livelihood refers to the need to ensure that one's way of earning a living in no way violates any of the Five Precepts.[89]

Meditation

The final three factors in the Eightfold Path are right effort (*samma-yayama*), right self-possession or mindfulness (*samma-sati*), and right meditation (*samma-samadhi*). These three factors are all very closely related, and basically involved "the cultivation of the wholesome (*kusala*) and rejection of the unwholesome (*akusala*)." They involve continuous striving to reject unwholesome states of mind, and to develop the mental quietness that leads to liberation.[90]

The ultimate goal of the Eightfold Path, as suggested here, is to avoid the ongoing cycle of death and rebirth, and to achieve Nirvana. This is done by leading a passion-free existence that has no karmic consequences, as is suggested by the term *Nirvana* itself, which actually refers to "the extinguishing of a flame from lack of fuel."[91]

For Westerners, one of the more puzzling aspects of Buddhism is its lack of concern for or interest in a personal God. Melford Spiro, for example, in his book *Buddhism and Society*, commented that:

Buddhism is a religion without a God. Just as the body has no soul which guides and directs its action, so the universe has no Creator who brought it into being, who guides its course, or who presides over the destiny of man. More important, there is no Being—no savior God—to whom man can turn for salvation. Each man, as it were, must save himself.[92]

It is important to note that the Buddha did not actually deny the existence of God. Rather, the Buddha argued that: "curiosity about such matters was like a man who, upon being wounded by a poisoned arrow, refused to have it pulled out until he was told the caste and origin of his assailant, his name, his height, the color of his skin, and all details about the bow and arrow. In the meantime, he died."[93] In other words, for Buddhism "speculations concerning the origin of the Universe are held to be immaterial.... They are not merely a waste of time but they may also postpone deliverance from suffering by engendering ill-will in oneself and in others."[94] In short, Buddhism is best understood simply as a "nontheistic" religion which does not, like other religions, presuppose the existence of a personal God.[95] Furthermore, while the monotheistic religions with which most of us are most familiar identify God with supreme good, for Buddhism it is emptiness—that is, the absence of both good and evil—that is the ultimate goal.[96] As Masao Abe explained:

[Buddhism] overcomes all duality completely and attains a nondualistic position. This means that both ends of duality, for instance good and evil, are equally overcome through the double negation of the two ends—i.e., good and evil. This double negation of both ends of duality does not entail the supreme good, but that which is neither good nor evil. This is the reason why in Buddhism ultimate reality is not God as the supreme good, but Emptiness, which is neither good nor evil.... Buddhism *completely* overcomes the duality of value judgment in the axiological dimension through the negation of negation, and thus reaches the religious dimension, which is entirely free from even the notion of absolute good.[97]

For the most part, the beliefs discussed thus far are common to all Buddhists. Within Buddhism, however, there coexist a number of different schools of thought. The two most important of these schools of thought are those of Theravada Buddhism and Mahayana Buddhism. The distinction between Theravada Buddhism and Mahayana Buddhism is one of both geography and emphasis. *Theravada Buddhism*, which emphasizes the original Buddhist scriptural tradition (hence its name, which means "Teaching of the Elders"), is sometimes called the Southern School since it is found primarily in the south Asian countries (Sri Lanka, Myanmar, Thailand, Kampuchea, and Laos). *Mahayana Buddhism* is, on the other hand, known as the Northern School, and is the kind of Buddhism found in Nepal, Tibet, China, Korea, Mongolia and Japan. Theravada Buddhism is a somewhat more austere kind of Buddhism and involves an emphasis not only on the early Buddhist scriptures, but also on the monastic life, while Mahayana Buddhism accepts a wider variety of scriptural traditions and gives greater freedom in terms of devotional and metaphysical beliefs and practices than does Theravada Buddhism, which tends to be more uniform.[98] At heart, however, there is an essential unity in Buddhism, as Edward Conze explained:

> Throughout its history, Buddhism has the unity of an *organism*, in that each new development takes place in continuity from the previous one. Nothing could look more different from a tadpole than a frog, and yet they are stages of the same animal, and evolve continuously from each other. The Buddhist capacity for metamorphosis must astound those who only see the end-products separated by long intervals of time, as different as chrysalis and butterfly. In fact they are connected by many gradations, which lead from one to the other, and which only close study can detect. There is in Buddhism really no innovation, but what seems so is in fact a subtle adaptation of pre-existing ideas.[99]

This essential unity includes not only Theravada Buddhism and Mahayana Buddhism, but also Tibetan Buddhism (which is actually a distinctive branch of Mahayana Buddhism) and Zen Buddhism, as well as the many different varieties of each that have developed in different social and cultural contexts.[100] With this brief introduction to Buddhism in mind, we turn now to a discussion of the educational thought and practice associated with Buddhism.

TRADITIONAL BUDDHIST EDUCATIONAL THOUGHT AND PRACTICE

Education in traditional Buddhism, at least in a formal sense, existed almost exclusively within the context of the monastery, both in terms of secular and religious education. As Radha Mookerji noted in his book *Ancient Indian Education*:

> The history of the Buddhist system of education is practically that of the Buddhist Order or *Sangha*. Buddhist education and learning centred round monasteries.... The Buddhist world did not offer any educational opportunities apart from or independently of its monasteries. All education, sacred as well as secular, was in the hands of the monks. They had the monopoly of learning and the leisure to impart it.[101]

In other words, our discussion of traditional Buddhist educational thought and practice brings us back to the final element of the Triple Refuge: the religious (i.e., monastic) community. As Heinrich Dumoulin observed:

> Taking refuge in the *sangha* is an essential co-condition of the other two refuges. From its beginnings, the Buddhist religion confronts us as a communal, and specifically as a monastic formation.... Though Buddhism has not yet developed a theology of community, it is clear that Buddhist faith has an essential communal dimension.[102]

The fact that traditional education was controlled by the *sangha*, however, in no way means that it was jealously guarded or hidden; indeed, quite the reverse is the case. Buddhist monasteries are not separate from the surrounding world. Rather, they are closely tied to the surrounding community in a sort of symbiotic relationship, and monasteries are commonly the center of village life.[103] Furthermore, at least in Theravadin societies, it is quite common for young men to take what are essentially temporary vows of monkhood (during, for instance, the rainy season when they are not required for agricultural work).[104]

A number of general themes characterized traditional Buddhist educational practice. Traditional Buddhist education was based on the close, intimate relationship that existed between the student and his teacher, whom he was to serve in much the same way as was expected in Vedic education. The relationship between student and teacher was a reciprocal one, however, and while the obligations of the student to the teacher were substantial, so too were the obligations of the teacher to the student.[105] All students observed the two fundamental principles that demarcate monastic life from that of the laity: celibacy and poverty.[106] Instruction was primarily oral, and was based on a knowledge of the Buddhist scriptural tradition, although an introduction to basic literacy was also provided.

The focus of education was on far more than mere memorization of texts, however. Debate played a central role in the educational process in traditional Buddhism. As Mookerji argued, "Buddhist education made dialectic skill and ability in argumentation a most important part of intellectual equipment essential to leadership."[107] The importance of such skill is made clear in a number of written texts in the Buddhist tradition, one of which, composed around the year 400 C.E., contains a detailed discussion of the subject of debate, the place in which debate should take place, the means by which a debate should be conducted, the qualifications of the debaters, the points of defeat in a debate, the fitness or appropriateness of a debate, and finally, the need for self-confidence in the debater.[108] It is interesting to note here that in a comparative study of traditional and contemporary education in Tibet, David Eckel observed that:

> In the traditional monastery, even with its emphasis on memorization and rote learning, students were required from an early age to defend what they had learned in formal debate. The debating hall was a lonely place, where rank and authority were no help. A student or teacher had to be able to defend his understanding before the whole assembly. It is hard to picture a 12-year-old monk standing up in a doctoral examination to question a scholar more than twice his age and still think of the traditional system as fostering only the values of dependence and submission. The irony of the Tibetan transition to modern styles of education is that it endangers not only the sense of dependence and respect for tradition, but the formal means for developing a sense of self-reliance and autonomy.[109]

Traditional Buddhist education, in short, involved what would today be called basic schooling for young boys, as well as more advanced education for monks (including a noteworthy university level educational system, as we shall see).[110] It did not, however, for the most part concern itself with the educational needs of girls and women and, although there were notable exceptions (including female monasteries where women were indeed well educated), traditional Buddhism paid relatively little attention to females' education.[111]

HIGHER EDUCATION IN ANCIENT INDIA

What we would today call university education, or at least something roughly equivalent to our understanding of higher education, existed in ancient India at least as early as the 7th century B.C.E. and probably much earlier. Indeed, by the 7th century B.C.E., Taxila (Takshasila) had already achieved considerable fame as a center of advanced learning. It drew scholars and students from throughout India, and was familiar to Greeks from the time of Alexander the Great.[112] Taxila never existed as a single institution in the way a modern university does; rather, it was an educational center where scholars and students met, studied, and interacted. Individuals could study a wide range of disciplines, among them medicine (and surgery), archery and the military arts, the Vedas and Vendanta philosophy, grammar, astronomy and astrology, accounting, commerce, agriculture, music, dancing, painting, magic, snake-charming, and even elephant-lore.[113]

Another well-known center of higher education in ancient India was Banaras, a seat of both Hindu and Buddhist learning that, like Taxila, consisted not of a single institution but rather functioned as an informal collection of masters, each teaching his own students. Banaras was described by one European visitor as the "Athens of India," which gives one some sense of its intellectual vitality. Unlike Taxila, which ceased functioning as an educational center around the 3rd century C.E., Banaras continued to be a significant intellectual center, and was in fact the center of the 16th—17th-century Hindu intellectual revival in northern India.[114]

Although there was extensive overlap between Hindu and Buddhist higher education and a great deal of intellectual and scholarly interaction which enriched both traditions, particular settings tended to be dominated by one or the other religion.[115] The most famous of the Buddhist centers of higher education in ancient India was Nalanda, which was founded at some point in mid-fifth century C.E. Nalanda was, unlike Taxila and Banaras, a single complex institution that consisted of a large campus, including large public halls for lectures, smaller classrooms, and a number of monasteries that functioned as dormitories for the students studying at Nalanda. The University also possessed three large libraries, and an astronomical observatory. An intellectual stronghold for Mahayana Buddhism, the University curriculum included the Vedas, the Upanishads, Jainism, grammar, logic, metaphysics and literature, and drew students and teachers from throughout southeast Asia. At its peak, the University had some 8,500 students and 1,500 teachers, and, perhaps most interestingly, "out of the income derived from its estates the University provided all its students with clothes, food, bedding and medicines."[116]

CONCLUSION

Given the highly decentralized nature of Buddhist institutions, as well as the tolerance for diversity within the Buddhist tradition, it is hardly surprising that traditional Buddhist education took somewhat different forms in different Buddhist societies. What is remarkable is the degree of uniformity that in fact seems to have existed on a number of important points. Perhaps most interesting in this regard is the role of the monastery as the sole educational institution in Buddhist societies and the reliance on the monasteries for both secular and religious education.[117] Also of significance here has been the emphasis on the individual teacher and the relationship between the teacher and the student—an emphasis that is to some extent indicated in the *Dhammapada*, in which we read the prescription that, "An intelligent man attends on a wise person."[118] Furthermore, it is clear that traditional Buddhist educational thought and practice had a powerful impact on the societies in which they existed, in many instances providing a cultural and intellectual base for the society concerned. This was, for instance, the case in Japan, as B. H. Chamberlain noted: "All education was for centuries in Buddhist hands, Buddhism introduced art, introduced medicine, moulded the folklore of the country, created its dramatic poetry, deeply influenced politics and every sphere of social and intellectual activity. In a word, Buddhism was the teacher under whose instruction the nation grew up."[119]

In short, traditional Buddhist educational thought and practice served a wide array of social, cultural, and spiritual functions as well as educational ones successfully, and did so in ways generally accepted in various Buddhist societies for centuries. This alone would merit our attention.

QUESTIONS FOR REFLECTION AND DISCUSSION

1. Given your understanding of the difference between *schooling* and *education*, do you think that the traditional Hindu educational practice of placing students in the homes of their teachers, where they become essentially part of the teacher's household, is an example of *schooling* or *education*? Why?
2. To a very great extent, the whole point of Hindu education is spiritual. What are the advantages of such a focus in education? What are the disadvantages? How does this emphasis on spirituality differ from the approaches to education found in contemporary American society?
3. It was suggested in this chapter that an oral tradition played an important role in traditional Hindu educational thought and practice, and yet,

the Hindu tradition is very much text-based. How can this seeming con-
tradiction be reconciled?

4. The six "methods of knowing" that are discussed in this chapter provide
us with an understanding of Hindu epistemology. In what ways, and to
what extent, do these "methods of knowing" differ from the "scientific
method"?

5. Traditional Hindu education is based on the student's progress through
three stages, *shravana, manana,* and *nididhyasana.* Are these stages reflected at all in contemporary American public schooling? What lessons
can be learned by considering these stages as we examine public schooling in our society?

6. The role of the *sangha* in traditional Buddhist education presents an interesting parallel to that of the monastery in medieval Europe. In what
ways are the educational undertakings of these two kinds of religious
communities similar, and in what ways do they differ? How can the similarities, and the differences, be explained?

7. Explain the educational significance of each of the three components of
the Triple Refuge. How do these three components relate to one another, and what are the social and educational implications of these relationships?

8. If the spiritual goal of Buddhism is "emptiness," then what purpose does
education serve? Why is education needed in the quest for Nirvana?

9. Given your own understanding of *religion,* was traditional Buddhist education a religious education? Was it a spiritual education? What, in your
view, is the difference between these two kinds of education?

10. What, in your view, were the strengths of traditional Buddhist education? What were its weaknesses? Can you identify any lessons from the
study of traditional Buddhist education for contemporary schooling in
our own society?

RECOMMENDED FURTHER READINGS

In terms of general introductions to Hinduism, some of the better works cur-
rently available are Stephen Cross, *The Elements of Hinduism* (Shaftsbury,
Dorset: Element, 1994); A. L. Herman, *A Brief Introduction to Hinduism: Re-
ligion, Philosophy, and Ways of Liberation* (Boulder, CO: Westview Press,
1991); and Ed Viswanathan, *Am I a Hindu? The Hinduism Primer* (San Francisco: Halo Books, 1992). Among the Hindu texts available in translation are
Juan Mascaró, trans., *The Upanishads* (Harmondsworth: Penguin, 1965);
Wendy Doniger O'Flaherty, trans., *The Rig Veda: An Anthology*
(Harmondsworth: Penguin, 1981); and S. Radhkrishnan (ed.), *The Principal
Upanishads* (New Delhi: Indus, 1994). In addition, the *Bhagavad Gita,* which
is considered to be one of the more accessible and readable Hindu texts, is
widely available in a number of translations. A very readable collection of short
essays on contemporary Hinduism is provided in Eleanor Zelliot and Maxine

Bernsten (eds.), *The Experience of Hinduism* (Albany: State University of New York Press, 1988).

Among the better general introductions to Buddhism that are readily available are Heinrich Dumoulin's *Understanding Buddhism: Key Themes* (New York: Weatherhill, 1994); Nolan Pliny Jacobson's *Understanding Buddhism* (Carbondale, IL: Southern Illinois University Press, 1986); and Nancy Wilson Ross' *Buddhism: A Way of Life and Thought* (New York: Vintage, 1980). An especially powerful contemporary work is Thich Nhat Hanh's *Old Path White Clouds: Walking in the Footsteps of the Buddah* (Berkeley, CA: Parallax, 1991). Also of considerable value is Eric Cheetham, *Fundamentals of Mainstream Buddhism* (Boston: Charles E. Tuttle, 1994). For an interesting and insightful personal account, see Tenzin Gyatso, *Freedom in Exile: The Autobiography of the Dalai Lama* (New York: Harper Perennial, 1990). Finally, there is a plethora of works readily available that deal explicitly with Zen Buddhism. Good basic introductions to Zen Buddhism include Kazuaki Tanahashi and Tensho David Schneider, *Essential Zen* (San Francisco: HarperCollins, 1994); David Scott and Tony Doubleday, *The Elements of Zen* (Shaftesbury, Dorset: Element, 1992).

NOTES

1. See Harold G. Coward (ed.), *Modern Indian Responses to Religious Pluralism* (Albany: State University of New York Press, 1987); Friedhelm Hardy, *The Religious Culture of India: Power, Love and Wisdom* (Cambridge, England: Cambridge University Press, 1994); Donald Lopez (ed.), *Religions of India in Practice* (Princeton, NJ: Princeton University Press, 1995). Although Jainism is not discussed in this book, it is a fascinating religious tradition well worth examination. See Subramania Gopalan, *Outlines of Jainism* (New York: Halsted, 1973); Paul Dundas, *The Jains* (London: Routledge, 1992); Caroline Humphrey and James Laidlaw, *The Archetypal Actions of Ritual: A Theory of Ritual Illustrated by the Jain Rite of Worshop* (Oxford, England: Clarendon Press, 1994).

2. Klaus Klostermaier, *A Survey of Hinduism* (Albany: State University of New York Press, 1989), 30–31; Madeleine Biardeau, *L'Hindouisme: Anthropologie d'une civilization* (Paris: Flammarion, 1981).

3. Mary Pat Fisher, *Living Religions*, 2nd ed. (Englewood Cliffs, NJ: Prentice Hall, 1994), 64–66.

4. Klostermaier noted that, "The very name *Hinduism* owes its origin to chance; foreigners ... extended the name of the province of Sindh to the whole country lying across the Indus river and simply called all its inhabitants *Hindus* and their religion *Hinduism*." See Klostermaier, *A Survey of Hinduism*, 31.

5. Klostermaier, *A Survey of Hinduism*, 31; see also Arvind Sharma, "Hinduism," in Arvind Sharma (ed.), *Our Religions: The Seven World Religions Introduced By Preeminent Scholars From Each Tradition* (San Francisco: Harper,

1993), 36–38; Robert C. Zaehner, *Hinduism* (London: Oxford University Press, 1962), 19–22; David Knipe, *Hinduism* (San Francisco: Harper, 1991), 17–25; K. M. Sen, *Hinduism* (Harmondsworth: Penguin, 1961), 17–21; David Kinsley, *Hinduism: A Cultural Perspective*, 2nd ed. (Englewood Cliffs, NJ: Prentice Hall, 1993), 11–25.

6. Klostermaier, *A Survey of Hinduism*, 45.

7. Fisher, *Living Religions*, 62; Zaehner, *Hinduism*, 2–4. Especially useful here is Gavin Flood, *An Introduction to Hinduism* (Cambridge, England: Cambridge University Press, 1996), 51–74.

8. Klostermaier, *A Survey of Hinduism*, 31.

9. Fisher, *Living Religions*, 62.

10. Troy Organ, *The Hindu Quest for the Perfection of Man* (Athens, OH: Ohio University Press, 1970), 4.

11. Stephen Cross, *The Elements of Hinduism* (Shaftesbury, Dorset: Element, 1994), 3. See also A. K. Banerjee, *Discourses on Hindu Spiritual Culture* (Delhi: S. Chand & Co., 1967), 3–4.

12. David Kinsley, *Hinduism: A Cultural Perspective*, 2nd ed. (Englewood Cliffs, NJ: Prentice Hall, 1993), 6.

13. Klostermaier, *A Survey of Hinduism*, 40–41.

14. Sharma, "Hinduism," 6.

15. Sharma, "Hinduism," 7–11.

16. Sharma, "Hinduism," 11.

17. Cross, *The Elements of Hinduism*, 3–4; see also Sharma, "Hinduism," 26–27.

18. Klostermaier, *A Survey of Hinduism*, 61.

19. Zaehner, *Hinduism*, 11–13.

20. Fisher, *Living Religions*, 66.

21. Colin Renfrew, *Archaeology and Language: The Puzzle of Indo-European Origins* (Cambridge, England: Cambridge University Press, 1987), 178–183.

22. Klostermaier, *A Survey of Hinduism*, 26; Cross, *The Elements of Hinduism*, 16–17.

23. Klostermaier, *A Survey of Hinduism*, 26; Cross, *The Elements of Hinduism*, 17.

24. Klostermaier, *A Survey of Hinduism*, 27; Sharma, "Hinduism," 26–27.

25. Sharma, "Hinduism," 27.

26. There is actually a third level of Hindu scripture as well, called *Itihasas*, which are essentially histories of individuals who, by virtue of the sanctity of their lives, have come to be seen as incarnations of God. Two works in particular are generally classified as *Itihasas*: the *Ramayana* ("The Deeds of Rama") and the *Mahabharata*, of which the *Bhagavadgita* is a part. See Sharma, "Hinduism," 29–30.

27. Sharma, "Hinduism," 27.

28. Sharma, "Hinduism," 27.

29. Klostermaier, *A Survey of Hinduism*, 67.

30. Gerald Larson, "Hinduism in India and in America," in Jacob Neusner (ed.), *World Religions in America* (Louisville, KY: Westminster/John Knox Press, 1994), 185–186.

31. Zaehner, *Hinduism*, 15–16.

32. Cross, *The Elements of Hinduism*, 12.

33. Victoria Fromkin and Robert Rodman, *An Introduction to Language*, 2nd ed. (New York: Holt, Rinehart and Winston, 1978), 295–296; Leonard Bloomfield, "Language," in Oscar L. Chavarria-Aguilar (ed.), *Traditional India* (Englewood Cliffs, NJ: Prentice Hall, 1964), 112–113; Robert H. Robins, *A Short History of Linguistics*, 2nd ed. (London: Longman, 1979), 134–135. Also of interest here is Winfred Lehmann, *Theoretical Bases of Indo-European Linguistics* (London: Routledge, 1993).

34. Quoted in Renfrew, *Archaeology and Language*, 9.

35. Quoted in Larson, "Hinduism in India and in America," 197. For an extensive presentation of contemporary Hindu beliefs, see Satguru Sivaya Subramuniyaswami, *Dancing with Śiva: Hinduism's Contemporary Catechism* (Concord, CA: Himalayan Academy, 1993); also of interest here is Bansi Pandit, *The Hindu Mind: Fundamentals of Hindu Religion and Philosophy for All Ages*, 2nd ed. (Glen Ellyn, IL: B & V Enterprises, 1993).

36. Fisher, *Living Religions*, 68; Cross, *The Elements of Hinduism*, 15–16; Biardeau, *L'Hindouisme*.

37. Cross, *The Elements of Hinduism*, 16; see also Sen, *Hinduism*, 27–31.

38. Cross, *The Elements of Hinduism*, 16; see also Sen, *Hinduism*, 27–31.

39. Cross, *The Elements of Hinduism*, 16; see also Sen, *Hinduism*, 27–31.

40. Larson, "Hinduism in India and in America," 189; Sharma, "Hinduism," 24; Biardeau, *L'Hindouisme*.

41. Larson, "Hinduism in India and in America," 189; Sharma, "Hinduism," 24; Biardeau, *L'Hindouisme*; Kinsley, *Hinduism: A Cultural Perspective*, 84–96.

42. Larson, "Hinduism in India and in America," 189. See also Patrick Olivelle, *The Ashrama System: The History and Heurmeneutics of a Religious Institution* (New York: Oxford University Press, 1993).

43. See Organ, *The Hindu Quest for the Perfection of Man*.

44. Organ, *The Hindu Quest for the Perfection of Man*, 173.

45. Organ, *The Hindu Quest for the Perfection of Man*, 47.

46. Klostermaier, *A Survey of Hinduism*, 69–70.

47. Organ, *The Hindu Quest for the Perfection of Man*, 47.

48. Organ, *The Hindu Quest for the Perfection of Man*, 48.

49. Organ, *The Hindu Quest for the Perfection of Man*, 48–49.

50. Klostermaier, *A Survey of Hinduism*, 69–70.

51. Organ, *The Hindu Quest for the Perfection of Man*, 49.

52. Organ, *The Hindu Quest for the Perfection of Man*, 49.

53. Organ, *The Hindu Quest for the Perfection of Man*, 50.

54. Radha Mookerji, *Ancient Indian Education* (Delhi: Motilal Banarsidass, 1969), xxiii.

55. Mookerji, *Ancient Indian Education*, xxiii–xxiv.

56. Mookerji, *Ancient Indian Education*, xxiii–xxiv.

57. Mookerji, *Ancient Indian Education*, xxxi–xxxiii.

58. Benjamin Walker, *The Hindu World: An Encyclopedic Survey of Hinduism* (New York: Praeger, 1968), vol. 1, 320.

59. Sures Banerji, *Society in Ancient India: Evolution Since the Vedic Times Based on Sanskrit, Pali, Prakrit and Other Classical Sources* (New Delhi: D. K. Printworld, 1993), 228–229.

60. For discussions of the role and place of women in Hindu society, see Julia Leslie (ed.), *Roles and Rituals for Hindu Women* (Rutherford, NJ: Fairleigh Dickinson University Press, 1991). Also of interest here are Christopher J. Fuller, *The Camphor Flame: Popular Hinduism and Society in India* (Princeton, NJ: Princeton University Press, 1992), 182–203; Arthur L. Basham, *The Origins and Development of Classical Hinduism* (Boston: Beacon Press, 1989), 104–106.

61. Walker, *The Hindu World*, 320; Mookerji, *Ancient Indian Education*, 173.

62. Mookerji, *Ancient Indian Education*, 174–175; see also David Miller and Dorothy Wertz, *Hindu Monastic Life and the Monks and Monasteries of Bhubaneswar* (Montreal: McGill-Queen's University Press, 1976), 3.

63. Walker, *The Hindu World*, 320–321.

64. Walker, *The Hindu World*, 321.

65. Walker, *The Hindu World*, 321.

66. Walker, *The Hindu World*, 321.

67. Mookerji, *Ancient Indian Education*, 366.

68. See Mookerji, *Ancient Indian Education*, 366–373; Walker, *The Hindu World*, 322.

69. See Sushila Raval, *Basic Education in Modern India: A Critique of Gandhian Educational Philosophy* (M.A. thesis, The American University, Washington, D.C., 1958), 2–8.

70. William T. de Bary (ed.), *The Buddhist Tradition in India, China and Japan* (New York: Modern Library, 1969), 3.

71. See, for example, Amamda Coomaraswamy, *Hinduism and Buddhism* (Westport, CT: Greenwood, 1971); Roderick Hindery, *Comparative Ethics in Hindu and Buddhist Traditions* (Delhi: Motilal Banarsidass, 1978); Pandit, *The Hindu Mind*, 85–86.

72. Coomaraswamy, *Hinduism and Buddhism*, 45.

73. Noble Ross Reat, *Buddhism: A History* (Berkeley: Asian Humanities Press, 1994), 1.

74. Reat, *Buddhism*, 1–2; see also Fisher, *Living Religions*, 113.

75. See David Kalupahana, *A History of Buddhist Philosophy: Continuities and Discontinuities* (Honolulu: University of Hawaii Press, 1992), 22–29; Fisher, *Living Religions*, 114.

76. Reat, *Buddhism*, 12.

77. Reat, *Buddhism*, 12.

78. Malcolm Eckel, "Buddhism in the World and in America," in Jacob Neusner (ed.), *World Religions in America: An Introduction* (Louisville, KY: Westminster/John Knox Press, 1994), 203.

79. See John Snelling, *The Buddhist Handbook: A Complete Guide to Buddhist Schools, Teaching, Practice, and History* (Rochester, VT: Inner Traditions, 1991), 103–189; Masao Abe, "Buddhism," in Arvind Sharma (ed.), *Our Religions* (San Francisco: Harper, 1993), 85–100.

80. Eckel, "Buddhism in the World and in America," 203.

81. Abe, "Buddhism," 73–74.

82. De Bary, *The Buddhist Tradition in India, China and Japan*, 9.

83. Melford Spiro, *Buddhism and Society* (New York: Harper & Row, 1970), 38–39; see also Hindery, *Comparative Ethics in Hindu and Buddhist Traditions*, 226–228; Mary Tucker and Duncan Williams (eds.), *Buddhism and Ecology: The Interconnection of Dharma and Deeds* (Cambridge, MA: Harvard University Press, 1977).

84. Fisher, *Living Religions*, 116; Abe, "Buddhism," 86; Heinrich Dumoulin, *Understanding Buddhism: Key Themes* (New York: Weatherhill, 1994), 21–24; Snelling, *The Buddhist Handbook*, 43–46.

85. Fisher, *Living Religions*, 117; Hardy, *The Religious Culture of India*, 179.

86. Reat, *Buddhism*, 40; see also Anthony K. Warder, *Indian Buddhism* (Delhi: Motilal Banarsidass, 1970), 100–106.

87. Reat, *Buddhism*, 40–41; Fisher, *Living Religions*, 117–118.

88. See Edward Conze, trans., *Buddhist Scriptures* (Harmondsworth: Penguin, 1959), 69–73.

89. Reat, *Buddhism*, 41–42; Fisher, *Living Religions*, 117.

90. Reat, *Buddhism*, 42; Fisher, *Living Religions*, 118–119.

91. Fisher, *Living Religions*, 120.

92. Spiro, *Buddhism and Society*, 7.

93. Fisher, *Living Religions*, 115.

94. Edward Conze, *Buddhism: Its Essence and Development* (New York: Harper & Row, 1975), 39.

95. Eckel, "Buddhism in the World and in America," 212.

96. The doctrine of emptiness (*sunyata*) is a very important one in Buddhist thought. In actuality, there are two distinct theories of emptiness in Buddhism, a moderate view and a more extreme view. See Kalupahana, *A History of Buddhist Philosophy*, 130–131; Reat, *Buddhism*, 56–58; Conze, *Buddhism*, 130–135.

97. Abe, "Buddhism," 119.

98. For discussions of the distinctions between Theravada Buddhism and Mahayana Buddhism, see de Bary, *The Buddhist Tradition in India, China and Japan*; Christmas Humphreys, *Buddhism: An Introduction and Guide* (Harmondsworth: Penguin, 1951).

99. Edward Conze, *A Short History of Buddhism* (Bombay: Chetana, 1960), xi–xii.

100. For Tibetan Buddhism, see Emil Schlagintweit, *Buddhism in Tibet*, 2nd ed. (London: Susil Gupta, 1968). For works that deal with Zen Buddhism, see David Scott and Tony Doubleday, *The Elements of Zen* (Shaftesbury, Dorset: Element, 1992); Daisetz Teitaro Suzuki, *An Introduction to Zen Buddhism* (New York: Philosophical Library, 1949); Trevor Leggett (ed.), *Zen and the Ways* (London: Routledge & Kegan Paul, 1978); Kenneth Kraft (ed.), *Zen: Tradition and Transition* (New York: Grove, 1988); Christopher Ives, *Zen Awakening and Society* (Honolulu: University of Hawaii Press, 1992).

101. Mookerji, *Ancient Indian Education*, 394.

102. Dumoulin, *Understanding Buddhism*, 56–57.

103. Abe, "Buddhism," 110.

104. Fisher, *Living Religions*, 123.

105. Mookerji, *Ancient Indian Education*, 403–405.

106. Mookerji, *Ancient Indian Education*, 409–412.

107. Mookerji, *Ancient Indian Education*, 454.

108. Mookerji, *Ancient Indian Education*, 454.

109. Quoted in Susan Pollak, *Ancient Buddhist Education (Papers from the Bernard Van Leer Foundation Project on Human Potential)* (Cambridge, MA: Harvard Graduate School of Education, 1983), 18. This publication, available through ERIC, is taken directly from Mookerji's earlier work.

110. Mookerji, *Ancient Indian Education*, 557–610.

111. Mookerji, *Ancient Indian Education*, 462–464. See also Diane Y. Paul, *Women in Buddhism: Images of the Feminine in the Mahayana Tradition* (Berkeley: University of California Press, 1985); Rita Gross, *Buddhism After Patriarchy: A Feminist History, Analysis and Reconstruction of Buddhism* (Albany: State University Press of New York, 1993); Lenore Friedman and Susan Moon (eds.), *Being Bodies: Buddhist Women on the Paradox of Embodiment* (Boston: Shambhala, 1997).

112. See Sunderrao R. Dongerkery, *University Education in India* (Bombay: Manaktalas, 1967), 2.

113. Dongerkery, *University Education in India*, 2.

114. Dongerkery, *University Education in India*, 2–3.

115. Dongerkery, *University Education in India*, 3.

116. Dongerkery, *University Education in India*, 4.

117. Pollak, *Ancient Buddhist Education*, 17.

118. Jaroslav Pelikan (ed.), *Sacred Writings, Volume 6: Buddhism, The Dhammapada* (New York: Quality Paperback Book Club, 1987), 23.

119. Quoted in Pollak, *Ancient Buddhist Education*, 16–17; see also Alicia Matsunaga, *The Buddhist Philosophy of Assimilation: The Historical Development of the Honji-Suijaku Theory* (Tokyo: Sophia University, 1969).

7

"Familiar Strangers":
The Case of the Rom

Gypsies have, throughout modern history, been synonymous in many peoples'
minds with colorfully painted caravans, exotic music and dance, trained animals, fortune-telling, and perhaps an enviably free "life on the road." They
have also been the ultimate "Other," maintaining their own language, customs,
values, social norms, and ethnic identity in virtually every setting in which they
have found themselves, and have all too commonly been seen as dishonest, im-
moral, criminal, and as a threat to society and "decent folk." As the "Other" in
every society in which they live, they have often suffered, and continue to experience, persecution and oppression. Although there are elements of truth in
the popular characterizations and stereotypes of Gypsies, there are also serious distortions that mask the complexity and diversity of a fascinating and re-
silient people. In this chapter, an overview of the history and complexity of the
Gypsy world is presented, its core cultural values explored, and the way in
which children in the community are raised and educated is discussed.

A WORD ABOUT LABELS

Terminology presents some incredible challenges in this chapter. The people
and communities with whom we are concerned share a common, distant origin
in India. Their ancestors arrived in Europe around the 14th century C.E. and
dispersed throughout the continent.[1] For the most part (although with some
notable exceptions), they share a number of characteristics, including speaking
varieties of a common language (Romani)[2] and, at least traditionally, often
maintaining a nomadic lifestyle. They are also, importantly, not only distinct
from but unrelated to other groups of nomadic peoples in Europe, such as the
Tinkers in Ireland and Scotland, and the Taters in Norway.[3]

The most common term to describe these people and communities historically has been "Gypsy" in English (roughly comparable to the use of "*Tsigane*"
in French, "*Ziguener*" in German, "*gitano*" in Spanish, etc.). Although etymo-
logically based on the mistaken notion that the Gypsies originated in Egypt,

this term (which is also sometimes perceived to be pejorative) does have the advantage of emphasizing the commonality of an internally very diverse group and is widely used not only in the scholarly literature but also among many Gypsies themselves to refer to the generic communal group (indeed, there is no equivalent term in Romani itself for the entire Gypsy population, but rather only terminology for specific subgroups). However, some contemporary scholars and political activists have strongly argued for the use of the term "Rom" or "Roma" to describe all of the diverse communities that make up the Gypsy world. The problem here is that "Rom" can refer either to all Gypsies or only to a particular subset (those whose ethnonym is *Rom*). In fact, some groups within the Gypsy world have explicitly rejected the use of the common label "Rom."[4] Further complicating the situation are debates among the Gypsies themselves about who constitute the "true Rom" or "true Gypsies."[5] Given the complexity of this situation, Matt Salo, in a study of Gypsy ethnicity, suggested that:

> It may be helpful to scholars to continue to use the term "Gypsy" only as a cover term for the totality of groups considered by scholarly tradition to be historically and/or linguistically related. The familiar designation is thus retained tentatively, but restricted to a single connotation. This is roughly analogous to the way the term "Slav" is used.... Since the term "Gypsy" does not denote any single group, we avoid the vicariously ethnocentric point of view.... "Gypsy" does not refer to an ethnic group, but to a set of groups tentatively considered related.... [6]

There is, however, still the problem of the pejorative overtones of the term "Gypsy," and given this problem, coupled with what I take to be the general preference among most of the people concerned, I have decided to use the term "Rom" here, with the understanding that it is being employed in its most general sense to refer to the overarching characteristics of the various communities that might be deemed to be "Gypsy" regardless of whether they would accept the term "Rom" to describe themselves. It is also, of course, very important to keep in mind that the people whom we are discussing are incredibly diverse in many ways and that any general claims made about "Rom" will be true of some, and untrue of others.

THE ORIGINS OF THE ROM

The historical origins of the Rom were very much clouded in mystery until the mid-18th and 19th centuries.[7] Indeed, the Rom themselves made use of a variety of fictitious origin stories to facilitate their travels and acceptance in different settings. In the 15th and early 16th centuries Rom throughout Europe, capitalizing on European fears of the expansion of the Ottoman Empire, sought and received letters of protection and safe passage, and even economic support in the form of alms from various European Christian rulers and communities,[8] by claiming that:

> their ancestors in Lesser Egypt [in minori Aegypto] had formerly abandoned for some years the Christian religion and turned to the error of the pagans and that, after their repentance, a penance had been imposed upon them that, for as many years, some members of their families should wander about the world and expiate in exile the guilt of their sin.[9]

This tale, which Angus Fraser has called "the Great Trick,"[10] was in fact merely an expedient ruse and was never believed by the Rom themselves.

Among the Rom, historical knowledge, passed on in their oral traditions, was quite limited and provided no real clues about their origin. Judith Okely noted that, "The Gypsies … have scarcely written their own history. Theirs is a non-literate tradition, so their history is found fragmented in the documents of the dominant non-Gypsy … society."[11] Not only is the historical record incomplete and written by outsiders, but it has been written by outsiders who all too often sought "to exoticise, disperse, control, assimilate or destroy" the Rom.[12] It was their language, Romani, that provided the necessary basis for tracing the history of the Rom, although more recently physical anthropology and genetics have provided additional support for hypotheses developed based on linguistic evidence.[13] As Alexandre Paspati commented in his book *Études sur les Tchinghianés* in 1870, "The true history of the Gypsy race is in the study of their language."[14] Romani is an Indo-Aryan language, historically related to Sanskrit, whose closest modern relative is Hindi.[15] This discovery, supported by other kinds of material evidence, provides the foundation for our contemporary understanding of the early history of the Rom. Thomas Acton summarized this understanding as follows:

> The ancestors of the Romani-speaking peoples left India some one thousand years ago, moving along trade routes trodden over the centuries by countless other migratory nations. Some two or three hundred years later, contemporary documents attest their arrival in eastern Europe; before the end of the fifteenth century their presence is recorded in the British Isles. They brought with them a language whose Indian construction was in the eighteenth century to betray their history to the learned world; but with the Indian base came loan words from every country on their path; and hybridisation and creolisation with other languages has fragmented the Romani language into hundreds of dialects. Today, like the Jews, they live throughout the world, sometimes intermarrying, sometimes not, disunited politically, heterogeneous culturally, and with the most diverse aspirations.[16]

Although it is probable that the Rom originally left northern India around 1000 C.E., we know very little about what motivated their exodus, or even whether they left as a single group or over time in smaller groups (although the latter appears to be more likely). Similarly, we do not know much about the role and place of the ancestors of the Rom in India before they left, although a number of possible scenarios have been proposed. Many scholars believe that the Rom began as a relatively low-caste group, in Sanskrit called the *domba* (from which the modern term *Rom* may be derived), who are known to have been musicians as early as the 6th century C.E.[17] Others, however, have suggested that the ancestors of today's Rom were more likely higher-caste *kshatriyas*, or warriors.[18] In any event, after leaving India the Rom entered Persia, and gradually moved through Armenia and on to the heart of the Byzantine Empire. They then traveled (and many remained and settled) in the Balkans and, between the 14th through 16th centuries, throughout Europe.[19]

THE CHALLENGE OF STUDYING THE ROM

If the origins and early history of the Rom are difficult to identify and understand, the same can be said, perhaps paradoxically, to be even more true of any effort to understand contemporary Rom life, values, behaviors, and so on. The world of the Rom is very much a secret one, neither particularly visible nor welcoming to outsiders.[20] The Rom have historically faced (and in many places continue to face) prejudice, discrimination, and persecution of incredible proportions, and so it is hardly surprising that they have developed not only suspicions of *gadje* (non-Rom), but very effective means of avoidance and deception to resist efforts to learn about them. While the Rom necessarily live in the midst of *gadje* and rely on contacts with *gadje* to survive, they nonetheless (and for good reason) "like being familiar strangers ... their status as strangers protects them in a number of ways. The less we know about them, the less we can harass them."[21] As William Kephart noted, "The boundaries between Rom and *gadje* are sharp, and the Rom have every intention of maintaining the sharpness. Deception, avoidance, misrepresentation, and lying are part of the Gypsies' arsenal, and they have had hundreds of years to perfect and embellish their defenses."[22] And yet, even given these barriers, there is a substantial and growing body of anthropological, sociological, and linguistic research about the Rom, some of it conducted by Rom scholars, which is opening a window into the world of the Rom.[23]

CULTURAL AND SOCIAL VALUES AND NORMS

Rom culture and society is fundamentally oppositional in nature, in the sense that the most basic distinction made is that between Rom and *gadje*. Regardless of the diversity present *within* the Rom world, this insider/outsider distinction is virtually universal amongst all Rom.[24] The distinction is not merely a social one; it is a *moral* one, grounded in Rom beliefs about ritual purity. Sutherland, for instance, noted that:

the Rom and *gadje* are moral opposites and constitute the most important social boundary in terms of behaviour. Relations with *gadje* are restricted to economic exploitation and political manipulation. Social relations in the sense of friendship, mutual aid, and equality are not appropriate with them.[25]

Wuzho and Marimé: Concepts of Ritual Purity and Impurity

At the heart of Rom culture is the concept of ritual purity, or *wuzho*. *Wuzho* suggests not merely ritual or ceremonial purity, however, but also "purity of a physical and moral nature."[26] It is contrasted with *marimé* that, in a superficial literal sense, refers to defilement or pollution.[27] *Marimé*, however, is a far more powerful concept than this definition might suggest. Carol Miller, in her discussion of what she terms the "ideology of defilement" among American Rom, commented that *marimé*:

> is pervasive to Rom categories of belief and thought, and extends to all areas of Rom life in some way, underwriting a hygienic attitude towards the world, themselves, and others. Pollution ideas work on the life of Rom society, especially in the sense of symbolizing certain dangers and expressing a general view of the social order. Lines are drawn between the Gypsy and the non-Gypsy, the clean and the unclean, health and disease, the good and the bad, which are made obvious and visible through the offices of ritual avoidance.[28]

In its most basic sense, the distinction between *wuzho* and *marimé* refers to the division of the human body into two parts: above the waist and below the waist. The area above the waist, and in particular the head and mouth, are considered *wuzho*, while the parts of the body below the waist (especially anal and genital areas) are *marimé*.[29] This distinction is seen as fundamental, and any contact between the two parts must be avoided, as must be any contact between any items and surfaces that are in any way associated with one or the other part of the body.[30] Thus,

> items that come into contact with these areas are separately maintained, washed in running water or special basins and stored apart from ordinary items; items like soaps, towels, razors and combs, clothes, pillows, furniture like the backs of chairs, the tops of tables, tablecloths, aprons, sinks, food utensils and, of course, food itself, which is prepared, served, and eaten with the greatest consideration for ritual quality.[31]

In practice, this means, for instance, that clothing worn above the waist and below the waist must be washed and kept separately. Otherwise, what was *wuzho* becomes *marimé*. As Ronald Lee, himself a Rom, explained:

> you can't wash clothes, dishes, and babies in the same pan, and every Gypsy has his own eating utensils, towels, and soap. Other dishes and utensils are set aside for guests, and still others for pregnant women. Certain towels are for the face,

and others for the nether regions—and there are different colored soaps in the sink, each with an allotted function.[32]

The concept of *marimé* applies not only to objects, but to people as well. *Gadje* are, by definition, *marimé*:

> The major offence of the *gadje*, the one offence that the Rom can never forgive, is their propensity to defilement. *Gadje* confuse the critical distinction between the pure and the impure. They are observed in various situations which the Rom regard as compromising; forgetting to wash in public bathrooms; eating with the fork they rescued from the floor of the restaurant; washing face towels and table-cloths with underwear at the local self-service laundry; relaxing with their feet resting upon the top surface of the table.[33]

Beyond this are common practices of *gadje* that strike the Rom as further evidence, should any be needed, of the impure practices and lifestyles of *gadje*:

> For their part, Gypsies can easily be stunned by examples of *gadjo* squalor that the *gadje* aren't even aware of. For example, keeping dogs as pets in the house, and, worse, tolerating cats, and indeed upholding them as unusually clean animals. Among Gypsies, the cat is *marimé* because it licks its fur and genitals and so brings dirt inside itself.[34]

It is important to understand that *marimé* does not mean merely "dirty"; something can be dirty (*melaló*) without being impure (*marimé*).[35] Rom believe that they are in constant danger of being polluted so long as they are in the midst of *gadje*, since not only the *gadje* themselves but anything they touch becomes *marimé*. This not only helps to explain the social barriers between Rom and *gadje*, but also demonstrates the incredible social control such a concept has for maintaining group boundaries.[36] As Salo observed:

> The separation of Gypsies from non-Gypsies is marked by differences of both values and other cultural traits. There seems to be a high degree of agreement among the Gypsies as to what the most basic and general values are. The most important values of family and group solidarity are exhibited by a host of symbolic objects and behaviors which so permeate all aspects of Gypsy life as to make contrast with outsiders constant and inevitable. The criteria for the ideal Gypsy man or woman are markedly lacking in most *gadje*, a fact that can be confirmed daily to the disgust and scorn of the Gypsy. Only the loosening of the Gypsy moral code could allow closer relationships to develop with the gadje.... [37]

Family and Kinship Patterns

If the contrast of Rom and *gadje* is the most basic for the Rom, internal divisions among different groups of Rom are nonetheless significant as well. Every individual Rom has a complex personal identity tied to an intricate pattern of family relationships.[38] At the core of this set of relationships is membership in the *familia*, or extended family, which functions both as an economic unit and as a support network. As Kephart noted:

> The *familia* is particularly effective as a *supportive institution*. Whether the problem is economic, social, political, or medical, the various family members unite in their efforts to provide aid. Should a police official, social worker, inspector, tax collector, or any other unwelcome *gadjo* appear on the scene, the intruder will be met with formidable—and generally effective—opposition. Should a family member fall ill, the *familia* will spare no expense in obtaining professional help, especially if it is a serious illness.[39]

Beyond the level of the *familia* is the *vitsa*, which is a collection of related *familiyi*. Although sometimes called "clans," the ties that hold members of a *vitsa* together are stronger than this would suggest. Membership in a *vitsa* is used by Rom as a "unit of identity" in determining their place in the broader Rom community, and certain obligations are owed to the other members of one's *vitsa*.[40] Finally, each *vitsa* is tied to one of the thirteen or more *natsiyi*, or "tribes," of the Rom world.[41] Different in kind from the kinship-based *familia*, each individual household is also a member of a *kumpania*, which is essentially an economically-based unit that also serves as "the basic political unit and its members can make decisions on moral, social, political and economic questions which are considered to be public rather than family matters."[42]

Gender Roles and Expectations

Within the Rom community, gender roles and expectations are both clearly defined and highly significant. As Sutherland noted:

> The male-female division is the most fundamental in Rom society. Men and women between puberty and old age are given entirely different status and rule within a relationship category. Actual physical separation of the sexes is very great, and this both exemplifies as well as reinforces the difference in treatment of men and women.[43]

The separation of men and women, at least traditionally,[44] includes social functions of various types, daily activities, duties and responsibilities, and occupational roles. For the Rom, the world of men and the world of women may overlap and interconnect, but they nonetheless remain very much separate. Kephart described these different worlds as follows:

> Women cook and take care of the household chores. Men are responsible for the acquisition and maintenance of transportation facilities. In many areas, the women bring in more money than the men ... the women's income seems to be steadier and more reliable than the men's. It is the men, nevertheless, who normally hold positions of power in the *familia*, the *vitsa*, and the *kumpania*.[45]

One way to conceptualize the differing roles of men and women in Rom society is in terms of the need for the community to concern itself with both biological and cultural/political survival. As Rena Cotten explained:

> [T]he woman is most active in those facets of life necessary for biological survival, but cultural survival is in male hands since the men are the initiators and major participants of group institutions. To phrase it another way: the focal point of interest for the men is the *vitsa* and its component extended families; the center of concern for the woman is her own conjugal biological family.[46]

The point at which gender roles most clearly intersect, of course, is in the context of marriage. Marriage is, for the Rom as for others, very important; in fact, for the Rom, marriage is a prerequisite for full participation in the life of the community.[47] The traditional view of the nature and purposes of marriage among the Rom, however, differs dramatically from that of most contemporary societies. As Rena Gropper explained in *Gypsies in the City*, the husband-wife dimension of marriage is among its *least* important facets:

> Aside from having a sex partner and someone besides his mother to fulfill his needs and give him money, the groom experiences little change in his lifestyle when he marries. His age-peers may joke about his sexual activities, and his mother and sisters may tell him to ask his wife for something because they are too busy. Gypsy marriage is not predicated on romantic love, and the Rom frown against any display of affection between husband and wife. The husband wants his wife to perform services for him, but he continues to spend much of his time with brothers and cousins. Husband and wife rarely go out together.[48]

Marriages are arranged only partly in terms of the *individuals* involved; although the husband and wife must be compatible, the marriage is a union not only of a man and a woman, but also a union of *families*. Thus, as Sutherland and others have observed, there is a strong preference for marriages between cousins, which is to say with "a person of one's own *vitsa*, or of the *vitsa* of one's female progenitors, that is, the mother, mother's mother, or father's mother."[49] Although marriages of first cousins are not considered the ideal, they do take place and are not restricted. In fact, with the exception of certain illegitimate *marimé* unions,[50] any marriage within the community is potentially possible and acceptable.[51] Marriage with *gadje*, however, is not acceptable, although on occasion a non-Rom woman will be allowed to marry into the community.[52] The business nature of the marriage is reinforced and made clear by the role of the *daro*, or "bride price," in the negotiations between the bride and groom's families.[53]

Earning a Living

Throughout their history, the Rom have survived by functioning as what some scholars call a "middleman minority."[54] There have been, and continue to be, a wide array of such "middleman minorities" in the world, including, in various contexts, the Chinese, the Indians, the Jews, and the Rom. These groups, whose position in any particular society is often tenuous at best because they remain "outsiders" in important senses, have, although they have been faced with considerable adversity, been "able to develop and perpetuate a cultural heritage involving a high degree of ethnocentrism and adaptive skills which enabled them to improve or maintain their competitive resources."[55] In the case of the Rom, vocational and occupational skills necessary for survival have developed over time in response to both changing social situations and needs. Judith Okely identified a set of 10 general skills that have served the Rom well in adapting to different host environments:

1. Knowing the local economy and its potential where demand and supply are irregular.
2. Knowing the local people, an alien population, and recognizing their psychological needs and weaknesses.
3. Opportunism and ingenuity in choice of occupation in the local context.
4. Flexibility in occupation at a given time and over a period of time.
5. Salesmanship.
6. Flexibility in role-playing.
7. Manual dexterity and mechanical ingenuity.
8. Bargaining skills.
9. Highly developed memory.
10. Physical strength and stamina.[56]

These skills are manifested in practice in a number of ways, but are perhaps most visible in the multioccupational approach to life taken by the Rom. As Sway commented:

> It has become a business principle among the Gypsies never to depend on one occupation. Since so many of the Gypsies' occupations are seasonal, temporary, marginal, and even precarious, they engage in a number of endeavors simultaneously.... The practice of being multioccupational affords the Gypsies a peculiar form of job security. Since the Gypsies never rely on one mode of work, they are never without a means to earn a living. If a particular market closes to them because it has been exhausted or they have been harassed by the police, they can quickly turn to other methods of earning a living. This occupational flexibility and pluralism should be viewed as a result of years of economic adaptation to unfriendly and unreliable market situations. The Gypsy practice of diversity enables them to survive the harshest of economic circumstances.[57]

In contemporary American society, there are a number of occupations pursued (often simultaneously) by Rom. For males, dealing in used cars and fender and body work have become major sources of income, supplemented by work as coppersmiths, farm labor, entertainers, junk dealers, and a host of other "free professions"[58]—but not, for the most part, as part of the normal wage-labor system in place in modern industrialized societies.[59] For women, fortune-telling remains the most common and respected occupation, if not necessarily a terribly lucrative one.[60] In fact, fortune-telling often provides the most consistent and reliable source of income for the Rom, and this is consistent with the economic role of the woman in Rom society:

> In all Gypsy societies, the woman functions as the family treasurer, and the Romany definition of the role differs considerably from ours. In Gypsy terms, part of the treasurer's responsibility is to ensure that there is always something in the treasury. It is the woman who is expected to bring in the daily money for routine expenses ... the woman is the one required to furnish daily food provisions and even pocket money for the men whenever they need it.[61]

Fortune-telling is more, however, than merely an essential economic activity. As Carol Silverman observed:

> Fortune-telling is the most widespread and traditional occupation of Rom women. It is not only their primary means of earning money, but also it is the way of being a Gypsy woman and of acquiring prestigious skills. As one Gypsy put it, "For a woman not to be able to read a palm is an insult." Every major American city hosts fortune-tellers. They are called "readers and advisers" because predicting the future for money is illegal. In New York City alone, there are hundreds of fortune-telling parlors. Customers are drawn exclusively from the non-Gypsy population. Since fortune-telling seems to strike a responsive chord in diverse cultures, it continues to be in demand in urban as well as rural settings among many ethnic groups.[62]

The Rom function in a perpetual symbiotic economic relationship with the surrounding *gadje* community; as Gropper noted, "no Gypsy group makes its living from other Gypsies."[63] A good example of this symbiosis can be found in Rom attitudes toward welfare benefits where they are available. As Marlene Sway commented:

> The Gypsies' historical willingness to undertake work that no one else wanted has led them to develop the attitude that earning money even under the most humiliating circumstances is still honorable and productive. As a result of this attitude, the Gypsies ... actively seek out and exploit welfare benefits in societies where they are obtainable.... The Gypsies do not view welfare as charity or aid; rather it is just one more method of outsmarting the non-Gypsy. Since collecting welfare is time-consuming in terms of hours required in agency offices, the Gypsies feel justified in being compensated for the income they lose while waiting. Additionally, since welfare agencies put restrictions on the Gypsies and the Gypsies have to "earn" their money by playing the role of a welfare recipient in a believable fashion, they feel they are justified in accepting the welfare benefits.[64]

Although it would be both misleading and dishonest to suggest that all, or even most, Rom engage in such practices, there is nevertheless something of an underside to Rom economic life. Working from the assumption that all *gadje* are fools who are asking to be cheated, many Rom do in fact engage in what Anne Sutherland has called "less legitimate ways of making a living." Such ways include the *xoxano baro*, or "Big Lie," of the fortune-tellers in its many forms (all of which involve, in some way, confidence games of some sort), as well as theft, pick-pocketing, and so on.[65] Another example given by Sutherland, which is still commonly taking place, is the following:

> Some groups of men travel around in trucks and camp in parking lots. They tar roofs or spray asphalt on driveways. Some of them have developed quite a racket from this by diluting the tar so much that it never dries, but it costs less to them and therefore their profits are higher. By the time the home-owners discover their dilemma, the men have packed up their trucks and moved to another city.[66]

For the most part, however, the Rom have been remarkably successful economically without resorting to such tricks. This is an especially impressive accomplishment when one considers that, "unlike … other middleman minorities, Gypsies are largely illiterate. As a consequence of their illiteracy, the educated and professional classes including attorneys, historians, sociologists, and politicians lack Gypsies who could represent their interests as an ethnic group on various levels. Yet despite this obvious liability, the Gypsies have managed to exploit one middleman niche after another and endure as a commercially successful ethnic group."[67]

Religious Belief and "Protective Coloration"

One of the ways in which the Rom are very different from most other "middleman minorities" is with respect to religion, religious belief, and religious practice. Religion often plays a central role in in-group identification for such groups and helps to maintain the boundaries between the group and the surrounding host society. This is not really the case with the Rom, who have tended, throughout their history, to adopt the dominant religion of whatever society they are in:

> Traditionally tolerant and respectful toward all religions, the Rom readily have absorbed practices around them. So, in Spain, Italy, and France, they became Roman Catholic; in England, usually Protestant; and in southeast Europe (occupied for so long by Muslim conquerors) they are either Muslim or Greek Orthodox.[68]

The outward adoption of the dominant faith of the surrounding community has functioned as "protective coloration" for the Rom, without seriously challenging or altering the core folk religious beliefs of their community.[69] Writing about Rom in Albania, for instance, Isabel Fonseca noted that:

> It is commonly said that Gypsies are irreligious, adopting the going faith as it suits them, in the hopes of avoiding persecution and possibly of reaping whatever ben-

efits group membership might bring. This is true. For one thing, they have often
been made to listen to sermons from outside the church. But the deeper reason is
that among themselves they have no need of the religions of other nations. It was
hard to say exactly what it meant to the Gypsies of Kinostudio to be Muslims, as
they claimed. Their women were chaste and wore long skirts, but this was the
code of "decent" Gypsies everywhere.[70]

To be sure, elements of adopted religions often permeate Rom life, but
these elements (such as holidays, naming patterns, etc.) are little more than
outward trappings rather than evidence of deep conviction. As Marlene Sway
compellingly argued, "The Gypsies are not Christian and never have been, although they have successfully convinced outsiders that they are."[71] This is not
to suggest, however, that the Rom are insincere in their religious beliefs.
Rather, their indigenous religious belief system simply allows for a wide range
of formal religious commitment and rejects the common Western assumption
that membership in a religious community must be exclusive in nature.[72]

Performance and "Impression Management"

One of the most intriguing and insightful studies of the Rom to appear in the
scholarly literature in recent years is Carol Silverman's study of "impression
management."[73] Silverman argued that:

> When Gypsies interact with non-Gypsies, they have various motives for influ-
> encing the impression received. To lawyers, they may be interested in demon-
> strating their credibility as American citizens; to welfare workers, their
> victimization as an afflicted minority; to fortune-telling customers, their spiritu-
> ality. By controlling the communicative situation, they control what is perceived
> by the "audience." Gypsies are highly skillful in performance.... Different per-
> formances are required for fortune-telling customers, for landlords, for truant
> officers, for welfare workers, etc. Various "impressions," "faces," or "identities"
> are managed by communicating highly selective information. Furthermore,
> Gypsies are highly skilled in face-shifting. Of course, this occurs in all groups and
> individuals, but the Gypsies have developed this process to an art, are quite con-
> scious and reflexive about it ... and have used it as a tactic for survival in hostile
> environments.[74]

Such behavior is interesting on a number of levels and can give us considerable insight not only into the way in which the Rom view the *gadje* world in
general, but also into the kinds of skills and knowledge that will be of greatest
value within the Rom community. Given the history of the Rom, it is hardly
surprising that the ability to hide one's identity as a Rom has proven to be both
necessary and expedient:

> An important and frequent Gypsy performance is "passing" as a non-Gypsy.
> Gypsies deliberately conceal their ethnicity to avoid confrontations with and ha-
> rassment by truant officers, landlords, the police, and the welfare department;

they pass as Puerto Ricans, Mexicans, Armenians, Greeks, Arabs, and other local ethnics in order to obtain jobs, housing, and welfare. Gypsies usually report themselves as members of other groups to census takers, causing Gypsy census statistics to be extremely unreliable. Gypsies have developed the skills of passing so well that many Americans are unaware that there are any Gypsies in America.[75]

"Passing," however, is but one of the many performances employed by the Rom. Another related phenomenon is that of "naming." In the American context, for instance, not only have many Rom adopted Americanized names (as have members of many other groups, of course), but further:

> Gypsies use a multiplicity of names to avoid visibility. One Gypsy family may list their apartment under one name, the telephone under another, and the fortune-telling business under yet another. The argument may be extended to addresses: because many urban Rom are semi-nomadic, addresses change continuously. The multiplicity makes Gypsies hard to identify and trace, producing precisely the effects the Gypsy seeks. In Western society, a name is an indelible mark which rarely changes. For Gypsies, on the other hand, changeable American names are a strategy they use to remain invisible, concealed, and untraceable.[76]

Yet another aspect of "impression management" that has been very effectively utilized by the Rom is attracting different clientele with group-specific advertising. For example, in discussing bilingual (Spanish-English) handbills used in California by one fortune-teller, Silverman reported that, "This handbill ... presents two sets of ascribed problems fitting two separate customer populations."[77] In other words, the appeal that is made to the middle class English-speaking population differs dramatically from that made to the working class *chicano* population. The handbill, in short, is really two separate documents, distinguished not only by language but also by target audience.

THE FEARS AND REALITIES OF PERSECUTION: "EVEN PARANOIDS HAVE ENEMIES"

The complexities of "impression management" discussed above reflect, among other things, serious concerns about the risk of persecution. It is only reasonable to ask how realistic such concerns and fears are; certainly in the contemporary American context, I suspect that many people would be astonished to discover such worries and would likely see them as evidence of group paranoia. Yet, not only the history of the Rom, but recent events, especially in Eastern Europe, would seem to strongly support such fears and worries. Gabrielle Tyrnauer, for example, powerfully reminded us that:

> The upheaval in Europe has had a strong impact on the Gypsies of the continent. Those from Eastern Europe are becoming refugees in unprecedented numbers, knocking on the gates of Western European countries, often afraid to acknowledge their ethnic identities, even as refugees.... Gypsies who remain in the East,

like Jews, are once more becoming strangers in their own lands, targets of diffuse hostility, scapegoats for the frustrations of societies in the convulsions of rapid change.... Hatred of the Gypsy minority is often all that unites the warring ethnic groups of ex-communist nations of eastern and central Europe.[78]

The Rom have been easy scapegoats and targets of persecution throughout their long history. Victims of prejudice, discrimination, disenfranchisement, forced migrations and expulsions, and even slavery and murder, the survival of the Rom can be attributed in no small measure to their (often quite legitimate) suspicions of *gadje*.[79]

Without a doubt, the most horrendous example of anti-Rom persecution in recent history has been the Holocaust. Although many individuals and groups suffered horribly at the hands of the Nazis, only two groups—the Jews and the Rom—were specifically "targeted for annihilation by National Socialist ideology and its state apparatus."[80] Although accurate figures are, as always with the Rom, difficult to determine, somewhere between at least a quarter and a half million Rom were murdered by the Nazis[81]—and the number could well be double this estimate according to some scholars.[82] In other words, as much as half the total Rom population in Europe may have been killed during the Holocaust. This aspect of the Holocaust, however, is relatively unknown, leading some to talk about the murder of the Rom as "the forgotten Holocaust."[83]

CHILD-REARING AND EDUCATION

In 1967, a report entitled *Children and Their Primary Schools* was issued by the Central Advisory Council for Education in London. The report, commonly called "The Plowden Report," asserted that Rom children "are probably the most severely deprived children in the country. Most of them do not even go to school and the potential abilities of those who do are stunted."[84] Such critical views are far from uncommon; a somewhat more recent publication of the Council of Europe makes clear the educational challenge facing those concerned with the schooling of Rom children:

> It is safe to assume that over one-half of Gypsies ... of school age in Europe are not attending school. Of those that are, many receive inappropriate instruction which is frequently trying for them as well as their families. Depending on the country, the attendance rate for children and young people below the statutory school-leaving age varies between 20% and 60% to 70%.... The illiteracy rate among those over the school-leaving age varies between 65% and 95%.[85]

The same general pattern has been historically true in the United States as well, but has been changing in recent years:

> Within the past decade, there has been a revolutionary trend among Gypsies of all countries to send their children to public school. While Gypsy parents would

like their children to learn how to read, write, and perform basic arithmetic, education is not the primary reason they send their children to school. In recent years, welfare workers have moved to tie welfare benefits to the children's attendance at public school.... Children help the Gypsies make money for the family through welfare benefits, and, additionally, the public school is a free babysitter.[86]

Such a description of contemporary Rom practice might lead one to agree with the conclusions of the "Plowden Report"—but if so, one would be very much mistaken. Such views, however common, are a serious distortion of both the Rom view of children and childrearing and do an important disservice to the nature of Rom family life.

The Rom value, love, and respect their children. Their response to public education is a reflection not of indifference or of a lack of concern, but rather of serious (and well-founded) reservations about the nature and purposes of such education. There is also a basic difference in the way in which the Rom and the dominant society view children and childhood. For the Rom, children are born as distinct individuals:

Children are considered miniature versions of adults, lacking only the motor strength and skill of adults and, of course, lacking experience in life. But willpower and desires, emotions and potential intelligence are all inborn and are functional immediately. It follows, therefore, that their rights are also the same as those of adults. Their wishes should be respected to the same extent as the wishes of other human beings.[87]

Such a view of children has important implications for education broadly conceived. Ultimately, because they are in no significant way different from adults, children "should have the right to participate in all the affairs of the adults; in such manner they can learn the ways of their forefathers."[88] In other words, within the Rom community children are prepared for adult life by observation and participation in that life, as well as through ongoing exposure to the oral tradition of the community.[89] As Okely explained, traditionally:

The Gypsy child learnt by direct participation.... Most Gypsy children spent the major part of the day with a parent or substitute parent, and at times were in the charge of older siblings. The skills required for earning a living were learnt when "calling" at houses or factories with parents or relatives, from the age of a toddler.... Children were encouraged to handle and earn money from an early age.... Children were also socialized into Gypsy life and values by long hours of observing and listening to adults' conversations and exchanges.... The children were generally treated as "little adults," being entrusted with secrets and given early responsibilities.[90]

Childcare is viewed as a responsibility of the entire family; interestingly, because of the relative economic importance of women (especially as fortune-tellers), childcare often becomes a male responsibility. Since children are considered a nuisance at a fortune-telling parlor, they spend long hours with their fathers, uncles, and grandfathers. Typically the children accompany the men wherever they go—on body and fender jobs, shopping, and visiting other Gypsies. When a Gypsy child is ill, often the father acts as nurturer, tending the child's needs and chauffeuring him or her to doctor and dental appointments.[91]

As for public education, from a Rom perspective the fundamental problem is that children should be separated as much as possible from the *gadje* world. Public education is, by its very nature, a means by which community ties are weakened—in essence, a door through which young Rom could go and not return. The lessons of public education go far beyond reading, writing, and basic arithmetic; public schools socialize children into the dominant, mainstream culture. Children are likely to form friendships with *gadje*; they are also unwittingly exposed to all sorts of *marimé*.[92] Ultimately, then, schools pose a very real threat to the continuity of the Rom community itself. It is with this aspect of public education that the Rom have their greatest problems. The solution most commonly adopted in Rom communities is to allow children to attend public schools until they are 10 or 11 years old. As one Swedish informant suggested, "It's no use telling children below the age of ten years, they don't understand anything till then."[93] After that point, however, public education becomes too great a threat to be tolerated. As Jean- Pierre Liégeois commented, "As an external element affecting the education of their children, the school is *a priori* disturbing, because it impinges on their upbringing within the group."[94]

CONCLUSION

The Rom present us with a fascinating example of a remarkably successful, highly adaptive cultural community in our midst, many of whose core values, among them beliefs about education, are radically different from those of the dominant society. The conception of education that motivates the Rom is one oriented to survival: economic and vocational survival, to be sure, but also physical and cultural survival. The bureaucratic institutions that modern governments have created and on which they rely (including, of course, schools) in some sense depend on the acquiescence and acceptance of their legitimacy by the population that they serve. It is this very legitimacy that is denied by the Rom, whose own core group identity outweighs any other social obligation, commitment, or identity. All that the Rom really want, of course, is to be allowed to be Rom—but this is the challenge for the societies in which they live, because being Rom necessarily means *not* being something else.

QUESTIONS FOR REFLECTION AND DISCUSSION

1. Write an essay in which you respond to the idea that children are just "miniature adults." Is this a reasonable conception of childhood in your view? How does this view differ from that offered by Rousseau? By Dewey? What educational advantages would such a notion have? What disadvantages?

2. What are the major challenges that would face the classroom teacher of Rom children in the United States today? How could teachers be better prepared to meet the needs of these children?

3. In the literature on the Rom, some writers have noted a number of common themes that would seem to make the Rom and the Jews (at least in traditional settings) somewhat analogous cases. To what extent, and in what ways, do you think that this is a credible comparison? How do the two groups differ? What are the social and educational implications of these similarities and differences?

4. The concept of *marimé* is a key one in understanding Rom cultural beliefs and practices. In this chapter, it is suggested that in public schools, Rom children are exposed to all sorts of *marimé*. What examples of *marimé* in the context of the typical elementary school classroom can you think of? What (if anything) might the classroom teacher do to address this problem?

5. Which of the ten general skills identified by Judith Okely are taught in the context of the public school? What does this tell you about the nature of public schooling? About the nature of Rom life?

6. "The educational practices of the Rom are in fact more sound than those of the typical public school classroom. Children learn by doing; they construct their own knowledge." Respond to this claim. To what extent is it true? In what ways is it misleading?

7. One of the core issues raised in this chapter is that of what the purposes of public schooling ought to be. With respect to culturally different groups in our society, what do you believe that the purposes of public schooling should be? To what extent do you believe that the school should seek to provide a common cultural experience for all children in our society?

8. What, in your view, is the greatest strength of the traditional Rom approach to childrearing and education? What is its greatest weakness?

9. The discussion of performance and "impression management" in this chapter raises a number of questions about education. How do *all* children engage in performance and "impression management" in the classroom? How do *teachers* engage in performance and "impression management"? Can you think of ways to make use of these behaviors in pedagogically useful ways?

10. In this chapter, it is argued that "Rom society and culture are fundamentally oppositional in nature." What does this mean, and what are its implications for educational practice in the school setting?

RECOMMENDED FURTHER READINGS

The best general introduction to Rom life and culture, especially in the United States, remains Anne Sutherland, *Gypsies: The Hidden Americans* (Prospect Heights, IL: Waveland, 1975). Two exceptionally powerful works that sympathetically, if not always entirely accurately, present views of the world of the Rom are Isabel Fonseca, *Bury Me Standing: The Gypsies and Their Journey* (New York: Vintage, 1995); and Michael Stewart, *The Time of the Gypsies* (Boulder, CO: Westview Press, 1997).

NOTES

1. See Francois de Vaux de Foletier, *Mille ans d'historie des Tsiganes* (Paris: Fayard,1970); Angus Fraser, *The Gypsies*, 2nd ed. (Oxford, England: Blackwell, 1995); Rena Gropper, *Gypsies in the City: Cultural Patterns and Survival* (Princeton, NJ: Darwin Press, 1975).
2. The spelling of terms in Romani (and, in fact, even the name of the language itself, which is also commonly written "Romany" and "Romanes") varies considerably, as a result both of the lack of a standardized written norm and the considerable diversity of dialects within Romani. See, for instance, Ian Hancock, "Romani and Angloromani," in Peter Trudgill (ed.), *Language in the British Isles* (Cambridge, England: Cambridge University Press, 1984), 367–383; Yaron Matras (ed.), *Romani in Contact: The History, Structure, and Sociology of a Language* (Amsterdam: John Benjamins, 1995); George Campbell, *Concise Compendium of the World's Languages* (London: Routledge, 1995), 419–424.
3. The Irish Tinkers, for instance, are Celtic in origin and speak Shelta, a Celtic language that is rapidly undergoing the process of lexical replacement and which has already become largely grammatically English; see Ian Hancock, "Shelta and Polari" in Peter Trudgill (ed.), *Language in the British Isles* (Cambridge, England: Cambridge University Press, 1984), 384–403; William Kephart, *Extraordinary Groups: The Sociology of Unconventional Lifestyles*, 2nd ed. (New York: St. Martin's Press, 1982), 8. For more detailed information about these groups, see Bettina Barnes, "Irish Travelling People," in Farnham Rehfisch (ed.), *Gypsies, Tinkers, and Other Travellers* (London: Academic Press, 1975), 231–256; A. and Farnham Rehfisch, "Scottish Travellers or Tinkers," in Farnham Rehfisch (ed.), *Gypsies, Tinkers, and Other Travellers* (London: Academic Press, 1975), 271–283; Fredrik Barth, "The Social

Organization of a Pariah Group in Norway," in Farnham Rehfisch (ed.), *Gypsies, Tinkers, and Other Travellers* (London: Academic Press, 1975), 285–299.

4. For example, a number of Gypsy groups use the term *Roma* to describe other Gypsy groups, but do not accept the term for themselves. This is the case for the Romanichal, Gitanos, Kalé, Sinti, and Manush. See Anne Sutherland, *Gypsies: The Hidden Americans* (Prospect Heights, IL: Waveland, 1975), 14–18.

5. See Sutherland, *Gypsies: The Hidden Americans*, 14–18; Thomas Acton, *Gypsy Politics and Social Change* (London: Routledge & Kegan Paul, 1974), 53–93.

6. Matt Salo, "Gypsy Ethnicity: Implications of Native Categories and Interaction for Ethnic Classification," *Ethnicity* 6 (1979): 94–95.

7. De Vaux de Foletier, *Mille ans d'historie des Tsiganes*, 13.

8. Fraser, *The Gypsies*, 63–78.

9. Quoted in Fraser, *The Gypsies*, 65.

10. Fraser, *The Gypsies*, 60–83.

11. Judith Okely, *The Traveller-Gypsies* (Cambridge, England: Cambridge University Press, 1983), 1.

12. Okely, *The Traveller-Gypsies*, 1.

13. Fraser, *The Gypsies*, 25; Gropper, *Gypsies in the City*, 2.

14. Quoted in Fraser, *The Gypsies*, 12.

15. Matt Salo and Sheila Salo, *The Kalderas in Eastern Canada* (Ottawa: National Museums of Canada, 1977), 1.

16. Acton, *Gypsy Politics and Social Change*, 1.

17. Fraser, *The Gypsies*, 25; see also Marlene Sway, *Familiar Strangers: Gypsy Life in America* (Urbana: University of Illinois Press, 1988), 31–33.

18. Fraser, *The Gypsies*, 25–26.

19. Gropper, *Gypsies in the City*, 6–12; see also David Crowe, *A History of the Gypsies of Eastern Europe and Russia* (New York: St. Martin's Griffin, 1996); David Crowe and John Kolsti (eds.), *The Gypsies of Eastern Europe* (London: M. E. Sharpe, 1991).

20. Kephart, *Extraordinary Groups: The Sociology of Unconventional Life-Styles*, 12–14; see also Saga Weckman, "Researching Finnish Gypsies: Advice from a Gypsy," in Diane Tong (ed.), *Gypsies: An Interdisciplinary Reader* (New York: Garland, 1998), 3–10. The more general problem with respect to insider/outsider status in research is discussed quite clearly in John Elliott, "Educational Research and Outsider-Insider Relations," *International Journal of Qualitative Studies in Education* 1, 2 (1988): 155–166.

21. Sway, *Familiar Strangers: Gypsy Life in America*, 6.

22. Kephart, *Extraordinary Groups: The Sociology of Unconventional Life-Styles*, 12.

23. See, e.g., Diane Tong (ed.), *Gypsies: An Interdisciplinary Reader* (New York: Garland, 1998).

24. Salo, "Gypsy Ethnicity," 81–82; Kephart, *Extraordinary Groups: The Sociology of Unconventional Life-Styles*, 17; de Vaux de Foletier, *Mille ans d'histoire des Tsiganes*, 213–224.

25. Sutherland, *Gypsies: The Hidden Americans*, 258; see also Kephart, *Extraordinary Groups: The Sociology of Unconventional Life-Styles*, 17–18.

26. Sutherland, *The Hidden Americans*, 258; Salo and Salo, *The Kalderas in Eastern Canada*, 115–129.

27. The term *marimé* actually has a double meaning in Rom culture. In addition to the meaning discussed in the chapter, it is also the word used to describe the most serious sanctions issued by a *kris*, a Rom judicial body. See Sway, *Familar Strangers*, 76–94; Sutherland, *Gypsies: The Hidden Americans*, 262–263.

28. Carol Miller, "American Rom and the Ideology of Defilement," in Farnham Rehfisch (ed.), *Gypsies, Tinkers, and Other Travellers* (London: Academic Press, 1975), 41.

29. Miller, "American Rom and the Ideology of Defilement."

30. Miller, "American Rom and the Ideology of Defilement"; see also Gropper, *Gypsies in the City*, 91–96.

31. Miller, "American Rom and the Ideology of Defilement," 42.

32. Quoted in Kephart, *Extraordinary Groups: The Sociology of Unconventional Life-Styles*, 15.

33. Miller, "American Rom and the Ideology of Defilement," 45.

34. Isabel Fonseca, *Bury Me Standing: The Gypsies and Their Journey* (New York: Vintage, 1995), 104.

35. Sutherland, *Gypsies: The Hidden Americans*, 268–270.

36. Kephart, *Extraordinary Groups: The Sociology of Unconventional Life-Styles*, 14. The comparison to *kashrut* in Judaism is obvious here; see Sway, *Familiar Strangers: Gypsy Life in America*, 24–26.

37. Salo, "Gypsy Ethnicity," 82.

38. Fraser, *The Gypsies*, 238.

39. Kephart, *Extraordinary Groups: The Sociology of Unconventional Life-Styles*, 21.

40. Fraser, *The Gypsies*, 238–239; Sutherland, *Gypsies: The Hidden Americans*, 181–184.

41. Fraser, *The Gypsies*, 238–239; Sutherland, *Gypsies: The Hidden Americans*, 185–188.

42. Fraser, *The Gypsies*, 239.

43. Sutherland, *Gypsies: The Hidden Americans*, 149.

44. For a discussion of recent changes with respect to gender roles and expectations among the Rom, see Rena Cotten, "Sex Dichotomy Among the American Kalderas Gypsies," in Diane Tong (ed.), *Gypsies: An Interdisciplinary Reader* (New York: Garland, 1998), 228–230.

45. Kephart, *Extraordinary Groups: The Sociology of Unconventional Life-Styles*, 38.

46. Cotten, "Sex Dichotomy Among the American Kalderas Gypsies," 223.

47. Sutherland, *Gypsies: The Hidden Americans*, 206.

48. Gropper, *Gypsies in the City*, 88.

49. Sutherland, *Gypsies: The Hidden Americans*, 206–207.

50. Sutherland, *Gypsies: The Hidden Americans*, 241–247. For example, marriages between individuals who are more closely related than first cousins, as well as between a man and his brother's wife or son's wife, would be *marimé*.

51. Sutherland, *Gypsies: The Hidden Americans*, 206–208.

52. Gropper, *Gypsies in the City*, 141. However, Matt Salo noted that in fact in the American context marriages between male Rom and female non-Rom were actually more common than intergroup marriages within the Rom communities (that is, between Rom, Ludari, and Romničel). He noted that,

> The reason for this apparent contradiction is simple enough. The *gažia* (feminine plural) were viewed as practically without culture and thus could be removed from their families and remodeled to fit into Gypsy life. This was considered much more difficult to do with members of other Gypsy groups. The Romničel view was that it would involve the confrontation of "two stubbornnesses." As one Romani phrased it, "You can't take the Gypsy out of a Gypsy and put in another Gypsy!" [Salo, "Gypsy Ethnicity," 92].

53. For detailed discussions of the *daro*, see Sutherland, *Gypsies: The Hidden Americans*, 220– 223; Sway, *Familiar Strangers: Gypsy Life in America*, 67–69; Kephart, *Extraordinary Groups: The Sociology of Unconventional Life-Styles*, 24–26.

54. Sway, *Familiar Strangers: Gypsy Life in America*, 16–30.

55. Sway, *Familiar Strangers: Gypsy Life in America*, 17.

56. Okely, *The Traveller-Gypsies*, 58–60.

57. Sway, *Familiar Strangers: Gypsy Life in America*, 110–111.

58. Sway, *Familiar Strangers: Gypsy Life in America*, 110–111; G, 91–94)

59. Okely, *The Traveller-Gypsies*, 53–56.

60. Sutherland, *Gypsies: The Hidden Americans*, 87.

61. Gropper, *Gypsies in the City*, 38–39.

62. Carol Silverman, "Everyday Drama: Impression Management of Urban Gypsies," *Urban Anthropology* 11, 3/4 (1982): 386.

63. Gropper, *Gypsies in the City*, 30.

64. Sway, *Familiar Strangers: Gypsy Life in America*, 96.

65. Sutherland, *Gypsies: The Hidden Americans*, 93–95; Gropper, *Gypsies in the City*, 41–43.

66. Sutherland, *Gypsies: The Hidden Americans*, 93.

67. Sway, *Familiar Strangers: Gypsy Life in America*, 95.

68. Gropper, *Gypsies in the City*, 109.

69. Sway, *Familiar Strangers: Gypsy Life in America*, 57–59; see also Silverman, "Everyday Drama: Impression Management of Urban Gypsies," 383.

70. Fonseca, *Bury Me Standing: The Gypsies and Their Journey*, 48.

71. Sway, *Familiar Strangers: Gypsy Life in America*, 59.

72. See, for instance, Salo and Salo, *The Kalderas in Eastern Canada*, 94–114; Elwood Trigg, *Gypsy Demons and Divinities: The Magic and Religion of the Gypsies* (Secaucus, NJ: Citadel Press, 1973).

73. Silverman, "Everyday Drama: Impression Management of Urban Gypsies," 377–398.

74. Silverman, "Everyday Drama: Impression Management of Urban Gypsies," 378.

75. Silverman, "Everyday Drama: Impression Management of Urban Gypsies," 382.

76. Silverman, "Everyday Drama: Impression Management of Urban Gypsies," 383.

77. Silverman, "Everyday Drama: Impression Management of Urban Gypsies," 391.

78. Gabrielle Tyrnauer, *Gypsies and the Holocaust: A Bibliography and Introductory Essay*, 2nd ed. (Montréal: Montréal Institute for Genocide Studies, Concordia University, 1991), iii.

79. See, for instance, Susan Tebbutt (ed.), *Sinti and Roma: Gypsies in German-Speaking Society and Literature* (New York: Berghahn, 1998); Rachel Tritt, *Struggling for Ethnic Identity: Czechoslovakia's Endangered Gypsies* (New York: Human Rights Watch, 1992); Ignacy-Marek Kaminski, *The State of Ambiguity: Studies of Gypsy Refugees* (Gothenburg, Sweden: Mobilis, 1980); Crowe, *A History of the Gypsies of Eastern Europe and Russia*; Crowe and Kolsti, *The Gypsies of Eastern Europe*; Fonseca, *Bury Me Standing: The Gypsies and Their Journey*; Stewart, *The Time of the Gypsies*. Although only tangentially concerned with the Rom, a work of considerable value in terms of recent developments in Eastern Europe is Christina Bratt Paulston and Donald Peckham (eds.), *Linguistic Minorities in Central and Eastern Europe* (Clevedon, Avon: Multilingual Matters, 1998). For a fascinating historical study of the interactions between the Rom and the Inquisition in Spain, see Maria Helena Sánchez Ortega, *La inquisición y los gitanos* (Madrid: Taurus Ediciones, 1988).

80. Tyrnauer, *Gypsies and the Holocaust*, vii. Actually, the Rom presented the Nazi race theory with a difficult challenge. As Tyrnauer explained,

> The Nazi's ideological dilemma, stemming from the presumed "Aryan" origin of the Gypsies, was nowhere more clearly seen than in the conflicting recommendations made by "racial scientists" and those in authority. While [some racial theorists] recommended sparing the more assimilated, those with "less than half Gypsy blood," others ... showed a marked preference for the nomadic "pure" Gypsies, and proposed special reserves where they could roam freely, speak their own language, preserve ancient "Aryan" customs and multiply for the study of future German "scientists." [Tyrnauer, *Gypsies and the Holocaust*, xiv].

In spite of this "academic" debate, however, in 1942 Himmler signed the "Auschwitz Decree" which sent nearly all of Germany's Rom to Auschwitz and their deaths.

81. Tyrnauer, *Gypsies and the Holocaust*, vii.

82. See, for instance, Ian Hancock, *The Pariah Syndrome: An Account of Gypsy Slavery and Persecution* (Ann Arbor, MI: Karoma, 1987).

83. Christian Bernadac, *L'Holocauste oblié: Le massacre des Tsiganes* (Paris: France-Empire, 1979); see also Sybil Milton, "Gypsies and the Holocaust," *The History Teacher* 24, 4 (1991): 375–387.

84. Quoted in Okely, *The Traveller-Gypsies*, 160.

85. Jean-Pierre Liégeois, *Gypsies and Travellers: Socio-cultural data, socio-political data* (Strasbourg, Germany: Council for Cultural Co-operation, 1987), 140.

86. Sway, *Familiar Strangers: Gypsy Life in America*, 72.

87. Gropper, *Gypsies in the City*, 130.

88. Gropper, *Gypsies in the City*, 32.

89. See, for instance, Zita Réger and Jean Berko Gleason, "Romani child-directed speech and children's language among Gypsies in Hungary," *Language in Society* 20 (1991): 601–617; Zita Réger, "A Preliminary Typology of Genres in the Oral Culture of Children Living in a Traditional Gypsy Community," paper presented at the Fourth International Conference on Romani Linguistics held at the University of Manchester, England, September 2–5, 1998.

90. Okely, *The Traveller-Gypsies*, 77–78.

91. Sway, *Familiar Strangers: Gypsy Life in America*, 104.

92. See Albert Vogel and Nan Elsasser, "Rom (Gypsy), Merimé, and the Schools," *Theory into Practice* 20, 1 (1981): 70–72.

93. Quoted in Sway, *Familiar Strangers: Gypsy Life in America*, 72.

94. Liégeois, *Gypsies and Travellers*, 59.

8

"No Gift is Better than Education": The Islamic Educational Enterprise

It is, in an important sense, inappropriate for a book concerned with non-Western educational traditions, such as this one, to include a chapter on Islam and the Islamic educational heritage. Islam is one of the world's three great monotheistic religions, along with Judaism and Christianity, and approximately one-fifth of the world's population are Muslim (see Fig. 8.1).[1] More important, Islam as a religion is not independent of the religions of the West in the way that Buddhism and Hinduism might be considered to be. Rather, Islam is part of what can be termed the *Judeo-Christian-Islamic tradition*, sharing with Judaism and Christianity many core beliefs, ideas, and values.[2] To be sure, the idea that all three religions are part of a single, unified tradition is for some people a problematic one, because just as they share many elements, so too do they disagree about key issues.[3] Nevertheless, historically the three faiths are closely related in ways quite different from their relationships with most other religions. This suggests, of course, that Islam is not really "non-Western" in the way that the other societies and religions we have examined thus far in this book can be said to be. Indeed, much of what we consider to be the basis for the Western tradition from the period of classical antiquity was preserved for us not in the West, but rather by Islamic scholars in the Middle Ages.[4] Why, then, is Islam included in this book?

The answer to this question is a pragmatic and straightforward one. While Islam may well be closely connected with Judaism and Christianity, it has, throughout Western history, been perceived to be alien and different.[5] This view of Islam as an "Other" in our own culture is in many ways as powerful today as ever before, encouraged by the resurgence of what has been called "militant Islam."[6] For many in the West, a lack of knowledge about and understanding of Islam is coupled quite closely with a fear and, in some cases, an active dislike for both the faith and its practitioners. In short, although Islam ought not be seen as non-Western, it nevertheless is seen in this light, and so should be treated here if for no other reason than to encourage a more accurate understanding of both Is-

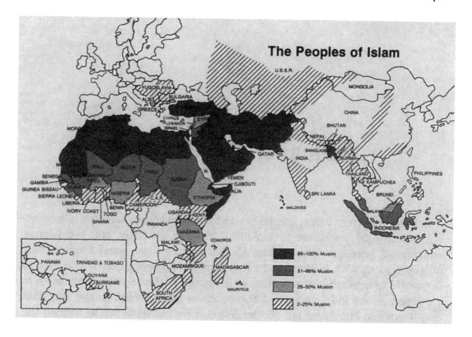

FIG. 8.1. The Islamic World [From John Esposito, *Islam: The Straight Path*, exp. and rev. ed. (New York: Oxford University Press, 1991), p. 2]. Reprinted with permission.

lam and the place of Islam in our own heritage. As John Esposito argued, "A basic knowledge of Islam is becoming essential for every American today. There are five million Muslims living in America. In fact, Islam is the third largest U.S. religion, and by the year 2010 it is expected to be second largest.... Islam, like Judaism and Christianity, is an American religion."[7]

Furthermore, given the historical relationship between the West and the Islamic world, one can offer an even stronger case for including the study of Islamic education in a book of this type. As Carolyn Fluehr-Lobban suggested in *Islamic Society in Practice*:

> Perhaps if the recent history of the world were different and Western society did not have the imperial advantage that it has inherited from the legacy of colonialism and economic domination, we might have studies of our culture by non-western people. A chapter entitled "Western Values and Social Practice" in such a study might include sections on individualism, self-sufficiency, entrepreneurial spirit, male supremacy, or optimism. The treatise, written in Arabic, might be read in translation by some "natives" who think it is reductionist and a simplification of their complex, multifaceted social reality.[8]

Just as such a chapter might have been written had recent history been different, then, so must a chapter such as this one be included in a book on non-Western educational traditions.

In this chapter, we begin by exploring the basic tenets of Islam as a religion, and then discuss the implications of these tenets for an understanding of what can be called an "Islamic philosophy of education." Finally, we examine the ways in which this Islamic philosophy of education has been manifested in traditional Islam education practice.

ISLAM: AN OVERVIEW

Discussions of Islam intended for non-Muslims often begin with Muhammad, but this is perhaps misleading. The word *Islam* actually means "submission," as in "submission to the will of God," and the real focus of Islam is not Muhammad, but rather, Allah (God).[9] Muhammad is important in his role as God's Prophet, as God's messenger bringing the word of God to humanity, and as an example of how a Muslim should seek to lead his life. As Mary Pat Fisher explained, "Muhammad's life story is important to Muslims, for his example is considered a key that opens the door to the Divine Presence."[10] Nevertheless, Muhammad was a man, the last prophet (*nabi*) in a long series of prophets sent by God to reveal His will—a series of prophets that included Adam, Abraham, Noah, Moses and Jesus, among others.[11] Islam, though, is far more than its messenger. With this in mind, we turn now to a brief account of the life of Muhammad.

The Life of Muhammad

Muhammad was born in 569 or 570 C.E. in the Arabian city of Mecca. His father had died before his birth, and his mother died when he was still quite young. He was initially cared for by his impoverished grandfather, but his grandfather died when Muhammad was only 8 years old. The boy was then raised by an uncle, Abu Talib, working first as a shepherd and later accompanying his uncle on caravan trade missions. As a young adult, Muhammad was well known in Mecca for his spirituality and his honesty. He was hired by a wealthy widow, Khadijah, who eventually married him.[12]

From the age of 35 on, Muhammad often spent time alone in spiritual retreats, in order to engage in prayer and meditation.[13] At the age of 40, during one of these retreats, the angel Gabriel appeared to him and told him that God had chosen him to be His messenger to all mankind. The angel insisted that Muhammad recite what he was told, and it was in this way that what we now know as the Qur'an was transmitted from Gabriel through Muhammad to humanity. Three years later, after a pause during which Muhammad continued to pray and meditate, Gabriel appeared again to Muhammad and commanded him to begin publicly proclaiming God's revelation. His message was simple and clear: "the belief in One Transcendent God, in Resurrection and the Last Judgment."[14] His message was a profoundly moral one, grounded in the revelations he was receiving from God—revelations that continued throughout his life, and which his followers were expected to learn by heart. It was also a message that contained hope for the oppressed, which helps to explain both the historical and contemporary power of Islam in many parts of the world.

Muhammad and his followers were persecuted by the Meccan leaders, who saw Muhammad as a social and political revolutionary, threatening the status quo, much as Jesus had been seen in his time. This led, in the year 622 C.E., to Muhammad's departure from Mecca to the more welcoming town of Yathrib (now Medina), where he established the first Muslim community.[15] This event, called the *hijrah* ("migration"), was a crucial one in the development of Islam, and it is from the date of the *hijrah*—not that of Muhammad's birth, or even of the first appearance of Gabriel to Muhammad—that the Muslim calendar begins. Ultimately, in 630 C.E., Muhammad and his followers returned triumphantly to Mecca, and then onward to northern Africa, the Persian states, and beyond.

The Central Beliefs of Islam

For Islam, there is a close interrelationship between belief and practice, and the distinction between being a believer (*mu'min*) and an unbeliever (*kafir*) is to a significant extent based on one's practice.[16] This is so because the basic beliefs of Islam in large part presume certain practices, as we see later in this chapter. This having been said, it is nonetheless possible for us to delineate the beliefs that are at the core of the Islamic worldview. These core beliefs of Islam are identified clearly in the *Qur'an* itself: "The Prophet believes in what has been revealed to him from his Lord, and so do the Believers. They all believe in God, His angels, His scriptures and His messengers, making no distinction among His prophets. And they say, 'We hear and we obey. Grant us Thy forgiveness, our Lord, and unto Thee is the journeying'" (Sura 2: 285).

As these core beliefs are discussed, it is important to keep in mind the following warning from Suzanne Haneef: "the principles on which the Islamic systems are based are constant, unalterable and universal ones originating in Divine revelation. However, the details of their application may certainly be adjusted as necessary within the Islamic framework to fit existing needs and circumstances."[17] In other words, although the core beliefs may be the same, the ways in which they will be manifested in practice may differ in various social and cultural contexts.[18]

The most fundamental belief of Islam is in the unity and Oneness of God. From a Muslim point of view, "the Oneness of God is the primordial religion taught by all prophets of all faiths. Muhammad merely served to remind people of it."[19] In Arabic, the concept of the unity of God is expressed in the term *tawhid*, which Khurshid Ahmad explained as follows: "*Tawhid* is a revolutionary concept and constitutes the essence of the teachings of Islam. It means that there is only One Supreme Lord of the universe. He is Omnipotent, Omnipresent and the Sustainer of the world and of mankind."[20]

Islam, as noted earlier, teaches that God has sent a series of prophets to mankind—in fact, according to a saying of Muhammad, there have been some 124,000 prophets, beginning with Adam.[21] Before Muhammad, each prophet was sent to renew the message of God's Oneness and unity to a particular people.[22] Only Muhammad, however, "was entrusted with the final and complete statement of God's guidance for the whole of humanity for all time to come."[23] Because of his special role, Muhammad is called the "Seal of the Prophets" in the Qur'an, and is believed by Muslims to be the last and final authority in the prophetic tradition.[24]

Two Islamic beliefs that are closely related to the role of the prophetic tradition are the belief in angels and the role of revealed Scriptures. It was the angel Gabriel who appeared to Muhammad, and this was necessary, as Haneef explained:

> Because the glory and majesty of the Creator is so awesome and overwhelming that a limited, flesh-and-blood human being is unable to bear direct contact with Him, God chose to convey His revelation to the prophets, including Muhammad … through the agency of an angel. … It is because of this vital role of angels as bringers of the Divine revelation to the prophets that belief in them is so important as to form a fundamental article of faith in Islam.[25]

Many of the prophets were also messengers (*rasul*), which is to say that the revelation they left was in written form. Thus, Islam accepts both the Hebrew Torah and the Christian Gospels as revealed Scripture, and Jews and Christians are both recognized in Islam as "people of the Book" (*ahl al-kitab*).[26] The status of the Qur'an, however, is somewhat different than that of other Scripture, as we see later in this chapter. For now, it is sufficient to note that for a Muslim, the "Qur'an is the only divinely-revealed scripture in the history of mankind which has been preserved to the present time in its exact original form."[27]

Finally, Muslims believe in both an afterlife and in a "Last Judgment" at which each person will have to answer for his or her sins. As stipulated in the Qur'an, "The works of each person We have bound about his neck. On the Day of Resurrection, We shall confront him with a book spread wide open, saying, 'Read your book. Enough for you this day that your own soul should call you to account'" (Sura 17: 13–14).

Islam teaches that there will be a physical, bodily resurrection, followed by either eternal paradise or eternal punishment, depending on God's judgment. Much has been made by writers about the descriptions of paradise found in the Qur'an, which emphasize physical and material pleasures. As John Esposito, using the *Qur'an* as his source, described it, the "Garden of Paradise is a heavenly mansion of perpetual peace and bliss with flowing rivers, beautiful gardens, and the enjoyment of one's spouses and beautiful, dark-eyed female companions."[28] Granting that such descriptions are indeed to be found in the *Qur'an*, Hamidullah compellingly pointed out, however, that:

> All this is easily explained when one thinks of the vast majority of men, of the common masses, to whom the Divine message is addressed. It is necessary to speak to every one according to his capacity of understanding and of intelligence.... The *Qur'an* speaks of Paradise and Hell simply as a means of persuading the average man to lead a just life and to march in the path of truth; it attaches no importance to details whether they describe a place or a state of things ... [29]

We turn now to a discussion of how these different core beliefs of Islam are manifested in practice in the lives of Muslims.

The Five Pillars of Islam

Although there is a great deal of diversity in the Islamic world with respect to religious practice, there is a core of practices shared by all Muslims. Specifically, there are five essential practices, commonly called the *pillars of Islam*, which are universally accepted throughout the Islamic world.[30] These five pillars of Islam are:

1. The profession of faith,
2. Prayer,
3. Almsgiving,
4. Fasting,
5. The pilgrimage to Mecca.[31]

The *profession of faith* (or *shahadah*, literally "witness" or "testimony") refers to the obligation of the Muslim to declare his or her faith that "There is no god but Allah, and Muhammad is His Prophet" ("*La ilaha illa Allah, Muhammadu Rasul Allah*" in Arabic)[32] (see Fig. 8.2). In other words, the believer accepts the absolute monotheism of Islam, the oneness and unity (*tawhid*) of God, and accepts Muhammad as God's final messenger to humanity. Furthermore, this implies that one accepts the obligation to inform others of the faith, although the *Qur'an* explicitly rejects the use of coercion in such efforts: "Let there be no compulsion in religion; truth stands out clear from error: whoever rejects evil and believes in God has grasped the most trustworthy handle, that never breaks" (Sura 2: 256).

The second pillar of Islam is prayer (*salah*); Muslims pray five times a day, at daybreak, noon, midafternoon, sunset, and evening.[33] Prayer is preceded by ritual ablutions (*wudu'*), normally done with water, which help to prepare the

FIG. 8.2.   A calligraphic presentation of the *Shadadah*.

individual for worship. The Muslim then faces Mecca and recites a series of prayers and Qur'anic passages. On Fridays, the noon prayer is a congregational one, led by a religious leader (called an *imam*). Prayer is thus both an individual and a communal obligation for the Muslim.

Almsgiving (*zakah*) "is an act both of worship or thanksgiving to God and of service to the community."[34] Although the basic goal of almsgiving is to redress economic inequities and to support the poor, it is not charity, in that it is obligatory rather than voluntary.[35] Muslims are required to donate at least 2.5% of their income in this manner,[36] and the funds are used both for the poor (including widows and orphans) and for the spread of the faith (which includes support for religious and educational institutions). This emphasis on the obligation to help those in need is one that occurs repeatedly in the Qur'an: "Who denies religion? It is the person who repulses the orphan and does not promote feeding the poor. Woe to those who worship but are neglectful, those who want to be noticed but who withhold assistance from those in need" (Sura 107: 1–7).

Once each year, during the entire month of Ramadan, all adult Muslims who are able are required to fast (*sawm*) from sunrise to sunset.[37] During the fast, Muslims must abstain from food, drink, smoking, and sexual activity. This is a time for reflection and self-discipline, and "a time to thank God for His blessings, repent and atone for one's sins, discipline the body and strengthen moral character, remember one's ultimate dependence upon God, and respond to the needs of the poor and hungry."[38] The fifth pillar of Islam is the pilgrimage (*hajj*) to Mecca.[39] All Muslims who can possibly do so are expected to make the pilgrimage at least once in their lifetime. The *hajj*:

> constitutes a form of worship with the totality of the Muslim's being: with his body, mind and soul, with his time, possessions and the temporary sacrifice of all ordinary comforts, conveniences and tokens of status and individuality which human beings normally enjoy, to assume for a few days the condition of a pilgrim totally at God's service and disposal, His slave who seeks only His pleasure.[40]

Underlying all five of the pillars of Islam is the unity of belief and practice, as well as the idea that Islam is not simply a body of religious beliefs, but is, rather, a unified and consistent way of life for both the individual and the community.[41] *Shari'a*, or Islamic religious law, provides the framework within which Islamic communities should exist, thus ensuring consistency with the mandates of the *Qur'an*.[42] As Ghulam Sarwar explained:

> Islam is a complete way of life. It is the guidance provided by Allah, the Creator of the Universe, for all mankind. It covers all the things people do in their lifetime. Islam tells us the purpose of our creation, our final destiny and our place among other creatures. It shows us the best way to conduct our private, social, political, economic, moral and spiritual affairs.[43]

One of the more controversial aspects of Islam has been the role and place of women in society, and this is an area about which there is considerable debate both in the West and in many contemporary Islamic societies.[44] There can be little doubt that in the time of the Prophet the status of women was improved markedly by Islam, and women are indeed accorded important rights and privileges by *shari'a*.[45] Islamic law grants women the right to enter into contracts, to earn money, and to possess goods in their own right, as well as ensuring their right to inherit.[46] Even more important for our concerns here, women are: "equal to [men] in the pursuit of education and knowledge. When Islam enjoins the seeking of knowledge upon Muslims, it makes no distinction between man and woman. Almost fourteen centuries ago, Muhammad declared that the pursuit of knowledge is incumbent on every Muslim male and female."[47]

There are, however, significant distinctions in the rights, duties, and responsibilities of men and women. The distinctions in treatment between them are argued to be manifestations of the different natures of the two sexes, and it is commonly asserted that men and women are indeed *equal* in Islam, but they are not the *same*, and that Islam therefore accords them appropriately different social positions and responsibilities.[48] As David Waines explained the "Islamic feminist" view:

> Women have the right to education, to religious instruction, to honor and respect, to the vote, and to employment. There are, however, restrictions sanctioned by the religious law for the welfare and stability of society as a whole. A woman can be

neither a political leader nor a judge; she must only appear in public modestly dressed, and her natural and sacred task is to keep the household smoothly functioning and to raise and instruct her children to be good Muslims. Men, for their part, must shoulder the burden of providing for the family in material ways. Liberation for a woman does not mean being like a male, or taking up male tasks, but rather being herself and fulfilling the destiny Allah created for her.[49]

In short, both with respect to the role of women and in terms of other aspects of social organization, Islam provides far more than a framework for social organization; it is a total, comprehensive way of life[50] in which religion is integral to economics,[51] politics,[52] law, and society.[53] Indeed, one of the areas in which a great deal of philosophical and theological work is being done by contemporary Muslim scholars is that of the "Islamization of knowledge."[54] The objectives of such an "Islamization of knowledge," according to Ismail Raji al-Farugqi, include:

1. To master the modern disciplines.
2. To master the Islamic legacy.
3. To establish the specific relevance of Islam to each area of modern knowledge.
4. To seek ways for a creative synthesis between the legacy and modern knowledge.
5. To launch Islamic thought on the trajectory that leads it to fulfilment of the divine patterns of Allah ... [55]

These objectives, as we shall see, have important implications for both the philosophy and practice of Islamic education.

The Role of the Qur'an

An understanding of Islam is possible only with an understanding of the Qur'an, which holds a unique place in Islam. While both Judaism and Christianity have scriptural traditions that include sacred texts, these texts are viewed by most believers in a way quite different from the view of the Qur'an in Islamic thought. The Qur'an is not the "inspired" Word of God, nor is it a record of what was reported to have been told to Muhammad. Rather, for the Muslim, the Qur'an is the exact, literal transcription of the words of God Himself, precisely as they were given to Muhammad.[56] In other words, the Qur'an is "the unadulterated word of God, which has become audible through Muhammad."[57] As Suzanne Haneef, writing as a Muslim herself, commented, "The Holy Qur'an is the only divinely-revealed scripture in the history of mankind which has been preserved to the present time in its exact original form."[58] This means, of course, that since the Qur'an was revealed in Arabic, it was spoken by God in Arabic, and should therefore only be read and recited in that language: "To recite the *Qur'an* is the most sublime and edifying occupation for the Muslim, even when he or she does not intellectually understand its words, as is the case with most non-Arab believers. Because the *Qur'an* is the Divine Word *par excellence*, Muslims consider it inconceivable to 'translate' it into any language."[59]

Nor is the *Qur'an* merely written in Arabic; the Arabic in which it is composed is believed by Muslims to be "inimitable and of superhuman beauty and power."[60] Not only do Muslims believe that it is not possible to match the beauty of the style of the *Qur'an*, but they use this style as compelling evidence for its divine origin.[61] Because Muhammad was illiterate, and because the records we have in the *Hadith* ("Traditions of the Prophet") of his speech makes clear that he spoke in a language quite different from that of the *Qur'an*, it follows that he was, as he claimed, only the means of transmission for the *Qur'an*.[62] Therefore it makes no sense to talk meaningfully about an English language *Qur'an*, nor can one really talk about a translation into English of the *Qur'an*. Instead, for Muslims English language translations are best discussed as "interpretations" of the *Qur'an*. As Haneef explained:

> Because of its extremely distinctive style and language, it is impossible for a translation to do more than convey its bare meaning. The great nobility of its form of expression, the earnest, moving, eloquent style which is its outstanding characteristic, cannot be translated, and hence any translation must be regarded (as all translators themselves confirm) as a mere approximation to the sense of the words.[63]

Finally, unlike both Jewish and Christian scriptures, which were in large part created as written texts, the *Qur'an* is, in essence, an oral text preserved in written form—in fact, the word itself is often translated, "the Recitation." The oral nature of the *Qur'an* is reinforced by the inclusion of *Qur'anic* passages in daily prayers and by the emphasis placed on its recitation by Muslims.[64]

This understanding of the nature of the *Qur'an*, of course, has important educational implications for the Muslim.[65] First, literacy becomes an important religious obligation. Indeed, the name of the *Qur'an* itself—which can also be translated as "that which is to be read"—entails a challenge to become literate. Muslims the world over not only read the *Qur'an* but, regardless of their native language, memorize the *Qur'an* in Arabic. Thus, the role of Arabic, as the language not only of the *Qur'an* but also of Islamic prayer, takes on a great significance for the believer as well. With this background in mind, we turn now to a discussion of what might be termed an *Islamic philosophy of education*.

ISLAMIC PHILOSOPHY OF EDUCATION

Education has, since the time of the Prophet, played a key role in Islam. As A. L. Tibawi commented, "the mosques, became the first schools in Islam [and] it would be equally true to say that the Qur'an was the first textbook."[66] In fact, *education* from an Islamic point of view makes little sense if one removes it from a religious context, and it is in the Qur'an that educational thought should be grounded.[67] As Abdul-Rahman Salih Abdullah explained:

> Since the Qur'an provides the Muslim with an outlook towards life, its princi-ples must guide Islamic education. One cannot talk about Islamic education without taking the Qur'an as one's starting point ... the Qur'an lays down the foundation for education aims and methods. Moreover, the Muslim educator will find in the Qur'an the guiding principles which help in selecting the content of the curriculum.[68]

Given the view of the nature of the Qur'an discussed earlier in this chapter, such a view of its centrality for educational thought is hardly surprising. Is-lamic educational thought, although based on the Qur'an and the *Hadith*, has, nevertheless, been further developed and articulated by Muslim scholars and educators. Among the best examples of such educational philosophers in the Islamic tradition is the theologian, mystic and teacher al-Ghazali, about whom Tibawi wrote, "Classical Arabic literature contains no theory of education more authoritative, systematic and comprehensive than had been bequeathed by al-Ghazali."[69] Al-Ghazali's philosophy of education provided the bedrock for Islamic educational thought for generations, and "practically all educa-tional literature down to the beginning of modernization in the nineteenth century is either inspired by his writings or directly derived from them."[70]

Al-Ghazali's view of education is characterized by a deep spirituality cou-pled with both a good deal of common sense and an obvious concern and affec-tion for children. In essence, al-Ghazali believed that there were two ways in which knowledge might be acquired: through human reason, and from "light from God." In a good educational setting, a balance will be achieved between these two, albeit one in which the latter is viewed as of greater significance than the former—a resolution of the faith/reason problem reminiscent of that of St. Thomas Aquinas. Furthermore, al-Ghazali believed that all children have the capacity to learn: "Knowledge exists potentially in the human soul like a seed in the soil; by learning the potential becomes actual."[71] The focus of education for al-Ghazali is largely on what might today be called *moral educa-tion* rather than on academic learning alone. As Tibawi explained:

> "The child," [al-Ghazali] wrote, "is a trust [placed by God] in the hands of his parents, and his innocent heart is a precious element capable of taking impres-sions." If the parents, and later on the teachers, brought him up in righteousness he would live happily in this world and the next and they would be rewarded by God for their good deed. If they neglected the child's upbringing and education he would lead a life of unhappiness in both worlds and they would bear the bur-den of the sin of neglect.[72]

It is worth noting here that within an Islamic framework, unlike in Christianity with its doctrine of "original sin," children are believed to have a basically good nature (*fitrah*),[73] and thus the purpose of education is not viewed as one of "correcting" or "remediating" a sinful nature but rather one of guidance—precisely the same goal as of the *Qur'an* itself.[74]

Another Islamic scholar who contributed important insights to the development of an Islamic philosophy of education was the historian Ibn Khaldun. Ibn Khaldun believed that education could only take place in a civilized social order, and, like the American philosopher of education John Dewey centuries later, he focused on the social nature of education: "Ibn Khaldun starts from first principles: education is a social phenomenon and teaching is one of the social crafts; man is a social animal and his prosecution of learning is conditioned by the nature of the material, intellectual and spiritual forces of the civilization in which he lives."[75]

Ibn Khaldun, like al-Ghazali before him, also addressed the role of reason in the learning process. It is reason that provides the base for education, on Ibn Khaldun's account. As he himself wrote, "Man is distinguished from animals by a capacity to reason. His reason guides him to make a living, to cooperate with other members of his society and to accept what God has revealed through His prophets for man's welfare in this world and the next. Man is therefore a reasoning animal, and reasoning is the foundation of all learning."[76] The ability to reason is not, however, given equally to all people, and there are innate intellectual differences among people. Furthermore, all learning ultimately rests on divine guidance—Ibn Khaldun recommends that learners "seek God's guidance which had illuminated the way of learners before you and taught them that which they knew not."[77] This is an important facet of Islamic educational thought, because it makes clear that any Islamic educational philosophy *must* be value-laden—in the words of Yusuf Waghid, "a theory of Islamic education cannot be epistemologically 'neutral'."[78]

It is possible for us to identify some of the broad outlines of an Islamic philosophy of education. Abdul-Rahman Salih Abdullah articulated some of the key elements in such a philosophy of education (although he prefers the term *hikmah*) as follows:

> The Islamic theory of education is fundamentally based upon the *Qur'anic* concepts. In this theory the door is left open for concepts which come from different fields of knowledge provided that they fit the *Qur'anic* perspective. All elements which cannot be reconciled with Islamic principles should be excluded. It has been pointed out that traditional philosophy which gives excessive weight to reason cannot offer any help to our theory.[79]

Islamic philosophy of education recognizes three distinct kinds of educational aims. Specifically, there are physical aims (*ahdaf jismiyyah*), spiritual aims (*ahdaf ruhiyyah*), and mental aims (*ahdaf 'aqliyyah*).[80] In essence, these aims taken together are concerned with ensuring that education results not merely in the Platonic goal of "a sound mind in a sound body," but rather in a thoroughly integrated personality grounded in the Qur'an and in Qur'anic morality, since "a person who truly accepts the message of Islam should accept all the ideals embodied in the Qur'an."[81] Underlying these different kinds of educational aims in Islamic philosophy of education are a number of common, unifying characteristics, including:

1. Islamic education should be concerned with developing the unique characteristics of the individual human being in such a way as to allow him/her to adapt to the standards of his/her society (which should share the ideals of Islam).
2. Islamic educational aims should be both realistic and idealistic. In other words, Islamic education must take into account biological needs, while at the same time not accepting an individual's yielding to temptation.
3. Because the Qur'an and its ideals are timeless and unchangeable, so too must educational ideals grounded in the Qur'an be seen as timeless and unchanging. The aims of Islamic philosophy of education are thus universal in nature.
4. Islamic education should be concerned both with preparation for this life and with preparation for the Hereafter.
5. Islamic educational aims and objectives should be translated into observable behavior.[82]

Having briefly discussed Islamic educational thought, we now turn to an examination of the ways in which this Islamic philosophy of education has been manifested in practice in traditional Islamic schools.

TRADITIONAL ISLAMIC EDUCATIONAL PRACTICE

The traditional Islamic educational system has varied from time to time and from place to place in a number of ways, but underlying the diversity in terms of curricula, teaching methods, and so on, there has been a common core that allows us to talk about a general approach to Qur'anic education in the Islamic world.[83] It is important to keep in mind, however, that what is being discussed here is the Islamic educational tradition, rather than the Western-inspired and derived, formal educational systems that are found today in most Islamic countries. Although such modern systems may include religious instruction, they are not "Islamic" in the same sense as traditional Qur'anic schools and often coexist with such Qur'anic schools, serving very distinct and different purposes, even today.

The basis of traditional Islamic education is the kuttab, or Qur'anic school, which had developed and become widespread by the 8th century.[84] This institution bears the responsibility for providing all children with the foundations necessary for the practice of their faith. The curriculum focuses on the memorization of the Qur'an[85] and the ability to read Arabic, although in some societies this basic curriculum was expanded to include the study of Arabic grammar, poetry, writing, and often penmanship.[86] However, it is important to note here that by "reading Arabic" what is often meant for non-Arabic speaking children is simply an ability to decode written Arabic for purposes of pronunciation, rather than fluent reading for meaning in what is for them a second language. As Lisbet Holtedahl and Mahmoudou Djingui noted,

> Young Muslims will begin by learning the Arabic alphabet, then go on to recognize letters and repeat them in speech, learn by heart some of the last suras (chapters) of the Quran, and conclude their studies by reciting the entire Quran without necessarily knowing its meaning. Throughout this period of study, they will learn all they need to know in order to say their prayers correctly. Having successfully recited the Quran, a young man may be called a *mallum* and may, if he wishes, establish a school for beginners.[87]

The skills taught in such basic Qur'anic schools are both valuable and necessary in the context of an Islamic society, and, in comparing such traditional schooling with that of other societies, it is clear that while such Qur'anic schooling:

> did not take [children] very far ... it fulfilled the requirements of the great mass of Muslims in the Middle Ages, indeed up to quite recent times, in that it gave them basic literacy. It is worth observing ... that the level of literacy among the masses of the people in the Islamic world during the Middle Ages, and perhaps even up to the establishment of state primary education in European countries, was probably higher than in Christendom.[88]

Beyond the level of the *kuttab* are other Islamic educational institutions that are responsible for the preparation of Islamic professionals—the scribes, theologians, magistrates, and so on, upon whom an Islamic society relies. Among these advanced institutions are mosque schools, mosque circles, bookshops, and universities (see Fig. 8.3). The most common and significant of these advanced institutions for most Islamic societies have traditionally been the *madaris* (singular, *madrasah*), which provided curricula that include the study of *tafsir* (Qur'anic exegesis), the *Hadith, shari'a, fiqh* (Islamic jurisprudence), and a variety of other appropriate subjects (see Fig. 8.4), often at very sophisticated levels of scholarship.[89] An important aspect of such higher education is the role of disputation or "dialectic" (*jadal*), which serves not only as an organizing framework for classroom teaching, but also gives considerable insight into the goals of Islamic higher education in general.[90] In the case of contemporary Shi'ite *madrasa* education, for instance, Roy Mottahedeh observes that:

> The image of education as disputation is so powerful that in theory when a student wins a disputation with the teacher, the teacher should cede his place to an-

PRESCHOOL	No formal organization; home-based.
BASIC SCHOOLING	Kuttab
TRANSITIONAL SCHOOLING (Secondary/College)	Palace Schools Masjid (Mosque Schools) Halqha (Mosque Circles) Madrasah
HIGHER EDUCATIONAL INSTITUTIONS	Bait-al-Hikmas (Houses of Wisdom) Bookshop Schools Literary Salons Universities Selected Mosques (e.g., Al-Azhar)

FIG. 8.3.   Traditional types of Islamic educational institutions
(8th–14th centuries C.E.).

Linguistic Studies	Arabic Grammar (al-Nahw wa'l-Sarf) Rhetoric (al-Balaghah) Literature (al-Adab)
Qur'anic and Islamic Studies	Scriptural (Qur'anic) Knowledge (al-Qira'at) Knowledge of the Hadith Scriptural Exegesis (al-Tafsir) Theology (al-Kalam) Jurisprudence (al-Fiqh)
"Philosophical" Studies	Alchemy (Chemistry) Anatomy Astrology Astronomy Botony Geology History Logic Mathematics (including arithmetic, algebra, and geometry) Medicine Meterology Music Philology Philosophy (non-Islamic) Physics Zoology

FIG. 8.4.   Curricular Areas of Study in Traditional Islamic Higher Education.

other teacher. While this seldom happens, and while there are limits beyond which challenges to the teacher might amount to unacceptable behavior and/or an unacceptable denial of fundamental precepts of Islam, teachers are likely to teach only those texts over which they feel they have complete mastery. This self-selection more or less decides what level teachers achieve in the system. And, since students can shop around and find which teacher teaches the set textbooks in a way most congenial to him, there is a natural selection that "retires" unpopular teachers to provincial seminaries or other tasks in the Shi'ite religious establishment.[91]

It is also worth noting at this point that traditional *madrasah* education has come under considerable criticism in many Islamic societies and is often perceived (not entirely incorrectly) to be a challenge to Western-oriented state schooling.[92] Typical of the criticisms of traditional *madrasah* education is A. H. Nayyar's claim that, "Present-day *madrasah* education indicates the existence of an ice age of the intellect."[93] It is interesting to note that such challenges, although grounded in and enunciated in Islamic societies, are in many ways similar to criticisms of some religiously-based educational institutions in the West.

CONCLUSION

Traditional Islamic educational thought and practice are, in short, inseparable from the fabric of Islamic religious thought and practice. As Carolyn Fluehr-Lobban commented about Islam in general, "Islam has been a powerful unifier because … its teachings blend religious, moral, and social practice into an indivisible whole for the believer-practitioner."[94] This unity of Islam is the context in which its educational thought and practice must be understood. To a very considerable extent, an understanding of the Qur'an is a necessary condition for a real understanding of traditional Islamic educational thought and practice. Indeed, the Islamic view of the importance of education is nowhere articulated more clearly than in the Qur'an itself, where we read, "And say, O Muhammad, 'My Lord, increase me in knowledge'" (Sura 20: 114). Finally, as we come to the end of this chapter, three beautiful passages from the *Hadith* provide as good a conclusion as one might wish:

> The Prophet prayed, "O my Lord, do not let the sun set on any day during which I did not increase in knowledge."

> No gift among all the gifts of a father to his child is better than education.[95]

> The person who goes in search of knowledge is on active service for God until he returns.

QUESTIONS FOR REFLECTION AND DISCUSSION

1. Memorization constitutes a central feature of traditional Qur'anic educational practice. What are the advantages of learning selected texts

(e.g., in the case of Islamic education, the *Qur'an*) by heart? Are there comparable advantages, in our own society, to memorizing other kinds of literature? What, in your view, are the problems associated with the use of extensive memorization in education?

2. In earlier chapters, we have discussed the distinction between "education" and "schooling." How does this distinction apply to the case of traditional Islamic thought and practice?

3. In this chapter, it is suggested that Muslims, when discussing the issue of gender and gender relations in Islam, commonly argue that men and women are indeed *equal* in Islam, but they are not the *same*, and that Islam therefore accords them appropriately different social positions and responsibilities. What are the educational implications for this argument? How does this view differ from those generally advocated by Western educators?

4. For the Muslim educator, what is the role of moral development in the educational process? Does moral education simply "come with the territory" for the educator, or is there an even stronger relationship between the two than this suggests?

5. In contemporary American society, are there other religious groups whose view of the role and purpose of education would parallel that found in Islam? What other commonalities are there between the groups you identify and Muslims? How might one explain these similarities?

6. From a Muslim perspective, the appropriate aims of education, since they are grounded in the *Qur'an*, are understood to be "timeless and unchanging." Does this view of the nature of philosophy of education differ from others with which you are familiar? What are the strengths of such a philosophy? The weaknesses?

7. Although not discussed explicitly in this chapter, an important feature of Islamic educational thought is its underlying epistemology. What generalizations can you make, from your knowledge of Islam and traditional Islamic educational thought and practice, about the epistemological beliefs of Islamic educational thought?

8. As increasing numbers of Muslim students begin attending American public schools in the years ahead, what kinds of changes and adjustments may be required of classroom teachers? What changes, if any, might be needed in the curriculum?

9. How do the three kinds of educational aims identified in this chapter (physical aims, spiritual aims, and mental aims) interrelate and overlap? What are the implications of such a view of educational aims for the curriculum? For teaching methods?

10. Do you agree with the author that there is, in fact, a "Judeo-Christian-Islamic" heritage? Why or why not? How would you describe the relationship among these three religious traditions?

RECOMMENDED FURTHER READINGS

There are a number of excellent introductions to Islam. David Waines' *An Introduction to Islam* (Cambridge, England: Cambridge University Press, 1995) is a recent work of this sort; John Esposito's *Islam: The Straight Path*, expanded edition (New York: Oxford University Press, 1991) is widely used and available. A very thorough guide to Islam is provided in Caesar Farah's *Islam: Beliefs and Observations*, 5th ed. (Hauppage, NY: Barron's Educational Series, 1994). Other good general works include George W. Braswell, Jr., *Islam: Its Prophet, Peoples, Politics and Power* (Nashville, TN: Broadman & Holman, 1996); Thomas Lippman, *Understanding Islam: An Introduction to the Muslim World*, 2nd rev. ed. (New York: Meridan, 1995); Kenneth Cragg, *The Event of the Qur'an: Islam and Its Scripture* (Oxford, England: Oneworld, 1994); Akbar S. Ahmed's *Discovering Islam: Making Sense of Muslim History and Society* (London: Routledge, 1988); and Frederick Denny's *Islam* (San Francisco: Harper, 1987). Suzanne Haneef provides an outstanding introduction to Islam from the perspective of an American convert to the faith in her book, *What Everyone Should Know About Islam and Muslims* (Des Plaines, IL: Library of Islam, 1985); and Ruqaiyyah Maqsood's *Islam* (London: NTC Publishing Group, 1994) provides a useful "hands on" introduction to Islam. Finally, a fascinating and sophisticated treatment of contemporary Islam is found in Akbar S. Ahmed's *Postmodernism and Islam: Predicament and Promise* (London: Routledge, 1992).

NOTES

1. See Mary Pat Fisher, *Living Religions*, 2nd ed. (Englewood Cliffs, NJ: Prentice Hall, 1994), 297.
2. Fisher, *Living Religions*, 297.
3. See, for example, the fascinating discussion of the way in which the three religions view Abraham in Hans Küng, *Judaism: Between Yesterday and Tomorrow* (New York: Crossroad, 1992), 11–18.
4. See George Holmes (ed.), *The Oxford Illustrated History of Medieval Europe* (Oxford, England: Oxford University Press, 1988), 50–51; see also Majid Fakhry, *A History of Islamic Philosophy*, 2nd ed. (New York: Columbia University Press, 1983); Franz Rosenthal, *The Classical Heritage in Islam* (London: Routledge, 1992).
5. See Edward Said, *Orientalism* (New York: Vintage, 1978).
6. Godrey H. Jansen, *Militant Islam* (New York: Harper & Row, 1979). Also of interest here are Maxime Rodinson, *L'Islam: Politique et croyance* (Paris: Fayard, 1993); Gilles Kepel and Yann Richard (eds.), *Intellectuels et militants de l'Islam contemporain* (Paris: Éditions du Seuil, 1990); John Voll, *Islam: Continuity and Change in the Modern World*, 2nd ed. (Syracuse, NY: Syracuse University Press, 1994).

7. John Esposito, "Islam in the World and in America," in Jacob Neusner (ed.), *World Religions in America: An Introduction* (Louisville, KY: Westminster/John Knox, 1994), 243. Also of interest here are Shahid Athar, *Reflections of an American Muslim* (Chicago: Kazi, 1994); George W. Braswell, Jr., *Islam: Its Prophet, Peoples, Politics and Power* (Nashville, TN: Broadman & Holman, 1996), 207–246; Yvonne Haddad, Byron Haines, and Ellison Findly (eds.), *The Islamic Impact* (Syracuse, NY: Syracuse University Press, 1984); Jane Smith, *Islam in America* (New York: Columbia University Press, 1999); Sha'ban Muftah Ismail, "Islamic Education in North America: A Reality, a Fact and a Responsibility," *Muslim Education Quarterly* 11, 3 (1994): 63–71.

8. Carolyn Fluehr-Lobban, *Islamic Society in Practice* (Gainesville: University of Florida Press, 1994), 44.

9. See Hammudah Abdalati, *Islam in Focus* (Indianapolis, IN: American Trust Publications, 1975), 1. This is a very important point, and helps to explain why the term "Mohammedan," which implies (falsely) that Muslims worship Muhammad, is deeply offensive to Muslims. See Maryam Jameelah, *Islam in Theory and Practice* (Lahore, Pakistan: Mohammad Yusuf Khan & Sons, 1986), 20– 21; Fluehr-Lobban, *Islamic Society in Practice*, 6–7.

10. Fisher, *Living Religions*, 298; see also Esposito, "Islam in the World and in America," 244– 245; Khurshid Ahmad (ed.), *Islam: Its Meaning and Message* (London: Islamic Foundation, 1980).

11. Esposito, "Islam in the World and in America," 244; M. Hamidullah, *Introduction to Islam* (Chicago: Kazi, 1981), 58–61.

12. A very thorough description of Muhammad's early life is provided in Muhammad Husayn Haykal, *The Life of Muhammad* (Indianapolis, IN: American Trust Publications, 1976). See also Karen Armstrong, *Muhammad: A Biography of the Prophet* (San Francisco: Harper, 1992); Ibn Ishaq, *The Life of Muhammad* (London: Oxford University Press, 1967); Martin Lings, *Muhammad: His Life Based on the Earliest Sources* (Rochester, CT: Inner Traditions, 1983); Abdul Hameed Siddiqui, *Life of Muhammad* (Des Plaines, IL: Library of Islam, 1991); Syed Ameer Ali, *The Spirit of Islam: A History of the Evolution and Ideals of Islam with a Life of the Prophet* (Delhi: Low Price Publications, 1990); Maxime Rodinson, *Mohammed* (New York: Vintage, 1974).

13. Hamidullah, *Introduction to Islam*, 6–7; see also Fazlur Rahman, *Islam*, 2nd ed. (Chicago: University of Chicago Press, 1979), 11–29; W. Montgomery Watt, *Muhammad at Mecca* (Karachi, Pakistan: Oxford University Press, 1953).

14. Hamidullah, *Introduction to Islam*, 8.

15. Esposito, "Islam in the World and in America," 245; see also W. Montgomery Watt, *Muhammad at Medina* (Karachi, Pakistan: Oxford University Press, 1956).

16. John Esposito, *Islam: The Straight Path* (New York: Oxford University Press, 1988), 68–69.

17. Suzanne Haneef, *What Everyone Should Know About Islam and Muslims* (Des Plaines, IL: Library of Islam, 1985), 93.

18. See Alfred Willms, "Nordafrika," in Michael Ursinus (ed.), *Der Islam in der Gegenwart* (München, Germany: Verlag C. H. Beck, 1984), 561–569; Lode Frank Brakel, "Indonesien," in Michael Ursinus (ed.), *Der Islam in der Gegenwart* (München, Germany: Verlag C. H. Beck, 1984), 570–581; Merwyn Hiskett, *The Development of Islam in West Africa*, 2nd ed. (Edinburgh: Edinburgh University Press, 1994); R. O. Lasisi, "French Colonialism and Islamic Education in West Africa, 1900–1939," *Muslim Education Quarterly* 12, 3 (1995): 12–22; Hassan Amdouni, *La famille musulmane: Relations familiales et éducations* (Paris: Al Qalam, 1992).

19. Fisher, *Living Religions*, 308.

20. Khurshid Ahmad, "Islam: Basic Principles and Characteristics," in Khurshid Ahmad (ed.), *Islam: Its Meaning and Message* (London: The Islamic Foundation, 1980), 29; see also Ghulam Sarwar, *Islam: Beliefs and Teaching* (London: Muslim Educational Trust, 1989), 19.

21. Sarwar, *Islam*, 27.

22. Haneef, *What Everyone Should Know About Islam and Muslims*, 20–21.

23. Haneef, *What Everyone Should Know About Islam and Muslims*, 20.

24. Fisher, *Living Religions*, 309.

25. Haneef, *What Everyone Should Know About Islam and Muslims*, 16–17; see also Fisher, *Living Religions*, 310–311; Sarwar, *Islam*, 27–28.

26. Annemarie Schimmel, *Islam: An Introduction* (Albany: State University of New York Press, 1992), 70; Hamidullah, *Introduction to Islam*, 57–58.

27. Haneef, *What Everyone Should Know About Islam and Muslims*, 18.

28. Esposito, *Islam*, 35.

29. Hamidullah, *Introduction to Islam*, 61.

30. Esposito, "Islam in the World and in America," 247; Fisher, *Living Religions*, 319; Fluehr- Lobban, *Islamic Society in Practice*, 23–37.

31. See Fisher, *Living Religions*, 320–323; Sarwar, *Islam*, 40–83; Shaykh Fadhlalla Haeri, *The Elements of Islam* (Shaftesbury, Dorset: Element, 1993), 37–42.

32. See Haneef, *What Everyone Should Know About Islam and Muslims*, 11–15, 42–43; Hamidullah, *Introduction to Islam*, 51–53; Fluehr-Lobban, *Islamic Society in Practice*, 23–24.

33. See Abdalati, *Islam in Focus*, 55–86; Haneef, *What Everyone Should Know About Islam and Muslims*, 43–46; Fluehr-Lobban, *Islamic Society in Practice*, 25–28.

34. Esposito, *Islam*, 92.

35. Esposito, *Islam*, 92.

36. Fisher, *Living Religions*, 321.

37. Sarwar, *Islam*, 76–78; Haneef, *What Everyone Should Know About Islam and Muslims*, 46–48.

38. Esposito, "Islam in the World and in America," 249.

39. For a fascinating history of the *hajj*, see Francis E. Peters, *The Hajj: The Muslim Pilgrimage to Mecca and the Holy Places* (Princeton, NJ: Princeton University Press, 1994).

40. Haneef, *What Everyone Should Know About Islam and Muslims*, 51.

41. Ahmad, "Islam," 35–37; Jansen, *Militant Islam*, 17–18. Also of interest here is Christoffel van Nieuwenhuijze, *The Lifestyles of Islam: Recourse to Classicism, Need of Realism* (Leiden, Netherlands: E. J. Brill, 1985), 93–132.

42. See Joseph Schacht, *An Introduction to Islamic Law* (Oxford, England: Clarendon Press, 1964); Bassam Tibi, *Islam and the Cultural Accommodation of Social Change* (Boulder, CO: Westview Press, 1990), 59–75; Ahmad Ibrahim, "Islam and the Law," in *Toward Islamization of Disciplines* (Herndon, VA: International Institute of Islamic Thought, 1989), 381–391; Hamidullah, *Introduction to Islam*, 122–138; Fluehr-Lobban, *Islamic Society in Practice*, 115–141; Ignaz Goldziher, *Introduction to Islamic Theology and Law* (Princeton, NJ: Princeton University Press).

43. Sarwar, *Islam*, 13.

44. See Sarwar, *Islam*, 166–170; Haneef, *What Everyone Should Know About Islam and Muslims*, 142–148; Abdalati, *Islam in Focus*, 184–191; John Esposito, *Women in Muslim Family Law* (Syracuse, NY: Syracuse University Press, 1982); Fatima Mernissi, *The Veil and the Male Elite: A Feminist Interpretation of Women's Rights in Islam* (Reading, MA: Addison-Wesley, 1987); Fatima Mernissi, *Beyond the Veil: Male-Female Dynamics in Modern Muslim Society* (Bloomington: Indiana University Press, 1987).

45. Sarwar, *Islam*, 166–167; Abdalati, *Islam in Focus*, 184–185.

46. Abdalati, *Islam in Focus*, 187.

47. Abdalati, *Islam in Focus*, 186.

48. Haneef, *What Everyone Should Know About Islam and Muslims*, 145–146; Abdalati, *Islam in Focus*, 187–191; Braswell, *Islam*, 148–156.

49. David Waines, *An Introduction to Islam* (Cambridge, England: Cambridge University Press, 1995), 255.

50. See Ahmad, "Islam," 37–38; Maxime Rodinson, *Islam et capitalisme* (Paris: Éditions du Seuil, 1966).

51. For detailed discussions about the nature of Islamic economics, see Hamidullah, *Introduction to Islam*, 139–154; Muhammad Najatullah Siddiqi, "Islamizing Economics," in *Toward Islamization of Disciplines* (Herndon, VA: International Institute of Islamic Thought, 1989), 253–261; Mahmoud Abu Saud, "Toward Islamic Economics," in *Toward Islamization of Disciplines* (Herndon, VA: International Institute of Islamic Thought, 1989), 265–270; Muhammad Abdul Mannan, "The Frontiers of Islamic Economics: Some Philosophical Underpinnings," in *Toward Islamization of Disciplines* (Herndon, VA: International Institute of Islamic Thought, 1989), 295–311.

52. See Johannes Reissner, "Die innerislamische Diskussion zur modernen Wirtschafts- und Sozialordnung," in Michael Ursinus (ed.), *Der Islam in der Gegenwart* (München, Germany: Verlag C. H. Beck, 1984), 155–169; Hamidullah, *Introduction to Islam*, 107–121; Aziz Al-Azmeh, *Islams and Modernities* (London: Verso, 1993), 89–103.

53. See Schacht, *An Introduction to Islamic Law*; Tibi, *Islam and the Cultural Accommodation of Social Change*, 59–75; Ahmad Ibrahim, "Islam and

the Law"; Hamidullah, *Introduction to Islam*, 122– 138; Fluehr-Lobban, *Islamic Society in Practice*, 115–141.

54. For detailed discussions of this topic, see Masudul Alam Choudhury, "A Critical Examination of the Concept of Islamization of Knowledge in Contemporary Times," *Muslim Education Quarterly* 10, 4 (1993): 3–34; M. A. Kazi, *Islamic Thought and Modern Science* (Amman, Jordan: Islamic Academy of Sciences, 1997); Talat Sultan, "The Role of Islamic Universities in the Islamization of Education," *Muslim Education Quarterly* 14, 3 (1997): 57–63.

55. Quoted in Mohammad Ishaq Khan, *Experiencing Islam* (Karachi, Pakistan: Oxford University Press, 1996), 99.

56. John Sahadat, "Divine Revelation and the Status of the Qur'an," *Muslim Education Quarterly* 13, 4 (1996): 4–17; see also Mohammad Kahn (ed.), *Education and Society in the Muslim World* (Jeddah, Saudi Arabia: King Abdulaziz University, 1981).

57. Schimmel, *Islam*, 29; see also Alfred Guillaume, *Islam* (Harmondsworth: Penguin, 1956), 55; Mohammed Arkoun, *Rethinking Islam: Common Questions, Uncommon Answers* (Boulder, CO: Westview Press, 1994), 35–39.

58. Haneef, *What Everyone Should Know About Islam and Muslims*, 18; see also Sarwar, *Islam*, 32–33.

59. Haneef, *What Everyone Should Know About Islam and Muslims*, 18.

60. Schimmel, *Islam*, 30; see also W. Montgomery Watt and Richard Bell, *Introduction to the Qur'an* (Edinburgh: Edinburgh University Press, 1970).

61. See Abdalati, *Islam in Focus*, 193; Esposito, *Islam*, 22–23.

62. Haneef, *What Everyone Should Know About Islam and Muslims*, 19.

63. Haneef, *What Everyone Should Know About Islam and Muslims*, 19.

64. See Waines, *An Introduction to Islam*, 23–24.

65. Helmut Gätje, *Koran und Koranexegese* (Zurich: Artemis Verlag, 1971); Allahbukhsh Brohi, "The Qur'an and Its Impact on Human History," in Khurshid Ahmad (ed.), *Islam: Its Meaning and Message* (London: The Islamic Foundation, 1980), 89–91; Charles Stanton, *Higher Learning in Islam: The Classical Period, A.D. 700–1300* (Savage, MD: Rowman & Littlefield, 1990), 1–20.

66. Abdul L. Tibawi, *Islamic Education: Its Traditions and Modernization into the Arab National Systems* (London: Luzac & Co., 1972), 24.

67. Seyyed Hossein Nasr, "Islamic Education and Science: A Summary Appraisal," in Yvonne Haddad, Byron Haines, and Ellison Findly (eds.), *The Islamic Impact* (Syracuse, NY: Syracuse University Press, 1984), 48; see also Seyyed Hossein Nasr, *Traditional Islam in the Modern World* (London: Routledge & Kegan Paul, 1987), 147–163; S. Waqar Ahmed Husaini, *Islamic Science and Public Policies: Lessons from the History of Science*, 2nd rev. ed. (Indianapolis, IN: Islamic Book Service, 1986), 16–24; Shmad Shalabi, *History of Muslim Education* (Beirut, Lebanon: Dar Al-Kashshaf, 1954), 15.

68. Abdul-Rahman Salih Abdullah, *Educational Theory: A Qur'anic Outlook* (Makkah, Saudi Arabia: Umm Al-Qura University, 1982), 25.

69. Tibawi, *Islamic Education*, 39.
70. Tibawi, *Islamic Education*, 41.
71. Quoted in Tibawi, *Islamic Education*, 40.
72. Tibawi, *Islamic Education*, 40.
73. Abdullah, *Educational Theory*, 31.
74. See Nasr, "Islamic Education and Science," 48.
75. Tibawi, *Islamic Education*, 42.
76. Quoted in Tibawi, *Islamic Education*, 42.
77. Quoted in Tibawi, *Islamic Education*, 43.
78. Yusuf Waghid, "Why a Theory of Islamic Education Cannot Be Epistemologically 'Neutral'," *Muslim Education Quarterly* 13, 2 (1996): 43–54.
79. Abdullah, *Educational Theory*, 43.
80. Abdullah, *Educational Theory*, 119.
81. Abdullah, *Educational Theory*, 121.
82. Abdullah, *Educational Theory*, 129–133.
83. See, e.g., Seydon Cissé, *L'enseignement islamique en Afrique noire* (Paris: L'Harmattan, 1992); Dale Eickelman, *Knowledge and Power in Morocco: The Education of a Twentieth-Century Notable* (Princeton, NJ: Princeton University Press, 1985), 59–65; J. Berkey, *The Transmission of Knowledge in Medieval Cairo: A Social History of Islamic Education* (Princeton, NJ: Princeton University Press, 1992). The development of Islam in sub-Saharan Africa in particular has been explored in depth by a number of scholars in enlightening and useful ways. See Eva Rosander and David Westerlund (eds.), *African Islam and Islam in Africa* (Athens, OH: Ohio University Press, 1997); Hiskett, *The Course of Islam in Africa;* Roman Loimeier, *Islamic Reform and Political Change in Northern Nigeria* (Evanston, IL: Northwestern University Press, 1997); René Otayek (ed.), *Le radicalisme islamique au sud du Sahara: Da'wa, arabisation et critique de l'Occident* (Paris: Éditions Karthala, 1993); Christian Coulon, *Les musulmans et le pouvoir en Afrique noire: Religion et contre-culture* (Paris: Éditions Karthala, 1988).
84. Bayard Dodge, *Muslim Education in Medieval Times* (Washington, DC: The Middle East Institute, 1962), 3–5; Mehdi Nakosteen, *History of Islamic Origins of Western Education, A.D. 800–1350* (Boulder, CO: University of Colorado Press, 1964), 44–45.
85. See Corinne Fortier, "Mémorisation et audition: L'enseignement coranique chez les Maures de Mauritanie," *Islam et Sociétiés au Sud du Sahara,* 11 (1997): 85–105.
86. See Tibawi, *Islamic Education*, 43.
87. Lisbet Holtedahl and Mahmoudou Djingui, "The Power of Knowledge," in Eva Rosander and David Westerlund (eds.), *African Islam and Islam in Africa* (Athens, OH: University of Ohio Press, 1997), 259.
88. Hiskett, *The Development of Islam in West Africa*, 55.
89. Hiskett, *The Development of Islam in West Africa*, 55; see Arkoun, *Rethinking Islam*, 35–48.

90. It is important to note here that the nature of such disputation as a means of study and understanding, although bearing some outward similarity to Talmudic study, is in fact firmly grounded in Aristotelean logic and methodology. Thus, its closest parallel in the West is probably to medieval scholastic philosophy. See Roy Mottahedeh, "Traditional Shi'ite Education in Qom," in Amelie Rorty (ed.), *Philosophers on Education: New Historical Perspectives* (London: Routledge, 1998), 451–457; Stanton, *Higher Learning in Islam*, 42–46, 53–90.

91. Mottahedeh, "Traditional Shi'ite Education in Qom," 453.

92. See, for example, Aziz Talbani, "Pedagogy, Power, and Discourse: Transformation of Islamic Education," *Comparative Education Review* 40, 1 (1996): 66–82.

93. A. H. Nayyar, "Madrasah Education Frozen in Time," in Pervez Hoodbhoy (ed.), *Education and the State: Fifty Years of Pakistan* (Karachi, Pakistan: Oxford University Press, 1998), 215.

94. Fluehr-Lobban, *Islamic Society in Practice*, 2.

95. Quoted in Haneef, *What Everyone Should Know About Islam and Muslims*, 162.

9
Themes and Lessons in the Study of Non-Western Educational Traditions: Toward a Beginning

In the first chapter of this book, it was suggested that "it is neither idealistic nor unrealistic to suggest that we can learn much from non-Western educational traditions." We have explored and examined a number of non-Western educational traditions in *Non-Western Educational Traditions: Alternative Approaches to Educational Thought and Practice*, and are now in a better position to evaluate this claim. In each of the traditions that we have studied, there have been similarities both to other non-Western educational traditions and to our own Western tradition, just as each of the traditions has offered unusual and even unique features. In this final chapter, we look at some of the themes that appear to be fairly common across the different traditions we have examined and try to determine what lessons might be learned from these common themes. We also briefly discuss some of the many non-Western educational traditions that have not been addressed in this book, but which might merit the attention of scholars and educators in the future.

SOME COMMON THEMES IN NON-WESTERN EDUCATIONAL TRADITIONS

Underlying the common themes that seem to be reflected in the various non-Western educational traditions that we have studied is a powerful answer to the question, "Have we lost something important and valuable in Western education?" Until recently, Western scholars tended to view non-Western educational traditions as largely irrelevant and unrelated to their concerns, and, when they have dealt with such areas at all, they all too often did so through a very potent and distorting lens. That lens was the assumption that non-Western educational traditions were in some significant way "primitive." Thus, when George Pettitt in the mid-1940s wrote what remains the single most comprehensive study of Native American educational thought and practice, he and others saw nothing odd about naming his monograph *Primitive Ed-*

ucation in North America.[1] And yet, if there is any single conclusion that can be reasonably reached from the cases that we have examined in this book, it is that there is much that those of us in the West can and should learn from the traditions of the non-Western world. In short, we have indeed lost something important and valuable, and that "something" can be found in the very traditions that were wrongly labeled "primitive." As Adam Kuper forcefully argued, the very idea of a "primitive society" is a concept developed by Western scholars to delegitimize the societies and social systems of others.[2] Given the evidence now available, it is simply not credible to believe that non- Western approaches to childrearing and education are in any way inferior to those with which we are more familiar. They are different, to be sure, and they functioned to prepare children and young people for very different kinds of societies—but they did so, for the most part, effectively and humanely.

Moving beyond the rejection of the view of non-Western educational traditions as primitive, we find that there are at least seven broad themes that seem to be fairly (although not universally) common among the different traditions that we have studied in this book. Each of these themes is now briefly discussed.

A fundamental distinction between contemporary Western conceptions of education and many of the non-Western systems that we have examined is that between formal schooling and education. Formal schooling played important roles in many non-Western traditions (consider, for instance, its potency in traditional Chinese education), and it was to some extent present in most of the traditions that we studied (for example, in initiation schools in Africa). However, it is also clear that the common tendency in our own society to conflate and confuse "formal schooling" with "education"—a tendency reflected in our concern with formal certification and degrees rather than with competence *per se*—has been far less common in non-Western traditions. To be sure, this may well be explained in large part by the nature and needs of different kinds of social organization. Our concerns with formal schooling no doubt reflect the nature of modern society, and in earlier times our tradition was far less concerned with formal schooling. The difference between formal schooling and education is, nonetheless, an important one for us to keep in mind, and the study of non-Western educational traditions certainly functions effectively to bring it to the forefront of our attention.

A second common theme in the non-Western educational traditions that we have studied is that education has tended to be community-based and communal in nature to a very great extent. Not only have adults and older children in the community tended to play important educational roles in the society, but with relatively few exceptions there has been relatively little focus on identifying educational specialists in non-Western societies. Education and childrearing have commonly been seen as a social responsibility shared by all of the members of the community. Although individuals may play greater or lessor roles in this undertaking, it is significantly seen as the province of everyone.

Thus, the concept of some adults being *teachers* and others (presumably) being *non-teachers* is a somewhat alien one to many traditions. Furthermore, it is interesting to note that in none of the cases examined here—even those with the most fully articulated formal educational systems—was there any explicit, formal training for those who would play teaching roles. The idea of teachers engaging in a profession, with specialized knowledge and expertise not held by others, appears to be a Western, and indeed relatively recent, innovation.

Related to the community-based focus of many non-Western educational traditions is the broadly shared concern with what might be called *civic education*. In every case we have studied, there is a concern with helping the child grow into the kind of adult who will function effectively and appropriately in his or her society. In many of the non-Western traditions that we have examined, this focus has clear political overtones, whereas in others a more spiritual concern is at issue. Furthermore, although there is a common concern with preparing the child for life in his or her society, this is not to say that there is a blind acceptance of the *status quo*. Indeed, just the opposite seems to be true—even in the more conservative instances, there is always room for the individual to challenge his or her society, albeit often at considerable personal cost. Thus, for instance, in the African tradition we find the role of the *imbongi*, whereas in the Chinese case we learn that in all relationships the rights and privileges of the educated person are seen in reciprocal terms; and in Aztec society, the higher one's rank, the greater the punishment for violating social norms.

Not only do non-Western educational traditions stress what can be called civic education, but they also emphasize the need for every child to be prepared to function economically in his or her society. Thus, what would today be called *vocational education* can be found in every case that we have studied. In some cases, occupations can be chosen by the child or the child's family, whereas in others special skills and aptitudes are required. Still other occupations are open only to selected individuals, often on the basis of birth. Finally, it is in the area of preparation to function economically that one finds the greatest degree of gender stratification. In most non-Western societies, the roles of men and women are different, and the differences are clearly demarcated. Thus, girls learn the skills they will need from the mothers (and, often, from other female relatives), while boys learn the skills that they will need from their fathers, uncles, and other adult male role models. It is also important in this context to note that although all of the traditions examined in this book pay attention to the vocational needs of the individual, this focus is different from that found in contemporary American society in a significant way. In modern capitalist societies in general, and in American society in particular, educational institutions are often expected to serve the needs of the economy (or, more accurately, of employers) rather than the needs of individual workers. To be sure, one could suggest that these two sets of needs ought to be, at least in the ideal, very similar, but they are by no means the same. In the cases examined in this book, the emphasis placed on vocational preparation is largely an empowering one, with the greater emphasis normally placed on the needs and aptitudes of the individual rather than on the needs of the employer.

The role of the family is, in every case we have examined, the central facet of education. Other social institutions may well play important and valuable roles, and non-family members may also perform important educational roles, but it is the family that is the key to the child's education. To be sure, different societies define the family in different ways, but what is common is the idea that it is the family as a unit that bears the ultimate responsibility for the child and for his or her education and upbringing. At the same time, in the cases examined here (and, in fact, in non-Western traditions generally), it is clear that the final say in decisions about childrearing and education almost always rests with the family rather than with the society at large.

The role of language plays a surprisingly important part in almost all non-Western educational traditions. Although many non-Western traditions do indeed have rich written traditions, others have been entirely oral. This has meant that the way in which language skills are taught and used may vary among different non-Western societies, but the concern with the *proper* use of language, knowledge of the spoken traditions of the community, and the ability to use language creatively to reason and to argue are all powerful components of language use, and they are virtually universal in the cases we have examined. Perhaps most interesting in this regard is the explicit Rom recognition of the role of performance and "impression management"—activities in which we all participate, but which are not generally discussed in our own society and culture.

Last, we come to the issue of values, morality, and spirituality in education. In every educational tradition that we have studied in *Non-Western Educational Traditions: Alternative Approaches to Educational Thought and Practice*, the principal goal of education seems to be the development of a *good person*. Although there may be differences of opinion about selective aspects of the nature of this good person, there are also a number of core features (such as honesty) that are agreed on in every case we have studied. As Jack Forbes, writing about Native American education, argued:

> The main thing I want to emphasize is that there can be no education that is multicultural involving the Native American tradition unless it gets into this area of the meaning of life, unless it gets into the area of values.... I don't have the answer as to how you bring a spiritual path into schools in a society which is going in the opposite direction. I don't have the answer as to how you do that, except that we must try.[3]

Each of these common themes that have been identified and briefly discussed here have much to teach us about not only what others have done and believed about education, but about what we ourselves seem to assume and believe about education. There are many valuable lessons that could be learned from the wisdom of others, and such insights should not be lightly put aside. We turn now to a discussion of some of the non-Western educational traditions that we have not examined in this book.

AREAS FOR FUTURE RESEARCH

In *Non-Western Educational Traditions: Alternative Approaches to Educational Thought and Practice* we have examined a number of different non-Western educational traditions, but there are, of course, far more non-Western educational traditions that have not even been mentioned thus far. It is certainly not the point of this chapter to cover all of the ground that remains; indeed, even if we wished to do so, it would not be possible. What we can do, however, is to simply identify other non-Western educational traditions that merit further, careful study. Among those traditions that have much to teach us, and that provide both interesting counterpoints to some of the cases discussed in this book and often strong support for the common themes that we have identified, are:

1. The traditional educational thought and practice of the different peoples in Oceania, including certainly the fascinating case of the Maori civilization.
2. The traditional educational thought and practice of different groups of the Australian Aborigines (the indigenous peoples of Australia).
3. A detailed study of both childrearing and formal education in the Inca empire before the Conquest.
4. Detailed, focused examinations of particular groups in Africa, the Americas, and so on.
5. The traditional educational thought and practice of various societies in Asia (and, in particular, those of Japan and Korea), especially with respect to how indigenous practices have interacted with those imported from China.

Another related area for future study is that of the interaction between traditional forms of educational thought and practice and imposed Western ones. There are relatively few instances today where formal schooling is anything but Western in structure; government schooling is virtually always fundamentally Western in orientation. As Levinson and Holland have observed:

Around the world, modern schools are central to the social and cultural shaping of the young. Relatively new to history, especially for those people situated on the margins of industrialization, institutions of mass schooling often remove children from their families and local communities, encouraging mastery of knowledges and disciplines that have currency and ideological grounding in wider spheres ... these schools have served to inculcate the skills, subjectivities, and disciplines that undergird the modern nation-state. No matter how the knowledgeable person is locally defined, regardless of the skills and sensibilities that count as indicators of "wisdom" and intelligence in the home and immediate locale, schools interject an educational mission of extra-local proportions.[4]

Needless to say, these topics and areas for future study are far from an exhaustive list. This book is intended to be at most a first step in our study of non-Western educational traditions, and it is a first step on a very long road. This having been said, it should also be kept in mind that every trip, no matter how long, must begin with a first step.

CONCLUSION

The first chapter of this book ended with an intriguing quote from Ali Mazrui. Mazrui, a noted African scholar, argued that: "I cannot help feeling that it is about time Africa sent missionaries to Europe and America, as well as teachers, engineers, doctors, and ordinary workers.... It is indeed time that Africa counter-penetrated the western world."[5]

If Mazrui is correct, then perhaps not only Africa, but the rest of the non-Western world as well needs to send us missionaries, for they do indeed have much to teach us. At the same time, we need not reject everything in our own tradition. In the operetta *The Mikado*, Gilbert and Sullivan speak disparagingly about "the man who loves every century but this and every country but his own." Other societies and traditions have many strengths, as does our own, just as they have many weaknesses, as does our own. The fundamental point of this book has been that there is much in *every* society that is worthwhile and valuable, and that we need to learn to do a better job of learning from one another.

QUESTIONS FOR REFLECTION AND DISCUSSION

1. What are some examples of educational activities in our own society that take place apart from, and are not connected with, formal schooling? What role, if any, do professional educators play in these activities?
2. It is pointed out in this chapter that "the idea of teachers engaging in a profession, with specialized knowledge and expertise not held by others, appears to be a Western, and indeed relatively recent, innovation." What are the benefits of viewing teachers as a specialized profession? What problems do you see with this development in our society?
3. One of the common themes identified in this chapter is that of the role of spirituality in education. In your view, should spirituality play a significant role in a secular, public education? What limits, if any, need to be observed in "spiritual education"?
4. How are the common themes found in the non-Western educational traditions discussed in this chapter reflected or manifested in contempo-

rary American education? What lessons can we learn from these themes?

5. In your view, what is the single most important idea that has emerged in our study of non-Western educational traditions and practices? How do you see that idea affecting your practice as an educator?

RECOMMENDED FURTHER READINGS

Although works that deal explicitly with non-Western educational thought and practice remain rare, a number of outstanding works have appeared in recent years. Among the best are Ladislaus Semali and Joe Kincheloe's edited collection, *What is Indigenous Knowledge? Voices From the Academy* (New York: Falmer Press, 1999), Seanna McGovern's *Education, Modern Development and Indigenous Knowledge: An Analysis of Academic Knowledge Production* (New York: Garland: 1999), and Maenette Benham and Joanne Cooper's edited work, *Indigenous Educational Models for Contemporary Practice: In Our Mother's Voice* (Malwah, NJ: Lawrence Erlbaum Associates, 2000). Works dealing with specific non-Western traditions are cited in the bibliography.

NOTES

1. George Pettitt, *Primitive Education in North America* (Berkeley: University of California Press, 1946).

2. See Adam Kuper, *The Invention of Primitive Society: Transformations of an Illusion* (London: Routledge, 1988).

3. Jack Forbes, "Traditional Native American Philosophy and Multicultural Education," in *Multicultural Education and the American Indian* (Los Angeles: American Indian Studies Center, University of California, 1979), 11.

4. B. Levinson and D. Holland, "The Cultural Production of the Educated Person: An Introduction," in B. Levinson, D. Foley, and D. Holland (eds.), *The Cultural Production of the Educated Person: Critical Ethnographies of Schooling and Local Practice* (Albany: State University of New York Press, 1996), 1.

5. Ali Mazrui, *The African Condition: The Reith Lectures* (London: Heinemann, 1980), 16.

Bibliography

Abdalati, H. (1975). *Islam in focus*. Indianapolis, IN: American Trust Publications.

Abdullah, A. R. S. (1982). *Educational theory: A Qur'anic outlook*. Makkah, Saudi Arabia: Umm Al-Qura University.

Abe, M. (1993). Buddhism. In A. Sharma (Ed.), *Our religions* (pp. 69–137). San Francisco: Harper.

Achebe, C. (1958). *Things fall apart*. London: Heinemann.

Achebe, C. (1960). *No longer at ease*. London: Heinemann.

Achebe, C. (1966). *A man of the people*. London: Heinemann.

Achebe, C. (1974). *Arrow of God* (2nd ed.). London: Heinemann.

Acton, T. (1974). *Gypsy politics and social change*. London: Routledge & Kegan Paul.

Adams, R. (1991). *Prehistoric Mesoamerica* (Rev. ed.). Norman: University of Oklahoma Press.

Adegbola, E. (Ed.), (1983). *Traditional religion in West Africa*. Nairobi, Kenya: Uzima.

Ahmad, K. (1980). Islam: Basic principles and characteristics. In K. Ahmad (Ed.), *Islam: Its meaning and message* (pp. 27–44). London: Islamic Foundation.

Ahmad, K. (Ed.), (1980). *Islam: Its meaning and message*. London: Islamic Foundation.

Ahmed, A. S. (1988). *Discovering Islam: Making sense of Muslim history and society*. London: Routledge.

Ahmed, A. S. (1992). *Postmodernism and Islam: Predicament and promise*. London: Routledge.

Aizpuro, P. (1990). *Historia de la educación en la época colonial: El mundo indígena* [History of education in the colonial period: The indigenous world]. México: Colegio de México.

Al-Azmeh, A. (1993). *Islams and modernities*. London: Verso.

Ali, S. A. (1990). *The spirit of Islam: A history of the evolution and ideals of Islam with a life of the Prophet*. Delhi: Low Price Publications.

Alonzo, G. Z. (1995). *An overview of the Mayan world* (11th ed.). Mérida, Yucatán, México: Author.

Amdouni, H. (1992). *La famille musulmane: Relations familiales et éducations* [The Muslim family: Familial and educational relations]. Paris: Al Qalam.

Andrews, J. (1975). *An introduction to classical Nahuatl*. Austin: University of Texas Press.

Ani, M. (1994). *Yurugu: An African-centered critique of European cultural thought and behavior*. Trenton, NJ: Africa World Press.

Appiah, K. (1989). *In my father's house: Africa in the politics of culture*. Oxford, England: Oxford University Press.

Archibald, J. (1990). Coyote's story about orality and literacy. *Canadian Journal of Native Education* 17, 2: 66–81.

Arens, W. (1979). *The man-eating myth: Anthropology and anthropophagy*. New York: Oxford University Press.

Argüelles, J. (1987). *The Mayan factor: Path beyond technology*. Sante Fe, NM: Bear & Co.

Arkoun, M. (1994). *Rethinking Islam: Common questions, uncommon answers*. Boulder, CO: Westview.

Armstrong, K. (1992). *Muhammad: A biography of the Prophet*. San Francisco: Harper.

Asante, M. (1988). *Afrocentricity* (Rev. ed.). Trenton, NJ: Africa World Press.

Asante, M. (1990). *Kemet, Afrocentricity and knowledge*. Trenton, NJ: Africa World Press.

Asante, M., & Asante, K. (Eds.), (1990). *African culture: Rhythms of unity*. Trenton, NJ: Africa World Press.

Athar, S. (1994). *Reflections of an American Muslim*. Chicago: Kazi.

Atwood, M. (1991). *Spirit healing: Native American magic and medicine*. New York: Sterling.

Austin, A. (1976). El fundamento mágico-religioso del poder [The magical-religious foundation of power]. *Estudios de Cultura Náhuatl* 12: 197–240.

Aveni, A. (Ed.), (1992). *The sky in Mayan literature*. Oxford, England: Oxford University Press.

Ayers, W. (1971). *Chang Chih-tung and educational reform in China*. Cambridge, MA: Harvard University Press.

Ayisi, E. (1979). *An introduction to the study of African culture*. London: Currey.

Ball, J. (1925). *Things Chinese, or, notes connected with China* (5th ed., revised by E. C. Werner). Shanghai: Kelly and Walsh.

Ball, S. (Ed.), (1990). *Foucault and education: Disciplines and knowledge*. London: Routledge.

Balme, M., & Lawall, G. (1990). *Athenaze: An introduction to Ancient Greek, book I*. New York: Oxford University Press.

Banerjee, A. K. (1967). *Discourses on Hindu spiritual culture*. Delhi: S. Chand & Co.

Banerji, S. (1993). *Society in ancient India: Evolution since the Vedic times based on Sanskrit, Pali, Prakrit and other classical sources.* New Delhi: D. K. Printworld.

Barrett, T. H. (1990). Religious traditions in Chinese civilization: Buddhism and Taoism. In P. Ropp (Ed.), *Heritage of China: Contemporary perspectives on Chinese civilization* (pp. 138–163). Berkeley: University of California Press.

Barman, J., Hébert, Y., & McCaskill, D. (1987). The challenge of Indian education: An overview. In J. Barman, Y. Hébert, & D. McCaskill (Eds.), *Indian education in Canada, volume 2: The challenge* (pp. 1–21). Vancouver: University of British Columbia Press.

Barman, J., Hébert, Y., & McCaskill, D. (Eds.). (1987). *Indian education in Canada, volume 2: The challenge.* Vancouver: University of British Columbia Press.

Barnes, B. (1975). Irish travelling people. In F. Rehfisch (Ed.), *Gypsies, tinkers, and other travellers* (pp. 231–256). London: Academic Press.

Barth, F. (1975). The social organization of a pariah group in Norway. In F. Rehfisch (Ed.), *Gypsies, tinkers, and other travellers* (pp. 285–299). London: Academic Press.

Bascom, W. (1975). *African dilemma tales.* The Hague: Mouton.

Basham, A. L. (1989). *The origins and development of classical Hinduism.* Boston: Beacon.

Bastid, M. (1987). Servitude or liberation? The introduction of foreign educational practices and systems to China. In R. Hayhoe & M. Bastid (Eds.), *China's education and the industrialized world* (pp. 3–20). London: Sharpe.

Bauer, W. (1976). *China and the search for happiness: Recurring themes in four thousand years of Chinese cultural history.* New York: Seabury.

Belenky, M. F., Clinchy, B. M., Goldberger, N. R., & Tarule, J. M. (1986). *Women's ways of knowing: The development of self, voice, and mind.* New York: Basic Books.

Bell, B. (Ed.), (1967). *Indian Mexico: Past and present.* Los Angeles: University of California at Los Angeles, Latin American Center.

Benham, M., & Cooper, J. (Eds.). (2000). *Indigenous educational models for contemporary practice: In our mother's voice.* Mahwah, NJ: Lawrence Erlbaum Associates.

Berdan, F. (1976). La organización del tributo en el imperio azteca [The organization of tribute in the Aztec empire]. *Estudios de Cultura Náhuatl* 12: 185–195.

Berdan, F., & Anawalt, P. (1997). *The essential Codex Mendoza.* Berkeley: University of California Press.

Berkey, J. (1992). *The transmission of knowledge in medieval Cairo: A social history of Islamic education.* Princeton, NJ: Princeton University Press.

Bernadac, C. (1979). *L'Holocauste oblié: Le massacre des Tsiganes* [The forgotten Holocaust: The massacre of the Gypsies]. Paris: France-Empire.

Bernal, M. (1987). *Black Athena: The Afroasiatic roots of classical civilization, volume 1: The fabrication of ancient Greece, 1785–1985*. New Brunswick, NJ: Rutgers University Press.

Bernal, M. (1991a). *Black Athena: The Afroasiatic roots of classical civilization, volume 2: The archeological and documentary evidence*. New Brunswick, NJ: Rutgers University Press.

Bernal, M. (1991b). Response to Edith Hall. *Arethusa* 24, 2: 203–214.

Bernal, M. (1992). Animadversions on the origins of Western science. *Isis* 83: 596–607.

Bernal, M. (1993). Response. *Journal of Women's History* 4, 3: 119–135.

Berrelleza, J. (1987). Offering 48 of the Templo Mayor: A case of child sacrifice. In E. Boone (Ed.), *The Aztec Templo Mayor: A symposium at Dumbarton Oaks* (pp. 131–143). Washington, DC: Dumbarton Oaks Research Library and Collection.

Besmer, F. (1983). *Horses, musicians, and gods: The Hausa cult of possession-trance*. Zaria, Nigeria: Ahmadu Bello University Press.

Biardeau, M. (1981). *L'Hindouisme: Anthropologie d'une civilization* [Hinduism: Anthropology of a civilization]. Paris: Flammarion.

Bill, M. (1991). Rhythmical patterning of Tsonga children's traditional oral poetry. *South African Journal of African Languages* 11, 4: 133–143.

Biot, É. (1847). *Essai sur l'histoire de l'instruction publique en Chine* [An essay on the history of public education in China]. Paris: Benjamin Duprat.

Birge, B. (1989). Chu Hsi and women's education. In W. de Bary & J. Chaffee (Eds.), *Neo-Confucian education: The formative stage* (pp. 325–367). Berkeley: University of California Press.

Bloom, I. (1987). *Knowledge painfully acquired: The K'un-chih chi by Lo Ch'in-shun*. New York: Columbia University Press.

Bloomfield, L. (1964). Language. In O. Chavarria-Aguilar (Ed.), *Traditional India* (pp. 112–113). Englewood Cliffs, NJ: Prentice-Hall.

Boateng, F. (1990). African traditional education: A tool for intergenerational communication. In M. Asante & K. Asante (Eds.), *African culture: Rhythms of unity* (pp. 109–122). Trenton, NJ: Africa World Press.

Bodde, D. (1967). *China's first unifier: A study of the Ch'in dynasty as seen in the life of Li Ssu*. Hong Kong: Hong Kong University Press. (Original work published 1938.)

Bodde, D. (1981). *Essays on Chinese civilization*. Princeton, NJ: Princeton University Press.

Boe, P. (1983). Circumcision: The rites of manhood in the Bille tribe. In E. Adegbola (Ed.), *Traditional religion in West Africa* (pp. 73–89). Nairobi, Kenya: Uzima.

Bol, P. (1989). Chu Hsi's redefinition of literati learning. In W. de Bary & J. Chaffee (Eds.), *Neo-Confucian education: The formative stage* (pp. 151–185). Berkeley: University of California Press.

Bol, P. (1992). *"This culture of ours": Intellectual transitions in T'ang and Sung China*. Stanford, CA: Stanford University Press.

Bond, M. (Ed.). (1986). *The psychology of the Chinese people.* Hong Kong: Oxford University Press.

Bond, M., & Kwang-kuo Hwang. (1986). The social psychology of the Chinese people. In M. Bond (Ed.), *The psychology of the Chinese people* (pp. 213–266). Hong Kong: Oxford University Press.

Boone, E. (Ed.). (1987). *The Aztec Templo Mayor: A symposium at Dumbarton Oaks, 8th and 9th October 1983.* Washington, DC: Dumbarton Oaks Research Library and Collection.

Boone, E., & Mignolo, W. (Eds.). (1994). *Writing without words: Alternative literacies in Mesoamerica and the Andes.* Durham, NC: Duke University Press.

Borland, C. H. (1969). The oral and written culture of the Shona. *LIMI: Bulletin of the Department of Bantu Languages, University of South Africa 8:* 1–27.

Boswell, J. (1988). *The kindness of strangers: The abandonment of children in Western Europe from late antiquity to the renaissance.* New York: Pantheon.

Boyer, R., & Gayton, N. (1992). *Apache mothers and daughters: Four generations of a family.* Norman: University of Oklahoma Press.

Brakel, L. F. (1984). Indonesien [Indonesia]. In M. Ursinus (Ed.), *Der Islam in der Gegenwart* (pp. 570– 581). München: C. H. Beck.

Braswell, G., Jr. (1996). *Islam: Its Prophet, peoples, politics and power.* Nashville, TN: Broadman & Holman.

Bray, W. (1968). *The everyday life of the Aztecs.* New York: Dorset.

Brodwin, P. (1996). *Medicine and morality in Haiti: The contest for healing power.* Cambridge, England: Cambridge University Press.

Brohi, A. (1980). The Qur'an and its impact on human history. In K. Ahmad (Ed.), *Islam: Its meaning and message* (pp. 81–97). London: Islamic Foundation.

Brown, D. (1971). *Bury my heart at Wounded Knee: An Indian history of the American West.* New York: Bantam.

Brundage, B. (1972). *A rain of darts: The Mexica Aztecs.* Austin: University of Texas Press.

Brundage, B. (1975). *Two heavens, two earths: An essay contrasting the Aztecs and the Incas.* Albuquerque: University of New Mexico Press.

Brundage, B. (1979). *The fifth sun: Aztec gods, Aztec world.* Austin: University of Texas Press.

Cajete, G. (1994). *Look to the mountain: An ecology of indigenous education.* Durango, CO: Kivakí.

Cajete, G. (1999). The making of an indigenous teacher: Insights into the ecology of teaching. In J. Kane (Ed.), *Education, information and transformation: Essays on learning and thinking* (pp. 161– 183). Upper Saddle River, NJ: Merrill.

Calnek, E. (1988). The *calmécac* and *telpochcalli* in pre–Conquest Tenochtitlán. In J. Klor de Alva, H. Nicholson, & E. Keber (Eds.), *The work of Bernardino de Sahagun: Pioneer ethnographer of sixteenth-century Aztec*

Mexico (pp. 169–177). Albany: Institute for Mesoamerican Studies, State University of New York.

Calvert, L.-J. (1984). *La tradition orale* [The oral tradition]. Paris: Presses Universitaires de France.

Campbell, G. (1995). *Concise compendium of the world's languages*. London: Routledge.

Campos, R. (1936). *La producción literaria de los Aztecas* [The literary production of the Aztecs]. México: Talleres Gráficos del Museo Nacional de Arqueología, Historia y Etnografía.

Carrasco, D. (1982). *Quetzalcoatl and the irony of empire: Myths and prophecies in the Aztec tradition*. Chicago: University of Chicago Press.

Carrasco, D. (1990). *Religions of Mesoamerica: Cosmovision and ceremonial centers*. San Francisco: HarperSanFrancisco.

Carrasco, D., with Sessions, S. (1998). *Daily life of the Aztecs: People of the sun and earth*. Westport, CT: Greenwood Press.

Carter, D. (1993). Recognizing traditional environmental knowledge. *IDRC Reports* 21, 1: 10–13.

Chaffee, J. (1979). *Education and examinations in Sung society*. Ph.D. dissertation, University of Chicago.

Chaffee, J. (1989). Chu Hsi in Nan-k'ang: *Tao-hsüeh* and the politics of education. In W. de Bary & J. Chaffee (Eds.), *Neo-Confucian education: The formative stage* (pp. 414–431). Berkeley: University of California Press.

Chase, D., & Chase, A. (Eds.). (1992). *Mesoamerican elites: An archeological assessment*. Norman: University of Oklahoma Press.

Chavarria-Aguilar, O. L. (Ed.). (1964). *Traditional India*. Englewood Cliffs, NJ: Prentice-Hall.

Cheetham, E. (1994). *Fundamentals of mainstream Buddhism*. Boston: Tuttle.

Chen Li-Fu. (1976). *Why Confucius has been reverenced as the model teacher of all ages*. New York: Center of Asian Studies, St. John's University, and the Institute of Chinese Culture.

Cheng Hanbang. (1991). Confucian ethics and moral education of contemporary students. In S. Krieger & R. Trauzettel (Eds.), *Confucianism and the modernization of China* (pp. 193–202). Mainz, Germany: Hase & Koehler.

Cheng Tien-Hsi. (1947). *China moulded by Confucius: The Chinese way in Western light*. London: Stevens & Sons.

Chew, P. (1991). The great Tao. *The Journal of Bahá'í Studies* 4, 2: 11–39.

Chisholm, J. (1983). *Navajo infancy: An ethological study of child development*. Hawthorne, NY: Aldine.

Choudhury, M. A. (1993). A critical examination of the concept of Islamization of knowledge in contemporary times. *Muslim Education Quarterly* 10, 4: 3–34.

Chu, R. (1989). Chu Hsi and public instruction. In W. de Bary & J. Chaffee (Eds.), *Neo-Confucian education: The formative stage* (pp. 252–273). Berkeley: University of California Press.

Chün-fang Yü. (1989). Ch'an education in the Sung: Ideals and procedures. In W. de Bary & J. Chaffee (Eds.), *Neo-Confucian education: The formative stage* (pp. 57–104). Berkeley: University of California Press.

Cissé, S. (1992). *L'enseignement islamique en Afrique noire* [Islamic education in Black Africa]. Paris: L'Harmattan.

Clarke, J. J. (1997). *Oriental enlightenment: The encounter between Asian and Western thought.* London: Routledge.

Clendinnen, I. (1991). *Aztecs: An interpretation.* Cambridge, England: Cambridge University Press.

Cleverley, J. (1985). *The schooling of China: Tradition and modernity in Chinese education.* Sydney: Allen & Unwin.

Cobb, P. (1994). Where is the mind? Constructivist and socioculturalist perspectives on mathematical development. *Educational Researcher* 23: 13–20.

Cobb, P. (1996). Where is the mind? A coordination of sociocultural and cognitive constructionist perspectives. In C. Fosnot (Ed.), *Constructivism: Theory, perspectives, and practice* (pp. 34–52). New York: Teachers College Press.

Cobern, W. (1993). Contextual constructivism: The impact of culture on the learning and teaching of science. In K. Tobin (Ed.), *The practice of constructivism in science education* (pp. 51–69). Hillsdale, NJ: Lawrence Erlbaum Associates.

Coe, M. (1987). *The Maya* (4th rev. ed.). London: Thames and Hudson.

Coe, M. (1992). *Breaking the Maya code.* London: Thames and Hudson.

Coetzee, P. H., & Roux, A. P. (Eds.). (1998). *The African philosophy reader.* London: Routledge.

Cohen, P., & Goldman, M. (Eds.). (1990). *Ideas across cultures: Essays on Chinese thought in honor of Benjamin I. Schwartz.* Cambridge, MA: Harvard University Press.

Coleman, M. (1993). *American Indian children at school, 1850–1930.* Jackson: University Press of Mississippi.

Collin, F. (1997). *Social reality.* London: Routledge.

Commeaux, C. (1970). *La vie quotidienne en Chine sous les Mandchous* [Everyday life in China under the Manchus]. Paris: Librairie Hachette.

Confrey, J. (1995). How compatible are radical constructivism, sociocultural approaches, and social constructivism? In L. Steffe & J. Gale (Eds.), *Constructivism in education* (pp. 185–225). Mahwah, NJ: Lawrence Erlbaum Associates.

Conrad, G., & Demarest, A. (1984). *Religion and empire: The dynamics of Aztec and Inca expansionism.* Cambridge, England: Cambridge University Press.

Conze, E. (1960). *A short history of Buddhism.* Bombay: Chetana.

Conze, E. (1975). *Buddhism: Its essence and development.* New York: Harper & Row.

Conze, E. (Trans.), (1959). *Buddhist scriptures.* Harmondsworth: Penguin.

Coomaraswamy, A. (1971). *Hinduism and Buddhism*. Westport, CT: Greenwood.

Cope, T. (Ed.). (1968). *Izibongo: Zulu praise poems*. Oxford, England: Oxford University Press.

Cordier, H. (1921). *Histoire générale de la Chine* (4 vols.) [General history of China]. Paris: Geuthner.

Cornog, E. (1998). American antiquity: How DeWitt Clinton invented our past. *The American Scholar* 67: 53–61.

Cornyn, J. (1930). *The song of Quetzalcoatl*. Yellow Springs, OH: Antioch.

Cotten, R. (1998). Sex dichotomy among the American Kalderas Gypsies. In D. Tong (Ed.), *Gypsies: An interdisciplinary reader* (pp. 219–232). New York: Garland.

Cotterell, M. (1997). *The supergods: They came on a mission to save mankind*. London: Thorsons.

Coulehan, J. (1980). Navajo Indian medicine: Implications for healing. *Journal of Family Practice* 10: 55–61.

Coulon, C. (1988). *Les musulmans et le pouvoir en Afrique noire: Religion et contre-culture* [Muslims and power in black Africa: Religion and counter-culture]. Paris: Éditions Karthala.

Coward, H. G. (Ed.). (1987). *Modern Indian responses to religious pluralism*. Albany: State University of New York Press.

Cragg, K. (1994). *The event of the Qur'an: Islam and its scripture*. Oxford, England: Oneworld.

Creel, H. (1949). *Confucius and the Chinese way*. New York: Harper & Row.

Cross, S. (1994). *The elements of Hinduism*. Shaftesbury, Dorset: Element.

Crowe, D. (1996). *A history of the Gypsies of eastern Europe and Russia*. New York: St. Martin's Griffin.

Crowe, D., & Kolsti, J. (Eds.). (1991). *The Gypsies of eastern Europe*. London: M. E. Sharpe.

Crystal, D. (1991). *A dictionary of linguistics and phonetics* (3rd ed.). Oxford, England: Blackwell.

Culin, S. (1975). *Games of the North American Indians*. New York: Dover.

Curtin, P., Feierman, S., Thompson, L., & Vansina, J. (1995). *African history: From earliest times to independence* (2nd ed.). London: Longman.

Davidson, B. (1991). *Africa in history* (Rev. ed.). New York: Macmillan.

Davidson, B. (Ed.). (1991). *African civilization revisited: From antiquity to modern time*. Trenton, NJ: African World Press.

Davies, C. (1973). *Los mexicas: Primeros pasos hacia el imperio* [The Mexicas: First steps to empire]. México: Universidad Nacional Autónoma de México, Instituto de Investigaciones Históricas.

Davies, N. (1982). *The ancient kingdoms of Mexico*. New York: Penguin.

Davies, N. (1987). *The Aztec empire: The Toltec resurgence*. Norman: University of Oklahoma Press.

Davis-Floyd, R., & Sargent, C. (Eds.). (1997). *Childbirth and authoritative knowledge: Cross-cultural perspectives*. Berkeley: University of California Press.

Dawson, R. (1978). *The Chinese experience*. London: Weidenfeld and Nicholson.

Day, J. (1992). *Aztec: The world of Moctezuma*. Niwot, CO: Denver Museum of Natural History and Roberts Rinehart Publishers.

Debaene, S. (1997). *The number sense: How the mind creates mathematics*. New York: Oxford University Press.

de Bary, W. (1981). *Neo-Confucian orthodoxy and the learning of the mind-and-heart*. New York: Columbia University Press.

de Bary, W. (1983). *The liberal tradition in China*. Hong Kong: Chinese University Press.

de Bary, W. (1989). Chu Hsi's aims as educator. In W. de Bary & J. Chaffee (Eds.), *Neo-Confucian education: The formative stage* (pp. 186–218). Berkeley: University of California Press.

de Bary, W. (Ed.). (1969). *The Buddhist tradition in India, China and Japan*. New York: The Modern Library.

de Bary, W., & Chaffee, J. (Eds.). (1989). *Neo-Confucian education: The formative stage*. Berkeley: University of California Press.

de Vaux de Foletier, F. (1970). *Mille ans d'historie des Tsiganes* [A thousand years of the history of the Gypsies]. Paris: Fayard.

de Villiers, S., & Hartshorne, S. H. (1981). Education. In A. Myburgh (Ed.), *Anthropology for Southern Africa* (pp. 145–153). Pretoria: van Schaik.

Denny, F. M. (1987). *Islam*. San Francisco: Harper.

Diamond, R. (1970). *Old English: Grammar and reader*. Detroit, MI: Wayne State University Press.

Diop, C. A. (1962). *The cultural unity of Negro Africa*. Paris: Presence Africaine.

Diop, C. A. (1989). *The cultural unity of Black Africa*. London: Karnak House.

Diop, C. A. (1991). *Civilization or barbarism: An authentic anthropology*. Chicago: Hill.

Dodge, B. (1962). *Muslim education in medieval times*. Washington, DC: The Middle East Institute.

Dongerkery, S. R. (1967). *University education in India*. Bombay: Manaktalas.

Donnelly, I. (1976). *Atlantis: The antediluvian world*. New York: Dover. (Original work published 1882)

Doolittle, J. (1966). *Social life of the Chinese: With some account of their religious, governmental, educational, and business customs and opinions* (2 vols.). Taipei: Ch'eng-Wen. (Original work published 1865)

Driver, R., Asoko, H., Leach, J., Mortimer, E., & Scott, P. (1994). Constructing scientific knowledge in the classroom. *Educational Researcher* 23: 5–12.

Duffy, T., & Jonassen, D. (Eds.). (1992). *Constructivism and the technology of instruction*. Hillsdale, NJ: Lawrence Erlbaum Associates.

Duminy, P. (1973). *African pupils and teaching them*. Pretoria: van Schaik.

Duminy, P. (Ed.). (1967). *Trends and challenges in the education of the South African Bantu*. Pretoria: van Schaik.

Dumoulin, H. (1994). *Understanding Buddhism: Key themes*. New York: Weatherhill.

Dundas, P. (1992). *The Jains*. London: Routledge.

Durán, D. (1964). *The Aztecs: The history of the Indies of New Spain*. New York: Orion.

Durán, D. (1971). *Book of the gods and rites and the ancient calendar*. Norman: University of Oklahoma Press.

Durant, W. (1963). *The story of civilization: Our Oriental heritage*. New York: Simon and Schuster.

Eberhard, W. (1977). *A history of China*. Berkeley: University of California Press.

Ebrey, P. (1989). Education through ritual: Efforts to formulate family rituals during the Sung period. In W. de Bary & J. Chaffee (Eds.), *Neo-Confucian education: The formative stage* (pp. 277–306). Berkeley: University of California Press.

Ebrey, P. (1990). Women, marriage and the family in Chinese history. In P. Ropp (Ed.), *Heritage of China: Contemporary perspectives on Chinese civilization* (pp. 197–223). Berkeley: University of California Press.

Ebrey, P. (1991). *Confucianism and family rituals in imperial China: A social history of writing about rites*. Princeton, NJ: Princeton University Press.

Ebrey, P. (Ed.). (1993). *Chinese civilization: A sourcebook* (2nd ed.). New York: Free Press.

Eckel, M. (1994). Buddhism in the world and in America. In J. Neuser (Ed.), *World religions in America: An introduction* (pp. 203–218). Louisville, KY: Westminster/John Knox Press.

Edmonson, M. (1988). *The book of the year: Middle American calendrical systems*. Salt Lake City: University of Utah Press.

Eichhorn, W. (1969). *Chinese civilization: An introduction*. New York: Praeger.

Eickelman, D. (1985). *Knowledge and power in Morocco: The education of a twentieth-century notable*. Princeton, NJ: Princeton University Press.

Elliott, J. (1988). Educational research and outsider-insider relations. *International Journal of Qualitative Studies in Education* 1, 2: 155–166.

Elvin, M. (1973). *The pattern of the Chinese past*. Stanford, CA: Stanford University Press.

Elzey, W. (1976). Some remarks on the space and time of the "center" in Aztec religion. *Estudios de Cultura Náhuatl* 12: 315–334.

Erlandson, D., Harris, E., Skipper, B., and Allen, S. (1993). *Doing naturalistic inquiry: A guide to methods*. Newbury Park, CA: Sage.

Esposito, J. (1982). *Women in Muslim family law*. Syracuse, NY: Syracuse University Press.

Esposito, J. (1988). *Islam: The straight path*. New York: Oxford University Press.

Esposito, J. (1991). *Islam: The straight path* (Exp. ed.). New York: Oxford University Press.

Esposito, J. (1994). Islam in the world and in America. In J. Neuser (Ed.), *World religions in America: An introduction* (pp. 243–258). Louisville, KY: Westminster/John Knox.

Eze, E. C. (Ed.). (1998). *African philosophy: An anthology.* Oxford, England: Blackwell.

Fadipe, N. (1970). *The sociology of the Yoruba.* Ibadan, Nigeria: Ibadan University Press.

Fafunwa, A. B. (1974). *A history of education in Nigeria.* London: George Allen & Unwin.

Fagan, B. (1984). *The Aztecs.* New York: Freeman.

Fairbank, J. (1992). *China: A new history.* Cambridge, MA: Harvard University Press.

Fairbank, J., & Kwang-Ching, L. (Eds.). (1980). *The Cambridge history of China, volume 11: Late Ch'ing, 1800–1911, part 2.* Cambridge, England: Cambridge University Press.

Fajana, A. (1986). Traditional methods of education in Africa: The Yoruba example. In J. Okpaku, A. Opubor, & B. Oloruntimehim (Eds.), *The arts and civilization of Black and African peoples: Volume 6, Black civilization and pedagogy* (pp. 42–59). Lagos, Nigeria: Center for Black and African Arts and Civilization.

Fakhry, M. (1983). *A history of Islamic philosophy* (2nd ed.). New York: Columbia University Press.

Farah, C. (1994). *Islam: Beliefs and observances* (5th ed.). Hauppage, NY: Barron's Educational Series.

Feyerabend, P. (1987). *Farewell to reason.* London: Verso.

Feyerabend, P. (1991). *Three dialogues on knowledge.* Oxford, England: Basil Blackwell.

Feyerabend, P. (1993). *Against method* (3rd ed.). London: Verso.

Finlayson, R. (1982). *Hlonipha:* The women's language of avoidance among the Xhosa. *South African Journal of African Languages (Supplement 1):* 35–59.

Finlayson, R. (1986). Linguistic terms of respect among the Xhosa. In P. Raper (Ed.), *Names 1983: Proceedings of the Second South African Names Congress* (pp. 128–138). Pretoria: Human Sciences Research Council.

Finnegan, R. (1970). *Oral literature in Africa.* Nairobi, Kenya: Oxford University Press.

Finnegan, R. (1992). Reflecting back on *Oral literature in Africa:* Some reconsiderations after 21 years. *South African Journal of African Languages* 12, 2: 39–47.

Fisher, M. P. (1994). *Living religions* (2nd ed.). Englewood Cliffs, NJ: Prentice-Hall.

Flood, G. (1996). *An introduction to Hinduism.* Cambridge, England: Cambridge University Press.

Fluehr-Lobban, C. (1994). *Islamic society in practice*. Gainesville: University of Florida Press.

Fonseca, I. (1995). *Bury me standing: The Gypsies and their journey*. New York: Vintage.

Forbes, J. (1979). Traditional Native American philosophy and multicultural education. In *Multicultural education and the American Indian* (pp. 3–13). Los Angeles: American Indian Studies Center, University of California.

Fortes, M. (1979). Foreword. In E. Ayisi, *An introduction to the study of African culture* (2nd ed., pp. vii–ix). London: Currey.

Fortier, C. (1997). Mémorisation et audition: L'enseignement coranique chez les Maures de Mauritanie [Memorization and recitation: Qur'anic teaching among the Maure of Mauritania]. *Islam et Sociétiés au Sud du Sahara* 11: 85–105.

Fosnot, C. (Ed.). (1996). *Constructivism: Theory, perspectives, and practice*. New York: Teachers College Press.

Fraser, A. (1995). *The Gypsies* (2nd ed.). Oxford, England: Blackwell.

Freidel, D., Schele, L., & Parker, J. (1993). *Maya cosmos: Three thousand years on the shaman's path*. New York: Morrow.

Friedman, L., & Moon, S. (Eds.). (1997). *Being bodies: Buddhist women on the paradox of embodiment*. Boston: Shambhala.

Fromkin, V., & Rodman, R. (1978). *An introduction to language* (2nd ed.). New York: Holt, Rinehart and Winston.

Fu Shufang. (1991). A brief account of the positive factors in Confucius' thinking. In S. Krieger & R. Trauzettel (Eds.), *Confucianism and the modernization of China* (pp. 175–192). Mainz, Germany: Hase & Koehler.

Fuller, C. J. (1992). *The camphor flame: Popular Hinduism and society in India*. Princeton, NJ: Princeton University Press.

Fung Yu–lan. (1948). *A short history of Chinese philosophy*. New York: Free Press.

Furlong, D. (1997). *The keys to the temple*. London: Piatkus.

Furniss, G., & Gunner, L. (Eds.). (1995). *Power, marginality and African oral literature*. Cambridge, England: Cambridge University Press.

Gallenkamp, C. (1985). *Maya: The riddle and rediscovery of a lost civilization* (3rd rev. ed.). New York: Penguin.

Galt, H. (1951). *A history of Chinese educational institutions* (vol. 1). London: Probsthain.

Gardner, M. (1998). Is cannibalism a myth? *Skeptical Inquirer* 22: 14–16.

Gätje, H. (1971). *Koran und Koranexegese* [The Qur'an and Qur'anic exegesis]. Zurich: Artemis Verlag.

Gendrop, P. (1992). *Les mayas* (5th ed.) [The Mayas]. Paris: Presses Universitaires de France.

Gergen, K. (1982). *Towards transformation in social knowledge*. New York: Springer.

Gergen, K. (1995). Social construction and the educational process. In L. Steffe & J. Gale (Eds.), *Constructivism in education* (pp. 17–39). Mahwah, NJ: Lawrence Erlbaum Associates.

Gernet, J. (1962). *Daily life in China on the eve of the Mongol invasion, 1250–1276.* Stanford, CA: Stanford University Press.

Gernet, J. (1982). *A history of Chinese civilization.* Cambridge, England: Cambridge University Press.

Gilligan, C. (1982). *In a different voice: Psychological theory and women's development.* Cambridge, MA: Harvard University Press.

Goetz, D., & Morley, S. (Trans.), (1950). *Popol Vuh: The sacred book of the ancient Quiché Maya.* Norman: University of Oklahoma Press.

Goldziher, I. (1981). *Introduction to Islamic theology and law.* Princeton, NJ: Princeton University Press.

Gomez, E. A. (1996). *Popol Vuh.* Mérida, Yucatán, México: Producción Editorial Dante.

Goody, J. (1987). *The interface between the written and the oral.* Cambridge, England: Cambridge University Press.

Gopalan, S. (1973). *Outlines of Jainism.* New York: Halsted.

Gossen, G. (1974). *Chamulas in the world of the sun: Time and space in a Maya oral tradition.* Prospect Heights, IL: Waveland.

Graham, C. (1998). *Ideologies of epic: Nation, empire, and Victorian epic poetry.* Manchester, England: Manchester University Press.

Granet, M. (1968). *La civilisation chinoise: La vie publique et la vie privée* [Chinese civilization: Public and private life]. Paris: Éditions Albin Michel.

Gropper, R. (1975). *Gypsies in the city: Cultural patterns and survival.* Princeton, NJ: Darwin Press.

Gross, R. (1993). *Buddhism after patriarchy: A feminist history, analysis and reconstruction of Buddhism.* Albany: State University of New York Press.

Guillaume, A. (1956). *Islam.* Harmondsworth: Penguin.

Guma, S. (1977). *The form, content and technique of traditional literature in Southern Sotho* (2nd ed.). Pretoria: van Schaik.

Gunnarsson, B. (1997). On the sociohistorical construction of scientific discourse. In B. Gunnarsson, P. Linell, & B. Nordberg (Eds.), *The construction of professional discourse* (pp. 99–126). London: Longman.

Gunnarsson, B., Linell, P., & Nordberg, B. (Eds.). (1997). *The construction of professional discourse.* London: Longman.

Gutek, G. (1993). *American education in a global society: Internationalizing teacher education.* New York: Longman.

Gyatso, T. (1990). *Freedom in exile: The autobiography of the Dalai Lama.* New York: Harper Perennial.

Haddad, Y., Haines, B., & Findly, E. (Eds.). (1984). *The Islamic impact.* Syracuse, NY: Syracuse University Press.

Haeri, S. F. (1993). *The elements of Islam.* Shaftesbury, Dorset: Element.

Haig-Brown, C., & Archibald, J. (1996). Transforming First Nations research with respect and power. *International Journal of Qualitative Studies in Education* 9, 3: 245–267.

Hall, R. N. (1969). *Ancient ruins of Rhodesia: Monomotapae Imperium* (2nd ed. revised and enlarged). New York: Negro Universities Press. (Original work published 1904.)

Hamer, R. (1970). *A choice of Anglo-Saxon verse.* London: Faber & Faber.

Hamidullah, M. (1981). *Introduction to Islam.* Chicago: Kazi.

Hammond, N. (1988). *Ancient Maya civilization.* New Brunswick, NJ: Rutgers University Press.

Hammond-Tooke, W. (Ed.). (1974). *The Bantu-speaking peoples of Southern Africa.* London: Routledge & Kegan Paul.

Hancock, I. (1984a). Romani and Angloromani. In P. Trudgill (Ed.), *Language in the British Isles* (pp. 367–383). Cambridge, England: Cambridge University Press.

Hancock, I. (1984b). Shelta and Polari. In P. Trudgill (Ed.), *Language in the British Isles* (pp. 384–403). Cambridge, England: Cambridge University Press.

Hancock, I. (1987). *The pariah syndrome: An account of Gypsy slavery and persecution.* Ann Arbor, MI: Karoma.

Handlin, J. (1983). *Action in late Ming thought: The reorientation of Lü K'un and other scholar-officials.* Berkeley: University of California Press.

Haneef, S. (1985). *What everyone should know about Islam and Muslims.* Des Plaines, IL: Library of Islam.

Hanh, T. N. (1991). *Old path white clouds: Walking in the footsteps of the Buddah.* Berkeley, CA: Parallax.

Hansen, C. (1992). *A Daoist theory of Chinese thought: A philosophical interpretation.* New York: Oxford University Press.

Hardy, F. (1994). *The religious culture of India: Power, love and wisdom.* Cambridge, England: Cambridge University Press.

Harrold, F., & Eve, R. (Eds.). (1995). *Cult archaeology and creationism: Understanding pseudoscientific beliefs about the past* (Exp. ed.). Iowa City: University of Iowa Press.

Hassig, R. (1985). *Trade, tribute, and transportation: The sixteenth century political economy of the Valley of Mexico.* Norman: University of Oklahoma Press.

Hassig, R. (1988). *Aztec warfare: Imperial expansion and political control.* Norman: University of Oklahoma Press.

Hassig, R. (1992). *War and society in ancient Mesoamerica.* Berkeley: University of California Press.

Hayhoe, R., & Bastid, M. (Eds.). (1987). *China's education and the industrialized world: Studies in cultural transfer.* London: Sharpe.

Haykal, M. H. (1976). *The life of Muhammad.* Indianapolis, IN: American Trust Publications.

Headland, I. (1914). *Home life in China.* London: Methuen & Co.

Hellbom, A. (1967). *La participación cultural de las mujeres: Indias y mestizas en el México precortesiano y postrevolucionario* [The cultural participation of women: Indians and mestizas in pre-Cortesian and post-revolutionary Mexico]. (Monograph Series, Publication 10.) Stockholm: The Ethnographic Museum.

Heren, L., Fitzgerald, C. P., Freeberne, M., Hook, B., & Bonavia, D. (1973). *China's three thousand years: The story of a great civilisation.* New York: Collier.

Herman, A. L. (1991). *A brief introduction to Hinduism: Religion, philosophy, and ways of liberation.* Boulder, CO: Westview.

Hersh, R. (1997). *What is mathematics, really?* New York: Oxford University Press.

Hindery, R. (1978). *Comparative ethics in Hindu and Buddhist traditions.* Delhi: Motilal Banarsidass.

Hiskett, M. (1994). *The development of Islam in West Africa* (2nd ed.). Edinburgh: Edinburgh University Press.

Ho Peng Yoke. (1985). *Li, qi and shu: An introduction to science and civilization in China.* Hong Kong: Hong Kong University Press.

Hogg, G. (1990). *Cannibalism and human sacrifice.* London: Hale.

Holmes, G. (Ed.). (1988). *The Oxford illustrated history of medieval Europe.* Oxford, England: Oxford University Press.

Holtedahl, L., & Djingui, M. (1997). The power of knowledge. In E. Rosander & D. Westerlund (Eds.), *African Islam and Islam in Africa* (pp. 254–285). Athens, OH: University of Ohio Press.

Horrocks, G. (1997). *Greek: A history of the language and its speakers.* London: Longman.

Horton, R. (1970). African traditional thought and western science. In B. Wilson (Ed.), *Rationality* (pp. 131–171). New York: Harper & Row.

Howe, S. (1998). *Afrocentrism: Mythical pasts and imagined homes.* London: Verso.

Hsiung-huei Lee. (1995). *Education in Taiwan during the Ch'ing dynasty, 1683–1895.* Ph.D. dissertation, University of Connecticut.

Hsü, I. C. Y. (1990). *The rise of modern China.* New York: Oxford University Press.

Huang, R. (1988). *China: A macro history.* London: Sharpe.

Hucker, C. (1975). *China's imperial past: An introduction to Chinese history and culture.* Stanford, CA: Stanford University Press.

Hulbert, J. (1935). *Bright's Anglo-Saxon reader.* New York: Henry Holt.

Humphrey, C., & Laidlaw, J. (1994). *The archetypal actions of ritual: A theory of ritual illustrated by the Jain rite of worship.* Oxford, England: Clarendon Press.

Humphries, C. (1951). *Buddhism: An introduction and guide.* Harmondsworth: Penguin.

Hurtado, A., & Iverson, P. (Eds.). (1994). *Major problems in American Indian history: Documents and essays.* Lexington, MA: Heath.

Husaini, S. W. A. (1986). *Islamic science and public policies: Lessons from the history of science* (2nd rev. ed.). Indianapolis, IN: Islamic Book Service.

Hymes, R. (1989). Lu Chiu-yüan, academies, and the problem of the local community. In W. de Bary & J. Chaffee (Eds.), Neo-Confucian education: The formative stage (pp. 432–456). Berkeley: University of California Press.

Ibrahim, A. (1989). Islam and the law. In Toward Islamization of disciplines (pp. 381–391). Herndon, VA: International Institute of Islamic Thought.

Icamina, P. (1993). Threads of common knowledge. IDRC Reports 21, 1: 14–16.

Infante, F. (1983). La educación de los Aztecas [The education of the Aztecs]. México: Panorama Editorial.

Irele, A. (Ed.). (1992). African education and identity. Ibadan, Nigeria: Spectrum.

Ishaq, I. (1967). The life of Muhammad. London: Oxford University Press.

Ishumi, A. (1986). Black civilization and pedagogy: A search for modern methods. In J. Okpaku, A. Opubor, & B. Oloruntimehin (Eds.), The arts and civilization of Black and African peoples: Volume 6, Black civilization and pedagogy (pp. 60–79). Lagos, Nigeria: Center for Black and African Arts and Civilization.

Ismail, S. M. (1994). Islamic education in North America: A reality, a fact and a responsibility. Muslim Education Quarterly 11, 3: 63–71.

Ives, C. (1992). Zen awakening and society. Honolulu: University of Hawaii Press.

Izquierdo, A. (1983). La educación maya en los tiempos prehispánicos. [Mayan education in pre- hispanic times]. México: Universidad Nacional Autónoma de México.

Jacobson, N. P. (1986). Understanding Buddhism. Carbondale, IL: Southern Illinois University Press.

Jameelah, M. (1986). Islam in theory and practice. Lahore, Pakistan: Mohammad Yusuf Khan & Sons.

Jansen, G. H. (1979). Militant Islam. New York: Harper & Row.

Jansen, J. (Ed.). (1991). Knowledge and power in South Africa: Critical perspectives across the disciplines. Johannesburg: Skotaville.

Jolly, J. (1989). Histoire de continent Africain (2 vols.) [History of the African continent]. Paris: Editions l'Harmattan.

Josephy, A. (1991). The Indian heritage of America. Boston: Houghton Mifflin. (Original work published 1968.)

Josephy, A. (1994). 500 nations: An illustrated history of North American Indians. New York: Knopf.

Josephy, A. (Ed.). (1991). America in 1492: The world of the Indian peoples before the arrival of Columbus. New York: Vintage.

Josserand, J. K., & Dakin, K. (Eds.). (1988). Smoke and mist: Mesoamerican studies in memory of Thelma D. Sullivan, part II. Oxford, England: B.A.R.

Kahn, M. (Ed.). (1981). Education and society in the Muslim world. Jeddah, Saudi Arabia: King Abdulaziz University.

Kalupahana, D. (1992). A history of Buddhist philosophy: Continuities and discontinuities. Honolulu: University of Hawaii Press.

Kaminski, I. (1980). *The state of ambiguity: Studies of Gypsy refugees.* Gothenburg, Sweden: Mobilis.

Karttunen, F., & Lockhard, J. (Eds.). (1987). *The art of Nahuatl speech: The Bancroft dialogues.* Los Angeles: UCLA Latin American Center Publications.

Kaschula, R. (1991). The role of Xhosa oral poetry in contemporary South African society. *South African Journal of African Languages* 11, 2: 47–54.

Kaschula, R. (Ed.). (1993). *Foundations in Southern African oral literature.* Johannesburg: Witwatersrand University Press.

Katengo, M., & Mwale, G. (1986). Can traditional education be integrated with the modern educational system? In S. Moyo, T. Sumaili, & J. Moody (Eds.), *Oral traditions in Southern Africa, vol 6.* (pp. 456–481). Lusaka, Zambia: Division for Cultural Research, Institute for African Studies, University of Zambia.

Katz, F. (1966). *Situación social y económica de los Aztecas durante los siglos XV y XVI* [The social and economic situation of the Aztecs during the 15th and 16th centuries]. México: Universidad Nacional Autónoma de México, Instituto de Investigaciones Históricas.

Kawagley, O. (1990). Yup'ik ways of knowing. *Canadian Journal of Native Education* 17, 2: 5–17.

Kazi, M. A. (1997). *Islamic thought and modern science.* Amman, Jordan: Islamic Academy of Sciences.

Keen, B. (1971). *The Aztec image in Western thought.* New Brunswick, NJ: Rutgers University Press.

Kefai, Y., & Risnick, M. (Eds.). (1996). *Constructionism in practice: Designing, thinking, and learning in a digital world.* Mahwah, NJ: Lawrence Erlbaum Associates.

Kelleher, M. T. (1989). Back to basics: Chu Hsi's *Elementary learning (Hsiao-hsüeh).* In W. de Bary & J. Chaffee (Eds.), *Neo-Confucian education: The formative stage* (pp. 219–251). Berkeley: University of California Press.

Kellogg, S. (1988). Cognatic kinship and religion: Women in Aztec society. In J. Josserand & K. Dakin (Eds.), *Smoke and mist: Mesoamerican studies in memory of Thelma D. Sullivan , part II* (pp. 665–681). Oxford, England: B.A.R.

Kepel, G., & Richard, Y. (Eds.). (1990). *Intellectuels et militants de l'Islam contemporain* [Intellectuals and militants in contemporary Islam]. Paris: Éditions du Seuil.

Kephart, W. (1982). *Extraordinary groups: The sociology of unconventional lifestyles* (2nd ed.). New York: St. Martin's Press.

Khan, M. I. (1996). *Experiencing Islam.* Karachi: Oxford University Press.

Kiang Kang-Hu. (1934). *On Chinese studies.* Shanghai: Commercial.

Kimmerle, H. (1991). *Philosophie in Afrika—Afrikanische Philosophie* [Philosophy in Africa—African philosophy]. Frankfurt/Main, Germany: Campus Verlag.

Kincheloe, T. S. (1984). The wisdom of the elders: Cross-cultural perspectives. *Journal of Thought* 19, 3: 121–127.

Kinsley, D. (1993). *Hinduism: A cultural perspective* (2nd ed.). Englewood Cliffs, NJ: Prentice Hall.

Klein, C. (1987). The ideology of autosacrifice at the Templo Mayor. In E. Boone (Ed.), *The Aztec Templo Mayor: A symposium at Dumbarton Oaks* (pp. 293–370). Washington, DC: Dumbarton Oaks Research Library and Collection.

Kleinman, A. (1980). *Patients and healers in the context of culture: An exploration of the borderland between anthropology, medicine, and psychiatry.* Berkeley: University of California Press.

Klor de Alva, J., Nicholas, H., & Keber, E. (Eds.). (1988). *The work of Bernardino de Sahagun: Pioneer ethnographer of sixteenth century Aztec Mexico.* Albany: Institute for Mesoamerican Studies, The University of Albany, State University of New York.

Klostermaier, K. (1989). *A survey of Hinduism.* Albany: State University of New York Press.

Kluckhohn, C., & Leighton, D. (1962). *The Navajo* (Rev. ed.). Garden City, NY: Doubleday.

Knipe, D. (1991). *Hinduism.* San Francisco: Harper.

Kraft, K. (Ed.). (1988). *Zen: Tradition and transition.* New York: Grove.

Krieger, S., & Trauzettel, R. (Eds.), (1991). *Confucianism and the modernization of China.* Mainz, Germany: Hase & Koehler.

Kroeber, K. (1981). The art of traditional American Indian narration. In K. Kroeber (Ed.), *Traditional literatures of the American Indian: Texts and interpretations* (pp. 1–24). Lincoln: University of Nebraska Press.

Kroeber, K (Ed.). (1981). *Traditional literatures of the American Indian: Texts and interpretations.* Lincoln: University of Nebraska Press.

Krugly-Smolska, E. (1994). An examination of some difficulties in integrating western science into societies with an indigenous scientific tradition. *Interchange* 25, 4: 324–334.

Kuang Yaming. (1991). Modern values of the positive elements in Confucius' ideas concerning the study of man. In S. Krieger & R. Trauzettel (Eds.), *Confucianism and the modernization of China* (pp. 7–17). Mainz, Germany: Hase & Koehler.

Kubik, G. (1990). *Visimu vya mukatikati:* Dilemma tales and "arithmetical puzzles" collected among the Valuchazi. *South African Journal of African Languages* 10, 2: 59–68.

Kubik, G. (1992). A Luchazi riddle session: Analysis of recorded texts in a south-central African Bantu language. *South African Journal of African Languages* 12, 2: 51–82.

Kuhn, T. (1970). *The structure of scientific revolutions* (2nd enlarged ed.). Chicago: University of Chicago Press.

Kuhn, T. (1977). *The essential tension: Selected studies in scientific tradition and change.* Chicago: University of Chicago Press.

Kuklick, H. (1991). *The savage within: The social history of British anthropology, 1885–1945*. Cambridge, England: Cambridge University Press.

Kunene, D. (1971). *Heroic poetry of the Basotho*. Oxford, England: Oxford University Press.

Küng, H. (1992). *Judaism: Between yesterday and tomorrow*. New York: Crossroad.

Kuper, A. (1988). *The invention of primitive society: Transformations of an illusion*. London: Routledge.

Lanczkowski, G. (1970). *Aztekische Sprach und Überlieferung* [Aztec language and traditions]. Berlin: Springer.

Larson, G. (1994). Hinduism in India and in America. In J. Neusner (Ed.), *World religions in America* (pp. 177–202). Louisville, KY: Westminster/John Knox Press.

Lasisi, R. O. (1995). French colonialism and Islamic education in West Africa, 1900–1939. *Muslim Education Quarterly* 12, 3: 12–22.

Last, M., & Chavunduka, G. L. (Eds.). (1986). *The professionalisation of African medicine*. Manchester, England: Manchester University Press, in association with the International African Institute.

Lau, D. C. (Trans.), (1970). *Mencius*. Harmondsworth: Penguin.

Lau, D. C. (Trans.), (1979). *The Analects*. Harmondsworth: Penguin.

Lee, G. (1967). *Crusade against ignorance: Thomas Jefferson on education*. New York: Teachers College Press.

Lee, T. (1989). Sung schools and education before Chu Hsi. In W. de Bary & J. Chaffee (Eds.), *Neo-Confucian education: The formative stage* (pp. 105–136). Berkeley: University of California Press.

Lee, T. H. C. (1985). *Government education and examinations in Sung China*. Hong Kong: Chinese University Press.

Lefkowitz, M. (1996). *Not out of Africa: How Afrocentrism became an excuse to teach myth as history*. New York: Basic Books.

Lefkowitz, M., & Rogers, G. M. (Eds.). (1996). *Black Athena revisited*. Chapel Hill: University of North Carolina Press.

Leggett, T. (Ed.). (1978). *Zen and the ways*. London: Routledge & Kegan Paul.

Lehmann, W. (1993). *Theoretical bases on Indo-European linguistics*. London: Longman.

León-Portilla, M. (Ed.). (1958). *Ritos, sacerdotes y ataviós de los dioses: Textos de los informantes de Sahagun, 1*. [Rites, priests and vestments of the gods: Texts from Sahagun's informants]. México: Universidad Nacional Autónoma de México, Instituto de Historia.

León-Portilla, M. (1963). *Aztec thought and culture*. Norman: University of Oklahoma Press.

León-Portilla, M. (1966). *La filosofia Nahuatl: Estudio en sus fuentes* [Nahuatl philosophy: A study of its origins]. México: Universidad Nacional Autónoma de México.

León-Portilla, M. (1967). *Trece poetas del mundo azteca* [Thirteen poets of the Aztec world]. México: Universidad Nacional Autónoma de México, Instituto de Investigaciones Históricas.

León-Portilla, M. (1968). *Tiempo y realidad en el pensamiento maya* [Time and reality in Mayan thought]. México: Universidad Nactional Autónoma de México.

León-Portilla, M. (Ed.). (1971). *De Teotihuacán a los Aztecas: Antología de fuentes e interpretaciones históricas* [From Teotihuacán to the Aztecs: Anthology of historical sources and interpretations]. México: Universidad Nacional Autónoma de México, Instituto de Investigaciones Históricas.

León-Portilla, M. (1988). *Time and reality in the thought of the Maya*. Norman: University of Oklahoma Press.

León-Portilla, M. (1992a). *The Aztec image of self and society: An introduction to Nahua culture*. Salt Lake City: University of Utah Press.

León-Portilla, M. (1992b). *Fifteen poets of the Aztec world*. Norman: University of Oklahoma Press.

León-Portilla, M. (1994). *Quince poetas del mundo náhuatl* [Fifteen poets of the Aztec world]. México: Editorial Diana.

León-Portilla, M. (1995). *Toltecáyotl: Aspectos de la cultura náhuatl* [Toltecáyotl: Aspects of Nahuatl culture]. México: Fondo de Cultura Económica.

Leslie, C., & Young, A. (Eds.). (1992). *Paths to Asian medical knowledge*. Berkeley: University of California Press.

Leslie, J. (Ed.). (1991). *Roles and rituals for Hindu women*. Rutherford, NJ: Fairleigh Dickinson University Press.

Levinson, B., Foley, D., & Holland, D. (Eds.). (1996). *The cultural production of the educated person: Critical ethnographies of schooling and local practice*. Albany: State University of New York Press.

Levinson, B., & Holland, D. (1996). The cultural production of the educated person: An introduction. In B. Levinson, D. Foley, & D. Holland (Eds.), *The cultural production of the educated person: Critical ethnographies of schooling and local practice* (pp. 1–54). Albany: State University of New York Press.

Lhuillier, A. (1963). El pensamiento náhuatl respecto de la muerte [Náhuatl thought concerning death]. *Estudios de Cultura Náhuatl* 4: 251–261.

Liégeois, J. (1987). *Gypsies and travellers: Socio-cultural data, socio-political data*. Strasbourg, Germany: Council for Cultural Co-operation.

Lincoln, Y., & Guba, E. (1985). *Naturalistic inquiry*. Newbury Park, CA: Sage.

Lings, M. (1983). *Muhammad: His life based on the earliest sources*. Rochester, VT: Inner Traditions.

Lippman, T. (1995). *Understanding Islam: An introduction to the Muslim world* (2nd rev. ed.). New York: Meridan.

Liu, J. (Ed.). (1974). *Political institutions in traditional China: Major issues*. New York: Wiley.

Liu Ts'un-Yan. (1970). Taoist self-cultivation in Ming thought. In W. de Bary (Ed.), *Self and society in Ming thought* (pp. 291–330). New York: Columbia University Press.

Llasera, I. (1987). Confucian education through European eyes. In R. Hayhoe & M. Bastid (Eds.), *China's education and the industrialized world* (pp. 21–32). London: Sharpe.

lo Liyong, T. (1969). *The last word.* Nairobi, Kenya: East Africa Publishing House.

Locust, C. (1988). Wounding the spirit: Discrimination and traditional American Indian belief systems. *Harvard Educational Review* 58, 3: 315–330.

Loewe, M. (1965). *Imperial China: The historical background to the modern age.* New York: Praeger.

Loewe, M. (1990). *The pride that was China.* New York: St. Martin's Press.

Loimeier, R. (1997). *Islamic reform and political change in northern Nigeria.* Evanston, IL: Northwestern University.

Lomawaima, K. T. (1994). *They called it prairie light: The story of Chilocco Indian school.* Lincoln: University of Nebraska Press.

Lopez, D. (Ed.). (1995). *Religions of India in practice.* Princeton, NJ: Princeton University Press.

Lowe, L. (1991). *Critical terrains: French and British orientalisms.* Ithaca, NY: Cornell University Press.

Luis de Rojas, J. (1988). *México Tenochtitlan: Economía y sociedad en el siglo XVI* [Mexican Tenochtitlan: Economy and society in the 16th century]. México: El Colegio de Michoacán, Fondo de Cultura Económica.

MacMillan, N. (1993). Indigenous peoples test the waters. *IDRC Reports* 21, 1: 6–8.

Magadla, L. (1996). Constructivism: A practitioner's perspective. *South African Journal of Higher Education* 10: 83–88.

Mahlangu, D. (1988). *Imiraro:* Ndebele riddles. *South African Journal of African Languages* 8 (Supplement 1): 147–172.

Manglapus, R. (1987). *Will of the people: Original democracy in non-western societies.* New York: Greenwood.

Mannan, M. A. (1989). The frontiers of Islamic economics: Some philosophical underpinnings. In *Toward Islamization of disciplines* (pp. 295–311). Herndon, VA: International Institute of Islamic Thought.

Maqsood, R. (1994). *Islam.* London: NTC.

Marcus, J. (1992). *Mesoamerican writing systems: Propaganda, myth, and history in four ancient civilizations.* Princeton, NJ: Princeton University Press.

Markus, M. (1963). Estudio comparativo entre la educación nahuatl y la griega [Comparative study of Nahuatl and Greek education]. *Estudios de Cultura Náhuatl* 4: 281–292.

Martin, C. (1994). Ethnohistory: A better way to write Indian history. In A. Hurtado & P. Iverson (Eds.), *Major problems in American Indian history: Documents and essays* (pp. 23–33). Lexington, MA: Heath.

Martin, J. R. (1982). The ideal of the educated person. In D. DeNicola (Ed.), *Philosophy of education: 1981* (pp. 3–20). Normal, IL: Philosophy of Education Society.

Martin, J. R. (1985). *Reclaiming a conversation: The ideal of the educated woman.* New Haven, CT: Yale University Press.

Martin, P., & O'Meara, P. (Eds.). (1995). *Africa* (3rd ed.). Bloomington: Indiana University Press.

Mascaró, J. (Trans.), (1965). *The Upanishads.* Harmondsworth: Penguin.

Maspero, H., & Escarra, J. (1952). *Les institutions de la Chine: Essai historique* [Chinese institutions: An historical essay]. Paris: Presses Universitaires de France.

Matras, Y. (Ed.). (1995). *Romani in contact: The history, structure, and sociology of a language.* Amsterdam: John Benjamins.

Matsunaga, A. (1969). *The Buddhist philosophy of assimilation: The historical development of the Honji-Suijaku theory.* Tokyo: Sophia University.

Mazrui, A. (1980). *The African condition: The Reith lectures.* London: Heinemann.

Mazrui, A., & Wagaw, T. (1985). Towards decolonizing modernity: Education and culture conflict in Eastern Africa. In *The educational process and historiography in Africa* (pp. 35–62). Paris: UNESCO.

Mbiti, J. (1989). *African religions and philosophy* (2nd ed.). Oxford, England: Heinemann.

McGovern, S. (1999). *Education, modern development, and indigenous knowledge: An analysis of academic knowledge production.* New York: Garland.

McIvor, M. (1990). Research into traditional First Nations healing practices: A beginning. *Canadian Journal of Native Education* 17, 2: 89–95.

McKay, A., & McKay, B. (1987). Education as a total way of life: The Nisga'a experience. In J. Barman, Y. Hébert, & D. McCaskill (Eds.), *Indian education in Canada, volume 2: The challenge* (pp. 64– 85). Vancouver: University of British Columbia Press.

McKnight, B. (1989). Mandarins as legal experts: Professional learning in Sung China. In W. de Bary & J. Chafee (Eds.), *Neo-Confucian education: The formative stage* (pp. 493–516). Berkeley: University of California Press.

McMullen, D. (1988). *State and scholars in T'ang China.* Cambridge, England: Cambridge University Press.

Medicine, B. (1987). My elders tell me. In J. Barman, Y. Hébert, & D. McCaskill (Eds.), *Indian education in Canada, volume 2: The challenge* (pp. 142–152). Vancouver: University of British Columbia Press.

Mernissi, F. (1987a). *Beyond the veil: Male-female dynamics in modern Muslim society.* Bloomington: Indiana University Press.

Mernissi, F. (1987b). *The veil and the male elite: A feminist interpretation of women's rights in Islam.* Reading, MA: Addison-Wesley.

Meskill, J., with J. Gentzler (Eds.). (1973). *An introduction to Chinese civilization.* New York: Columbia University Press.

Miller, C. (1975). American Rom and the ideology of defilement. In F. Rehfisch (Ed.), *Gypsies, tinkers, and other travellers* (pp. 41–54). London: Academic Press.

Miller, D. (1988). Hopi education: Before schools and teachers. *Tennessee Education* 18, 2: 28–32.

Miller, D., & Wertz, D. (1976). *Hindu monastic life and the monks and monasteries of Bhubaneswar.* Montreal: McGill-Queen's University Press.

Miller, M. E. (1986). *The art of Mesoamerica from Olmec to Aztec.* London: Thames and Hudson.

Milton, S. (1991). Gypsies and the Holocaust. *The History Teacher* 24, 4: 375–387.

Mitchell, B. (1995). *An invitation to Old English and Anglo-Saxon England.* Oxford, England: Blackwell.

Mitchell, B., & Robinson, F. (1992). *A guide to Old English* (5th ed.). Oxford, England: Blackwell.

Moctezuma, E. (1987). Symbolism of the Templo Mayor. In E. Boone (Ed.), *The Aztec Templo Mayor: A symposium at Dumbarton Oaks* (pp. 185–209). Washington, DC: Dumbarton Oaks Research Library and Collection.

Moll, L. (Ed.). (1990). *Vygotsky and education: Instructional implications and applications of sociocultural psychology.* Cambridge, England: Cambridge University Press.

Mookerji, R. (1969). *Ancient Indian education.* Delhi: Motilal Banarsidass.

Morales-Gómez, D. (1993). Knowledge, change and the preservation of progress. *IDRC Reports* 21, 1: 4–5.

Morton, W. S. (1995). *China: Its history and culture.* New York: McGraw-Hill.

Moses, W. J. (1998). *Afrotopia: The roots of African American popular history.* Cambridge, England: Cambridge University Press.

Mote, F., & Twitchett, D. (Eds.). (1988). *The Cambridge history of China, volume 7: The Ming dynasty, 1368–1644, part I.* Cambridge, England: Cambridge University Press.

Mottahedeh, R. (1998). Traditional Shi'ite education in Qom. In A. Rorty (Ed.), *Philosophers on education: New historical perspectives* (pp. 451–457). London: Routledge.

Moumouni, A. (1968). *Education in Africa.* New York: Praeger.

Moyo, S., Sumaili, T., & Moody, J. (Eds.). (1986). *Oral traditions in Southern Africa, vol 6.* Lusaka, Zambia: Division for Cultural Research, Institute for African Studies, University of Zambia.

Mudimbe, V. (1988). *The invention of Africa: Gnosis, philosophy, and the order of knowledge.* London: Currey.

Muller, C. F. J. (1986). *Five hundred years: A history of South Africa* (5th ed.). Pretoria: Academica.

Myburgh, A. (Ed.). (1981). *Anthropology for Southern Africa.* Pretoria: van Schaik.

Mzolo, D. (1988). Social function of clan praises. In A. Nkabinde (Ed.), *African linguistics and literature* (pp. 132–138). Johannesburg: Lexicon.

Nadel, S. (1942). *Black Byzantium: The kingdom of the Nupe in Nigeria*. London: International African Institute.

Nakosteen, M. (1964). *History of Islamic origins of Western education, A.D. 800–1350*. Boulder, CO: University of Colorado Press.

Nasr, S. H. (1984). Islamic education and science: A summary appraisal. In Y. Haddad, B. Haines, & E. Findly (Eds.), *The Islamic impact* (pp. 47–68). Syracuse, NY: Syracuse University Press.

Nasr, S. H. (1987). *Traditional Islam in the modern world*. London: Routledge & Kegan Paul.

Nayyar, A. H. (1998). Madrasah education frozen in time. In P. Hoodbhoy (Ed.), *Education and the state: Fifty years of Pakistan* (pp. 215–250). Karachi, Pakistan: Oxford University Press.

Needham, J. (1981). *Science in traditional China: A comparative perspective*. Cambridge, MA: Harvard University Press.

Nelson-Barber, S. (1990). Considerations for the inclusion of multiple cultural competencies in teacher assessment: A Yup'ik Eskimo case study. *Canadian Journal of Native Education* 17, 2: 33–42.

Neusner, J. (Ed.). (1994). *World religions in America*. Louisville, KY: Westminster/John Knox Press.

Nicholson, H. (1967). The efflorescence of Mesoamerican civilization: A resume. In B. Ball (Ed.), *Indian Mexico: Past and present* (pp. 46–71). Los Angeles: University of California at Los Angeles, Latin American Center.

Nkabinde, A. (Ed.). (1988). *African linguistics and literature*. Johannesburg: Lexicon.

Nkara, J. (1992). *Bisisimi* or the language of the wise. *South African Journal of African Languages* 12, 4: 144–149.

Noddings, N. (1990). Constructivism in mathematics education. In R. Davis, C. Maher & N. Noddings (Eds.), *Constructivist views on the teaching and learning of mathematics* (pp. 7–18). Reston, VA: National Council of Teachers of Mathematics.

Noddings, N. (1995). *Philosophy of education*. Boulder, CO: Westview.

Norman, J. (1988). *Chinese*. Cambridge, England: Cambridge University Press.

Nwosu, S. (1986). Pedagogic problems in Africa today. In J. Okpaku, A. Opubor, & B. Oloruntimehin (Eds.), *The arts and civilization of Black and African peoples: Volume 6, Black civilization and pedagogy* (pp. 102–118). Lagos, Nigeria: Center for Black and African Arts and Civilization.

Nyembezi, C. (1974). *Zulu proverbs*. Johannesburg: University of the Witwatersrand Press.

Obanewa, O. (1973). *Education of the children and youth in Ile-Ife: A comparison of formal and non-formal systems of education*. M.Ed. thesis, University of Ife, Nigeria.

O'Flaherty, W. D. (Trans.). (1981). *The Rig Veda: An anthology*. Harmondsworth: Penguin.

Ogbalu, F., & Emenanjo, E. (Eds.). (1982). *Igbo language and culture, vol. 2*. Ibadan, Nigeria: Ibadan University Press.

Ogundijo, M. (1970). *Indigenous education in the Ejigbo District of Oshun Division in the pre-colonial days and the coming of the missionaries*. B.A. thesis, Faculty of Education, University of Ife, Nigeria.

Okeke, A. (1982). Traditional education in Igboland. In F. Ogbalu & E. Emenanjo (Eds.), *Igbo language and culture, vol. 2* (pp. 15–26). Ibadan, Nigeria: Ibadan University Press.

Okely, J. (1983). *The Traveller-Gypsies*. Cambridge, England: Cambridge University Press.

Okpaku, J., Opubor, A., & Oloruntimehin, B. (Eds.). (1986). *The arts and civilization of Black and African peoples: Volume 6, Black civilization and pedagogy*. Lagos, Nigeria: Center for Black and African Arts and Civilization.

Olaniyan, R. (1982). African history and culture: An overview. In R. Olaniyan (Ed.), *African history and culture* (pp. 1–12). Lagos, Nigeria: Longman.

Olaniyan, R. (Ed.). (1982). *African history and culture*. Lagos, Nigeria: Longman.

Olivelle, P. (1993). *The Ashrama system: The history and heurmeneutics of a religious institution*. New York: Oxford University Press.

Opland, J. (1983). *Xhosa oral poetry: Aspects of a Black South African tradition*. Cambridge, England: Cambridge University Press.

Opland, J. (1990). Xhosa *izibongo:* Improvised line. *South African Journal of African Languages* 10, 4: 239–251.

Orellana, C. (1997). *Historia de la educatión en Guatemala* (5th ed.) [History of education in Guatemala]. Guatemala: Editorial Universitaria, Universidad de San Carlos de Guatemala.

Organ, T. (1970). *The Hindu quest for the perfection of man*. Athens, OH: Ohio University Press.

Orr, D. (1992). *Ecological literacy: Education and the transition to a postmodern world*. Albany: State University of New York Press.

Ortega, M. (1988). *La Inquisición y los gitanos* [The Inquisition and the Gypsies]. Madrid: Taurus Ediciones.

Ortiz de Montellano, B. (1990). *Aztec medicine, health, and nutrition*. New Brunswick, NJ: Rutgers University Press.

Ortiz de Montellano, B. (1995). Multiculturalism, cult archaeology, and pseudoscience. In F. Harrold & R. Eve (Eds.), *Cult archaeology and creationism: Understanding pseudoscientific beliefs about the past* (Exp. ed.) (pp. 134–151). Iowa City: University of Iowa Press.

Otayek, R. (Ed.). (1993). *Le radicalisme islamique au sud du Sahara: Da'wa, arabisation et critique de l'Occident* [Islamic radicalism in sub-Saharan Africa: Da'wa, Arabization, and critique of the west]. Paris: Éditions Karthala.

Othón de Mendizábal, M. (1971). La cultura azteca y los sacrificios humanos [Aztec culture and human sacrifices]. In M. León-Portilla (Ed.), *De Teotihuacán a los Aztecas: Antología de fuentes e interpretaciones históricas* (pp. 208–214). México Universidad Nacional Autónoma de México, Instituto de Investigaciones Históricas.

Oxendine, J. (1988). *American Indian sports heritage.* Champaign, IL: Human Kinetics.

Ozmon, H., & Craver, S. (1995). *Philosophical foundations of education* (5th ed.). Englewood Cliffs, NJ: Prentice-Hall.

Palter, R. (1996). *Black Athena,* Afrocentrism, and the history of science. In M. Lefkowitz & G. Rogers (Eds.), *Black Athena revisited* (pp. 209–266). Chapel Hill: University of North Carolina Press.

Pandit, B. (1993). *The Hindu mind: Fundamentals of Hindu religion and philosophy for all ages* (2nd ed.). Glen Ellyn, IL: B & V.

Parrinder, G. (1969). *Religion in Africa.* Harmondsworth: Penguin.

Patton, M. (1978). *Utilization-focused evaluations.* Beverly Hills, CA: Sage.

Patton, M. (1990). *Qualitative evaluation and research methods* (2nd ed.). Newbury Park, CA: Sage.

Paul, D. Y. (1985). *Women in Buddhism: Images of the feminine in the Mahayana tradition.* Berkeley: University of California Press.

Paulston, C., & Peckham, D. (Eds.). (1998). *Linguistic minorities in central and eastern Europe.* Clevedon, Avon: Multilingual Matters.

p'Bitek, O. (1967). *Song of Lawino and Song of Ocol.* Ibadan, Nigeria: Heinemann.

p'Bitek, O. (1971). *African religions in Western scholarship.* Nairobi, Kenya: East African Literature Bureau.

Pei-yi Wu. (1989). Education of children in the Sung. In W. de Bary & J. Chaffee (Eds.), *Neo-Confucian education: The formative stage* (pp. 307–324). Berkeley: University of California Press.

Pelikan, J. (Ed.). (1987). *Sacred writings, volume 6: Buddhism, The Dhammapada.* New York: Quality Paperback Book Club.

Peters, F. E. (1994). *The Hajj: The Muslim pilgrimage to Mecca and the holy places.* Princeton, NJ: Princeton University Press.

Pettitt, G. (1946). *Primitive education in North America.* Berkeley: University of California Press.

Phillips, D. C. (1995). The good, the bad, and the ugly: The many faces of constructivism. *Educational Researcher* 24: 5–12.

Phillips, D. C. (1996). Response to Ernst von Glasersfeld. *Educational Researcher* 25: 20.

Phillips, H. (1975). *Basic education: A world challenge.* New York: Wiley.

Piaget, J. (1979). *L'epistémologie génétique* (3rd ed.) [Genetic epistemology]. Paris: Presses Universitaires de France.

Ping-Ti Ho. (1962). *The ladder of success in imperial China.* New York: Columbia University Press.

Pollak, S. (1983). *Ancient Buddhist education (Papers from the Bernard Van Leer Foundation Project on Human Potential).* Cambridge, MA: Harvard Graduate School of Education.

Prakash, G. (1990). Writing post-orientalist histories of the third world: Perspectives from Indian historiography. *Comparative Studies in Society and History* 32: 383–408.

Pretorius, W. J. (1990). A comparative look at the development of heroic poetry in Northern Sotho. *South African Journal of African Languages* 10, 3: 125–131.

Radhkrishnan, S. (Ed.). (1994). *The principal Upanishads*. New Delhi: Indus.

Rahman, F. (1979). *Islam* (2nd ed.). Chicago: University of Chicago Press.

Rampal, A. (1992). A possible "orality" for science? *Interchange* 23, 3: 227–244.

Ramsey, S. R. (1987). *The languages of China*. Princeton, NJ: Princeton University Press.

Raper, P. (Ed.). (1986). *Names 1983: Proceedings of the Second Southern African Names Congress*. Pretoria: Human Sciences Research Council.

Raum, O. (1967). An evaluation of indigenous education. In P. Duminy (Ed.), *Trends and challenges in the education of the South African Bantu* (pp. 89–105). Pretoria: van Schaik.

Raval, S. (1958). *Basic education in modern India: A critique of Gandhian educational philosophy*. M.A. thesis, The American University, Washington, DC.

Rawski, E. (1979). *Education and popular literacy in Ch'ing China*. Ann Arbor: University of Michigan Press.

Ray, B. (1976). *African religions: Symbol, ritual, and community*. Englewood Cliffs, NJ: Prentice-Hall.

Raymond, J. (1982). Medicine as patriarchal religion. *Journal of Medicine and Philosophy* 7: 197–216.

Reagan, T. (1993). Educating the "reflective practitioner": The contribution of philosophy of education. *Journal of Research and Development in Education* 26, 4: 189–196.

Reat, N. R. (1994). *Buddhism: A history*. Berkeley, CA: Asian Humanities Press.

Réger, Z. (1998). A preliminary typology of genres in the oral culture of children living in a traditional Gypsy community. Paper presented at the Fourth International Conference on Romani Linguistics held at the University of Manchester, England, 2–5 September.

Réger, Z., & Gleason, J. (1991). Romani child-directed speech and children's language among Gypsies in Hungary. *Language in Society* 20: 601–617.

Regnier, R. (1995). Bridging western and First Nations thought: Balanced education in Whitehead's philosophy of organism and the sacred circle. *Interchange* 26, 4: 383–415.

Rehfisch, A., & Rehfisch, F. (1975). Scottish travellers or tinkers. In F. Rehfisch (Ed.), *Gypsies, tinkers, and other travellers* (pp. 271–283). London: Academic Press.

Reissner, J. (1984). Die innerislamische Diskussion zur modernen Wirtschafts- und Sozialordnung [The internal Islamic discussion on modern economics and social order.] In M. Ursinus (Ed.), *Der Islam in der Gegenwart* (pp. 155–169). München, Germany: C. H. Beck.

Renfrew, C. (1987). *Archeology and language: The puzzle of Indo-European origins.* Cambridge, England: Cambridge University Press.

Reynolds, P. (1986). The training of traditional healers in Mashonaland. In M. Last & C. Chavunduka (Eds.), *The professionalization of African medicine* (pp. 165–187). Manchester, England: Manchester University Press.

Richardson, V. (Ed.). (1997). *Constructivist teacher education: Building a world of new understandings.* London: Falmer.

Ricoeur, P. (1965). *History and truth.* Evanston, IL: Northwestern University Press.

Robins, R. H. (1979). *A short history of linguistics* (2nd ed.). London: Longman.

Rodinson, M. (1966). *Islam et capitalisme* [Islam and capitalism]. Paris: Éditions du Seuil.

Rodinson, M. (1974). *Mohammed.* New York: Vintage.

Rodinson, M. (1993). *L'Islam: Politique et croyance* [Islam: Politics and belief]. Paris: Fayard.

Rogers, J., & Wilson, S. (Eds.). (1993). *Ethnohistory and archaeology: Approaches to postcontact change in the Americas.* New York: Plenum.

Ronan, C. (1978). *The shorter science and civilisation in China, volume 1: Volumes I and II of the major series.* Cambridge, England: Cambridge University Press.

Ronan, C. (1981). *The shorter science and civilisation in China, volume 2: Volume III and a section of volume IV, part I of the major series.* Cambridge, England: Cambridge University Press.

Ronan, C. (1986). *The shorter science and civilisation in China, volume 3: A section of volume IV, part I and a section of volume IV, part 3 of the major series.* Cambridge, England: Cambridge University Press.

Ronan, C. (1994). *The shorter science and civilisation in China, volume 4: The main sections of volume IV, part 2 of the major series.* Cambridge, England: Cambridge University Press.

Ron-guey Chu. (1989). Chu Hsi and public instruction. In W. de Bary & J. Chaffee (Eds.), *Neo-Confucian education: The formative stage* (pp. 252–273). Berkeley: University of California Press.

Ropp, P. (Ed.). (1990). *Heritage of China.* Berkeley: University of California Press.

Rosander, E., & Westerlund, D. (1997). *African Islam and Islam in Africa.* Athens, OH: Ohio University Press.

Rosenthal, F. (1992). *The classical heritage in Islam.* London: Routledge.

Ross, N. W. (1980). *Buddhism: A way of life and thought.* New York: Vintage.

Rubin, V. (1976). *Individual and state in ancient China: Essays on four Chinese philosophers.* New York: Columbia University Press.

Rycroft, D., & Ngcobo, A. (1981). *Say it in Zulu.* Pietermaritzburg: Language and Reading Laboratories, University of Natal.

Sáenz, J. (1988). Reto y educación en el México prehispánico [Challenge and education in pre-hispanic Mexico]. In J. Josserand & K. Dakin (Eds.), *Smoke and mist: Mesoamerican studies in memory of Thelma D. Sullivan, part II* (pp. 681–695). Oxford, England: B.A.R.

Sagan, E. (1993). *Cannibalism: Human aggression and cultural form.* Santa Fe, NM: FirstDrum.

Sahadat, J. (1996). Divine revelation and the status of the Qur'an. *Muslim Education Quarterly* 13, 4: 4– 17.

Sahagun, B. (1981). *El Mexico antiguo: Selección y reordenación de la historia general de las cosas de Nueva España* [Ancient Mexico: Selection and reordering of the general history of the matters of New Spain]. Caracas: Biblioteca Ayachucho.

Sahlins, M. (1995). *How "natives" think: About Captain Cook, for example.* Chicago: University of Chicago Press.

Said, E. (1978). *Orientalism.* New York: Vintage.

Said, E. (1993). *Culture and imperialism.* New York: Vintage.

Sakai, T. (1970). Confucianism and popular educational works. In W. de Bary (Ed.), *Self and society in Ming thought* (pp. 331–366). New York: Columbia University Press.

Salo, M. (1979). Gypsy ethnicity: Implications of native categories and interaction for ethnic classification. *Ethnicity* 6: 73–96.

Salo, M., & Salo, S. (1977). *The Kalderas in eastern Canada.* Ottawa: National Museums of Canada.

Sarwar, G. (1989). *Islam: Beliefs and teaching.* London: Muslim Educational Trust.

Saud, M. A. (1989). Toward Islamic economics. In *Toward Islamization of disciplines* (pp. 265–270). Herndon, VA: International Institute of Islamic Thought.

Saunders, C. (1988). *The making of the South African past: Major historians on race and class.* Cape Town: David Philip.

Schacht, J. (1964). *An introduction to Islamic law.* Oxford, England: Clarendon.

Schapera, I. (1965). *Praise-poems of Tswana chiefs.* Oxford, England: Oxford University Press.

Schele, L., & Freidel, D. (1990). *A forest of kings: The untold story of the ancient Maya.* New York: Morrow.

Schele, L., & Mathews, P. (1998). *The code of kings: The language of seven sacred Maya temples and tombs.* New York: Simon & Shuster.

Schimmel, A. (1992). *Islam: An introduction.* Albany: State University of New York Press.

Schlagintweit, E. (1968). *Buddhism in Tibet* (2nd ed.). London: Susil Gupta.

Schwartz, B. (1985). *The world of thought in ancient China.* Cambridge, MA: Harvard University Press.

Scott, D., & Doubleday, T. (1992). *The elements of Zen.* Shaftesbury, Dorset: Element.

Semali, L., & Kincheloe, J. (Eds.). (1999). *What is indigenous knowledge? Voices from the academy.* New York: Falmer Press.

Sen, K. M. (1961). *Hinduism.* Harmondsworth: Penguin.

Senese, G. (1991). *Self-determination and the social education of Native Americans.* New York: Praeger.

Shalabi, A. (1954). *History of Muslim education.* Beirut, Lebanon: Dar Al-Kashshaf.

Sharer, R. (1994). *The ancient Maya* (5th ed.). Stanford, CA: Stanford University Press.

Sharer, R. (1996). *Daily life in Maya civilization.* Westport, CT: Greenwood Press.

Sharer, R. (1998). *La civilización maya.* México: Fondo de Cultura Económica.

Sharma, A. (1993). Hinduism. In A. Sharma (Ed.), *Our religions: The seven world religions introduced by preeminent scholars from each tradition* (pp. 1–67). San Francisco: Harper.

Sharma, A. (Ed.). (1993). *Our religions: The seven world religions introduced by preeminent scholars from each tradition.* San Francisco: Harper.

Sherzer, J. (1991). A richness of voices. In A. Josephy (Ed.), *America in 1492: The world of the Indian peoples before the arrival of Columbus* (pp. 251–275). New York: Vintage.

Shipps, J. (1985). *Mormonism: The story of a new religious tradition.* Urbana: University of Illinois Press.

Siddiqi, M. N. (1989). Islamizing economics. In *Toward Islamization of disciplines* (pp. 253–261). Herndon, VA: International Institute of Islamic Thought.

Siddiqui, A. H. (1991). *Life of Muhammad.* Des Plaines, IL: Library of Islam.

Siegel, H. (1997). *Rationality redeemed? Further dialogues on an educational ideal.* New York: Routledge.

Silverman, C. (1982). Everyday drama: Impression management of urban Gypsies. *Urban Anthropology* 11, 3/4: 377–398.

Siméon, R. (Ed.). (1889). *Annales de Domingo Francisco de San Anton Muñon Chimalpahim Quauhtlehuanitzin sixième et septième relations* [The annals of Domingo Francisco]. Paris: Maisonneuve et Ch. LeClerc.

Siméon, R. (1963). *Dictionnaire de la langue Nahuatl ou Mexicaine* [Dictionary of the Nahuatl or Mexican language]. Graz, Germany: Akademische Druck U. Verlagsanstalt.

Sinclair, H., Berthoud, I., Gerard, J., & Venesiano, E. (1985). Constructivisme et psycholinguistique génétique [Constructivism and genetic psychology]. *Archives de Psychologie* 53: 37–60.

Sirayi, M. (1996). Oral African drama in South Africa: The Xhosa indigenous drama forms. *South African Theatre Journal* 10, 1: 49–61.

Smith, J. (1999). *Islam in America.* New York: Columbia University Press.

Smith, K. (1988). *The changing past: Trends in South African historical writing.* Johannesburg: Southern.

Smith, R. (1983). *China's cultural heritage: The Ch'ing dynasty, 1644–1912.* Boulder, CO: Westview.

Snelling, J. (1991). *The Buddhist handbook: A complete guide to Buddhist schools, teaching, practice, and history.* Rochester, VT: Inner Traditions.

Snively, G. (1990). Traditional Native Indian beliefs, cultural values, and science instruction. *Canadian Journal of Native Education* 17, 1: 44–59.

Sokal, A., & Bricmont, J. (1998). *Fashionable nonsense: Postmodern intellectuals' abuse of science.* New York: Picador.

Solana, N. G. (1985). *Códices de México: Historia e interpretación de los grandes libros pintados prehispánicos* [Mexican codices: History and interpretation of the great pre-hispanic painted books]. México: Panorama Editorial.

Soustelle, J. (1961). *Daily life of the Aztecs on the eve of the Spanish conquest.* Stanford, CA: Stanford University Press.

Soustelle, J. (1979). *The Olmecs: The oldest civilization in Mexico.* Norman: University of Oklahoma Press.

Soustelle, J. (1991). *Les aztèques* (6th ed.) [The Aztecs]. Paris: Presses Universitaires de France.

Spiro, M. (1970). *Buddhism and society.* New York: Harper & Row.

Spores, R. (1984). *The Mixtecs in ancient and colonial times.* Norman: University of Oklahoma Press.

Sprenger, A. (1991). Confucius and modernization in China: An educational perspective. In S. Krieger & R. Trauzettel (Eds.), *Confucianism and the modernization of China* (pp. 454–472). Mainz, Germany: Hase & Koehler.

Spring, J. (1995). *The intersection of cultures: Multicultural education in the United States.* New York: McGraw-Hill.

Staiger, B. (1991). The image of Confucius in China. In S. Krieger & R. Trauzettel (Eds.), *Confucianism and the modernization of China* (pp. 116–125). Mainz, Germany: Hase & Koehler.

Stanton, C. (1990). *Higher learning in Islam: The classical period, A.D. 700–1300.* Savage, MD: Rowman & Littlefield.

Stewart, M. (1997). *The time of the Gypsies.* Boulder, CO: Westview Press.

Stover, L. (1974). *The cultural ecology of Chinese civilization: Peasants and elites in the last of the agrarian societies.* New York: Pica.

Stuart, G. (1981). *The mighty Aztecs.* Washington, DC: National Geographic Society.

Stumpfeldt, H. (1991). Confucius and Confucianism: On their history and status and on their present theoretical and practical potential. In S. Krieger & R. Trauzettel (Eds.), *Confucianism and the modernization of China* (pp. 18–28). Mainz, Germany: Hase & Koehler.

Suárez, J. (1983). *The Mesoamerican Indian languages.* Cambridge, England: Cambridge University Press.

Subramuniyaswami, S. (1993). *Dancing with Śiva: Hinduism's contemporary catechism.* Concord, CA: Himalayan Academy.

Sudarkasa, N. (1982). Sex roles, education and development in Africa. *Anthropology and Education* 13, 3: 279–288.

Sullivan, T. (1963). Nahuatl proverbs, conundrums and metaphors collected by Sahagun. *Estudios de Cultura Náhuatl* 4: 93–178.

Sultan, T. (1997). The role of Islamic universities in the Islamization of education. *Muslim Education Quarterly* 14, 3: 57–63.

Sutherland, A. (1975). *Gypsies: The hidden Americans.* Prospect Heights, IL: Waveland.

Suzuki, D. T. (1949). *An introduction to Zen Buddhism.* New York: Philosophical Library.

Swartz, L. (1998). *Culture and mental health: A Southern African view.* Cape Town: Oxford University Press.

Sway, M. (1988). *Familiar strangers: Gypsy life in America.* Urbana: University of Illinois Press.

Szasz, M. (1974). *Education and the American Indian: The road to self-determination, 1928–1973.* Albuquerque: University of New Mexico Press.

Talbani, A. (1996). Pedagogy, power, and discourse: Transformation of Islamic education. *Comparative Education Review* 40, 1: 66–82.

Tanahashi, K., & Schneider, T. D. (1994). *Essential Zen.* San Francisco: HarperCollins.

Tebbutt, S. (Ed.). (1998). *Sinti and Roma: Gypsies in German-speaking society and literature.* New York: Berghahn.

Telushkin, J. (1992). *Jewish humor.* New York: Morrow.

Temple, R. (1986). *The genius of China: 3,000 years of science, discovery, and invention.* New York: Simon and Schuster.

Thomas, N. W. (1969). *Proverbs, narratives, vocabularies and grammar: Anthropological report on the Ibo-speaking peoples of Nigeria, part III.* New York: Negro Universities Press. (Original work published 1913.)

Thompson, J. (1933). *Mexico before Cortez: An account of the daily life, religion, and ritual of the Aztecs and kindred peoples.* New York: Scribner's.

Thompson, J. E. (1962). *A catalog of Maya hieroglyphs.* Norman: University of Oklahoma Press.

Tibawi, A. L. (1972). *Islamic education: Its traditions and modernization into the Arab national systems.* London: Luzac & Co.

Tibi, B. (1990). *Islam and the cultural accommodation of social change.* Boulder, CO: Westview.

Tong, D. (Ed.). (1998). *Gypsies: An interdisciplinary reader.* New York: Garland.

Townsend, R. (1992). *The Aztecs.* London: Thames and Hudson.

Tozer, S., Violas, P., & Senese, G. (1998). *School and society: Historical and contemporary perspectives* (3rd ed.). New York: McGraw-Hill.

Trigg, E. (1973). *Gypsy demons and divinities: The magic and religion of the Gypsies.* Secaucus, NJ: Citadel Press.

Tritt, R. (1992). *Struggling for ethnic identity: Czechoslovakia's endangered Gypsies.* New York: Human Rights Watch.

Tucker, M., & Williams, D. (Eds.). (1997). *Buddhism and ecology: The interconnection of Dharma and deeds.* Cambridge, MA: Harvard University Press.

Tu Wei-ming. (1989). The Sung Confucian idea of education: A background understanding. In W. de Bary & J. Chaffee (Eds.), *Neo-Confucian education: The formative stage* (pp. 139–150). Berkeley: University of California Press.

Tu Wei-ming. (1990). The Confucian tradition in Chinese history. In P. Ropp (Ed.), *Heritage of China: Contemporary perspectives on Chinese civilization* (pp. 112–136). Berkeley: University of California Press.

Tu Wei-ming. (1993). Confucianism. In A. Sharma (Ed.), *Our religions: The seven world religions introduced by preeminent scholars from each tradition* (pp. 139–227). San Francisco: Harper.

Turner, B. (1994). *Orientalism, postmodernism, and globalism.* London: Routledge.

Turner, N. (1988). Comparison of the *izibongo* of the Zulu royal women, Mnkabayi and Nandi. *South African Journal of African Languages* 8, 1: 28–33.

Twitchett, D. (Ed.). (1979). *The Cambridge history of China, volume 3: Sui and T'ang China, 589–906, part I.* Cambridge, England: Cambridge University Press.

Twitchett, D., & Loewe, M. (Eds.). (1986). *The Cambridge history of China, volume 1: The Ch'in and Han empires, 221 B.C.–A.D. 220.* Cambridge, England: Cambridge University Press.

Twumasi, P., & Warren, D. (1986). The professionalization of indigenous medicine: A comparative study of Ghana and Zambia. In M. Last & C. Chavunduka (Eds.), *The professionalization of African medicine* (pp. 117–135). Manchester, England: Manchester University Press.

Tyrnauer, G. (1991). *Gypsies and the Holocaust: A bibliography and introductory essay* (2nd ed.). Montréal: Montréal Institute for Genocide Studies, Concordia University.

Übelhör, M. (1989). The community compact *(Hsiang-yüeh)* of the Sung and its educational significance. In W. de Bary & J. Chaffee (Eds.), *Neo-Confucian education: The formative stage* (pp. 371–388). Berkeley: University of California Press.

Uka, N. (1986). Continuity and change: A challenge to African educators. In J. Okpaku, A. Opubor, & B. Oloruntimehin (Eds.), *The arts and civilization of Black and African peoples: Volume 6, Black civilization and pedagogy* (pp. 129–144). Lagos, Nigeria: Center for Black and African Arts and Civilization.

UNESCO. (1985). *The educational process and historiography in Africa.* Paris: UNESCO.

Ungar, S. (1986). *Africa: The people and politics of an emerging continent* (Rev. ed.). New York: Simon & Schuster.

Ursinus, M. (Ed.). (1984). Der Islam in der Gegenwart [Islam in the Modern World.] München, Germany: C. H. Beck.

Vaillant, G. (1995). *La civilización azteca* [The Aztec civilization]. México: Fondo de Cultura Económica.

van der Vliet, V. (1974). Growing up in a traditional society. In W. Hammond-Tooke (Ed.), *The Bantu-speaking peoples of Southern Africa* (pp. 211–245). London: Routledge & Kegan Paul.

van Jaarsveld, F. A. (1975). *From Van Riebeeck to Vorster, 1652–1974.* Pretoria: Perskor.

van Nieuwenhuijze, C. (1985). *The lifestyles of Islam: Recourse to classicism, need of realism.* Leiden, Netherlands: Brill.

van Zantwijk, R. (1985). *The Aztec arrangement: The social history of pre-Spanish Mexico.* Norman: University of Oklahoma Press.

Vansina, J. (1985). *Oral tradition as history.* Madison: University of Wisconsin Press.

Veytia, M. (1944). *Historia antigua de Mexico* (2 vols.) [History of ancient Mexico]. México: Editorial Leyenda.

Viswanathan, E. (1992). *Am I a Hindu? The Hinduism primer.* San Francisco: Halo Books.

Vogel, A., & Elsasser, N. (1981). Rom (Gypsy), merimé, and the schools. *Theory into Practice* 20, 1: 70– 72.

Voll, J. (1994). *Islam: Continuity and change in the modern world* (2nd ed.). Syracuse, NY: Syracuse University Press.

von Däniken, E. (1968). *Chariots of the gods: Unsolved mysteries of the past.* New York: Berkley.

von Däniken, E. (1995). *The return of the gods.* Shaftesbury, Dorset: Element.

von Däniken, E. (1996). *The eyes of the Sphinx.* New York: Berkley.

von Däniken, E. (1997). *Arrival of the gods.* Shaftesbury, Dorset: Element.

von Glasersfeld, E. (1984). An introduction to radical constructivism. In P. Watzlawick (Ed.), *The invented reality: How do we know what we believe we know?* (pp. 17–40). New York: Norton.

von Glasersfeld, E. (1989). Cognition, construction of knowledge, and teaching. *Synthese* 80: 121–140.

von Glasersfeld, E. (1993). Questions and answers about radical constructivism. In K. Tobin (Ed.), *The practice of constructivism in science education* (pp. 23–38). Hillsdale, NJ: Lawrence Erlbaum Associates.

von Glasersfeld, E. (1995a). *Radical constructivism: A way of knowing.* London: Falmer.

von Glasersfeld, E. (1995b). A constructivist approach to teaching. In L. Steffe & J. Gale (Eds.), *Constructivism in education* (pp. 3–15). Hillsdale, NJ: Lawrence Erlbaum Associates.

von Glasersfeld, E. (1996). Footnotes to "The many faces of constructivism." *Educational Researcher* 25: 19.

Vygotsky, L. (1978). *Mind in society: The development of higher psychological processes.* Cambridge, MA: Harvard University Press.

Vygotsky, L. (1986). *Thought and language.* Cambridge, MA: MIT Press.

Waghid, Y. (1996). Why a theory of Islamic education cannot be epistemologically "neutral." *Muslim Education Quarterly* 13, 2: 43–54.

Waines, D. (1995). *An introduction to Islam.* Cambridge, England: Cambridge University Press.

Waley, A. (Trans.), (1938). *The Analects of Confucius.* New York: Vintage.

Wall, S. (1994). *Shadowcatchers: A journey in search of the teachings of Native American healers.* New York: HarperCollins.

Walker, B. (1968). *The Hindu world: An encyclopedic survey of Hinduism, vol. 1.* New York: Praeger.

Walton, L. (1989). The institutional context of neo-Confucianism: Scholars, schools, and Shu-yüan in Sung-Yüan China. In W. de Bary & J. Chaffee (Eds.), *Neo-Confucian education: The formative stage* (pp. 457–492). Berkeley: University of California Press.

Wang Gungwu. (1991). *The Chineseness of China.* Hong Kong: Oxford University Press.

Warder, A. K. (1970). *Indian Buddhism.* Delhi: Motilal Banarsidass.

Watson, B. (Trans.), (1961). *Records of the grand historian of China* (2 vols.). New York: Columbia University Press.

Watt, W. M. (1953). *Muhammad at Mecca.* Karachi, Pakistan: Oxford University Press.

Watt, W. M. (1956). *Muhammad at Medina.* Karachi, Pakistan: Oxford University Press.

Watt, W. M., & Bell, R. (1970). *Introduction to the Qur'an.* Edinburgh: Edinburgh University Press.

Weaver, M. (1981). *The Aztecs, Maya, and their predecessors: Archeology of Mesoamerica* (2nd ed.). New York: Academic Press.

Weckman, S. (1998). Researching Finnish Gypsies: Advice from a Gypsy. In D. Tong (Ed.), *Gypsies: An interdisciplinary reader* (pp. 3–10). New York: Garland.

Weibust, P. (1989). Tradition as process: Creating contemporary tradition in a rural Norwegian school and community. *International Journal of Qualitative Studies in Education* 2, 2: 107–122.

White, J. (1971). *Cortés and the downfall of the Aztec empire: A study in a conflict of cultures.* New York: St. Martin's Press.

Wilkinson, E. (1973). *The history of imperial China: A research guide.* Cambridge, MA: Harvard University Press.

Williams, S. W. (1907). *The Middle Kingdom: A survey of the geography, government, literature, social life, arts, and history of the Chinese empire and its inhabitants* (2 vols.). New York: Scribner's.

Williamson, A. (1997). Decolonizing historiography of colonial education: Processes of interaction in the schooling of Torres Strait Islanders. *International Journal of Qualitative Studies in Education* 10, 4: 407–423.

Willms, A. (1984). Nordafrika [North Africa]. In M. Ursinus (Ed.), *Der Islam in der Gegenwart* (pp. 561–569). München, Germany: C. H. Beck.

Wing-tsit Chan. (1989). Chu Hsi and the academies. In W. de Bary & J. Chaffee (Eds.), *Neo-Confucian education: The formative stage* (pp. 389–413). Berkeley: University of California Press.

Witherspoon, G. (1977). *Language and art in the Navajo universe*. Ann Arbor: The University of Michigan Press.

Wright, R. (1992). *Stolen continents: The "new world" through Indian eyes*. Boston: Houghton Mifflin.

Wyatt, D. (1990). A language of continuity in Confucian thought. In P. Cohen & M. Goldman (Eds.), *Ideas across cultures: Essays on Chinese thought in honor of Benjamin I. Schwartz* (pp. 33–61). Cambridge, MA: Harvard University Press.

Yellow Bird, R. (1990). Position paper on Native Education. *Humanity & Society* 14, 3: 297–301.

Young, R. (1990). *White mythologies: Writing history and the West*. London: Routledge.

Young, R. E. (1981). The epistemic discourse of teachers: An ethnographic study. *Anthropology and Education Quarterly* 12: 122–144.

Yuan Zheng. (1994). Local government schools in Sung China: A reassessment. *History of Education Quarterly* 34, 193–213.

Yu Dunkang. (1991). The concept of "great harmony" in the Book of Changes *(Zhou Yi)*. In S. Krieger & R. Trauzettel (Eds.), *Confucianism and the modernization of China* (pp. 51–62). Mainz, Germany: Hase & Koehler.

Zaehner, R. C. (1962). *Hinduism*. London: Oxford University Press.

Zelliot, E., & Bernsten, M. (Eds.). (1988). *The experience of Hinduism*. Albany: State University of New York Press.

Zürcher, E. (1989). Buddhism and education in T'ang times. In W. de Bary & J. Chaffee (Eds.), *Neo-Confucian education: The formative stage* (pp. 19–56). Berkeley: University of California Press.

Author Index

A

Abdalati, H., 199, 200, 201, 202, 213
Abdullah, A. R. S., 191, 192, 202, 203, 213
Abe, M., 145, 155, 156, 213
Achebe, C., 26, 49, 213
Acton, T., 159, 175, 213
Adams, R., 57, 74, 213
Adegbola, E., 52, 213, 216
Ahmad, K., 185, 199, 200, 201, 202, 213, 217
Ahmed, A. S., 198, 213
Aizpuro, P., 76, 213
Al-Azmeh, A., 201, 213
Ali, S. A., 199, 213
Allen, S., 19, 222
Alonzo, G., 75, 213
Amdouni, H., 200, 214
Anawalt, P., 81, 215
Andrews, J., 77, 214
Ani, M., 54, 214
Appiah, K., 49, 214
Archibald, J., 97, 214, 225
Arens, W., 23, 214
Argüelles, J., 13, 23, 214
Arkoun, M., 202, 203, 214
Armstrong, K., 199, 214
Asante, K., 25, 49, 50, 214, 216
Asante, M., 25, 45, 49, 50, 54, 214, 216
Asoko, H., 20, 221
Athar, S., 199, 214
Atwood, M., 98, 214

B

Austin, A., 214
Austin, L., 66, 214
Aveni, A., 75, 214
Ayers, W., 126, 214
Ayisi, E., 49, 50, 52, 214, 224

B

Bahá'u'lláh, xv
Ball, B., 236
Ball, J., 123, 124
Ball, S., 2, 18, 214
Balme, M., 21, 214
Banerjee, A. K., 140, 214
Banerji, S., 152, 154, 215
Barman, J., 88, 98, 215, 234
Barnes, B., 174, 215
Barrett, T. H., 126, 215
Barth, F., 174, 215
Bascom, W., 36, 51, 215
Basham, A. L., 154, 215
Bastid, M., 123, 129, 215, 226, 233
Bauer, W., 122, 215
Belenky, M. F., 18, 215
Bell, B., 77, 78, 215
Bell, R., 202, 247
Benham, M., xv, 211, 215
Berdan, F., 78, 81, 215
Berensten, M., 151, 248
Berkey, J., 203, 215
Bernadac, C., 178, 215
Bernal, M., 5, 18, 54, 55, 216
Berrelleza, J., 79, 216

Subject Index